EXCURSIONS IN WORLD MUSIC

Bruno Nettl
Charles Capwell
Isabel K. F. Wong
Thomas Turino

University of Illinois
Urbana-Champaign

Philip V. Bohlman

University of Chicago

Prentice Hall
Englewood Cliffs, New Jersey, 07632

Library of Congress Cataloging-in-Publication Data

Excursions in world music / by Bruno Nettl ... [et al.].
        p.   cm.
    Includes bibliographical references and index.
    ISBN 0-13-299025-3
    1. Music appreciation. 2. Ethnomusicology.   I. Nettl, Bruno,

MT6.E98 1992
780'.9--dc20   91-32258
                                                                   CIP
                                                                    MN

Editorial/production supervision and interior design: **Jordan Ochs**
Acquisitions editor: **Bud Therien**
Prepress buyer: **Herb Klein**
Manufacturing buyer: **Patrice Fraccio**
Cover design: **Bruce Kenselaar**
Cover art: **Folklore Musicians; Hammamet, Tunisia. Photo Courtesy of *Four by Five*.**

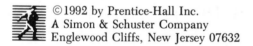 ©1992 by Prentice-Hall Inc.
A Simon & Schuster Company
Englewood Cliffs, New Jersey 07632

Printed in the United States of America
10 9 8 7 6 5 4 3

ISBN   0-13-299025-3

Prentice-Hall International (UK) Limited, *London*
Prentice-Hall of Australia Pty. Limited, *Sydney*
Prentice-Hall Canada Inc., *Toronto*
Prentice-Hall Hispanoamericana, S.A., *Mexico*
Prentice-Hall of India Private Limited, *New Delhi*
Prentice-Hall of Japan, Inc., *Tokyo*
Simon & Schuster Asia Pte. Ltd., *Singapore*
Editora Prentice-Hall do Brasil, Ltda., *Rio de Janeiro*

CONTENTS

To the Memory of
John Blacking (1928-1990)

"In a world such as ours . . .
it is necessary to understand why
a madrigal by Gesualdo or a Bach Passion,
a sitar melody from India or a song from Africa,
Berg's *Wozzeck* or Britten's *War Requiem*,
a Balinese gamelan or a Cantonese opera,
or a symphony by Mozart, Beethoven, or Mahler,
may be profoundly necessary for human survival . . ."

How Musical Is Man? (1973)

1

INTRODUCTION: STUDYING MUSICS OF THE WORLD'S CULTURES

Bruno Nettl

OUR PURPOSE: PRESENTING THE WORLD OF MUSIC

In this book we wish to present, in an introductory fashion, the world of music. Directing ourselves to students—particularly those without a technical background in music—and to general readers, we want to show the character of music and musical life of all of the world's peoples. Clearly we can do this only by sampling and by judicious synthesis, and yet we hope to go beyond the scope of other treatments of "world music" or "ethnic music." Rather than considering this book only as an introduction to non-Western music, we include also the musical culture of Europe, with its academic or art music, among the musics of the world. We have divided the world into ten major culture areas or blocks, devoting a chapter to each, mindful of course that within each of these areas dwells a plethora of cultural and musical diversity. We have tried to be representative in each region and of the world as well; even so, there are large areas which we have had to leave untouched.

In order to provide a degree of depth as well as breadth, we have had to be selective. We can do no more than provide excursions. Thus, in each chapter we first focus upon detailed description of a musical event which may be considered broadly representative of its culture area; ordinarily, this is followed by an introduction to the cultures and societies of the area, and then a more synthetic treatment of musical life and ideas about music, of musical style (described in terms comprehensible by nonspecialists), music history, and musical instruments, a brief description of a few additional musical genres or contexts, and finally a consideration of recent developments. We describe musical cultures as they exist in the twentieth century, but wherever possible we provide some information about their history. We do this in some measure in order to dispel the notion that Western academic or art music lives in a sense through its history, while the musics of other societies have no history at all, or at best a very different sort of history.

We wish to help the reader understand music as a cultural phenomenon. We do hope that these pages will stimulate readers to listen to music of at least some of the world's many societies, and we hope they will enjoy this music. But the notion that music is principally to be "enjoyed" is characteristic of Westerners, and much of the music we discuss has purposes far beyond enjoyment. It is music of great significance in religion and in the integration of society. It identifies clans and social classes, confirms political status, expresses communication from the supernatural, and cures the sick. Thus, while readers will wish to know how the musical pieces of the world's cultures are put together and what general principles of composition may dominate in a given society, it is perhaps even more important for them to understand each culture's ideas of what music is, what its powers are, how it relates to other aspects of life, and how it reflects important things about its people and their view of the world. For this reason, while we wish to explain the nature of musical sound, we have also tried to present a holistic picture of musical life and musical culture.

NOTES ON *THE MARRIAGE OF FIGARO*

Our purpose, then, is to present the varieties of the world's musics, and to present several ways of looking at music, all of them needed to understand a particular work of music as it interacts with its culture in many ways. Let me use as an example Mozart's opera *The Marriage of Figaro* (*Le Nozze di Figaro*). Its structure is an alternation of recitatives, in which the action is carried forward through quick dialogue barely sung, with arias and musical ensembles such as trios and quartets, in which characters make lyrical and contemplative statements, or comment on what has just happened. This tells us something about the aesthetics and, if you will, attention span of the patrons. But it also tells us about the relationship of opera to spoken drama, about the way Mozart and his colleagues and his audience perceived the relationship of music and language.

The fact that this is an opera with Italian words, composed by a German-speaking Austrian for a German-speaking audience in Vienna, speaks to this relationship as well. The well-educated audience of patrons for whom *Figaro* was composed presumably understood Italian and thought that this knowledge set them off from the general population, which would have wished for operas in German, and so we see this work as directed towards an elite segment of society. But it is a segment that comes up for criticism in the content of the opera, for the latter depicts a mild social revolution. Figaro, the lowly but clever barber, wants to protect his fiancee from having to spend a night with his boss, the count, as was once an aspect of the relationship between landowners and their employees. He succeeds, of course, without violence and through his wit, and everyone lives happily ever after, but the opera when first presented raised the eyebrows of the Austrian aristocracy.

Mozart was not generally regarded as a great composer in his own day, but now he holds that status more than any other. In his day, actually, the concept of "great master" of music was not really developed, and composers did not write music with the feeling that it should be great art for all times. *Figaro* was considered, at best, to be fine entertainment, not something for edifying the human spirit. To be sure, in Mozart's time the difference in musical style between academic music and music for popular entertainment was not very great; the two sounded rather alike. This began to change around 1800, and today we expect academic music, which we call "classical" or "art" music, to be quite different from popular music.

So Mozart has become a minor deity, and much is said and written about the greatness of *Figaro* and the reasons for it. In our society today, the concept of genius is important to musical culture, as is the notion of talent. It is very important to us to know that Mozart composed acceptable music at the age of seven. And that Mozart composed works with enormous speed—or so it has been thought. We have, it seems, a kind of athletic view of music: We are impressed when something takes many hours, or when someone can do important work quickly, or when someone, composer or performer, can carry out an extremely difficult task.

A quick look at *The Marriage of Figaro* tells us certain important things about our own musical culture as North Americans. But from the viewpoint of this book, it is essential now for us to accept the idea that doing something difficult musically may not be a criterion in American Indian societies, and that the notion of the musical masterwork, which may not be altered and must always be performed as the composer intended it, is not relevant to understanding the music of India. At the same time, we should realize that many societies have drama rather like opera, in which the characters sing; that many have forms of communication which, like recitative, fall between ordinary speech and song; that music is frequently used to express criticism of society; that a social elite has musical ways of showing its superiority—artistic resources such as the orchestra, linguistic techniques such as having opera in a foreign language. And we will need to remember that just as the European view of Mozart has changed since his death, all societies change in their views of music as well as in their musical styles. And, further, that Western academic musical culture requires constant innovation and rapid change as a hallmark of its series of masterworks, while other societies may restrict and inhibit change as detrimental to the function of music.

Ideas about music, and contexts of creation and performance, help us to understand the music itself, which in turn provides insight into the values that led to it and the culture of which it is a part. And a look at a single work or performance gives us insight into the entire musical system.

CERTAIN BASIC ASSUMPTIONS

This book, in presenting the world's musical cultures, employs certain basic assumptions, the most important of which should be understood by the reader at the outset.

A Relativistic View

If *The Marriage of Figaro* is a great work of music, this must be because it satisfies certain criteria: It is a work of great complexity; its structure has internal logic; it has harmony and counterpoint, whereby several simultaneous melodies are both independent and united; the composer shows ability to write music particularly suited to voices, instruments, and orchestra, and ability to relate words and music; the work carries a particular social and spiritual message; and so on. Using these criteria to judge the musics of other cultures, we would quickly conclude that Western music is the best and greatest. But from the viewpoint of an Indian musician whose task is improvising within a framework of melodic and rhythmic rules, the performers of *Figaro* don't come off so well, since they must reproduce an existing work precisely and rely on notation to keep them from deviating, thus finding little opportunity to be creative. An American Indian who considers a song to be a way for spirits to communicate with humans might marvel at the counterpoint of a Bach but also feel that the whole notion of what is "good" or "better" music makes no sense. Performers in a West African percussion ensemble might find the melodic and harmonic structure of *Figaro* interesting but its rhythms simpleminded.

As students of world music, we cannot reconcile these divergent viewpoints and are instead best off taking a relativistic attitude. We—the authors—believe that each society has a musical system that suits its culture, and while we may compare them with each other in terms of their structure and function, we don't make these comparisons the basis of qualitative judgments. Instead, we recognize that each society evaluates its own works of music by its own criteria. In our society, we take it for granted that music should be an enjoyable auditory experience; elsewhere, the ideal of music may be quite different. We want to understand each music as an aspect of its culture and recognize that each culture creates the kind of music it needs to serve its purposes and reflect its principal values.

World Music Is a Group of Musics

We think of the world of music as consisting of a group of musics. It makes sense to think of a music somewhat as if it were a language. Each society has its own principal music, and the members of a society know and respond to their music with a kind of common understanding, just as they communicate through their language. Just as languages borrow words from each other, musics influence each other. And just as a society sometimes replaces one language with another (the Anglo-Saxons learned Middle English after the Norman invasion in 1066, and native peoples of South America learned Spanish after the arrival of Columbus), a group of people may cease using a traditional kind of music and replace it with another. Some individuals and some entire communities are bilingual; this is true of many North American Indian peoples today. Similarly, many Indian communities are "bimusical," using traditional Indian music and Western music equally but for different purposes.

We think of each music as a system in the sense that changes in one of its components cause changes in the rest. Thus, if a society begins using the Western piano to perform its traditional musical repertory, this music is also likely to change in its melodic and harmonic aspects. The contexts in which it is performed may also change. Consider, for example, a kind of music performed by itinerant street musicians. If this music were taken up by the piano it would no longer be itinerant, and if the piano were located in a concert hall the idea of what this music should be and do would also change radically.

The Three-Part Model

This brings us the third basic assumption. Music is, to most of us, a group of sounds, but in order to study it interculturally we must also be interested in the ideas about music that a society has, and in the events in which music plays a part. The ideas determine to some extent what the contexts for music will be and how the music will sound. If innovation is an important component of the system of ideas about music, then the music will change frequently. If the notion of masterworks is present in the culture, then great technical complexity and stylistic uniqueness may characterize its pieces. If the idea of conformity is important, then well-disciplined orchestral performances may result; but if individualism is important, then solo performances or improvised jam sessions may be the musical counterpart. If a society has complex music, then the notion of virtuosity in the realm of ideas may be reinforced, and social contexts for performances by virtuosi may be established. Using a model suggested by Alan P. Merriam, we look at music, therefore, as a phenomenon with three aspects: *sound, behavior,* and *conception.* These three are closely related; each plays a role in determining the nature of the others.

UNIVERSALS OF MUSIC

Throughout the following chapters, there will be emphasis on the great differences among musics. Each society has a unique musical system related to the character of its culture. But are there not some things about music that all, or virtually all, societies share? Such phenomena are called "universals."

The most obvious one is music itself. It is a cultural universal in the sense that all societies, to our knowledge, have something that sounds to us like music. But the matter is more complicated. First, just because it sounds like music to us—reminds us, however distantly, of Western music—does not mean that it *is* music. Moreover, many societies do not have a concept of music as it has developed in Western culture. For us Americans, music is a broad concept—it may be vocal or instrumental, sacred or secular, solo or ensemble—and it has its metaphoric extensions, such as the notion that a pleasant sound is musical. The notion that all of these sounds—singing and instruments, ritual and entertainment, human and animal—can be brought together under one concept is not shared by all societies.

So, if we are to defend the proposition that music is a cultural universal, we can perhaps do it by suggesting that all cultures have some kind of vocal sound production that they distinguish from ordinary speech. Much of this is clearly singing, but various kinds of ceremonial speech are included. It follows from this that singing is a cultural universal: All peoples sing. There may be a few that have no instruments, but this situation, if indeed it obtains, is so rare that the existence of instruments can also be called a universal. In all societies, music is used in religious ritual. Virtually everywhere, music is presented in units that can be identified as songs or pieces. Nowhere do people "just" sing;

they always sing something, and in this respect music contrasts with some other art forms such as dance.

Everywhere, people can recognize a tune, a configuration of pitches, whether it is performed high or low, sung by a man or a woman. The principal melodic interval in most musics is approximately a major second, the distance in pitch between two white keys on the piano if they are separated by a black key. It seems that, in all cultures, music is used in some sense for transforming ordinary experience—producing anything from trance in a ritual to edification in a concert. The function of music everywhere may be to help society reinforce boundaries between social groups, who can then view their music as an emblem of identity. There are, clearly, some aspects of music that have a well-nigh universal distribution throughout the globe.

MUSICAL CHANGE, TRANSMISSION, AND HISTORY

It is tempting to think of Western music as dynamic and all other musics as static. We often hear about the "Stone Age" music of tribal peoples and the great age of the music of China and India. But all musics have a history and all of them change, though at various rates and not always in the same direction. It would be a great mistake to assume that the music of India, because it is largely melodic and without harmony, somehow represents an earlier stage through which Western music has already passed; or that Europeans, in the days when they lived in tribes, had music similar to that of American Indians. Musics do not uniformly change from simple to complex. Each music has its own unique history. If there are patterns, they have to do with the relationships of cultures to one another. Thus, in the twentieth century, as Western culture has affected most others, most non-Western musics now show some influence of Western music. But the results of this influence vary.

For example, when the violin was introduced into the music of South India, it was incorporated into the Indian soundscape and began to be used in imitation of the Indian singing style. The same instrument, when introduced to Iran, brought with it the Western sound of violin playing, thus effecting changes in the Iranian notion of how music should sound. Brought to Amerindian peoples in the southwestern United States, it motivated the Navajo and Apache to develop the single-string "Apache fiddle," combining aspects of the violin and the traditional hunting-bow–like musical bow.

One of the things that determines the course of history in a musical culture is the method of transmission. In most societies, music lives in oral (or better, "aural") tradition; that is, it is passed on by word of mouth and learned by hearing live performance. It is often assumed that such a form of transmission inevitably causes songs to change, as each person who learns one develops his or her own variant, lacking the control of notation. Societies differ, however, in their attitude toward musical stability; to some it is important that a song remain stable and unchanged, while in others individual singers are encouraged to have their personal versions. In aural traditions, music can perhaps not go beyond a certain degree of complexity, as limits of memory and coordination of simultaneous performers or components must function in the end as inhibitions.

Western academic music is traditionally notated, and there are also notation systems for some Asian musics, although these are usually not as detailed as the Western and are not normally used by performers while they play or sing. Notated traditions may also be divided into written and printed. Musical notation appeared in Europe long before the development of music printing in the late fifteenth century, but the number of handmade copies of one piece was inevitably small, and they could differ. The change from written to printed music surely led to a different set of ideas about the nature and stability of a musical work. The development of sound recording has affected both aural and written traditions, as a recording allows someone learning a piece to hear it repeatedly in identical form, incorporating those aspects of music often inadequately represented in Western notation—such as tone color, ornaments, and phrasing. The nature of a musical tradition is affected greatly by the way it is transmitted and by the way its content is taught and learned.

MUSICAL INSTRUMENTS

Virtually all cultures have instruments, as we have said. In one sense, there is an infinite variety of instruments, but there is also a good deal of similarity among instruments across cultures. Bowed, stringed instruments held vertically, like the cello, appear throughout Asia, Europe, and parts of Africa; as we have just seen in the case of the Apache fiddle, they probably developed in the native cultures of the Americas as a result of culture contact with Europeans. Xylophonelike instruments were highly developed in Indonesia, Africa, and Central America. Flutes, drums, and rattles are found throughout the world. Yet each culture has its own version of an instrument type, its own set of ideas about it, and its own terminology. Thus, the African instrument sometimes known as "thumb-piano" or "finger-xylophone"—its metal or reed keys are actually attached to a bridge and plucked, and therefore it is neither a piano nor a xylophone—is known in African languages as *mbira, sansa, kalimba, likembe, kasai*, and many other names.

What to call such an instrument in scholarly literature or even in this book? Whenever possible, we use the native designation—sitar instead of "North Indian lute," erhu instead of "Chinese spike fiddle." In some cases of terminological variety, one term has come to be widely used; for the thumb-piano, for example, mbira is now the most common term. But for more general groupings, it is useful to draw on a classification of instruments. Musicians in Western culture use a four-fold grouping—strings, woodwinds, brass, and percussion—which is actually derived not from the nature of the instruments themselves but from their roles in the eighteenth-century orchestra of Mozart and Haydn, as each group fulfilled certain functions in the music. This is a European kind of classification which one needs to know in order to understand European ideas about music, and most of the world's cultures have their own ways of classifying instruments.

But in order to talk about instruments of different cultures comparatively, students of world music commonly use a classification system that divides instruments into four main groups on the basis of the way in which the sound is produced. Developed by two prominent German scholars of the early twentieth century, Erich M. von Hornbostel and Curt Sachs, it is based on the way a Belgian museum curator, Victor Mahillon, arranged a large and varied instrument collection in Brussels in the nineteenth century, and ultimately on a way of grouping instruments in philosophical treatises of India.

One of the four classes consists of *aerophones*, basically wind instruments, subdivided into flutelike, trumpetlike, and reed instruments, among others. A second is *chordophones*, or stringed instruments. These are divided principally into *zithers*, which consist of sets of strings stretched in parallel fashion along a board, and *lutes*, on which strings are stretched along a fingerboard and its attached resonator. Most of the stringed instruments of Western culture—violins, double basses, guitars, mandolins—are lutes that are bowed or plucked. A third group is *idiophones*, instruments whose bodies themselves vibrate; among these are rattles, xylophones, bells, gongs, and many other instruments that are struck or rubbed. This is actually the largest group of instruments by far, and there are societies that have representatives of this class only and of no other. Finally, there are *membranophones*, instruments in which a membrane vibrates—basically drums.

Each of these classes is elaborately subdivided, so that the system provides a space for each of the world's instruments and perhaps even for instruments not yet discovered.

WHY DO DIFFERENT CULTURES HAVE DIFFERENT KINDS OF MUSIC?

If the following chapters succeed in making it clear that each culture has a unique musical system, it is natural that the reader should ask why there are these differences and what it is that determines the particular music that a culture has. Why indeed *did* Western music develop its pervasive system of harmony, and why *do* Indians of the North

American Plains sing in a harsh and tense manner, and why *do* sub-Saharan African peoples stress rhythmic complexity and the concept of improvised variation? Though these are the questions that we may wish ultimately to answer in this kind of a book, we will not be able to do so definitively.

But we can suggest some answers. There are some factors that we should eliminate from serious consideration at the outset. One is the genetic. There is no evidence that the musical style of a society is determined by heredity. It is true, for example, that black societies in Africa and the New World share certain musical traits; these are not, however, the result of the same factors that determine their physical similarity, but come rather from their common African cultural roots. After all, it has been amply demonstrated by such artists as Zubin Mehta, Yo-Yo Ma, and Seiji Ozawa that members of non-Western societies can become leading musicians in the sphere of Western music; and despite the problems occasioned by exposure delayed until adult life, there are Americans and Europeans who have become accepted as excellent performers of African and Indian music. As is the case with language, anyone can learn any music; but to become as much at ease and as proficient as a native, to speak musically without accent, requires exposure early in life or special talent and effort.

We should also eliminate, as already suggested the notion that all musics pass through a set of stages, and that we can explain the variety of world musics by suggesting that we are observing each of them at a different stage of the same development. It is possibly true that musics evolve in a sense similar to that of biological species. But just as it was not inevitable that "lower" species would eventually lead to humans, it is not inevitable (or even likely) that a non-Western music would gradually change to become like Western. Rather, the concept of evolution suggests that musical systems change in accordance with the needs of the social environment so as thus to be able to survive.

Take, for example, the role of music in human migration. In the late nineteenth century many European peasants moved to North America in search of jobs and a higher standard of living, settling in cities and becoming factory workers. They brought with them their rural folk songs from Poland, Italy, Rumania, or Greece to Cleveland, Detroit, and Chicago. But in these cities they no longer need ritual songs to accompany agricultural festivals, or social songs to sing on the village square while courting, or narrative ballads to entertain on evenings, because instead they work in factories, go to high-school dances, and watch television. But they do need music to help remind them of their European heritage and of their special origins. Therefore folk songs passed down in aural tradition become national songs learned from songbooks and taught in classes on Saturday mornings and sung at special Polish or Hungarian concerts. In the course of these kinds of performances, they change from melodies sung unaccompanied to choral settings with harmony, and from songs that exist in many variants to standardized versions. In this way the music changes in order to satisfy a new social need.

_� This suggests that a society develops its music in accordance with the character of its social system. While this statement surely does not account for all the aspects of a music or all the differences among musics, it may come closest to answering the general question raised above. A typical ensemble in South Indian classical music has a clear hierarchy, somewhat along the lines of the Hindu caste system. The solo vocalist is highest and most prestigious, socially and musically; the accompanying drummer is next, followed by the accompanying violinist, the second percussionist, and finally the player of the drone instrument. Among the Mambuti Pygmies of Zaire, an egalitarian society with no formal leadership, musical ensembles also have no formal leaders, and the singers in choruses blend their voices.

The Western symphony orchestra began to develop seriously about the time of the industrial revolution. It is in effect a factory for producing music, in which group precision plays a great role, as does specialization. Each section has its boss, the concertmaster is a kind of factory foreman, and the conductor—who is symbolically different, making no sounds but standing on a pedestal and getting his name on the recording package—represents management. In those societies in which the social roles of men and women are extremely different, the genders have separate repertoires and different ways of using the voice. It has been suggested that those societies in which there is good cooperation and relative equality create large ensembles in which this cooperation is reflected, while others in which a part of the population is dominated by an elite develop soloistic music.

One should not carry the argument too far. Surely music is created in part to support and symbolize important aspects of culture, but it also has other functions, as, for example, to counteract rather than support the dominant cultural characteristics. There are, after all, societies in which one may say in music what one may not express in words and in which music and musicians represent deviation from societal norms. And yet, if we wish to identify what it is that determines the nature of a music, we should look first to the general character of its culture and particularly the types of relationships among people within its society, and to the way the society relates to other societies.

THE FIELD OF ETHNOMUSICOLOGY

The subject of this book properly belongs to the field of enthnomusicology, which may be defined as the comparative study of the musics of the world and the study of music as an aspect of culture. Ethnomusicologists customarily regard themselves as either members of the discipline of musicology (the scholarly study of music from historical and social viewpoints) or of sociocultural anthropology (the study of humans with emphasis on culture). Ethnomusicology can also be regarded as the anthropological study of music.

Most enthnomusicologists are specialists in one culture or a small number of cultures, in whose locations they carry out field research for periods upwards of a year to collect data, and with whose cultures and languages they become conversant. Their field techniques include sound and video recording along with interviewing of many kinds, often along with participation in the culture. Thus, a field-worker frequently puts himself or herself into the hands of a music teacher or master, studying the musical system as it is taught to members of the society, learning it, so to speak, from the inside. Ethnomusicologists try to combine their own detached observations as cultural outsiders with the views of a society about its own musical culture. The following chapters attempt to maintain this combination of viewpoints.

INTRODUCTION BIBLIOGRAPHY

The Field of Enthnomusicology   Alan P. Merriam, *The Anthropology of Music* (Evanston, Ill.: Northwestern University Press, 1964); Mantle Hood, *The Ethnomusicologist* (New York: McGraw-Hill, 1971); John Blacking, *How Musical Is Man?* (Seattle: University of Washington Press, 1973); Bruno Nettl, *The Study of Ethnomusicology* (Urbana: University of Illinois Press, 1983); Bruno Nettl and Philip Bohlman, eds., *Comparative Musicology and Anthropology of Music: Essays in the History of Ethnomusicology* (Chicago: University of Chicago Press, 1991); Charles Seeger, *Essays on Musicology 1935–1975* (Berkeley: University of California Press, 1977).

Surveys of World Music: William P. Malm, *Music Cultures of the Pacific, the Near East, and Asia*, 2nd ed. (Englewood Cliffs, N.J.: Prentice-Hall, 1977); Bruno Nettl, *Folk and Traditional Music of the Western Continents*, 3rd ed. (Englewood Cliffs, N.J.: Prentice-Hall, 1990); Elizabeth May, ed., *Musics of Many Cultures* (Berkeley: University of California Press, 1980); David Reck, *Music of the Whole Earth* (New York: Scribner's, 1977); Jeff Titon and others, *Worlds of Music* (New York: Schirmer Books, 1984).

Musical Change: Bruno Nettl, ed., *Eight Urban Musical Cultures: Tradition and Change* (Urbana: University of Illinois Press, 1978); Bruno Nettl, *The Western Impact on World Music* (New York: Schirmer Books, 1985); Gerard Béhague, ed., *Performance Practice: Ethnomusicological Perspectives* (Westport, Conn.: Greenwood, 1984).

Instruments: Curt Sachs, *The History of Musical Instruments* (New York: W. W. Norton, 1940); Sibyl Marcuse, *Musical Instruments: A Comprehensive Dictionary* (Garden City, N.Y.: Doubleday, 1964); *The New Grove Dictionary of Musical Instruments* (New York: Macmillan, 1984).

Determinants of Music: Curt Sachs, *The Wellsprings of Music* (The Hague: Martinus Nijhoff, 1961); Alan Lomax and others, *Folk Song Style and Culture* (Washington, D.C.: American Association for the Advancement of Science, 1968).

Views of Western Music: Henry Kingsbury, *Music, Talent, and Performance: A Conservatory Cultural System* (Philadelphia: Temple University Press, 1988).

2

THE MUSIC OF INDIA

Charles Capwell

ATTENDING A MUSIC CONFERENCE IN CALCUTTA

Getting There

As the sun disappeared from the late afternoon sky of a January day, a mild temperature inversion progressively trapped more and more visible pollutants in the thickening air hovering above the streets and buildings of Calcutta. Ignoring my smarting eyes and abandoning the search for a taxi, I settled on taking a more economical bus ride downtown. The first bus to arrive at the stop, however, was full to overflowing and was besieged by a group far hardier than I, some of whom managed to buffet their way onto the stair landing or grab on to the rear of the bus for a free but perilous ride. The situation didn't improve much with the arrival of the second bus, so when the third one showed up I joined the siege and succeeded in intimidating enough of my rivals with a judicious use of elbows and feet to get a purchase on the first stair. Pressure from those descending the bus threatened to wrest this foothold from me until the impatience of those boarding behind me propelled me upward into the aisle. Having gotten *inside*, all of us who viewed one another as opponents to be overcome *outside* suddenly felt a comradely warmth towards our neighbors, and a flurry of apologies and wry comments accompanied the liberties we were compelled to take with one another's bodies, though a moment earlier these would have been deliberate and unexcused.

As the bus lurched into traffic, I necessarily struck up an acquaintance with the young man against whom I fell and on whose toes I trampled as I tried to steady myself. My excessive clumsiness tested his fading spirit of camaraderie, but when he learned that we were both headed towards the same "music conference"—series of recitals, that is—he overlooked my assaults and began to chat enthusiastically about the musicians we were going to hear.

When we reached the southeast corner of the Maidan, Calcutta's enormous equivalent of Central Park, Swarup—that was my new acquaintance's name—and I extricated ourselves from the bus and walked the short distance to the entrance of Rabindra Sadan, the modern concert hall named for Rabindranath Tagore.[1]

Preliminaries

Although we had arrived just on time at 6 P.M., the hall was sparsely populated because the conference was to extend over several days, and the lesser-known artists appear earliest in the series as well as at the beginning of each evening. Swarup had come early because the first performer was to be a young dancer who was his classmate at the University of Calcutta, where they both studied physics. Many young dancers these days come from the middle class and are well educated, he told me, although traditionally professional performers in music and dance had little education outside their art and held relatively low social positions. His friend Premlata was just about to complete her M.A. and was torn between continuing her studies in physics and trying to establish a reputation as a professional dancer; if she chose the latter, he said, she would face fierce competition and relatively small rewards.

As people milled about in the audience greeting one another and chatting, a few people began to appear on stage adjusting microphones and vases of flowers; at last, a couple of musicians came out, removed their sandals at the edge of the stage, and placed a few instruments on the carpet at the right. Swarup named them for me: There was a harmonium, a small box with a bellows and a keyboard; a sitar, remotely related to a guitar with a very long, wide neck; a tambura, similar to the sitar but with no frets, since its strings were simply plucked to provide a drone; a pair of small drums called tabla; and another drum,

---

[1]Rabindranath Tagore (1861–1941), winner of the Nobel Prize for poetry in 1913, was one of India's greatest artists. Besides being a poet, he was also a novelist, dramatist, composer, painter, and educator.

Figure 2–1. North Indian *tambura*.

barrel-shaped and having two heads, called pakhavaj (See Figures 2–1 and 2–2). Since no one paid the musicians any attention and they left once again, I started to wonder if something were amiss, but as no one else seemed to be concerned, I relaxed. Soon all the musicians came out, sat on the carpet, and started tuning their instruments. I was a little startled when the tabla player picked up a hammer and started striking his instrument with it; after a few taps at the edge of the skin, however, he would tap the head with his fingers, and I realized he was simply tuning.

The audience still did not seem very interested in the musicians, and even after they started playing many people continued their conversations as others began to settle down. Not until the dancer made her entrance and gracefully made obeisance to the musicians, the in-

Figure 2–2.   A *tabla* maker lacing a new head to the *dahina* or
right drum of the pair.

struments, and the audience in the Indian way by bringing her palms
together in front of her face did most of the audience direct their attention to the stage.

Kathak Dance—Nritta (Abstract Dance)

Since everything had struck me as being rather casual so far, I was totally
unprepared for what happened next. Premlata suddenly leapt into action, flailing her arms, flicking her wrists in circles, snapping her head
from side to side, twitching her brows, and madly pirouetting about,
all the while jingling her ankle bells in crisp rhythms that mimicked
the drum, which she punctuated by sharply slapping the soles of her
bare feet against the floor of the stage. Then in an instant all this diz-
zying activity was coordinated into one brilliant movement, bringing
everything to a complete and astonishing halt, and the dancer froze—
one arm straight out and the other arched above her head, fingers twitch-

ing and eyebrows quivering as though to express the uncontainable kinetic vitality the rhythms inspired in her.

Watching her repeat these waves of activity and repose, I began to understand why this music conference had begun with a dancer. It was as though she were simply a physical realization of the musical rhythms the drummer played, all of which seemed to be magically transmitted to Premlata's feet, while the rest of her body exquisitely ornamented these rhythms. Sometimes the drummer and Premlata would speak to one another in a string of special rhythmic syllables called bols, whose rhythms they would then reproduce on the drum and with the feet.

Kathak Dance—Abhinaya (Mimed Dance)

There was more to it than just this, I soon discovered. As the harmonium player started to sing, Premlata's physical abstractions of rhythm gave way to mime, and she began to act out the words of his song with gestures and facial expressions but no props. Swarup interpreted for me the words to the beautiful melody, which the sitar and harmonium duplicated, as is customary, without adding any harmony.

It is a very familiar story to many Indians, in large part because it has been retold for many generations in many different media such as kathak, the kind of dance we were enjoying. The Hindu god Krishna is said to have been inordinately fond of butter as a child. As the story begins, Krishna's foster mother, Yashoda, is churning butter. When she has finished her tiring household chore, she puts the butter into a clay pot and hangs it from a rafter in her simple cottage—otherwise, it would be too easy for Krishna to help himself to the butter. (This made me think of the cookie jar naughty American kids are always said to be stealing from.) Then Yashoda leaves the cottage to do some other chore. As the dancer depicts Yashoda's departure, she suddenly twirls about and transforms herself into an impish child to show us the mischievous Krishna intent on retrieving the butter. Frustrated by its being out of reach, he pouts and frets until he thinks of hurling a stone at the pot. At last he succeeds in breaking it and is covered with a torrent of butter, which he greedily licks from hands and arms. Satisfied and very pleased with himself, Krishna quickly realizes he is in trouble, for he sees the look on Yashoda's face when she returns home and discovers his mischief. Now Premlata shifts quickly from one character to the other; she shows Yashoda, beside herself with fury, dragging Krishna about by the ear as she scolds him, then the terrified child cowering in expectation of a beating. Just as Yashoda is indeed raising her hand to give Krishna a solid box on the ear, she sees the terror in the little boy's face and comes to her senses; rather than lashing out at the frightened child, she is overwhelmed with motherly protectiveness. Subject to the irresistible charm of childish innocence that Krishna embodies, she scoops him up in a fond embrace and cuddles and fondles him in delight.

Although the audience was small and was a little inattentive at the start, there were many appreciative cries of "Bah, bah!" (Bravo!) and "Bahut accha!" (Very good!) for her skill both in abstract dance and in mime. Swarup seemed pleased with the response, which he had done his best to encourage as a less than impartial critic.

During the brief interval before the next item on the program we stepped outside for a cup of tea, and I mentioned to him my initial surprise at having a dancer in a music concert.

"Not surprising at all,"he replied. "After all, the name of the sponsoring association is 'Kolkata Sangita Mela.'"

"That's the Calcutta Music Festival, right?" I asked.

"Yes, but *sangita*, which we generally translate as 'music,' means not just the melody and rhythm of instrument and voice, but also the embodiment of rhythm in dance and the dramatic expression of story and mood through dance and song as well."

Vocal and Instrumental Performance: Khyal and Gat-Tora

Two days later, Swarup and I had tea together again during a break in the last evening's group of performances, which were continuing throughout the night. As it was four in the morning, I desperately needed the stimulant and wished that I had taken the opportunity for a catnap during one of the earlier performances, as some of my neighbors had surprised me by doing. I certainly did not want to fall asleep during the next performance, since the artist was considered among the foremost musicians in India and had been given the position of honor as the final performer. We had just heard a singer, however, who was also considered one of the great musicians performing today, and I wanted Swarup's opinion about his performance. I confessed that I had difficulty keeping awake at the start because the pace seemed so slow.

"Well, that's not surprising, since you don't know what to listen for," Swarup told me rather baldly, I thought. But of course he was right, I admitted to myself—that's why I wanted his opinion. "A full-scale performance of khyal, the kind of piece we just heard, begins in vilambit lay, slow tempo, and concludes—maybe thirty of forty minutes later—in drut lay, or fast tempo. You probably found the faster part more enjoyable, right?"

"That's right!" I readily agreed. "I could hardly believe my ears when he sang those rapid passages, the virtuosity was so astonishing."

"Yes, his tans are exceptionally clean and precise, but is alap is even more satisfying to the connoisseur."

"That's the slow part?"

"Right. In the beginning the singer's task is to show subtlety rather than virtuosity in the artistry he employs to reveal the rag, the particular set of pitches, that he has chosen to sing."

"He must have been very successful, then," I suggested, "because I noticed many people in the audience shaking their heads and making other gestures and comments of approval."

"Oh, yes, he was in particularly good form tonight—but then, artists are often inspired to do their best in Calcutta because they know the audience is especially sophisticated and demanding here."

We decided to finish our tea quickly and return to the hall in order not to miss the beginning of the final performance. I noticed a palpable air of excitement in the hall as people roused themselves for the arrival of the last star performer just as the dawn was breaking outside. Appreciative applause greeted the famous sitarist's presence on stage, and a murmur of excitement went round the audience as he announced the raga he would play—one that he himself had created, Swarup said.

Like the singer's performance of khyal, the sitarist's performance of gat-tora began slowly with a careful step-by-step revelation of the raga that began in a low range and slowly worked its way higher, setting each pitch in its particular melodic relationship to the others. No tabla accompaniment was used for the sitarist's alap, however, and only after he had explored the whole range of the raga did the sitarist introduce a steady pulse into his melody. I had mentioned to Swarup that in the slow khyal I had been distracted by the drone pitches that were constantly played on the tamburas, but as he had assured me I would do, I was beginning to learn to focus on the melody and to be aware of the drone only subliminally. With no other harmony to distract me, I began to appreciate the individual pitches of the melody as they stood out against the tonal backdrop of the droning tamburas and began to understand why others would occasionally shake their heads or murmur in approval of something the artist did. Rather than feeling drowsy, I began to be entranced by the contemplation of these beautiful sounds (Figure 2–3).

The contemplative mood changed to a more active one, however, when, as with the khyal, the tempo picked up and the playing became more dazzling and virtuosic, the sitarist strumming driving rhythmic patterns on the drone strings to accompany his melody. After this flashy climax the whole procedure was begun over, but with the added interest of tabla accompaniment and tala—that is, meter. At the climax the tabla player, too, displayed an amazing skill that rivaled the soloist's, whereas in the fast khyal, the tabla had only occasionally drawn my attention. At the end, the two performers engaged in a kind of duel in which the intricate rhythms the soloist initiated on the sitar were reproduced by the tabla player as a sort of answer to a challenging rhythmic question. After a while the patterns became shorter and shorter,

Figure 2–3. Nikhil Banerjee playing *sitar* at a 1971 concert in the former princely state of Maihar on the occasion of a birthday celebration for his teacher "Baba" Alauddin Khan, who was once the court musician there. Alauddin Khan was also the teacher of his son, the *sarod* player Ali Akbar Khan, and of the *sitariya* Ravi Shankar.

until the sitar and tabla merged for a hair-raising finish that brought the house down.

Leaving the hall thinking we had certainly gotten our money's worth during the previous night, Swarup and I decided to walk home and take advantage of the brisk morning air to refresh ourselves for the long day ahead. Having patiently answered many of my questions during the last few days, Swarup now proceeded to interrogate me about how I perceived the differences between his classical music tradition and my own.

"The most striking difference," I began, "is certainly that every performance we've seen in the last few days has focused on solo perform- ance, vocal or instrumental or dance, with the accompaniment of a drum and the support of a drone. At home, I've attended concerts ranging from true solo recitals to performances by a couple of hundred instrumentalists and singers."

"That's the very thing I like about Western music," Swarup agreed enthusiastically. "There's such a wide range of groups. But you know, when I visited my uncle in London last year and he took me to a performance of Handel's *Messiah*, he complained afterwards about its all sounding the same to him—though he's been in London twenty years now! He said, I remember, 'It's all the same rag.'"

Laughing, I nonetheless had to agree with Swarup's uncle. "Yes, I guess he's right. We have a variety of combinations of voices and instruments but are limited in much classical music to major or minor, whereas you use an enormous variety of rags. How do you remember them all, anyway? We must have heard at least a dozen different ones in these recitals, and yet you seemed acquainted with them all. For us it doesn't matter whether a piece is in E-flat or C-sharp; it's still the same old scale just placed a little higher or lower. And for the great majority of music lovers, knowing the difference between one chord and another doesn't enter into it."

"Well, most of the audience here doesn't recognize more than a few common rags either, but those who've studied music seriously, as I have, eventually come to recognize dozens, while any good performer has to be able to keep a couple of dozen or so active in his performing repertory."

"Without the use of notation, either," I added in admiration.

"Not for performance, no, but students often do write down a short composition they're learning in order to record a kind of capsule summary of the way a rag should go."

"That can't be too much help," I objected, "since a performance is almost entirely improvised. As you pointed out to me, the composition is simply used as a kind of cadence, an occasional resting place for the soloist to plan what's coming next and to let the tabla player do more than simply keep time."

"Speaking of the tabla," Swarup interrupted, "you've not said anything about tal so far."

"You mean how I feel it is different from Western meter?"

"Yes. You see, I'm afraid that as regards meter I feel somewhat similarly about Western music to the way my uncle felt about keys or major and minor. Although something like the waltz is very catchy, it's all pretty limited, don't you think?"

Again I laughed and agreed. "Our meters are basically simple and repetitive—until the twentieth century, anyway, when all sorts of possibilities have arisen to replace the idea of key as well as regular meter."

By this time we had arrived in front of Swarup's home, and we decided to continue our discussion sometime in the future—when we would, we hoped, be a little less sleepy. As we parted, we thought of the old saw, "Music is a universal language." Perhaps, we agreed, it had started out as something closer to "Music, like language, is universal," since we both felt that, though music might be everywhere, to understand someone else's music was like learning to understand someone else's language.

ROOTS

The Vedas

Music in India is a lively phenomenon of contemporary life, but of course it has a history and is founded on the continuity of tradition. As the record of India's civilizations and learning stretch back for millennia, it is not surprising to find music as one of the elements figuring in that record. A charming statuette of a dancing girl, for example, is found among the archeological remains of one of the world's oldest civilizations, the Harappan, located in Pakistan and northwestern India, which had connections with the early agricultural theocracies of Mesopotamia in the second millennium B.C.E. During this period new people were arriving in the area from further north and west who, though they apparently had a more primitive culture than that of the people in Harappan urban centers, nevertheless managed through a combination of circumstance and force to supplant the culture of their predecessors.

One of the attributes of the Harappan civilization was a writing system, but the newcomers were nonliterate, and for them the power of sound embodied in speech was an aspect of the divine. Speakers of an Aryan language related to most of those spoken in Europe today, the newcomers extolled the power and beauty of their gods in a body of poems they had brought with them which they preserved through oral transmission. Eventually, these poems of the Rig-Veda came to be the special responsibility of the top-ranking of the four divisions or *varnas* of society, whose many ramifications we call "castes." The Brahmins (also spelled Brahmans), as the members of the top varna were called, were entrusted with supernatural and intellectual matters and were given a long and intensive education from childhood, the purpose of which was to ensure the correct transmission and the correct pronunciation of the Vedic hymns. Particular care had to be taken to preserve these because their very sounds were considered to be the necessary means for coercing the gods to provide for the needs of the people, and after many generations in a new land the people feared that the archaic language and pronunciation of the Vedas would be lost. In order to preserve the accent patterns of ancient Vedic, for example, the Brahmins adopted the practice of associating the three types of spoken accent with a relative pitch level; this gives the recitation of Rigvedic texts the quality of chant, a chant whose melodic contour depends precisely upon the succession of accent in the sung syllables. A further musical component is evident in the durations of the pitches; these too depend on the syllables, since Vedic, like classical Latin or Greek, based its prosody on the relative length of syllables rather than on a pattern of feet as English verse does. So important was the *sound* of the text that, long after the enormously elaborate ritual sacrifices of Vedic religion had died out, the Vedas continued to be preserved in oral transmission; the habit of writing them down is relatively recent. Even today some Brahmin boys are trained to memorize the Vedas in chant, although contemporary Hinduism, while venerating the Vedas, has little connection with the ancient ritualistic religion founded upon them.

The Antiquity of Theory

A further musical element entered into the preservation of the Rig-Veda texts when these were rearranged for use as hymn texts in the Sama-Veda and were sung to a collection of special tunes called Samagana. It is these religiously based traditions of chant and song to which the early Sanskrit writers on musical theory and practice refer as the source for the secular art music with which they are concerned. Being intellectuals themselves, the theoretical and prescriptive writers on music naturally looked to the intellectual tradition that preserved the Vedas as a means to provide their own tradition with prestige and dignity; therefore, in the dramaturgical treatise Natyasastra, written sometime before the fifth century C.E., the performing arts are considered a "new" Veda, more suited for the enlightenment of humankind in a degenerate age than its predecessors.

Music, as one of the performing arts, is treated at some length in the Natyasastra, since it is considered an adjunct of drama, or natya. The purpose of drama-according to Bharata, the eponymous author of this work—is to create an experience of aesthetic pleasure, or rasa, in the spectator. To effect this the dramatist must use a panoply of particular devices in certain ways, and these are carefully codified in the Natyasastra. Among them, for example, are special types of scales and patterns derived from them and distinct types of songs, all of which have prescribed uses for certain types of scenes or situations.

Continuity and Divergence of Theory and Practice

While the technical matter of the musical discussion in the Natyasastra is not entirely clear today and it is certain that much has changed over the centuries, it is nevertheless evident that some aspects of musical practice today are related to some of those mentioned in the treatise. To cite one aspect, the matter of prescribing a variety of scales and their characteristic patterns (that is, the defining of modes, or ragas, as they were later to be called in India) continues to be one of the main theoretical concerns of classical music in India. In the Natyasastra the scale that completely filled in an octave was said to contain twenty-two steps, and this continues to influence the way many musicians and theorists think about the octave today, even though for all practical purposes only twelve steps are now used, as in the Western scale. (Play, for example, twelve successive keys on the piano, white and black, and the thirteenth will sound much like the pitch you began with, only higher or lower). Such is the prestige of ancient theory that, though it may contradict current practice, it is nevertheless accommodated.

But how is it possible to say that twelve and twenty-two are the same? On an instrument like the piano, this is indeed difficult to conceive, but the distinct and precise pitches of the piano can, when sung or played on a violin, be made to slide from one to another, the space between them being imperceptibly filled. Such flexibility is used to great advantage in Indian melody, which is expressively ornamented to a much greater degree than in the West. The ornamentation is therefore integral to Indian melody and not incidental, and in these ornaments, a musician may say, lie the ancient twenty-two divisions of the scale, which have given their name—sruti—to the modern subtleties of intonation and ornamentation of the twelve-pitch modern scale. Herein, too, lies the Western misconception that Indian music uses scales constructed on pitches quite different from those of the Western chromatic scale of twelve pitches. While a musician of Tehran who uses the piano to play a dastgah may, in fact, have to tune it differently from "normal," harmonium players in India find that a single set of twelve pitches suffices to play any raga.

North and South: The Hindustani and Karnatak Systems

The concept of raga has been used in the previous paragraphs to suggest the continuity of musical thought over many centuries in India, but it may also help us to understand the current dichotomy in Indian classical music, which today exists in two related systems, the Hindustani system of North India and the Karnatak (Carnatic) system of South India. Along the lines laid down over the centuries by theorists, both the Hindustani and Karnatak systems represent ragas as more than just a collection of pitches in a scale. For example, specifying certain pitches for particular emphasis, or forbidding some pitch or pitches from being used in ascending or descending the scale, or requiring that the scale double back on itself before continuing in the original direction, or stating what form a note is to take (sharped, flatted, or natural) in ascent or descent—all these are common features of raga in both systems. Although a raga in the Hindustani system may be essentially the same as its Karnatak counterpart according to such rules and may be recognizably similar in performance, the styles of performance are nevertheless sufficiently different to make it difficult for someone acquainted with one style to appreciate the other. This is a difficulty encountered more, perhaps, by the Hindustani music lover listening to Karnatak music than vice versa; the smoother, more sensuous quality of North Indian performance often seems more melodious and therefore more accessible than the intricately ornamented and demanding melodies of the South, which require longer familiarity and attention to appreciate—even for North Indians.

This distinction in style has developed over the last seven centuries, according to the documentation of theory, which has, since the thirteenth-century treatise Sangitaratnakara, tended to reflect a divergence in musical culture that nevertheless remains founded on a common heritage. One may now find ragas of the North and South that have a common name—bhairavi, to name a popular example—although their different evolutions have resulted in their having quite different musical features, even different scales.

Hindu/Muslim Attitudes toward Music and Its Transmission

In part, this divergence in musical culture is attributable to the fact that North India came under the increasing political and cultural influence of a new group of people who entered from the northwest in the manner of the ancient invaders who brought the Vedas with them. Millennia ago, the Aryan-speaking invaders settled in the North and had the profoundest influence there, and the Dravidian speakers of the South although they adopted Vedic practices, the Sanskrit language of learning, and many elements of social culture such as caste—retained their own regional languages and many other aspects of their regional heritage. From the thirteenth century on, the influence of Persian and Turkish culture and of the Islamic religion, which had been sporadically encountered during the previous five centuries, became of singular importance for North India when the foreigners established political control over the area from the city of Delhi.

As the importance of Persian culture and language grew, the significance of Sanskrit learning waned, and expertise in music came largely to mean knowledge of a repertory and style of performance learned through oral transmission in certain families of professional musicians, mostly Muslim. By the time the British had made the last Mughal Emperor a puppet in the early nineteenth century, the lineages, or gharanas, established by these families and their students jealously guarded their various musical heritages as trade secrets to be shared only with talented sons or especially dedicated and loyal men from outside the family. To become the shagird (pupil) of an ustad (master) was to become an apprentice in a closed guild. While this apprentice system still obtains to a degree in India, and many people feel it is the only proper way to be trained as a professional musician, it is also felt that the remnants of exclusivity and jealousy of the old system of training have hampered the development of Hindustani music.

In Karnatak music the attitude toward musical preservation and transmission has been somewhat different from that of the North. The gharanas of the North ultimately derive their legitimacy from the famous sixteenth-century musician Tansen, who was brought to the imperial court near Delhi by Akbar at the high point of the Mughal reign (Figure 2–4). In the South the name to conjure with is that of Tyagaraja, who

Figure 2–4.   A pavilion surrounded by water in the imperial city Fatehpur Sikri where Tansen is said to have performed for the Mughal Emperor Akbar in the sixteenth century.

is remembered not simply as a great musician but also as a remarkable saint. Unlike Tansen, who during his lifetime accepted positions at various courts, Tyagaraja steadfastly refused an appointment to the southern court of Tanjore, where Karnatak musical culture was flourishing at the end of the eighteenth century. Instead he composed his songs exclusively for his chosen deity Rama, and not being a professional musician he was not concerned about keeping these songs as the inheritance of his family tradition alone. Over the last couple of centuries, as the songs of Tyagaraja and his contemporaries came to form the core of Karnatak music and were passed from guru (teacher) to shishya (disciple), different traditions of repertory and style inevitably arose, but these did not acquire the same sense of familial exclusivity and professional secrecy as did the northern gharanas.

In the stories of the careers of Tansen and Tyagaraja, we touch upon some distinctions between Hindu and Muslim attitudes toward music as well. Tansen, himself a Hindu, established himself and his Muslim descendants essentially as professional entertainers, with the association of relatively low status. His legendary predecessor Gopal Nayak, like Tyagaraja, remained primarily a Hindu religious devotee, and the Hindu view that music is a worthy religious offering and a means to spiritual enlightenment continues to ensure him, as it does Tyagaraja, great respect and high status. The orthodox Muslim fear of music as a sensual enticement that may lead to debauchery rather than to spiritual advancement has tainted the practice of music, particularly in the North, and musicians have carefully tried to maintain a distinction between music as high art and music as mere sensual gratification. Musicians who were members of Hindustani gharanas, for example, fought to keep exclusive control of their heritage, in part to guarantee them higher status than that accorded to their accompanists, who often accompanied women dancers and served as their teachers.

A similar distinction prevailed in dance. The dance we encountered in the Calcutta concert, kathak, began as an elaborate form of storytelling employing music and gesture for the recounting of religious tales. In the nineteenth century, it reached its apogee as an art form preserved by Brahmin men at the Shi'a Muslim court of Lucknow, where the dance was so admired that even the Shi'a king Wajid Ali Shah was a student of the dance—by all accounts quite a competent one, too! Being based in the Hindu religion and performed by Brahmin men, kathak had as much respectability as a performing art could have—which is to say, not a great deal. Other types of dance—or nautch, as it was known during the British period—were performed by professional female dancers for the enjoyment of male audiences, who sometimes paid for sexual entertainment as well; naturally these were less respectable.

In the South, trained dancers were required at temples and courts for various rituals and ceremonies. Thje devadasis, or "servants of the gods," were dedicated as children to the service of the temple and received an intensive training in the art of dance; being "married" to the temple deity, they were not allowed to marry in the usual sense and were therefore not constrained to the limited world of the respectable housewife. Living outside the normal social role for women, they did not have the housewife's "respectability"; but being married to a deity, they could never become widows, who were believed to bring misfortune to all, including themselves. In fact, because of their good fortune in this regard, devadasis were also known as "ever auspicious," and their presence at rites and ceremonies was believed to ensure the welfare of all involved.

While not permitted to marry, the devadasis often became the concubines of prominent men, and the children they had by them often became dancers, if girls, or musicians and dance teachers, if boys. These families, having a hereditary association with music and dance, had a lesser status than did Brahmin musicians like Tyagaraja; thus in South India there was a difference in status among musicians similar to that found in the North between gharana members and the men who accompanied them as well as accompanying dancing girls.

In the late nineteenth and early twentieth centuries, some prominent intellectuals sought to remove the stigma associated with the performing arts and to rehabilitate them, so that the growing middle class could take over their patronage and development as the importance of the aristocracy and religious institutions waned in this regard. The change they effected just before independence from Britain in 1949 was perhaps most noticeable in the dance, where, as we have seen in the description of the concert in Calcutta, women of the middle class may now take up a career in dancing without necessarily losing their status. In the South, too, there are probably more middle-class women dancing Bharata Natyam, the classical style of Karnatak dance, than women from the traditional families of performers. The traditional distinction between the high caste of Brahmins and the low castes associated with musical professions has created a social tension in the musical life of South India, as the latter naturally feel they have been the respository for real musical competence, while the former feel they have made it possible to continue the heritage of Karnatak music in the new venue of the public concert hall.

THE KARNATAK RECITAL AND TYPES OF PIECES

In our discussion of a concert series in Calcutta we briefly mentioned some aspects of the performance of dance, instrumental music, and vocal music. Now let us consider the components of a music recital and a dance recital in South India as we might encounter them in the major South Indian city of Madras. In doing so, we can make a comparison with what we have learned about Hindustani performance and elaborate upon it as well (Figure 2–5).

Vocal music has a special importance in South India because it also provides the repertory for instrumental music; in other words, instrumentalists play the tunes of vocal music, and in doing so they generally try to maintain the articulation of the tune as determined by the pronunciation of the words in the original text. Where a syllable of text would be enunciated in a song, for example, a vina player (see p. 34) will pluck a string. Vocal music is important in Hindustani music, too,

Figure 2–5. *Sarod*

but instrumentalists rarely reproduce it, and then only as an item of light classical music at the end of a recital.

A Karnatak recital normally starts with a piece called varnam, whose purpose is to allow the performer to warm up with a familiar item. Often compared to a Western "etude"—a technical "study," as the name indicates—this is a kind of musical exercise that prepares the musician for the demands of the rest of his or her program.

The major portion of the program normally consists of pieces called kritis, which consist of three sections—pallavi, anupallavi, and caranam. The first portion of the pallavi serves as a refrain, recurring at the end of the pallavi as well as at the end of the anupallavi and of the caranam. The kritis of Tyagaraja and of his contemporaries Syama Sastri and Muttuswami Dikshitar, all stemming from the late eighteenth and early nineteenth centuries, form a significant part of the repertory of most performers; though these pieces were not written down by their composers, they are "compositions" in the sense of being fixed songs preserved through oral transmission. They have, in fact, been notated in recent times as an alternative to preservation through performance.

In the performance of a kriti, the singer or instrumentalist has several options despite the "fixed" aspect of the composition. First, he or she may decide to precede the composition itself with an improvised exposition of the ragam (as raga is named in the South) in which the kriti is composed. This performance, which is itself also called ragam or, alternatively, alapanam, allows the artist to demonstrate accomplishment in depicting the specific musical characteristics of the ragam in which the kriti has been composed. The audience thereby either learns the nature of the ragam, if it is unfamiliar, or, if it is well known, can judge the skill and expertise of the artist in his or her rendition.

The alapanam is in free rhythm; that is, it is without a regular pulse. It is also, therefore, unaccompanied by percussion; only the tambura provides a drone. Eventually the alapanam progresses to tanam when the artist introduces a regular pulsation into the improvisation. Although there is now a pulse, there is no regularity in its arrangement that would produce a meter, or talam (the Karnatak version of tala), and the percussion is still absent. The equivalent procedures in Hindustani instrumental music like the sitar performance discussed earlier are called alap-jor; jor is often followed—again, as in the sitar recital—with a flashy section of rhythmic drone strumming called jhala, but this lacks an equivalent in Karnatak music.

Melodic accompaniment of the Karnatak soloist is generally provided by a violinist who tries to imitate the soloist, immediately reproducing every turn of phrase. The violinist also alternates with the soloist in providing his or her own rendition of ragam and tanam, but during these periods the soloist is silent.

After the ragam-tanam has been concluded, the soloist begins the kriti, which, being in a regularized meter, or talam, is accompanied by percussion. If the artist has preceded the kriti with an improvised ragam-tanam, then he or she will likely insert appropriate kinds of improvisation into the composition as well. These are of two types: niraval and svarakalpana. In the former, the articulation of the melody—derived from the text—is maintained while the pitch content is varied within the prescriptions of the ragam; in the latter, the names of the pitches—sa, re, ga, ma, pa, dha, ni—are sung instead of the text or, if played instrumentally, each pitch is articulated separately. This practice is somewhat similar to Western solfège or solfeggio, a kind of vocal exercise that uses *do*, *re*, *mi*, etc., in place of words.

The beginner who wants to determine when improvisation is being used in the kriti should try to notice when the violinist and soloist no longer perform in unison. During the unison, of course, they both have the composition in mind, but when the soloist improvises, the accompanist must follow as in the alapanam. And there will normally be an alternation between soloist and accompanist as well, so that the accompanist temporarily becomes a soloist, too, again as in the improvised alapanam.

After the kriti, if the soloist is particularly good at improvisation, ragam-tanam-pallavi may be performed. In this case the pallavi that follows the ragam-tanam may be the first section of a kriti or may be newly composed by the soloist, but it is merely a composed fragment that is not followed by the remainder of a full-scale composition. Instead the artist immediately begins to perform niraval and svarakalpana on a more extensive scale than would be usual in a kriti. Yet a third kind of improvisation may be used; this is trikala, in which the artist will alter the relation of the pallavi to the talam by, for example, doubling, then tripling, then quadrupling the duration of its notes, and then perhaps reversing the process to return to the original note values. The purpose of this type of improvisation is to demonstrate virtuosic control over the time component of performance, since the most important feat in any type of improvisation is to never lose one's place in the talam and to be able to conclude precisely at its first beat, samam, or at the beginning of the pallavi.

Ragam-tanam-pallavi is considered the ultimate test of a musician, since it requires exceptional training, great confidence, and spontaneous creative ability. Although composed songs play a very great role in Karnatak music, improvisation nevertheless has special prominence. In Hindustani music, serious vocal and instrumental styles are both almost entirely improvised and in this regard are more like pallavi in Karnatak music. Relatively fixed songs are used only in so-called light classical music, the repertory for which derives from regional folk styles, religious devotional music, and lyric songs of an erotic nature associated with dance.

After a performance of ragam-tanam-pallavi, the mood of a Karnatak recital generally changes to something less profound and demanding, and as in Hindustani recitals, pieces of a lyrical, erotic mood may be sung. Padams and javalis constitute this repertory; these are pieces associated with the lighter side of the bharata natyam dance style, in which emphasis is placed on mime and gesture for the interpretation of the songs' lyrics. Similar in construction to kritis, padams and javalis also have pallavi, anupallavi, and caranam sections. In performing these, the artist is expected to display a sensitively expressive style rather than the technical virtuosity of the earlier part of the recital.

In a Hindustani recital the pieces comparable to padam and javali would be, for example, thumri, associated with the female dancers of Lucknow and Benares, or dhun, a folk tune from a particular region of India. A Hindu vocalist may also conclude with a devotional bhajan, particularly if he or she wants to avoid any stigma of impropriety.

The Karnatak recitalist may likewise conclude with songs of a devotional nature. While the bulk of Karnatak performance is of fixed compositions, improvisation is of great importance; in Hindustani music it is fair to say that it is all-important, since the "fixed" composition is often no more than a tag of recognizable melody. Such a tag—the eduppu in Karnatak music, the mukhra in Hindustani—is important, however, because it plays a role similar to that of the first beat of the tala, called the sam. It is a reference point which the performer must skillfully pick up at the end of an improvisatory passage to demonstrate that he or she has maintained an awareness of the meter during the improvisation.

To illustrate this, let us consider the kriti "Banturiti" by Tyagaraja. It is in the commonest talam, called adi, which has eight beats indicated by a clap on samam and two other claps on beats 5 and 7; the three beats following samam are indicated by tapping the fingers of the right hand, starting with the little finger, on the palm of the left, and "waving" the right hand, i.e., turning it palm upwards on the palm of the left hand, for beats 6 and 8. The eduppu, or beginning, of this song is midway between beats 2 and 3—that is, after a clap and a tap of the little finger—and the performer must return to this point accurately whenever finishing a passage of niraval or svarakalpana. Alternatively, the performer may choose to conclude at samam.

In a sitar performance that uses the similarly common Hindustani tal called tintal, a composition, or bandis, in slow tempo would normally begin on beat 12 of this sixteen-beat tala, which is kept by clapping on beats 1, 5, and 13 and waving the hand on beat 9. The portion of the bandis between beats 12 and 1 is the mukhra, which the performer will pick up precisely at the right place in concluding a passage of improvisation. Again, alternatively, the performer may conclude on sam.

INSTRUMENTS

Our discussion of Hindustani music has often mentioned the sitar and tabla for the reason—as many of you may have guessed—that these are the most familiar instruments to foreigners. Ever since George Harrison of the Beatles became the temporary disciple of Pandit Ravi Shankar in the mid-sixties, these instruments have occasionally cropped up in Euro-American pop music, and their sounds have become relatively familiar to our ears if not always immediately identifiable. Many other instruments are used in India, of course; the list below is limited to some of the most important.

Sitar: As a group, plucked stringed instruments are the most important in Indian music. A plucked stringed instrument with a long neck, the sitar has frets which allow for shortening a string to produce a change in pitch as on a guitar. The frets do not cover all pitches, however, and are therefore adjustable according to the needs of a particular raga. Many pitches may be played from the same fret by pulling the string sideways and increasing the tension; the neck is particularly wide, to accommodate this technique. The pitches played in this way are, of course, joined seamlessly to one another rather than discretely separated. The strings are of three categories—those used for melody, those used for a drone, and those which are not usually plucked but vibrate in sympathy with the vibrations of the other strings. These "sympathetic" strings and the peculiar construction of the bridge that transmits the sound of the melody and drone strings to the soundboard help to produce the typical buzzing tone color of the sitar. A wire plectrum or pick is worn on the index finger of the right hand to pluck the strings.

Vina: Somewhat similar to the sitar but without sympathetic strings, this instrument has fixed rather than moveable frets. It is the most important Karnatak instrument. The Hindustani vina (also called bin) is much less common and is associated with an old style of vocal music called dhrupad and may have fixed or moveable frets.

Violin: This Western instrument has become so totally assimilated into Indian music over the last two hundred years that it is sometimes difficult for Indians to think of it as nonnative. The performer plays the violin, like other Indian instruments, while seated cross-legged on the floor. This position allows the instrument to be propped between the chest and the ankle, thus freeing the fingering hand to slide up and down the fingerboard with ease to join pitches smoothly to one another. Much more common in the South than in the North, it is very frequently used for accompaniment there, as well as for solo performance; the Hindustani violin is normally a solo instrument.

Harmonium: Introduced by Christian missionaries in the mid-nineteenth century, the harmonium quickly became established in the homes of wealthy Indians of Calcutta, who used it for their own musical entertainment. Now modified to portable size, its bellows are pumped with one hand while the melody is played on the keyboard by the other. Despite being considered a foreign adulteration of Indian music by the British who founded All-India Radio, it has nevertheless managed to become a universal favorite among Indians, who find it eminently useful for accompanying all kinds of vocal music.

Tabla: The common drums for Hindustani music, these paired drums have individual heads and are played with the hands. The treble drum is called dahina, meaning "right," although it may be played with the left hand by a left-hander; the baya, or "left," drum is the bass. The dahina can be tuned, in part, by means of a spot of black, hardened paste in the center of its head; it is normally tuned to sa, or *do*. The baya also has a spot, but it is not precisely tuneable and merely aims at a clear bass resonance.

Mridangam: The common drum for Karnatak music, the mridangam is a single, barrel-shaped drum having two heads, a treble one normally at the right and a bass one at the left. Like the dahina of the tabla, the right head of the mridangam is normally tuned to sa, while the left is not tuned to a pitch. Unlike the baya, however, the left head of the mridangam has no permanent spot of dried paste; instead the player applies a small spot of a porridgelike substance during performance to attain the desired resonance from this head. From time to time, as it dries out, this will be removed and reapplied. A similar drum of Hindustani music is the pakhavaj, mentioned in the discussion of kathak dance; this drum is also used to accompany the Hindustani vina.

Shehnai: A kind of oboe, the Hindustani shehnai has a Karnatak equivalent in the nagasvaram. Both have traditionally been associated with temple rituals, court ceremonies, wedding festivities, and other public music. Now brought into the concert hall to play the concert repertory, they still maintain strong associations with their traditional roles.

The drums used for these oboes are different from the usual tabla of the North and mridangam of the South: louder drums than these were needed for large outdoor ceremonies. The shehnai is accompanied by a small pair of kettledrums called khurdak, although the tabla are often used today, too. A single-barrel drum with two heads, the tavil, is used to accompany nagasvaram. To increase the sound from this drum, the player uses a stick for one head and wears hard thimbles of a plasterlike substance on the fingers of the other hand.

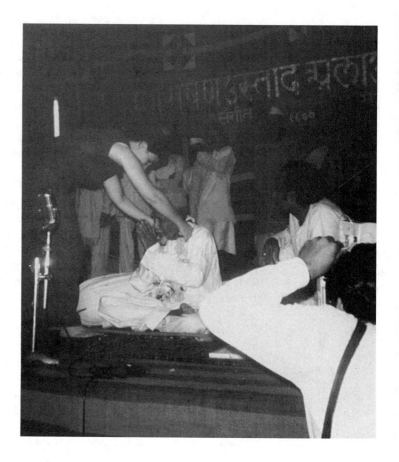

Figure 2–6. Alauddin Khan being garlanded by a visiting
American student at the concert honoring him in Maihar (see
Figure 2–3).

Sarod: Next to the sitar, the sarod is the most popular Hindustani
instrument (Figure 2–6). It too is a plucked stringed instrument, but
it has no frets. To produce a smooth transition from one pitch to another,
the player often slides a finger along the string rather than pulling it
to the side as is done on fretted instruments. To facilitate this, the fingerboard is covered with a chrome-plated sheet of metal, and the finger-
nail rather than the pad of the fingertip is used to stop the string. A
plectrum, or pick, of coconut shell is used to pluck the strings. Deriving from a popular Afghani instrument, the sarod has been indigen-
ized for about the last two hundred years. It has undergone greater
change than the violin during that period and has become just as firmly established in its importance for Indian music.

Bansuri. The Indian flute known as the bansuri has a special significance since it is the instrument played by the Hindu god Krishna, who is said to bewitch his devotees with its seductive music. The Karnatak version is called venu or kuzhal. Both Hindustani and Karnatak flutes are among the simplest instruments, being made from a tube of bamboo with the necessary holes bored into it. Despite the simplicity of their technology, Indian flutes are capable of producing the most sophisticated and technically demanding music in the hands of a skilled performer. Particularly in the South, flutes are connected with dance and temple music and are also used in folk music, but like oboes they have also become "naturalized" into the concert hall.

Less common instruments than those discussed above also play a role in India's music. Just a few of these are mentioned below.

Guitar: Played in slide-guitar fashion, this Western instrument has been adopted for Hindustani music quite successfully. Perhaps the existence of a type of vina, also played in slide fashion, helped to prepare entry of the instrument into Indian music. The Hindustani slide vina (vichitra vina) is now rarely heard, but its Karnatak counterpart, the gottuvadyam, is more common.

Santur: Counterparts of this instrument, all related to the Persian santur, are found throughout the world, from the hammered dulcimer of American folk music to the cimbalom of Hungarian Gypsies and the yang qin of China. The santur's recent entry into Hindustani music came via the northwestern state of Kashmir, where it has traditionally been used in music accompanying ceremonies of the Sufi sect of Islam.

Saxophone: Another instrument borrowed from the West, this instrument, like its relative the clarinet, has become a substitute for the nagasvaram in Karnatak music, and like the latter it is accompanied by tavil (see shehnai).

Jalatarangam: This instrument is a collection of small porcelain bowls whose pitch is regulated by filling them with different amounts of water. The bowls are sounded by being struck with a stick.

THE REALM OF INDIAN MUSIC

In considering the instruments of Indian music, we necessarily had to mention that influence from outside has made a significant contribution to this aspect of Indian culture; but India itself has had a profound influence on music outside its borders as well. First of all, we should remember that borders are political entities brought about through circumstances that do not always reflect "natural" linguistic and ethnic groupings. The India that came into existence as an independent state in 1947 when British rule ended, for example, was not the same as "British India." The latter included the present-day countries of Pakistan and Bangladesh but not, technically speaking, the independent princedoms of the Indian subcontinent, which were compelled to join the Indian union only upon the dissolution of British India. Not surprisingly, Hindustani music is an important part of the musical life of Bangladesh and Pakistan. In Afghanistan, too, Hindustani music is viewed as having great prestige. Because in the past the court at Kabul favored Hindustani music, musicians from other areas of Afghanistan as well have come to accept its performance and its theory as a standard of excellence. In this Muslim country, the technical and theoretical apparatus associated with Hindustani music helps to distance it from the stigma of sensual indulgence and thereby to raise the status of musicians. Regional styles still persist, of course, and are generally more favored by the masses of people than the Hindustani. Hindustani music performed for the guests at a wedding may lend prestige to the affair, but the familiar chaharbeiti songs and atan, the national dance, are what will get the audience most involved.

The island country of Sri Lanka (formerly Ceylon) has long-standing cultural links with India, and both Hindustani and Karnatak music are to be heard there. The indigenous Sinhalese population, speaking an Aryan tongue, and the Tamil-speaking immigrant community from South India naturally tend to view the difference in musical styles as yet another of the differences that separate their unfortunately antagonistic ethnic groups.

While India's musical links with nearby countries might be expected, we should not overlook the fact that many Indians—and Pakistanis and Bangladeshis—now live abroad and have brought elements of their musical culture with them. In Europe and America many communities of immigrants from the subcontinent have formed societies for sponsoring musical events that serve as potent reminders to those recently settled abroad of their cultural heritage. They also serve to introduce traditional cultural values to the younger generation born abroad.

Of course, the younger generation, whether born in India or abroad, is often more interested in something less highfalutin than classical music, and there is no doubt that the most widely supported type of Indian music is that associated with the film industry. An Indian film without musical numbers is almost unheard-of, and India makes more films than any other country; it stands to reason, therefore, that films are the greatest source of popular music. A filmigit ("film song") hit is virtually impossible to escape even if one does not attend the movies or listen to the radio in India, because it is sure to be broadcast over the public-address systems used by neighborhood organizations to help celebrate numerous festivals that occur throughout the year. Many kinds of music serve to provide filmigit with material—from folk songs and classically based melodies to rock and jazz—and a variety of instruments and studio recording techniques all help to make it a diverse music with something for nearly every taste. Because the early filmmaking practice of dubbing musical numbers has been continued to the present, actors lip-synch to the recordings of famous singers. Dozens of actresses, for example, have appeared on the screen all singing with the voice of the enormously popular Lata Mangeshkar! Lata's voice alone could offer the hope of rescue to a film that might otherwise have been a flop. The well-educated and musically sophisticated often denigrate this enormous quantity of mass-produced music; in so doing, however, they often miss out on a good deal of musical pleasure.

New experiments fusing Western popular music and jazz with Indian music are taking place both in India and abroad, with the impetus coming from Western as well as Indian musicians. For example, Ananda Shankar, son of the dancer Uday Shankar and nephew of the sitarist Pandit Ravi Shankar, has developed a sophisticated stage show of music and dance that is an original amalgam of Western and Indian ideas—not surprising in a man whose father and uncle were already entertaining Europeans with original music and dance in the thirties. Abroad, the Karnatak violinist L. Shankar (not related) and the tabla player Zakir Hussain have had great success playing a remarkably Indianized jazz with artists like the American guitarist John McLaughlin.

Perhaps one of the most interesting and successful blends of Indian and Western music is taking place in a type of song with roots in Islamic culture but with a broad appeal to all who appreciate the tradition of romantic Urdu poetry. The ghazal is a well-loved poetic form that consists of a chain of related couplets—each of which, however, expresses a self-contained idea—often culminating in a kind of "punchline" couplet that will bring exclamations of appreciation from a group attending a traditional poetry-reading session called a mushaira. Ghazals are also sung and may be performed by singers with considerable classical training; in the past, singing ghazals was often one of the accomplishments of courtesans. While these types of ghazal recitation and singing are at the sophisticated and elegant end of the spectrum, more popular types of ghazal are to be found, for example, among filmigit, in which the form has an important place.

Popular ghazal has reached a new level of sophistication and refinement in its own right in a blend of Western jazz harmony and synthesized instrumentation with more traditional features of ghazal performance produced in modern multitrack recording studios in London. The flexibility of ghazal has made it an excellent medium for experimentation and is sure to guarantee it continued vitality in the musical life of Indian communities throughout the world.

The kind of blend we find in the new London ghazal raises the possibility of crossover from the Indian community to its host environment. There has not been much evidence of this so far, but a type of Indo-British pop music combining aspects of rock with a folk-music and dance style from the state of Punjab called bhangra has made some slight inroads in this direction and may point to possibilities for the future. The rock-bhangra style has special appeal for London teenagers of Indian parentage. It allows them to identify themselves ethnically and at the same time to participate in social dancing at clubs, which lets them distance themselves from their parents' heritage and participate in a style of life more similar to that of other young people.

PROSPECTS

While Indian music has had an influence on international pop styles, it is perhaps overshadowed today by the phenomenal spread of Afropop, which is now becoming well known in Europe and America. But since the advent of groups like the Beatles, Oregon, and Shakti, Western pop and jazz have acquired new possibilities through an awareness of Indian music.

This is not to say that Western classical music has remained uninfluenced, however. Western composers have always had an interest in "exotic" music, such as that of the Janissaries, the Turkish military guards. (Listen to Mozart's opera *The Abduction from the Seraglio* or to the finale of Beethoven's Ninth Symphony, for example, and you will hear the bass drum, triangle, and cymbals used to conjure up the Janissary band.) In the twentieth century, composers like the Frenchman Olivier Messiaen and the American John Cage have found inspiration in the abstract theoretical components of Indian music. The former, for example, found in the theoretical descriptions of ancient talas material that helped him construct his *Turangalila Symphony*, while the latter, in his piano sonatas, attempted to write pieces that would reflect his understanding of the theory of rasa, which we encountered in our discussion of the Natyasastra.

During the last twenty to thirty years, recordings of Indian music have become widely available, making the sounds as easy to refer to on disk and tape as the theory is in books, and ease of travel has allowed Indian artists to appear abroad. The result has been a more readily apparent influence of the sounds and performance practice of Indian music in the works of composers like Terry Riley, Steve Reich, and Philip Glass, many of whom have taken the time to study with musicians from India and other countries (as have, for that matter, a number of pop musicians).

The vitality of Indian music does not depend, however, solely on its vicarious existence in transformation; the latter merely confirms that Indian music is becoming a significant component of world music. The musical traditions of India continue to have a vital role in the cultural life of Indians at home, and despite the influential role of Western music, classical and pop, around the world, it does not yet seem to coexist on an equal footing with, much less be supplanting, filmigit or kriti or khyal in India. Compared with the importance of East Asians in the world of Western classical music, too, the lesser role played by Indians would seem indirectly to imply the strength of Indian musical traditions. Those traditions are undergoing considerable change in the modern world, but their ability to adapt and respond to new circumstances is also an indication of their vitality.

INDIA BIBLIOGRAPHY

Indian Music as a Whole: Bonnie C. Wade, *Music in India: The Classical Traditions* (Englewood Cliffs, N.J.: Prentice Hall, 1979); Bonnie C. Wade, ed., *Performing Arts in India: Essays on Music, Dance, and Drama*, Monograph Series No. 21 (Berkeley: University of California Press, 1983); Peggy Holroyde, *The Music of India* (New York: Praeger, 1972); M. R. Gautam, *The Musical Heritage of India* (New Delhi: Abhinav, 1980); Peter Manuel, *Popular Musics of the Non-Western World* (New York: Oxford University Press, 1988).

North Indian Music: Nazir Jairazbhoy, *The Rags of Northern Indian Music: Their Structure and Evolution* (Middletown, Conn.: Wesleyan University Press, 1971); Daniel Neuman, *The Life of Music in North India: The Organization of an Artistic Tradition* (Detroit: Wayne State University Press, 1980); Bonnie C. Wade, *Khyal: Creativity within North Indian Classical Music Tradition* (Cambridge: Cambridge University Press, 1984); James Kippen, *The Tabla of Lucknow* (Cambridge: Cambridge University Press, 1988); Regula Qureshi, *Sufi Music of India and Pakistan* (Cambridge: Cambridge University Press, 1986); Stephen Slawek, *Sitar Technique in Nibaddh Forms* (Delhi: Motilal Banarsidas, 1987); Walter Kaufmann, *The Ragas of North India* (Bloomington: Indiana University Press, 1968); Edward O. Henry, *Chant the Names of God: Musical Culture in Bhojpuri-speaking India* (San Diego: San Diego State University Press, 1988).

South Indian Music: Walter Kaufmann, *The Ragas of South India: A Catalog of Scalar Materials* (Bloomington: Indiana University Press, 1976); P. Sambamoorthy, *South Indian Music*, 5 vols., (Madras: Indian Music Publishing House); R. Rangaramanuja Ayyangar, *History of South Indian (Carnatic) Music from Vedic Times to the Present*

(Madras: privately published, 1972); Mrinalini Sarabhai, *Understanding Bharata Natyam* (Ahmedabad: Darpana, 1981).

INDIA DISCOGRAPHY

Anthologies: *A Musical Anthology of the Orient*, Vols. 6,7,18 (Bärenreiter 30L 2006,2007,2018); *Classical Indian Music* (Odeon MOAE 147–9).

North India: *Parween Sultana* (khyal) (Gramophone Co. of India ECSD 2785); *Ram Chatur Mallick* (dhrupad and dhamar), *Musiques de l'Asie Traditionelle*, Vol. 9 (Inde du Nord); *Ravi Shankar* (sitar) (Gramophone Co. of India EASD 1307); *Ananda Shankar and His Music* (modern instrumental pop) (Gramophone Co. of India ESCD 2528); *Begum Akhtar Sings Ghalib* (ghazal) (Gramophone Co. of India ECSD 2399); *Film Hits from Hit Films*, Vol. 2 (Gramophone Co. of India ECLP 5470).

South India: *Kaccheri* (vocal) (Nonesuch H-72040); *Vidwan* (vocal) (Nonesuch H-72023); *Dhyanam/Meditation* (vocal) (Nonesuch H-72018); *Musik für Vina* (Telarc MC8); *S. Balachander: Veena Maestro of South India* (Odeon MOCE 1026); *Pallavi* (flute) (Nonesuch H-72052).

3

MUSIC OF THE MIDDLE EAST

Bruno Nettl

CONCERTS IN TEHRAN

In the Great Concert Hall

We are in Tehran, the capital of Iran, a rather modern city of about four million people, close to the last years of the reign of the Shah—that is, about 1970. We are in a modern concert hall, have paid about $3.00 for each ticket, and sit in the seventh row; there are some 1200 seats, only half occupied. The audience is well dressed, in modern Western clothes; we see ladies in very fine dresses of Paris fashion and we recognize academics, professional people, and a fairly large number of foreigners. We have been shown to our seats by ushers and given printed programs, and we feel as if we were in a concert hall in an American city ready to hear a string-quartet concert. On the stage are a few chairs and some music stands.

The program tells us that we will hear several pieces, that there will be an intermission, and that there will be some ensemble music at the beginning and end, with several solo or duet numbers in between. The labeling of the numbers gives us, in a couple of cases, the composers of the music, and in all cases, an unfamiliar designation which turns out to be the name of the mode—or, in Persian, dastgah—of each piece.

Fifteen minutes after the official beginning time, six male musicians appear on the stage with instruments and sit down on the chairs. They are dressed in costumes approximating the clothes one sees on seventeenth- and eighteenth-century Persian miniatures. They are greeted with applause and begin tuning. The instruments are quite different from each other. There is a heavy-looking lute with long neck and frets, the tar, which turns out to be played with a pick; also a kamancheh, a spiked fiddle with a small round body and four strings, which will be held upright on a peg like a miniature cello and bowed with the palm upward, like an early European viol player rather than a modern cellist. There is a trapezoidal zither or dulcimer, the santour, with seventy-two strings (tuned to twenty-seven different pitches), which sits on a stand and will be played with two small balsa-wood mallets. A fourth player brings an ordinary Western violin, and a fifth, a cane flute, which he will play by blowing across the end (rather than across a hole in the side, as on the standard Western flute). Finally there is a drummer, who brings out a goblet-shaped drum with one skin, called dombak or zarb. These are most of the principal instruments of Persian classical music (Figures 3–1 to 3–6).

Figure 3–1. Iranian *Tar.*

The program says that the first section of the concert will be in the dastgah of Shur. I ask my neighbor what that means and am told that there are in Persian music twelve dastgahs, which provide the basic material for all music making in the Persian classical system. Each has a scale or collection of pitches from which composers or improvisors make selections, and each has a unique configuration of intervals. But each dastgah also has a basic musical motif, a tune consisting of some five or six tones which characterizes it. My neighbor softly sings the main musical motif of Shur into my ear and says, "This is the heart of the

Figure 3–2.   The *Santour*, used in Iran and neighboring countries.

Figure 3–3.   Left: Darbucca, the most widely used drum type in the Middle East. Right: Iranian *zarb* or *dombak*.

Figure 3–4.   Iranian *sehtar*.

Figure 3–5. Older and highly decorated *kamancheh*.

dastgah of Shur; when you play Shur, you must always keep coming back to it, otherwise your audience will say you don't really know our music."

In the first piece all of the musicians play together, sitting behind music stands. (I strain to see whether they actually have music, and conclude that they either don't or are just barely looking at it.) They are playing a type of piece called pishdaramad, which means "before the introduction," and it is by Darvish Khan, who I'm told was a great musician early in the century. They play in unison, but hardly perfect unison, and it's easy to pick out the flute's ornamented tune, the nasal voice of the kamancheh, the heavy plucked sounds of the tar, and the brilliant runs of the santour. The drummer keeps meter and tempo, and the piece is obviously in slow three-quarter time. As I make out the form, I discover that it consists of a line of music which is repeated with a final ending; and this pair of lines keeps reappearing, alternating with other pairs, so that the piece could be represented by letters like this: A^1A^2, B^1B^2, C^1C^2, A^1A^2, D^1D^2, B^1B^2, A^1A^2, C^1C^2. In form it's a bit like an eighteenth-century European rondo, but also like the dances

Figure 3–6. *Kamancheh* used by students and folk musicians.

of the European Middle Ages, and for that matter some European instrumental folk music.

The audience applauds. In the front are a few young men, music students from a conservatory, who wag their heads sideways and cry out gently, "Bah, bah!" For the next section all the musicians remain onstage, but it is performed by only two of the group, the santour player and the drummer. The santour plays a very rapid piece in which a rhythmic pattern keeps being repeated as the basis of a short bit of melody, which is itself repeated many times with variations, alternates with other tunes, and eventually returns. All this is done with enormous emphasis on virtuosity. The santour player throws his arms around to show his expertise; halfway through, he takes out a cloth and places it over the strings to show that he can play correctly even without seeing the instrument. It's a great show. In all of this he is accompanied by the drummer, who takes a modest stance musically and physically. At those points when it hears something particularly difficult, the audience bursts into brief applause while the musicians go on uninterrupted. The name of this kind of piece is chahar mezrab, which means "four picks" or "four hammers," possibly because it is so fast that it sounds as if there were four hands flying over the instrument.

For the third section, the group is joined by a female singer who comes onstage to enthusiastic applause. Dressed in modern evening dress, flamboyant and colorful, she sings, accompanied by the tar, music whose words, as my neighbor tells me, are a poem from the fourteenth century by Hafez, "our greatest poet." This section of the performance is called Avaz, and it is the part everyone has perhaps been waiting for. She sings short phrases—and I hear the motif of Shur (still sounding a bit out of tune to me, with its intervals that don't quite fit into the scale of our piano) at the beginning, and again at various times—moving gradually from the low part of her range to the higher. She doesn't sound at all like an American opera singer, or someone with a rock group, or for that matter a country-and-western singer. She has a strong, husky chest-voice, free of vibrato, but she uses lots of ornaments, and as she moves to the higher part of her range the lines get longer and she dwells for two, three, then fifteen or twenty notes on one syllable. Eventually, she sings lines without using words at all, long passages simply on "Aaah," with a tone that sounds like a combination of yodeling and sobbing, and the audience breaks into applause. Finally, after some fifteen minutes of singing, the performer allows her song to draw to a close, moving to lower pitches and softer sounds. Meanwhile, the tar player has been accompanying in an interesting style, following the singer but lagging a note or two behind, and at the end of a phrase quickly repeating what she has just sung, precisely or approximately.

We have just heard what is clearly the high point of the performance. Now we hear another number sung by the same lady, this time accompanied by the entire ensemble, and with a meter—a rather vigorous three-quarter time—set by the drum. This is a song in stanzas, roughly the length of stanzas in American folk music or in hymns, and the ensemble plays interludes between them as well as short introductory and closing sections. The instruments play in approximate unison with the singer except for an occasional flourish or quick passage between stanzas. The printed program tells me that this is a type of song called tasnif, and that both the music and the words are by 'Aref Qazvini, the most noted composer of tasnifs, who lived in the first half of our century. The words are those of a love song, but my helpful neighbor tells me that many tasnifs are about social and political matters and criticize the social system.

There follows another number played by the ensemble, but without singer. In the same dastgah, it has a rollicking rhythm and sounds a bit as if its composer had been hearing old English folk songs. In the program it is called a reng, which is a kind of dance, but of course no one comes on stage to dance. At the end of the performance there is applause and, things so far having taken up some fifty minutes, the audience is ready for the intermission, which has the flavor of intermissions at concerts and operas in London, New York, or Vienna. What we have just heard is a full-blown performance of one mode, or dastgah, that of Shur. If done properly it has five parts, always in the order given here, but one or several of the movements may be omitted. I am told that this was really a "very classical" performance, and that things will be lighter in the second half.

To be sure, they are. There is first another tasnif, sung by a male singer this time. Then the performer on the goblet-shaped zarb comes out alone and puts on a display of pyrotechnics, showing many rhythms and imitating on his drum various sounds from nature as well as the sound of a moving steam engine. A new group of performers—a singer in peasant costume, a player of a long-necked two-string lute called dotar, and a drummer with a kind of tambourine—appears and performs three short folk songs, but they are greeted and dismissed with little applause. Five ladies in costume join them for a few folk dances, and then our original ensemble, with its classical instruments, comes out to play a couple of pieces rather like the first piece of the evening, stately and metric. But while the program gives names and composers, it does not indicate that they are cast in some traditional type. The audience applauds with modest enthusiasm, there are no encores, and everyone leaves in search of buses and taxis.

The Majles

As the audience breaks up, I tell my neighbor that it has been fun but that I was a bit puzzled. I had been told that Middle Eastern classical music is largely improvised, but here out of some ten movements, only one was clearly in that category. And I had thought that the music would be contemplative, but it struck me as more of a variety show. "Yes," my neighbor agreed, "but that's the modern way of performing Iranian classical music. But perhaps I can invite you to a place where they perform the same music in a much more traditional way."

I took him up on it, but the invitation was long in coming. Finally, after two months, I was asked to come on a particular evening to an address in the wealthier section of northern Tehran, at dinnertime. It was made clear that I should not (as would most Americans) bring along wife, daughter, or date, but that I should come alone, and that being invited to this gathering was a rather special thing. Those who attend this kind of event don't usually accept outsiders into their midst.

A bit apprehensive, I showed up. It was a modern home, but in the living room there were no chairs, and six men were sitting in a circle leaning against large pillows. Three of them were wearing loose, pajamalike garments. I recognized two of them, one a physicist and the other a doctor, and it was clear that they were all old friends, although they spoke to each other in rather formal terms. One heard women's voices—there must have been half a dozen—from the kitchen, but no women were to be seen that evening. Some of the men smoked (a bit of opium in one case), a servant brought some wine and brandy, eventually we were served a traditional meal, and as soon as we had finished eating one of the men present opened an instrument case and began tuning his setar. This was a small lute, like a mandolin but with a much longer neck; it had not been used in the formal concert but now I was told that it was really the truest, most characteristic instrument of Persian traditional music. It had four strings and frets, and was strummed with the forefinger's long nail, melody and drone together; the tone is usually very soft but sometimes it can be loud and vigorous.

The setar player followed the same plan as the ensemble in the first half of the formal concert, but the introductory pishdaramad was very short, while the chahar mezrab, obviously improvised this time, went on at length. The musician made a great deal of the nonmetric avaz, in which he moved from low pitches very gradually up the scale over a good half-hour, clearly watching the reactions of his audience and obviously stimulated by it to move gradually into excited and emotional musical utterances. There followed a brief tasnif, but there was no fifth section. In contrast to the public concert, the nonmetric and improvised sections were clearly featured here. During the performance there was a bit of conversation, but usually in the way of comments on the music, such things as "He always does this very well," and "I heard so-and-so play hesar [the section being performed] quite differently last week." At the end there was a bit of conversation about music, local politics, and the weather, and the guests left, this time bidden farewell at the door by the host's wife. My friend accompanied me to my taxi. "Don't tell people you were here," he said. "A lot of people don't approve of sessions like this."

MUSICAL AND CULTURAL VALUES

Attributes of Music

These are two contexts in which one could hear Persian classical music around 1970, and these experiences tell us some important things about Middle Eastern music: certain forms of music, the interaction between improvisation and composition, the role of modernization in musical life, some of the instruments, and most important, the attitude of society toward music. It is the last of these that may be most significant in explaining the peculiarities of Middle Eastern musical culture.

Perhaps we may begin by asking a basic question: Is music a "good" thing? Does one even need to ask the question? In American society we think of music unequivocally as a good thing. All of it may not be good, but music improves an action or context, adding dignity or formality, marking its subdivisions, or providing an entertaining component. If a person is singing or whistling, he or she is assumed to be happy. Sounds we like are "music to our ears." A beautiful sound, such as a beautiful speaking voice, is said to be "musical." On the other hand, music is not thought to be seriously significant; it does not seriously affect the essence of life.

It may be a surprise to some that not all societies have this view. But in many cultures, music is a principal form of mediation between humans and the supernatural. Many American Indian peoples believe that their songs are taught to them by supernatural figures. Tibetan Buddhists have loudly playing orchestras to attract the attention of deities. In these instances, music is surely regarded as extremely important; but the notion that one should "like" it in the American sense and even decide which of its pieces one should prefer might be strange to those peoples. Similarly, in Middle Eastern Muslim societies, music is sumultaneously feared and loved, enjoyed but viewed with suspicion; it is subject to a kind of ambivalence.

This sort of attitude is actually widespread in the world. In earlier periods of European and American culture, music was regarded as acceptable only when it was religious. Musicians have been viewed with suspicion in many parts of the world. But in the Middle East, the character of the entire musical culture seems to be the result of this ambivalence.

Just why music should be held in low esteem is not quite clear, as the Koran does not direct this attitude, although it cautions believers to avoid the kinds of music that lead to frivolous and lewd behavior.

But whatever the roots, in Islamic society in the Middle East music must be kept far from the centers of religion; devout Muslims should avoid it; instruments in particular are to be viewed with suspicion; dancing, even more. But these undesirable aspects of music are mitigated by the fact that in Islamic societies there is great respect for scholarly activity and for poetry, there is a place for non-Muslims, and there is a tradition of intellectual argumentation that can justify exceptions to rules.

So, on the one hand, we find that musicians are held in low esteem. On Islamic holidays, they dare not appear in the streets with their instruments. There is no tradition of instrumental religious music, and there are no concerts in the mosques. There is also no tradition in Arabic or Persian rhetoric of using metaphorical extensions of the concept of music to symbolize the good and beautiful. And while Iranians and Turks take their traditions of poetry and visual art, their miniatures and their carpets, very seriously, they usually cannot imagine that music deserves the same dignified treatment.

At the same time, Middle Eastern societies have a lot of what we consider to be music, and they are very good at it. But they have found ways to reconcile their religion's ambivalence toward music and their own desire to have music, some of which should be briefly mentioned.

A great deal of musical activity has been turned over to members of non-Muslim minorities, particularly Jews and to a smaller extent Christians. While there have certainly been many Muslim musicians, there has always been a disproportionate number of Jewish musicians. Instrument making and selling, as well, has been in the hands of non-Muslims; in Tehran around 1970, most instrument makers were Armenian Christians.

If music making was dangerous, the intellectual study of music was not, and thus there developed in Islamic society a tradition of scholarship in music theory which resulted in the writing, between 900 and 1900, of almost 2000 treatises in Arabic, Persian, and Turkish. Among the philosophical and scientific branches of learning, music played a major part.

In visual art, architecture, literature, even in political and social structures, the heartland of Islam has always showed an interest in and an aptitude for grand designs. Large structures with complicated interrelationships such as Persian carpets and long, complex works of literature such as the *Shahnameh* of Ferdowsi, the national epic of Iran, are illustrative. Music was sometimes treated in such a grand manner, but only in treatises. In practice it was composed of small units with tenuous relationships. Only in the late nineteenth century, under the influence of Western musicianship with its own grand designs, did Persian musicians organize a comparable work, the radif (to be described later), a large repertory of music which is memorized and becomes the basis for improvisation and composition. It seems significant that the radif came into existence precisely at the time when the more positive Western approach to music became known in Iran. The previous Middle Eastern system of music could be considered quite analogous to that of India, except that there was simply much less in the way of content and structural sophistication.

Defining Music

The definition of music was narrower. In Persian, for example, there are two terms to denote music—musiqi, derived from Greek and meaning "music," and khandan, meaning "to sing, to recite, to read." A particular sound or context of music may be considered one or the other, or in some respect both. Thus we may say that certain sounds have more "musicness" about them than others. The kinds of music (in our sense) that are least objectionable are those that are khandan. They include, most importantly, the reading of the Koran, which in formal situations is always sung (but in a way that emphasizes the words), is nonmetric, has no instrumental accompaniment, and, in accordance with certain rules, is improvised.

Slightly more "musical" is the music of the Zurkhaneh, a kind of traditional gymnasium where men exercise to the chanting of a specialized singer, or morshed, who accompanies himself on drum and bells, using the latter also to direct the participants to change exercises. Chanting secular literature such as the Iranian national epic, he is somewhat more metric in his improvisation and does use some instruments; but even secular music has a dignified function and is not just for entertainment.

Going further, a rather more "musical" type of sound (which might actually be called musiqi) is the vocal performance of avaz, the improvised nonmetric section of a classical performance. It would be considered a bit more dangerous because it is often accompanied, is performed for entertainment (if indeed of a high order), emphasizes some vocal pyrotechnics, and is frequently performed by women. Instrumental avaz, the same kind of music but using one of the things most symbolic of the dangerous in music, would be next—and definitely called musiqi.

A similar degree of "musicness" might be enjoyed by vocal tasnifs, which are songs in a more Western sense, as they are metric and usually sung with instrumental accompaniment, but not improvised, less associated in their sound with spoken language, and also often sung by women. Quite close to the extreme of musicness would be metric instrumental pieces such as the introductory pishdaramad in a classical performance, followed by virtuosic instrumental pieces such as the chahar mezrab, in which rhythmic predictability is greatest on account of the use of repeated rhythmic patterns as well as steady meter.

The classical genres just described are nevertheless not totally unacceptable. Classical music is entertainment, but it has intellectual components, being associated with music theory and musical scholarship. To traditionalists, the most "undesirable" kind of music is the popular, and at the extreme end would be music explicitly for dancing such as the ensemble music that accompanies belly dance.

Music in the Middle East, then, is a phenomenon about which people have ideas quite different from those held in North America or India. How do the two performances in Tehran that we described above fit into this set of attitudes? They were performances of the same kind of music, but they were surely different. The second one was part of a tradition called dowreh, a word denoting a small group of men who meet periodically for a special purpose such as reading the Koran to each other, or reading poetry, or hearing music. Such a group is often based on an extended family, and certainly its members belong to the same social class and perhaps even occupation. They feel very close to each other and depend on the ambience provided by this sense of belonging and of privacy. In earlier times, music was often heard in such venues, and the notion of music as dangerous accompanies the concept of keeping it within a closed social circle. But the familiarity of the dowreh also goes with the concept of freedom that is essential in an improvised music. In any event, while the improvised sections of a program were very much controlled in the public concert and were relatively short compared to the composed materials, improvisation played a much greater role in a small private performance.

The Musician

In many parts of the world, musicians are looked down on or are regarded as a peculiar group of people. In Europe throughout history, musicians were of low status. One expected foreigners to take the roles of musicians, and there is folklore in which the musician is somehow associated with the supernatural, in league with the devil. His ability to be creative and virtuosic was ascribed to the supernaturally tinged concept of talent. He was permitted and even expected to engage in unconventional social, sexual, and even religious behavior.

In the Middle East, although being a musician was not generally a good thing, there were a number of different types of musician. In the classical-music scene of Tehran, one might be a professional musician or an amateur, as is the case here; but contrary to Western practice, technical competence aside, the well-trained and artistic amateur has higher status than the professional. It has to do with the status of music, but also with the notion of freedom. The professional musician may be looked down upon because he must perform when ordered and play whatever his patron wishes to hear at whatever length is desired. An amateur, who plays for his own pleasure and for his friends, may make these decisions himself, and particularly those that involve the modal system and improvisation. Considering that in Persian music the selection of mode, or dastgah, has a lot to do with the musician's mood, as each mode has its own character, the notion of freedom gives amateur status its higher prestige. And since improvised music has the greatest prestige but requires the greatest degree of freedom for the performer, the amateur (assuming he is really as well trained and as knowledgeable as the professional) is able to indulge his own musical desires best.

One other group of individuals in Islamic society is particularly associated with music—the Sufi. Sufism is a mystical movement in Islam, which is able to overcome the disapproval of music by saying, in effect, "Music is just another way of knowing and being close to God." Thus many Middle Eastern musicians, if they are Muslims, are members of Sufi sects.

In rural or small-town culture of the Middle East, the classical-music systems are hardly known. But the kinds of music used in the countryside are not principally performed by the general population (as they are in some of the world's rural societies), but rather by specialists. Individuals are not known as "musicians" per se, but there are various genres of music and each is the province of a particular specialist-class with a name.

In his study of the music of Khorasan, Stephen Blum identified a large number of musician-types, recognized as such by society, each of whom specialized in one genre or context. The naqqal recited the *Shahnameh* in teahouses. The darvish (any of a number of different kinds of individual all associated with Sufism), might recite the same work, and recent religious poetry, on the streets. The bakhshi performed narratives dealing with war and romance at weddings and similar events. The rouzeh-khan performed rouzeh, songs of the martyrdom of Hossein; the monaqeb-khan sang about the virtues of Ali and his descendants. The motreb performed vocal and instrumental music at teahouses; the asheq sang romantic narratives in towns and encampments. One person could perform several functions and have several of these designations, but the point was that none of them associated himself with music as such, none was a "musician." The relationship between art and folk music is quite different from that found in Western Europe, where folk music is performed by people who are not specialists. In the Middle East, folk music is the province of the specialist; art music, ideally of the amateur. All this comes, of course, from the different kinds of value placed on music in the two culture areas (Figures 3–7 and 3–8).

Figure 3–7. The *Oud*, the most famous of the Arabic lutes.

MIDDLE EASTERN CULTURE AND HISTORY

A Culture Area: Common Features and Diversity

The Middle Eastern culture area is centered in the region of Iran, Turkey, and the heartland of Arabic culture—Saudi Arabia, Syria, Iraq, Lebanon, Egypt. It is in these nations that the cultural characteristics of the area are most pronounced, and from which they radiated over a period of more than a thousand years in several directions. What most characterizes the culture is the religion and general way of life of Islam. Islam is monotheistic and basically egalitarian—all men are equal before God—while insisting on greatly differing cultural roles for men and women. The culture places emphasis on urban life, and trading and business are the ideal occupations. The extended family and, in more traditional Arabic societies, the tribe play a major role in social life, and ethnicity is associated with small population units rather than peoples. It is a culture in which quality of speech, elegance in writing, and direct verbal exchange among individuals play a major role. It is important for people in positions of authority—everyone from kings to

Figure 3–8. *Dotar* or *dutar*, used in Turkey and Afghanistan.

religious leaders to teachers—to be directly accessible to those under them, as one looks for leadership and guidance directly to the figure of authority, not to intermediaries.

With the Islamic religion—which was brought by the Arabs to the Persians and other peoples of Iran and to the various Turkic peoples of the area—came the Arabic alphabet, now long held in common by most peoples of the area. The Middle Eastern heartland is an area of major literary, and particularly poetic, accomplishments, and of great architecture and abstract art, such as carpets, as well as grand traditions of miniature painting. What may appear as a lower level of musical accomplishment results, no doubt, from the culture's ambivalence toward music.

But the Middle Eastern heartland is certainly not completely homogeneous. There is much cultural, linguistic, and religious diversity. To speak simply of "Arabs" neglects the existence of many Arabic-speaking cultures, from tribal units to urban societies. Then there are a number of different Turkic-speaking peoples, as well as Kurds, Armenians, Baluchis, and many more ethnic groups. Further, while most Middle Easterners are Muslims (largely Sunni Muslims in Arabic and Turkish areas, Shi'ites in Iran), there are also Armenian, Nestorian, and Assyrian Christians, as well as Jews, Bahais, and Zoroastrians (Zoroastrianism being the original religion of Iran).

The Middle East stretches in several directions and has no precise boundaries. What we label here as the Middle Eastern culture and music area goes beyond the heartland and includes North Africa, all the way to Morocco (a largely Arabic-speaking area); the Caucasus, largely in the Soviet Union; and Afghanistan and Soviet Central Asia, areas with largely Persian and Turkic speakers. Furthermore, some of the characteristics of Middle Eastern music are held in common with South Asia, and it would be difficult to draw a precise line separating the musics of Iran, Afghanistan, and Pakistan. And finally, because of its proximity but also because of a period of some 500 years of occupation by the Turkish Empire, much of the Balkan peninsula has music clearly related to and often even definitely a part of the music of the Middle East.

History of Music in the Middle East

Since Middle Eastern music, like most musics, lives in oral tradition, we know much more about its workings in the twentieth century than we do about its history. But as the Middle East generally has long been an area of special interest to Europeans and Americans, its history has been greatly explored by archeologists and historians. We have some knowledge of its cultures long before the Christian era, and we know a bit about its music history. Archeological sites indicate that the entire area had a large variety of instruments already some 3000 years ago. There is evidence that the Sumerians, around 2000 B.C.E., had a rather complex system of musical notation. The Bible suggests that in ancient Jewish society music was regarded as a joyful activity, and that the ambivalence about music that is characteristic of Islam came to this culture area later on.

We can get some sense of the age of the Middle Eastern system of modes (maqams or dastgahs) by looking at the modal system of ancient Greece, which in its time was culturally closely associated with Egypt and Persia and should probably be regarded as part of the Middle Eastern rather than the European culture area at that time.

The ancient Greek modes—Dorian, Aeolian, Phrygian, Lydian, and so on—whose names are still used in modern modal analysis in Western music, appear to have been units somewhat like maqams or dastgahs. They were units with scales, but named after regions and probably derived from the folk-tune types of geographic areas in the Greek world, and they were thought to have some specific character. Though it was only in Greece that theorists and philosophers wrote about the modes, it seems likely that this system of making music was known throughout a far broader area, probably all the way to India, and that the present-day modal systems of South and West Asia are descendants of long-standing traditions.

After Islam was established in 622 C.E., empires led successively by Arabic, Turkish, and Persian forces dominated the area for a thousand years. At the courts of these empires, art-music establishments were developed (despite the Muslim ambivalence about music), and famous individual musicians such as the Persian Barbod (who lived in the tenth century C.E.), Yunus al-Katib (d. 765), and Ibrahim al-Mausili (d. 850) flourished even during the Middle Ages. Except for verbal descriptions, we have no knowledge of the sound of their music.

More influential on the later tradition was the large body of music theory that was produced in hundreds of treatises written by musicians, scientists, and philosophers, many of them attached to the courts of the Middle Eastern empires. These treatises dealt principally with two topics, the value and acceptability of music and the tuning of the modal scales. Interestingly, however, the precise measurements of pitch which these treatises imply may never have played much of a role in performance, in which intonation is less emphasized than the appropriate musical themes and motifs. Among the authors of these treatises, however, are some of the great names in Arabic philosophy—Al-Farabi, Al-Kindi, and Ebn-e Sina (Avicenna)—who included music among the systems of knowledge to be described.

An important aspect of Middle Eastern music history is the interaction of the area with neighboring culture areas. In the Middle Ages, probably as a result of the Crusades, Arabic musical ideas and theories came to Europe, as did the 'oud, the Arabic lute with short neck, which became the European lute so widely used in art music of the Renaissance. In the sixteenth century , the Moghul emperor Akbar brought Persian musicians to India, and they are said to have had a major impact, establishing a musical system in north India distinct from the possibly older South Indian or Karnatak. In the nineteenth century, Western musical culture began to play a major role, and Western institutions such as concerts, conservatories of music, notation, and musical technology, along with Western ideas about music such as the eminence of the composed piece as compared to the improvised, began to affect the Middle East substantially.

One of the major events in the area in the twentieth century was the establishment of the state of Israel in 1948. The gathering of representatives of Jewish populations from many cultures and countries stimulated the development of a distinctive folk and popular music culture based mainly on a combination of Eastern European and Middle Eastern elements. At the same time, the arrival of many Jewish musicians from MIddle Eastern Muslim countries encouraged the preservation and also the interaction of Middle Eastern traditions within Israel.

A Musical Area

This very large area—which does not, incidentally, take in the entire region of Islam, as Pakistan, Bangladesh, and Indonesia are actually the nations with the largest Muslim populations—is surely quite diverse musically, but it nevertheless holds in common certain characteristics of musical culture and musical style. We have described important elements of musical thought; what now of the sound of the music?

Whether classical or folk, urban or rural, Middle Eastern music has a very distinctive sound. It is almost always monophonic—there is only one melody, not several melodies proceeding together, as might be the case in a European chorus, and no system of harmony to guide or accompany the melody. This statement is generally correct but also an oversimplification, as one sometimes does hear more than one pitch at a time. A vocalist improvising may be accompanied by an instrument that follows a note or two behind him or her; or there may be parallel polyphony, that is, two voices or instruments playing the same melody at different pitch levels, say a fifth apart. But in principle, Middle Eastern music is monophonic (Figure 3-9).

With this goes a prevailingly ornamented style of singing and playing. Many if not most tones are "bent" or are embellished with trills, glissandos, or short secondary notes—all kinds of techniques to transcend a simple, straightforward rendering of a pitch. Middle Eastern musicians consider that this ornamentation gives the music its special regional character and accounts for its emotional impact. The more ornamented a passage, the better and more expressive its audience perceives it to be.

Figure 3–9. Middle Eastern wind instruments. Top: Two *zornahs*, double-reed instruments used throughout the Middle East. Bottom: Arabic *Zummarah*s, double clarinets with parallel finger-holes.

Along with the ornamentation comes a characteristic singing style or instrumental tone color. The basic way the voice is used, the kind of sound made by singers and instrumentalists—in other words, the ideal musical sound—is one of the most important characterizing feature of any musical style. It is also something that tends to be, on the whole, the same within any one culture, no matter how varied the structure of the music may otherwise be. Thus, singers of Persian, Arabic, and Turkish classical music and of the many regional folk and tribal musics of the area tend to sound rather alike. It is difficult to describe the ideal sound, much easier to grasp it by hearing the music. But we could attempt to convey its effect by saying that Middle Eastern singing is tense-sounding and has a harsh, throaty, nasal tone, with a certain flatness. It has ornaments, but no vibrato. Men sing high in their range, and women usually low. The kinds of sound made by the human voice are usually imitated by instruments. Thus, the traditional spiked fiddle, kamancheh, has a flat, nasal tone without vibrato, in contrast to the fuller and vibrated sound of the Western violin.

MELODY AND RHYTHM

Melodic Modes: Maqam, Makam, Mugam, and Dastgah

The most important structuring device for composers and improvisers is the modal system. Musicians and musicologists argue unendingly about the definition of "mode," but for our purposes we may say that it is a pattern or set of rules for composing melody. Modes are found in many of the world's culture areas, but particularly in European art music of earlier periods, in South and Southeast Asia, Indonesia, and of course the Middle East. In the Arabic world, the term for mode is maqam, and also in Turkey, where it is respelled makam (in the Caucasus, mugam); and in Iran the term dastgah is most used. A maqam has a particular scale—that is, a collection or group of pitches (somewhat like the Western major and minor scales) from which the composer draws and to which he is limited when creating one piece.

The tones are separated by distances in pitch called intervals. In Western major and minor scales, the consecutive intervals are major and minor seconds, also called whole- and half-tones. (You can identify them on the piano: half-tones are made by playing adjacent keys, whole-tones by skipping a key, but be sure to include the black keys in your calculation.) But in Middle Eastern music, there are, besides these intervals known in the West, others not compatible with the standard Western system. They are three-quarter-tones, slightly larger than our half-tone, and five-quarter-tones, slightly larger than our whole-tone. From various combinations of these, the scales of maqams and dastgahs are made up.

But there is more to a maqam: Along with a scale, there are typical kinds of order in which the tones should appear, and short three- or four-note motifs or musical gestures which a composer or improviser must use, bringing them back every ten, twenty, or thirty seconds to maintain the proper character of the mode. To play just anything with the use of a prescribed scale isn't enough.

Every maqam or Persian dastgah has a name. Some give place of origin. Thus, there is Isfahan (name of a city in Iran), Rak (probably a Persian form of the Indian word "raga," thus indicating Indian origin), Hijaz (a section of Saudi Arabia), Nahawand (a village in Turkey), and so on. The name may instead suggest something of the character of the music: Homayoun (royal), Shur (salty), and the like. In some cases, notions from technical music theory play a role; for example, Mokhalef ("opposite," indicating that the scale is, as it were, turned around), Chahargah ("fourth place," or "fourth fret"), Segah ("third place"), Panjgah ("fifth place"). The systems of Turkish, Arabic, and Persian music are quite different, but they share many of these terms, a preponderance of which come from the Persian language. While it is impossible to know whether the name of a maqam or dastgah really indicates musical relationship to a place or nonmusical character, there is no doubt that Middle Eastern musicians consider each mode to have a particular character. And so, while much of the music of this area is improvised, it is a matter of music making within rather specific sets of rules and patterns.

If you are performing in one mode, you may wish to change, or modulate, to another; and in Arabic and Turkish music, each maqam has certain others to which a musician would typically move. Thus, if you perform in Nahawand, you are likely to move to Rast, Hijaz, and Ajam, but not typically to others. In twentieth-century Iranian music the system has become formalized, with each dastgah including within its purview several gushehs, units that are like the Arabic maqams and are performed one after the other. If for instance you want to play the dastgah of Chahargah, you will not only tend to move to particular other modal units as in Arabic music, but you must select your modulations from the gushehs belonging to Charhargah—Zabol, Mokhalef, Hesar, Mansuri, and others.

Rhythmic Structure

The modal system of Middle Eastern music is complex and fascinating, and has been the focus of musicological attention. Rhythm has received less attention, but it is equally complex. Take the matter of metric and nonmetric music. In standard Western music, we assume that there is always a meter—a cycle of beats, possibly with subdivisions, which organizes the rhythmic experience. It is usually rather simple, with main stress on the first beat and secondary stress halfway through; for example, "1 2/3 4" or "1 2 3/4 5 6." In twentieth-century Western art music, other cycles and combinations are sometimes found; and in liturgical chant, such as Medieval Gregorian chant, there is no meter. And so we tend to classify non-Western music as either metric or nonmetric. But although some Middle Eastern music can be described in this way, it actually has a more complicated system of rhythm.

For one thing, Middle Eastern music is metric, or nonmetric, or somewhere between. One can say about the chanting of the Koran that it is nonmetric; but when we get to singing in the zurkhaneh, by a morshed who chants epic poetry to percussion accompaniment, we have to admit that while it too is nonmetric it has more of a metric feel. The same is true of the improvised avaz in classical music, in which varying degrees of "metricness" can be found at various times and a performer can switch almost unnoticed between short metric and nonmetric passages. The stately, introductory ensemble pieces are definitely metric; but fast virtuoso pieces such as the Persian chahar mezrab are not only metric but are dominated by a short rhythmic pattern (such as 1 2 3

4–6/1 2 3 4–6), which gives an even greater degree of rhythmic predictability than the meter alone.

In Arabic and Turkish music—and evidently in Persian music too, before the twentieth century—the metric part of the music was organized by rhythmic modes of a sort. They are not too different from the talas of Indian music and involve a series of beats—up to twenty or twenty-five, but usually from seven to sixteen—some of which are stressed to provide a set of subdivisions. These rhythmic modes, which are called iq'a in Arabic and usul in Turkish, have names, like the melodic maqams, and serve as an underlying structure articulated by the drum, which uses different kinds of strokes on the drumhead for stressed and unstressed beats. The melodies that the drums accompany fit in with the rhythmic mode, but sometimes so subtly that one can hardly tell just what the relationship is. Just as the concept of melodic mode has been widespread, extending from Europe (in the Middle Ages) to Southeast Asia, systems of rhythmic modes are found in the same area. But they have been abandoned in European music, and now play less of a role in the Middle East than formerly; they remain important only in the two classical music systems of India.

WAYS OF MAKING MUSIC

Improvisation, Form, and Process

One of the central features of Middle Eastern music is improvisation. We have stressed that much of the music is composed—put together by a known or unknown composer, memorized, and then taught to others who perform it more or less precisely as they have learned it, and also more or less exactly the same way each time they render it. Whether this music is written in notation or not is not really relevant. Until the twentieth century, Middle Eastern musicians did not use notation, but they composed pieces. Even so, much of the music is indeed improvised.

Improvisation is a central feature of many of the world's musics. A great deal of African music is improvised in the sense that musicians create, in the course of performance, variations on a short theme or musical unit. And in many African cultures, no sharp distinction is made between performance of memorized music and the spinning-out of improvised variations. In most of Western musical culture, improvisation is regarded rather as a craft, subordinate to the concept of composition and performance carefully worked out in advance. In jazz, however, a set of chords, or a popular tune, becomes the basis of improvisation. In the gamelan music of Java and Bali, members of the ensemble improvise variations on a theme that is being played at the same time by other instruments. In the classical musics of India and the Middle East, improvised and composed musics coexist, and the two are regarded as distinct processes. The general system of Indian improvisation is rather related to that of the Middle East, except that different types of improvisation—slow, fast, metric, and nonmetric (vistar alap, jor, jhala in North India; alapana, tanam, kalpana svaram in South India)—are recognized. Such differences are found in the Middle East as well, but they are not recognized by separate terminology.

As in all musics in which improvisation takes place, Middle Eastern musicians do not simply perform any old thing that comes into their minds. Their improvised pieces have more or less predictable form and musical content.

The rules by which one improvises fall into two categories. One may be termed form, the overall design of a performance. The most widely known Middle Eastern improvised forms are the taqsim of Arabic and Turkish music and the avaz of Persian. In each case, the piece is cast in a mode (maqam, makam, or dastgah), which tells the performer the scales, the identities of the pitches, and the typical motifs that must be used. Moreover, the rhythmic structure—not consistently metric, though metric bits may appear—is predetermined. Beyond this the performer has certain choices, but if we analyze a lot of recorded performances we see that they follow a limited set of patterns. He may decide to move from the main mode into others; and in the case of Persian music, he is almost obliged to do so, moving gradually from a low part of the range to a higher part. He may decide to how many and which secondary modes he may modulate, in what order, and just how long to stay with each one. The overall form is set, but the details are determined by the improviser.

But beyond the matter of overall form, there is a matter of style on a more detailed level. It is this aspect of the music that causes it to sound Middle Eastern—or Iranian, or from a particular place, or by a particular performer—in the first place. It is the way in which musical materials are handled, repeated, changed, developed, alternated. In Middle Eastern music it is important to repeat a motif two or three times, but not more. It is important to present a highly characteristic motif occasionally and to surround it with more general material. Most melodic movement should take place in accordance with the scale of the maqam or dastgah, with few large intervals that skip tones. It is expected that the music be ornamented, that one move from lower to higher areas of the scalar range. These are general rules of style, but how they are applied in detail is up to the improviser.

And yet Arabic and Persian improvisations have a very consistent style. You can always identify a Persian avaz when you hear it, and you can almost instantly identify the mode. When you hear a snatch of it you can even guess whether the performer is near the beginning or the end of his rendition, and you can often identify the performer. How does such a system live, with its balance of freedom and restriction?

Learning to Improvise

In the case of Iran, it has much to do with the way musicians learn the classical system, and the way in which they learn to improvise. They do this by studying the repertory of music known as the radif. It's not quite right to speak of *the* radif, because each musician, each teacher has his own version of it. But all of these versions have a great deal in common; they are different only in the way that different American or English folksingers have different versions of one folk song. A radif consists of some 300 pieces of music, most of them quite short—thirty seconds to four minutes—and they are organized in the twelve modes, or dastgahs, of Persian music. Thus, each mode has a section of the radif devoted to it. For example, the dastgah of Shur has some thirty pieces. The first is Shur itself—that is, a piece that has the main scalar and thematic characteristics of Shur. Then come others clearly related to Shur but with their own peculiarities; these are called gushehs (corners). Some have the same names as Arabic maqams, and there is reason to believe that the way Arabic musicians combined maqams informally in a performance of a taqsim, for example, was codified by Iranian musicians into the much more formal radif.

A student memorizes the radif; it takes about four years to learn, and some eight to ten hours to play through all the way. The radifs for various instruments are essentially alike, the vocal ones slightly different. The radif teaches a musician how to improvise. How can a piece of music do this? It incorporates the various techniques Iranian musicians need, ideas of how to take a musical motif and transform it into various versions, ways of moving gradually from metric to nonmetric rhythm, ways of repeating and then extending a theme, notions of when to present a memorable theme or motif of highly distinct character, and when to "noodle around." The content and structure of the radif isn't really different from the improvised avaz; but once you are an accomplished musician you should not perform the radif in public, but rather practice it and use it as a model, a point of departure, for improvisation.

One may ask how it was that the Iranians established this large, formal radif as a basis for its classical music system when Arabic and Turkish musicians did not. Questions of this sort are always difficult to answer, and one cannot be sure that one's speculation is right, but the following is a possibility:

Iranian culture has for a long time developed a sense for large, complex structures. The complicated carpet designs, the tendency of literary artists to produce grand, compound works, including a very long national epic, and the complexity of the imperial political system show us this. But until the twentieth century, music—and art that was looked down on—did not partake of such development. In the late nineteenth century, Iranians became acquainted with European music, as the emperor brought French and Italian musicians to modernize the music of his military establishment. Iranian musicians saw Western music as a grand design—a system with a unified theory, notation, and great control over the sonic environment—and they also saw Western musicians as more respected members of their society. This, it would seem, stimulated them to develop the radif, a large, complex work. Organized by musicians who were members of the middle class, it reflected certain important values of Iranian culture—the tension between equality and hierarchy (that is, equality of all before God in Islam and the hierarchy of a political empire), the value of individualism and surprise, and a characteristic way of ordering the subdivisions of an event.

Take an example from Iranian social life as a model. In ordinary relationships between members of a family or close friends, what is important comes first: a father goes through the door before his son, an older friend before the younger, and this is done without much ceremony. In a more formal relationship, people shuffle around deciding who should go first (although it's really been settled in advance that the older, more prestigious, higher-placed must precede). And in a truly formal event, the amount of introductory behavior preceding the main substance is substantial; a formal dinner, for example, will be preceded by hours of chitchat and tea-with-cookies. The radif is like the family: what is important, main dastgahs, gushehs, motifs, comes first. When the radif is transformed into a more formal performance, the most prestigious part, the improvised avaz, comes later and is preceded by less prestigious composed compositions. In this way, the radif itself and the music derived from it reflect important values of Iranian culture and principles of social behavior.

The general structure of Middle Eastern art music is complex, perhaps most so in Iran. But the rural and vernacular repertories are based on similar principles. Take a major genre of folk music sung in Khorasan, the northeastern province of Iran. It is called chaharbeiti, which means something like "four lines," and it is a poem with four lines dealing with any of a variety of subjects, ordinarily lyrical and expressing a mood or sentiment. There are many hundreds of these poems. But ordinarily they are sung to one of the variants of one tune, which is actually called the "chaharbeiti tune." Variants are alike in that they follow the same general melodic contour, use the same selection of pitches, and emphasize the same notes. They are like variations on a theme. Musicologists call this a "tune type." But the fact that the society recognizes them as closely related and gives them a collective name is significant. Probably much of the radif was built up by the inclusion of such tune types, perhaps abstracting them into standardized short tunes. If one listens to Middle Eastern folk music in general, one finds a relatively small number of distinct tunes, but many, many variations on each of them. Probably many of these tune types became the bases of the maqams.

Other Genres, Styles, and Contexts

There are many other kinds of music in the Middle East; here is a sampling. Classical music in the Middle East is often performed in suites or sequences of pieces. In North Africa, a widespread name for such a suite is naubat; in Iraq, it is the so-called Iraqi maqam. In Turkey, the ceremony of the Mevlevi (Sufis following in the tradition of the founder of Sufism, the Persian poet Mowlavi or Rumi, who lived in Turkey) is in the form of such a suite. The form consists of several movements. Some of them are composed, some improvised; some are soloistic, others for ensemble; some are usually vocal, others always instrumental. Among the types of pieces that make up a Middle Eastern suite, the best known are the taqsim (Turkish, taksim), an improvised, usually nonmetric solo instrumental number in which the musician may move from the main maqam to others, eventually returning to the original; and the *beshrav* or *peshrev*, a metric, composed piece usually performed by an ensemble.

In Western classical music, opera, a play in which the characters sing rather than speak, is one of the most valued genres. In the Middle East there is no similarly complex form, but there is a type of play in Iran, called ta'azieh, in which the characters sing as well as speak. Like Middle Eastern music generally, it is monophonic, and since it has religious content there is no instrumental accompaniment. The plots ordinarily involve the martyrdom of the Imam Hossein, the son of the prophet Mohammed's son-in-law, in a battle in 680 C.E. at which the lines between the two main sects of Islam, Sunni and Shi'ite, were drawn.

And we must mention the singing or chanting of the Koran, not classified as music in the Middle East but structurally very much like classical nonmetric improvisation. Anyone may sing the Koran, but in the mosque it is professionals who render the holy word. There is a system of modes similar to the maqam system, but different in terminology. There are different ways of chanting, schools with different practices—for example, the Meccan, Egyptian, Damascus, and Western North African. The chanting is improvised, but the Koran may be written with a kind of notation that indicates whether a tone is to be ornamented or not, and in which direction the melody should move.

At the other end of the spectrum of acceptability is the music for belly dancing, performed by a group called takht (literally, "platform"), which consists ordinarily of a hammered dulcimer, a violin, a lute, a goblet-shaped drum, and a tambourine. The music is rapid and is accompanied by fast, complex, but repeated drum figures. While belly dancing has recently become a genre of popular and somewhat vulgar entertainment, it was traditionally a high art performed by highly trained dancers and musicians.

And while Western music in its many aspects—concerts and opera, nightclubs, rock groups and jazz ensembles, instruments, notation, the mass media—is making the Middle East in certain ways a subdivision of the Western cultural system, there are many forms of music that combine traditional styles of music with features of Western music to create new forms.

Among the characteristic kind of venue is the traditional music hall, as found in some of the large cities in the period around 1970. Here a large audience (mostly of men, and often from the same social or occupational group) may attend a long series of entertainment numbers while eating a standard supper and drinking beer. The entertainment may consist of some twenty to thirty acts, some of them political or humorous skits, others folk dances and acrobatics, but the most prominent being musical. Typically, a female singer will be accompanied by a small ensemble of traditional and Western instruments which plays in unison with her while also providing some very simple, rudimentary Western harmony.

Songs of the sort heard in the music halls could also be heard on radio or bought on 45-RPM disks, and some come from films. They constitute the Middle Eastern version of urban popular music, a type of music that almost everywhere combines indigenous and Western elements and employs certain Western instruments and Western harmony. In general, the popular music of the Middle Eastern cities has a homogeneous style; what one could hear in Cairo, Beirut, and Tehran in the 1970s was very much one kind of music. The culture of the Middle East of centuries past was a relatively unified combination of the confluence of Arabic, Persian, Turkish, and other elements, and its popular music in the twentieth century constitutes to reflect this homogeneity.

MIDDLE EAST BIBLIOGRAPHY

Middle Eastern Music as a Whole: Kristina Nelson, *The Art of Reciting the Qur'an* (Austin: University of Texas Press, 1985); Harold S. Powers, ed., "Symposium on the Status of Traditional Art Musics in Muslim Nations," in *Asian Music* 12/1 (1980); Owen Wright, *The Modal System of Arab and Persian Music A.D. 1250–1300* (London: Oxford University Press, 1978); Hans Engel, *Die Stellung des Musikers im arabisch-islamischen Raum* (Bonn: Verlag für systematische Musikwissenchaft, 1987); Amnon Shiloah, *The Theory of Music in Arabic Writings c. 900–1900* (Munich: Henle, 1979); William P. Malm, *Music Cultures of the Pacific, the Near East, and Asia*, 2nd ed. (Prentice Hall, Englewood Cliffs, N.J.: 1977), Chap. 3; Peter Manuel, *Popular Musics of the Non-Western World* (New York: Oxford University Press, 1988), Chaps. 5 and 6.

Iran: Ella Zonis, *Classical Persian Music: An Introduction* (Cambridge, Mass. Harvard University Press, 1973); Bruno Nettl and others, *The Radif of Persian Music: Studies in Structure and Cultural Context* (Champaign, Ill.: Elephant & Cat, 1987); Stephen Blum, "Persian Folksong in Meshhed (Iran), 1969," *Yearbook of the International Folk Music Council* (1974); Hormoz Farhat, *The Dastgah Concept in Persian Music* (Cambridge: Cambridge University Press, 1990).

Arabic Music: Lois Ibsen al-Faruqi, *An Annotated Glossary of Arabic Musical Terms* (Westport, Conn.: Greenwood, 1981); Jürgen Elsner, *Der Begriff Maqam in Aegypten in neuerer Zeit* (Leipzig: Deutscher Verlag für Musik, 1973); Henry George Farmer, *History of Arabian Music to the XIIIth Century* (London: Luzac, 1929); Habib Hassan Touma, *Die Musik der Araber* (Wilhelmshaven: Heinrichshofen, 1975).

Afghanistan: Hiromi Lorraine Sakata, *Music in the Mind* (Kent, Ohio: Kent State University Press, 1983); Mark Slobin, *Music in the Culture of Northern Afghanistan* (Tucson: Viking Fund Publications in Anthropology, 1976); John Baily, *Music of Afghanistan* (Canbridge: Cambridge University Press, 1988).

Israel: Eric Werner, *A Voice Still Heard . . . The Sacred Songs of the Ashkenazic Jews* (University Park: Pennsylvania State University Press, 1976); Philip V. Bohlman and Mark Slobin, eds., *Music in the Ethnic Communities of Israel*, Special Issue, *Asian Music* 17/2 (Spring/Summer 1986); Philip V. Bohlman, *The Land Where Two Streams Flow: Music in the German-Jewish Community of Israel* (Urbana: University of Illinois Press, 1989).

Turkey: Laurence Picken, *Folk Music Instruments of Turkey* (London: Oxford University Press, 1975); Karl Signell, *Makam: Modal Practice in Turkish Art Music* (Seattle: Asian Music Publications, 1977); Béla Bartók, *Turkish Folk Music from Asia Minor* (Princeton, N.J.: Princeton University Press, 1976).

MIDDLE EAST DISCOGRAPHY

Iran: *A Persian Heritage* (Nonesuch H-72060; 1974); *Tradition Classique de l'Iran: Le Tar* (Harmonia Mundi, France HM 1031; 1980); *Iranian Dastgah*—UNESCO Collection Musical Sources (Philips

6586–005; 1971); *Iran*, 2 disks UNESCO Collection: A Musical Anthology of the Orient (Bärenreiter Musicaphon BM 30 L 2004; ca. 1965).

Arabic Nations: *Iraq: Ud Classique Arabe par Munir Bashir* (Ocora OCR 63; 1983); *Arabian Music: Maqam*, UNESCO Collection Musical Sources (Philips 6586–0006; 1971; *Tâqâsim—The Art of Improvisation in Arabic Music* (Lyrichord LLST 7374; ca. 1984).

Turkey: *Musik aus der Türkei*, 2 disks (Museum Collection Berlin–West MC1; ca. 1985); *Turkey*—An Anthology of the World's Music (Anthology AST 4003; 1971); *Turkish Village Music* (Nonesuch H–72050; ca. 1969).

Other Areas: *Heritage: Authentic Songs of Ambience and Ritual from the Musical Heritage of Jewish Communities in Israel* (CBS 63437; ca. 1970); *Jewish Music*, UNESCO Collection Musical Sources (Philips 6586 001; 1971); *Afghanistan*—An Anthology of the World's Music (Anthology AST 4001; 1969); *Azerbaijani Mugam*, UNESCO Collection Musical Sources (Philips 6586 027; 1975).

4

CHINA

Isabel K.F. Wong

THE CONTEMPORARY SCENE

In mid-April of 1989, like many people in the world I was glued to the television screen, watching the dramatic events unfolding in Beijing's Tiananmen Square. (*Tiananmen*, ironically, means "Gate of Heavenly Peace.") The students of Beijing staged a sit-in, beginning April 17th, to call for an end to corruption and nepotism in government, for more democratic participation in decision making, and for better conditions in the universities. Eventually the students began a hunger strike to press their demands. Millions of Chinese people echoed these demands and joined the students in massive prodemocracy demonstrations. Finally, on June 4th, the armies moved into Tiananmen Square to crush the demonstration. The world watched helplessly as the massacre took place.

Up until May 22nd, two days after the declaration of martial law, the spirits of the demonstrators had been high; the students made speeches, danced, and sang "Songs for the Masses" and pop songs to amuse themselves. The former included the loyal Communist songs like the "Internationale" and "Without the Communist Party There Is No New China," while the latter included "A Blood-Soaked Image," a love song bidding farewell to a soldier of the Sino-Vietnamese skirmishes of the late 1970s.

Watching the demonstrating students singing "Songs for the Masses" brought back memories to my mind, for I am very familiar with these songs. When I was a young student in the People's Republic of China in the early 1950s, the singing of political songs called "Songs for the Masses" constituted most of our musical diet. These songs, whose origins may be traced back to Western Protestant hymns and school songs, modern Japanese school songs, Chinese folk songs, and Russian revolutionary songs, are short and simple, use the diatonic scale, and have texts that are sloganlike ideological messages of Communism. We sang these songs in classes and in numerous political rallies and parades where thousands of people were gathered under hundreds of fluttering red banners; we sang them during labor sessions in the countryside, where we were often brought to do physical labor as a show of patriotism; and finally, we sang them in our leisure time to amuse ourselves, for they were the only songs we were allowed to sing or hear.

When I returned to China in the early 1980s after some thirty years of absence, I was very surprised to learn that students seldom sang "Songs for the Masses" nowadays. Instead, students and young people in general prefer to sing Chinese pop songs, or pop songs imported from Taiwan or Hong Kong (all of these influenced by pop songs from the West and from Japan), and some particularly like country music.

Pop Music Today

Since the Chinese government adopted some measures of economic reform and an open-door foreign policy in the early 1980s, political pressure on the Chinese people—quite strong since the establishment of the People's Republic of China in 1949—has become relatively relaxed. As a result, some forms of pop music, which the government prefers to call "light music," have been tolerated. In recent years, the popularity of pop music has eclipsed all forms of traditional music, particularly in the cities.

Modern Chinese pop song first came into being in Shanghai in the late 1920s. These early pop songs were hybrids of jazz, Hollywood film songs, and popular Chinese urban ballads of the entertainment quarters, generically known as xiaodiao. More recent pop songs, particularly those of Taiwan and Hong Kong, which have been emulated by Chinese pop songs today, show the strong influence of white rock from the United States of the 1950s.

Pop songs, or "light music," are included in Chinese radio programs and in television programs of song-and-dance numbers, which are very popular with today's urban audience and which feature pop songs almost exclusively. Cassettes of pop songs are in great demand

and are readily available in shops, as many Chinese possess cassette recorders. Walking in any Chinese city today, one cannot avoid the sound of pop songs being blasted out to the streets from stores or homes.

In the last two years the kara-oka pop-song singing craze has swept some major cities. Kara-oka, a Japanese invention of the 1970s, is a kind of nightclub version of "music minus one." The venue of kara-oka is usually a bar, a nightclub, or a restaurant equipped with a video machine, a video monitor, a microphone, a large screen hung where most of the customers can see it, and MTV-like video films of the current hits, mostly from Taiwan and Hong Kong. The singing, however, is provided by the customers. When one or more customers desire to sing, they let the management know of their choice, and then take their place in front of the monitor and the microphone. When the music begins—electronic accompaniment only, without the vocal part—the customer sings along with it. At the same time the video relating to the song appears on the monitor in front of the singer, and the song text also appears on the screen to serve as a prompter. These same images are simultaneously projected on the big screen for the rest of the customers to watch. Since the singing is not always expertly done, there are some comical moments, and these have come to be expected as part of the entertainment. I have been to kara-oka bars a few times in China, and I have noticed that both singers and listeners tend to giggle a great deal; thus the atmosphere is always one of great merriment. People usually dance with the music, and food and drinks are served. (Food and drink always seem to be an integral part of Chinese musical entertainment.) Kara-oka has become so popular nowadays that it is the in thing to do for private parties as well, such as weddings and birthday celebrations; dancing, food, and drink are always part of these parties.

Since the mid-1980s, rock music has become increasingly popular among university students, particularly among the reform-minded ones who advocate emulating the political and economic systems of the West. Even though rock music is not banned outright, the authorities construe it as representing Western capitalistic decadence and ideas of nonconformity and individualism that are frowned upon.

The most popular rock band is the one led by Cui Jian, a former trumpet student of the prestigious Central Conservatory of Music of Beijing; his song "I Have Absolutely Nothing," first released in 1985, has remained a perennial hit. During the prodemocracy demonstration in Tiananmen, Cui Jian and his band volunteered to give a performance in the square to show solidarity with the demonstrators. The audience, which gave him a tremendous reception, sang along with him and danced to the music. The British Broadcasting Corporation later produced a film on Cui Jian, as did an independent U.S. documentary filmmaker, whose film, *No More Disguise*, was shown on New York public television in 1989.

The Creation of "Songs for the Masses" in Modern China

The foundation for the development of "Songs for the Masses" such as I had learned in the early years of Communist rule and which had been sung—with, I think, ironic intent—by the students in Tiananmen Square had been laid at the beginning of this century by educational reformers. At the outset of education reform, famous scholars and reformers like Kang Youwei (1858–1927) and Liang Qizhou (1873–1929) had advocated the use of a new type of school song, with simple melodies and didactic texts, somewhat similar to those used in Western or Japanese schools, to inculcate a new ethic of discipline and nationalism. The reformers contended that traditional Chinese music was languid and passive and therefore unsuitable for school use. These opinions touched off a debate between the traditionalists and the reformers on the pros and cons of traditional music versus modern school music. The reformists' most representative views were summed up in a 1903 article entitled "On the Reform of Chinese Music," written by the pseudonymous Fei Shi. Fei Shi strongly attacked the two dominant kinds of traditional music: the yayue, or ritual music of the court, and the popular entertainment music of the theater. The yayue, said Fei Shi, was an antiquated vehicle of the state, bolstering the prestige and authority of the ruling monarch, and as such it had no relevance to the common people. The popular theatrical music, on the other hand, was too narrowly confined to entertainment and therefore also not suitable for the education of children. Fei Shi argued that China at this time of change needed to have her music reformed, or to create new music that would be accessible to a large segment of the Chinese people, including children, and capable of arousing in them a new morale of self-strengthening. Further, he argued that China's habitual fondness for antiquity and disregard of things contemporary was suicidal, according to the evolutionary theory of social Darwinism. Fei Shi's view anticipated the development of modern Chinese music from the following decades up to our own time.

As didactic school songs were urgently needed when education reform first began in the beginning of the twentieth century, a selective adaptation of school songs from misssionary schools in China and those from Japan brought back by Chinese students studying there was put into practice. By the end of the first decade of the century, however, Chinese songwriters, many of whom had received some elementary music training in Japan, began themselves to write didactic school songs. The three most notable were Zheng Zhiwan (1879–1929), Shen Xingong (1869–1947), and Li Shutong (1880–1942), all of whom had been trained in Japan. The songs they wrote were simple and short, with a limited range and a square, marchlike rhythm, and were predominantly syllabic, reflecting the influence of early Japanese school songs. The song texts have simple and direct messages concerned with patriotism, self-discipline, military readiness, and civic-spiritedness, reflecting the national concerns of the Chinese intellectuals of that time. With these early songs, the modern genre of Chinese song emerged. In the following decades the descendants of these didactic songs became the main musical diet of the majority of Chinese students.

After the fall of the Qing emperor in 1911 and the establishment of a republic in 1912 under the leadership of Dr. Sun Yat-sen, a parliament was formed. In the same year a new political party called the Guomindang (kuomintang, or Nationalist Party, often abbreviated as KMT) was brought into being by Dr. Sun. Lacking an army, Sun was impotent to compete with the powerful new army chief, Yuan Shikai, the founder of the modern Imperial army who soon became the dictator of China. Yuan's death in 1915 left the central government in a weak position, and warlords came to power in various parts of China. In 1914, when World War I broke out, Japan on the allied side moved to take over the German concession in Shangdong province in northern China, and in 1915 set before the central government in Beijing its Twenty-one Demands, which would have placed China under Japanese protection. Immediately, the Chinese people expressed their outrage in protests, demonstrations, and strikes. Songs denouncing Japanese aggression and the weak central government were part of the protest movement; they circulated widely in schools, universities, and nationwide demonstrations. The musical style of these protest songs resembled that of the didactic school songs, but what set them apart was the messages of the texts. Whereas the texts of school songs usually expounded the general principles of good citizenship, discipline, patriotism, and nationalism, those of the protest songs focused on the current political issues and used terse, sloganlike language. These protest songs may be regarded as the predecessors of the later political songs—known as Revolutionary Songs, or "Songs for the Masses"—which were developed by the Chinese communists.

In 1917 China entered World War I, declaring war on Germany in the hope of recovering Shangdong province, then claimed by Japan. The confirmation of the Japanese claim to Shangdong by the Western powers at the Versailles Peace Conference of 1919 brought a storm of protest in China. Protest songs denouncing the Conference and Western and Japanese imperialism immediately appeared and circulated in nationwide strikes and demonstrations. On May 4th, 1919, the intellectual and political ferment culminated in a mass student demonstration at the National Peking University. This was the first time that the new intellectual *class*, educated along modern non-Confucianist lines, was able to make its mark on Chinese politics. The political activities and the intellectual currents set in motion by these modern students developed into a broad national intellectual awakening known as the May 4th Movement.

The May 4th Movement affected the development of modern Chinese music profoundly. The hub of the Movement was Beida (National Peking University),which under the administration of its remarkable and liberal Chancellor Cai Yuanpei (1867–1940) was fostering freedom of thought and education. Cai was a scholar well versed in the tenets of Confucianism as well as in Western philosophy; his thinking represented an attempt to synthesize the Chinese classical tradition and the libertarianism of the modern European West that characterized the May 4th Movement. When he became Chancellor, Cai endeavored to create opportunities for the students to receive an aesthetic education that included music and art, which he maintained were essential subjects in modern education.

Like his contemporary Fei Shi, Cai felt that the reform of traditional Chinese music was necessary in order to bring it up to date, and that elements in Western music should be borrowed to moderenize Chinese music. In 1916 Cai established at Beida an extracurricular music study group, staffed by both Chinese and Western teachers, which offered students instruction in Chinese and Western vocal and instrumental music; the teachers were also charged with the responsibility of finding ways to modernize traditional Chinese music. This music group eventually was reorganized and expanded to become China's first academic music department. Under the leadership of the composer Xiao Youmei (1884–1940), who was trained in Japan and Germany, this music department offered instruction in music theory, composition, as well as the academic study of music, in addition to instrumental and vocal instruction. Sharing Cai's enthusiasm and belief in modernizing Chinese music, Xiao pioneered in the reform of Chinese music by borrowing Western elements, notably harmony, and by so doing he put into musical practice for the first time the realization of the self-strengthening slogan of 1898, "Chinese culture as the essence, and Western learning for practical use."

Another development initiated at Beida during the May 4th period that had significant implications for the future development of the field of Chinese musicology was the Folk-Song Campaign. Inspired by the Russian Narodnik Movement of the 1870s, which called for educated youth to go to the countryside to educate the peasants, a group of Beida students did just that. Through the process of discovering rural problems, the young intellectuals encountered folk song and folk art (which were considered unworthy of attention by most of the members of the elites of the old regime); they came to recognize their value and realized that they were important areas to be studied. Out of these efforts eventually came the systematic collection and scholarly research of folk song, which laid the foundation for the future collection and study of other types of Chinese music, and thereby contributed to the development of the modern field of Chinese musicology.

The May 4th Movement also affected the development of modern Chinese music by promoting the use of Chinese vernacular language as a written medium of communication in all fields, including scholarship, in place of the cumbersome literary Chinese that had continued as the language of literature and scholarship for millennia. Using the vernacular, the young writers introduced a new popular literature that emulated Western forms and spread it through numerous periodicals and newspapers. Inspired by this development, some songwriters began to set new vernacular poems to music. The pioneer in this endeavor was Y. R. Chao (1892–1982), an internationally known linguist and a composer trained in the United States. Combining elements of traditional Chinese music with Western ones such as harmony, Chao wrote songs with vernacular poetic texts and piano accompaniment. He is now considered the creator of the modern Chinese art song.

The creation of songs specifically for young children was yet another development inspired by the promotion of the vernacular language. Some songwriters, notably Li Jinhui (1891–1967), developed songs of a recreational nature for young schoolchildren. This effort eventually led to the development of a kind of song-and-dance skit for stage performance by children, which came to be enjoyed by adults as well because of its novelty. Realizing there was a ready market for this new form of entertainment, Li transformed it into a kind of modern musical for adults and organized his own song-and-dance troupe to give performances in big cities. In the 1920s Li's musicals were quite a commercial success; through radio and sound recordings, songs from these musicals became widely circulated, and the modern medium of Chinese popular song was born. During the 1930s and '40s, Li's younger brother Li Jinguang (b. 1916) further developed this new genre. Drawing his inspiration from Hollywood hit songs, jazz, cabaret versions of Latin American rhythms such as the tango and rumba, and urban popular xiaodiao, all of which could be heard in cosmopolitan Shanghai, Li, with his facile ability for writing catchy melodies, brought unprecedented attention to the pop-song medium. Li was employed by the French record company Pathé in Shanghai, which monopolized the Chinese market, and he also wrote for movies and for live performances in nightclubs. His famous hit "Shangri-la," which was written and released in the 1930s, can still be heard on Chinese radio today (the instrumental version only), and the older generation of Americans will remember Bing Crosby's recording of his "Rose, Rose, I Love You!" I visit him often in Shanghai, where he still lives.

One of the most enduring aspects of the May 4th Movement was the change in the ideology of China's educated class, brought about by the attack upon Confucian values. Using newspapers and such journals as *The New Youth*, modern scholars condemned as tyranny the subordination of subject to ruler, of wife to husband, of son to father, and of individual to family, all of which were regarded as remnants of a feudal society. Since the stories portrayed in the traditional Chinese musical theater adhered primarily to the values of the feudal society, a debate on the merits of the traditional theater was touched off by the journal's editors and contributors. Some writers advocated the total elimination of traditional theater; others advocated reform by emulating the theater of the West. Though these debates lasted only a few years (mainly from 1917 to 1919) and failed to produce any immediate, tangible reform, they may rightly be regarded as having initiated a lasting trend toward theater reform, which came to fruition after the establishment of the People's Republic in 1949.

At the time of the May 4th Movement authoritarian parties were proving successful in Europe. The Fascists came to power in Italy during the period after World War I, and the Russian Revolution had just concluded with the triumph of the Communist Party there. Marxism-Leninism found adherents among many of the leading writers and thinkers of the May 4th Movement; it also affected music activities. In 1921 members of a Marxist study group at Beida attempted to organize the railroad workers of Beijing and to introduce Marxism to them. They established an adult school and a recreation center for these workers, and the activities in these facilities included the teaching and singing of protest songs, which were later used in strikes by the workers.

The Chinese Communist Party (CCP) was founded in 1921 by a leader of the May 4th Movement. There began a competition between the two groups—the KMT, or Nationalists, and the CCP, or Communists—for control of China that was to last for many decades.

By 1923 the impact of Marxism-Leninism on Chinese thought and on Chinese arts and music began to be felt. Arts and music are regarded by the Marxists as political tools for propaganda. The introduction of the "Internationale" to China in 1923, a song closely identified with the European labor movement of the 1890s and with the Bolshevik revolution in Russia, came to be regarded as the signal of China's entrance into the world communist movement.

The increase of Japanese aggression in China in the ensuing years stimulated many more protest songs against Japanese aggression; and Russian revolutionary songs began to be heard in leftist circles. The war of resistance against Japan of 1937–45 stimulated a further outpouring of songs with patriotic themes; composers of all political persuasions joined forces to produce songs in support of the war. Through being sung in war films, many of these songs became very popular with general audiences, thus constituting a true mass medium. After the establishment of the People's Republic in 1949, the production of thousands of "Songs for the Masses" became one of the important functions of the propaganda machine.

Western Art Music

Western art music has been imported to China since the early 1920s. Today, it has a sizable audience in the big cities. Since the government instituted an open-door policy in the early 1980s, it has become rather common to have performances by visiting Western orchestras and virtuosi in big cities such as Beijing, Shanghai, and Guangzhou. As most Chinese cities are not yet equipped with big concert halls, these performances usually take place in large sports auditoriums, where the acoustical conditions are not always ideal and a great deal of amplification is needed. The audience for Western classical music performances is made up mainly of members of the modern educated classes, as well as influential government officials (called cadres in China) and their families. Tickets are quite expensive, yet they are always in great demand.

Some Chinese people genuinely enjoy Western art music, but others come to these performances with extramusical motives. For example, one of my friends, a university professor who had been to the United States as a visiting scholar recently, told me that he attends these concerts because they make him feel that he still has some link with the outside world; another friend, the daughter of a high official, told me that she likes to attend Western art-music concerts because they represent prestige and status.

I have often had opportunities to attend Western art-music concerts during my frequent visits to China in recent years. I particularly remember a concert in Beijing by a famous opera singer from the West, whose program consisted of arias from popular Italian operas such as *Madama Butterfly*, *La Traviata*, *Tosca*, and *Aida*, which are among the great favorites of Chinese concertgoers. Chinese audiences respond to performances of works like these with great enthusiasm. They applaud whenever they feel like it, which is often; they exchange appreciative remarks with their friends about the quality of the singing, often loudly; and they also move about a great deal during the performance. The singer graciously ignored all the commotion and gave a wonderful performance.

I remember thinking to myself: someone must have informed the singer that most Chinese concertgoers, except the aficionados of Western art music, are unaccustomed to listening to music in complete silence. The Chinese are used to talking and moving about a great deal during musical performances because traditionally music has always served as background for a social gathering.

A few of China's major cities have modern music conservatories. Concerts of Western classical music performed by native Chinese musicians take place in these conservatories regularly, usually to a smaller and more knowledgeable and select audience.

AN INSTRUMENTAL PERFORMANCE AT A TEAHOUSE IN SHANGHAI

Traditional Chinese music includes instrumental music (both solo and ensemble), musical theatricals, and musical narratives. Each of China's three great topographical regions—northern, western, and eastern—has its own forms and styles of these genres.

One kind of traditional instrumental music I often go to hear in Shanghai is the chamber ensemble of winds and strings called Jiangnan sizhu. Jiangnan, meaning "south of the river" (the river being the Yangzi), is the designation for the Yangzi Delta region in southeastern China, of which Shanghai is a part. Si literally means "silk," and it denotes stringed instruments because strings used to be made of silk (nowadays the strings are usually made of steel for greater volume). Zhu literally means "bamboo," and it denotes wind instruments because they are made of bamboo.

Instruments belonging to the "silk" category include plucked strings, bowed strings, and struck strings. The plucked strings of the ensemble are one pipa (a pear-shaped, four-stringed plucked lute with a short, bent neck and twenty-four frets), one or two sanxian (a three-stringed lute with a long, fretless neck and an oval-shaped sound box), and one qinqin (a two- or three-stringed plucked lute with a long, fretted neck). The bowed strings are one or two erhu (two-stringed fiddles with hollow wooden cylindrical sound boxes having one side covered by snakeskin). And the struck string is the yangqin (a dulcimer struck with a pair of bamboo sticks).

Instruments of the ensemble belonging to the "bamboo" category include one dizi (a transverse bamboo flute with six fingerholes, a mouth hole, and another hole covered by a thin membrane which vibrates to give the instrument a reedy sound), one xiao (an end-blown bamboo flute with five frontal fingerholes, one hole in the back, and a blowing hole on the top), and one sheng (The sheng is a free-reed mouth organ made of a series of bamboo pipes arranged in a circle, each with a reed on its lower end, and all inserted into a base made of copper, wood, or gourd, to which a mouthpiece is attached. Two or more tones may be produced simultaneously on the instrument).

The Jiangnan sizhu ensemble also includes an assortment of percussion instruments. These are: a small flat drum called the gu, a paired wooden clapper called the ban (the gu and ban are played by one person), a muyü, or "wooden fish" (a carved, hollow, wooden instrument stuck with a pair of wooden sticks), and finally a pair of small handbells called pongzhong, which may be used in certain pieces in the repertory.

Jiangnan sizhu was formerly a favorite pastime of the gentry and educated classes of the urban centers in the Jiangnan region. There were many private clubs where people gathered to play and while away a pleasant evening. As a rule, the performers of Jiangnan sizhu are amateurs; they perform not for payment but for their own enjoyment. In Shanghai today there are still half a dozen or so Jiangnan sizhu clubs whose members are retired urban workers; many belonged to the gentry class before 1949.

Jiangnan sizhu performances usually take place in neighborhood teahouses. The teahouse where I usually go to listen to Jiangnan sizhu is located in the Square of the Temple of the City God in the Old City of Shanghai, a picturesque area lined with many small shops selling all kinds of traditional wares and souvenirs. The old teahouse, always thronged with people, is an elegant structure built on an artificial lake teeming with goldfish, and it is approached via a zigzag footbridge. It is a hexagonal wooden building of two stories, lacquered with dark-brown paint, with intricate latticework windows open on all sides. It has double-tiered black tile roofs with elongated eaves swooping out in a complex pattern of upturned curves.

As an entrance fee, customers are required to pay a modest price for a pot of tea—they can choose their favorite kind of tea leaves—but there is no extra charge for the Jiangnan sizhu, which is played on the second floor every afternoon from 1:30 to 5:00. Tea is served to the customers seated at the dozen or so teakwood tables by a waiter who brings a very elegant, small, brown ceramic pot and matching cup. One may also order snacks, such as watermelon or sunflower seeds.

Every afternoon before playing time, the players arrive one by one, place their instruments on a big table situated at one side of the teahouse, and then wander off to chat with friends, waiting for the rest of the ensemble to gather. Around 1:30 they sit down around the big table and start to play. The string players and the player of the drum and clapper sit in an inner circle, while the rest sit in an outer one. There is no conductor, but the player of the drum and clapper (gu ban) beats time. Everybody plays from memory, and no written music is used (Figures 4–1 and 4–2).

There is no formal announcement of the program, nor are there program notes, for the audience is familiar with the small repertory, which consists of only about two dozen pieces that all have descriptive titles (the composers are anonymous). The first piece for the afternoon is always a short, slow, and simple piece, and is always played by novices. Pieces played during the afternoon progress from simple to complex. Each piece usually lasts ten minutes or more, and some may be played more than once. After one piece is finished, some players may get up from the table, and other players sitting among the customers may come up to the big table to join the performers. There is no formal intermission between pieces. Around 4:30 the most skillful and respected players of the club will join in to perform pieces that are fast and require great skill.

Figure 4–1. Instruments are put on tables before a performance; from left to right: the hammer dulcimer *yanqqin*, the plucked lute *qinqin*, the back of the plucked lute *pipa*, the two-stringed fiddle *erhu*, and an unidentified instrument.

When the novices are not playing, they usually sit around the big table listening to and watching the more skilled players. This is how the music is transmitted—there is no formal instruction, and learning is entirely by imitation. When it is felt that some novices are ready to join the more skilled players to play complicated pieces, they will be asked to do so; after they have finished playing a piece, the skilled players will give them criticism or suggestions.

Like most traditional Chinese instrumental music, Jiangnan sizhu pieces always begin slowly and gradually accelerate, ending in a fast tempo. There are no fixed tempo indications associated with any of the pieces; the tempi are left up to the discretion of the players. The drum-and-clapper player is supposed to provide the beat for the music, but the players typically are not overly concerned with rhythmic exactitude.

As in other genres of instrumental music, all the instruments in Jiangnan sizhu play together most of the time. The overall timbral quali-

Figure 4–2. A *Jiangnan sizhu* performance; the instruments are (clockwise from front left): the horizontal flute *dizi*, the hammer dulcimer *yanqqin*, the end-blown flute *dong xiao*, the plucked lute *pipa*, the mouth organ *sheng*, the two-stringed fiddle *erhu* (partially shown), the percussion *muyu* slit drum, and the plucked lute *qinqin* (partially shown).

ty of this music is a combined strings-and-winds sound (the strings being plucked, bowed, and struck) in a relatively high register. A variety of musical temperaments exists because individual instruments are tuned differently. The resultant sonic quality of the melody is slightly fuzzy and thick, which is characteristic of traditional Chinese music.

When I first heard Jiangnan sizhu music, I could discern no break within a given piece; it seemed to me that, once started, it went on without break until the end. I later found out that every piece is divided into sections, but because the end of a section is always overlapped by the beginning the next, a piece usually gives the impression of being through-composed.

Another characteristic of Jiangnan sizhu, I later learned, is the extensive use of improvised embellishments on the basic melody. Every melodic instrument plays the same basic melody, but each player applies the improvised embellishments according to the idiomatic conventions of that instrument, creating a complicated texture of heterophony which—like the variations in tuning—gives a kind of "thickness" to the melody. Because of this freedom in adding improvised embellishments, no two performances of one piece are exactly alike, and the more skilled the performers, the greater the differences may be.

The teahouse where Jiangnan sizhu is performed is always noisy. The customers chat among themselves and some of them play chess, while others come and go during the performance. The waiters crisscross between tables constantly, bringing tea to new customers and adding hot water to pots whose lids have been left open—an unspoken sign they are quick to notice. The players are oblivious to the commotion, and when some of them are not playing they also chat with their friends. Jiangnan sizhu, like many other kinds of traditional Chinese music of a popular nature, is considered a kind of background music to enhance the ambience of a pleasant social environment (Figures 4–3 and 4–4).

Figure 4–3.   The two-stringed fiddle *erhu*.

Figure 4–4.   A Chinese visiting scholar playing the *erhu* at a Chinese New Year party at the University of Illinois at Urbana-Champaign.

THE QIN AND ITS MUSIC

The qin (pronounced "chin"), a seven-stringed zither, is the most highly regarded of Chinese musical instruments because of its antiquity and its rich legacy of associations. Made from a hollowed, slightly convex board approximately four feet long and eight centimeters deep, the qin has seven strings of varying thickness stretched over the entire length of the board. It has neither frets nor bridges. The most common tuning is C-D-F-G-A-c-d. The body is painted with layers of lacquer. Thirteen studs or position markers, called hui, made of mother-of-pearl or other semiprecious material, are embedded along the outer edge of the instrument and indicate finger positions for stopping the strings. The flat, smooth underside of the instrument has two openings called "sound pools" and is usually engraved with the name of the owner and the given name of the instrument. This indicates that the qin is a highly personalized instrument (Figures 4–5 and 4–6).

Figure 4–5.   The seven-stringed zither *qin*.

Figure 4–6.   The famous *qin* master, the late Professor Wu Jing-le, giving a
qin lesson to his students at the Central Conservatory of Music in Beijing.

Qin playing involves various ways of plucking the strings with the
fingers of the right hand (except the little finger) and stopping them
with the fingers of the left hand (except the little finger), as well as the
use of ornaments such as portamento, vibrato, mordents, and harmonics.
Around the sixth century C.E., a type of directions for qin playing was
devised, which explained in detailed prose the techniques required for
producing each and every sound; this type of prose tablature is known
as wenzipu. Later, in the Tang dynasty (618–906 C.E.), a new type of
tablature was created that consisted of clusters of abbreviated symbols
derived from Chinese characters; these specified the string number, the
stopping positions, and the hand, finger, and direction of plucking. This
tablature is called jianzipu ("abbreviated-character tablature"), and its
later form is still in use today.

The qin enjoys great prestige because all through Chinese history
it has been associated with sages and scholars. The earliest mention of

the qin is found in the Shujing (*Book of History*), which contains references to the many ideas and concepts associated with the qin that were further developed later. Learning the qin was already a requirement for scholars and gentlemen before the third century B.C.E. At that time, however, the qin was employed primarily to accompany poetry recitation, as a member of the large orchestra for the court ceremonial music known as yayue (elegant music) or to form a duet with the se (a twenty-stringed plucked zither). A duo of qin and se symbolized a harmonious spousal relationship or friendship. After the Han dynasty (206 B.C.E.–290 C.E.), as ceremonial music at court gradually declined, the qin emerged as both a solo instrument and the accompanying instrument for chamber vocal genres. During the end of the Han period and thereafter, the literati initiated the scholarly study of the qin and wrote compositions specifically for the solo qin, and thus its status and prestige were established. In the subsequent periods of the Sui and Tang dynasties and the Five Dynasties (581–618, 618–907, 907–960), the playing of qin and qin scholarship were restricted to court circles only; outside of the court, the qin was neglected.

It was not until the Song dynasty (960–1027) that there was a renaissance of qin music. An ideological system for the qin was developed by fusing Confucian philosophy with Daoist (Taoist) and Buddhist mystical symbolism. According to this ideology, the playing of the qin is an act of contemplation, self-purification, and self-regulation; hence it should be played in private, amidst charming scenery, under pine trees and beside running creeks, in the privacy of one's garden, or in the cloister of one's own library with incense burning.

The qin vogue among the scholars reached its height in the Ming dynasty (1368–1644), when numerous treatises and handbooks of qin music were printed. Prince Zhu Quan, the sixteenth son of the first Ming emperor, was a qin scholar and the first person to print a qin handbook, in 1425. But in the early twentieth century rapid social change brought about a sharp decline in interest. Good qin players were very few, and qin scholarship came to a virtual halt. After the establishment of the People's Republic in 1949, under government encouragement, research in qin music and its history reached a higher level of competence, particularly during the 1950s. In recent years, the qin has been brought into the new context of the modern concert stage; and with the appearance of a younger generation of qin virtuosi, interest in the qin has been revived among members of the educated circle. Among the general populace, however, the qin, with its associations with past literary and philosophical traditions, is too exclusive and inaccessible and has therefore been totally neglected.

The earliest extant qin manuscript, dating from the Tang dynasty, contains the composition "Youlan" ("Orchids in a Secluded Valley"), which is written out in prose tablature. The first printed qin handbook, the Shenqi mipu (The Mysterious Secret Handbook), compiled by Prince Zhu Quan of Ming, appeared in 1425 and was followed by numerous other woodblock handbooks, together comprising more than three thousand compositions notated in the abbreviated-character tablature. However, only about eighty pieces have survived in the oral performance tradition.

In qin handbooks tempo is indicated by terms such as "Slow down," or "Speed up," but durational symbols are totally absent. Such omissions indicate the importance placed upon oral tradition and the realization and interpretation of the music by the performing artist. A process of reconstructing ancient pieces from qin tablature through the aid of oral tradition is called dapu (literally, "to obtain from the notation"). This recreating process, done by the qin player, has been a venerable qin composition/realization tradition. Qin meters vary among free meter, duple meter, and sometimes triple meter, often within the same piece.

Qin notation is very difficult to read, even for those who are literate and cultivated, and this contributes to the exclusive nature of the qin. In the famous eighteenth-century novel *The Story of the Stone* (also known as *The Dream of the Red Chamber*) by Cao Xueqin (d.1763), there is a passage that conveys this well. This greatest of Chinese novels depicts in meticulous detail life in a very wealthy and influential family, in particular the love and fate of the hero Jai Baoyu and his cousin Lin Daiyu, two extremely talented, cultivated, and precocious teenagers. In Chapter 86 Baoyu seeks Daiyu out in her quarters and learns something about qin tablature and the philosophy of the qin—although his wry concluding comment seems to indicate he takes it all with a grain of salt.

> Daiyu was sitting at her desk reading. Baoyu approached her, saying cheerfully, "I see that you left Grandmother's place early." Daiyu responded with a smile and said, "Well, you wouldn't speak to me, so why should I stay any longer?"
>
> "There were so many people there, I didn't have a chance." As he replied he tried to see what she was reading, but he couldn't recognize a single word. Some looked like the character for "azalea," some looked like the character for "hazy." Some had the radical "big" on the left, the character for "nine" next to it, and a large hook underneath them with the character for "five" written inside. . . .
>
> Baoyu was curious and puzzled. He said, "Sister, I am more and more impressed by you. You must be reading a secret Book of Heaven!"
>
> Daiyu couldn't help laughing. "Here is an educated man! Don't tell me you have never seen a musical score!"
>
> "Of course I have," he replied, "but I don't know any of those characters. . . . Why don't you teach me to read some of it? . . . For example, what do you make of this character 'big' with that long hook and a character 'five' stuck in the middle?"
>
> With a laugh Daiyu replied, "This character 'big' and the character 'nine' mean that you press on the ninth stud with your left thumb, and this big hook with the character 'five' inside means that you hook inward

the fifth string with your right hand. This whole cluster is not a word; it stands for a musical note. There is really nothing to it. You have also many kinds of left-hand techniques such as the quick vibrato, broad vibrato, upward glide, downward glide, trill, quick glide, and so forth."

Baoyu was hopping with joy, saying, "Come on, dear sister, since you know so much about it, why don't we try it out?"

"It is said that the zither is synonymous with the word for self-restraint. The ancients intended it to be used for discipline, for tranquilizing one's emotions, and for suppressing excessive and frivolous desires. In playing the zither, you must select a quiet and secluded place. It could be in the top story of a building, in the forest among the rocks, at a mountain precipice, or at the edge of the water. The weather should be calm, with a light breeze or a clear moon. You have to burn some incense and meditate for a while. . . .

"As to the performance itself, the fingering and the intonation have to be good enough . . . the position of your heart should be in a line with the fifth stud on the instrument. . . . Now you are ready, bodily, and spiritually. . . .

Baoyu said, "Can't we just do it for fun? It's next to impossible if we have to go through all that rigmarole!" (Adapted from a translation by Rulan Chao Pian)

Practically all qin compositions have programmatic titles either deriving from common poetic images or alluding to Chinese history or legends. The titles serve to evoke a mood or atmosphere familiar to the Chinese.

A typical qin composition usually contains several sections. The first part, known as sanqi ("introduction"), begins slowly in free rhythm. Its function is to introduce the principal notes of the mode used in the following particular piece. In the second part, known as rudiao ("entering the music," or exposition), the meter is established and the principal motives of the piece are introduced, which are then varied by means of extension, reduction, and changes in timbre, tempo, and register. This part is usually the longest and musically the most substantial. During the third part, known as ruman ("becoming slower"), the principal motives undergo further rhythmic variation, and modulation to other keys may occur. In some larger compositions, motivic materials occurring in the second part may be restated and reinterpreted here; this is called fuqi ("restatement"). Finally, in the fourth part, a short coda known as weisheng ("tail sounds") concludes the composition. The coda, always played in harmonics and in a slackening tempo, reiterates the important notes used in the composition.

PROMINENT FEATURES IN CULTURE AND MUSIC

In the foregoing descriptions of performances of music in varying contemporary Chinese contexts, I have already touched upon some salient features of Chinese music and of Chinese attitudes toward music and music performance. In the following I shall give a more detailed description of these features under separate headings.

The Value and Functions of Music

Since ancient times, the Chinese have equated enjoyment of music with the natural human desire for aesthetic and sensual gratification such as the taste for food, the need for sex, and the satisfaction of seeing beautiful things. Music has traditionally been treated as one of the component phenomena that make up an environment for living. Thus music has not only served as a means of expressing emotions such as joy and sadness or as a vehicle for spiritual or religious contemplation, but it has also always been integrated into events such as rituals, banquets, weddings, funerals, festivals, harvest celebrations, and so forth. In addition, music has always been conceived of as an integral part of other performing arts such as dance and drama. Furthermore, reference to some types of music has conventionally been used to evoke certain moods and atmospheres in literature, poetry, and painting. This complex and integral view of music and its functions had already become well established in the Zhou dynasty in the first millennium B.C.E.

Kong Fuzi, or Master Kong (551–479 B.C.E.), known to the West as Confucius, who founded the school of philosophy (popularly called Confucianism) that had the greatest effect on subsequent Chinese thought, maintained that music has positive and negative power to stimulate allied behavior and desire. Positive music, or shi yin ("proper sound"), which he believed to have attributes of harmoniousness, peacefulness, and appropriateness, was to Confucius an important educational tool capable of inspiring virtue and appropriate attitudes; whereas negative music, or chi yue ("extravagant music"), which had the attributes of inappropriate loudness ("like thunder and lightning") and wanton noisiness, stimulated excessive and licentious behavior.

Confucius, who lived during the end of the Zhou period in a time of constant warfare and chaos, sought to restore China to the peaceful feudalism of the early Zhou years, but felt that the only way the hierarchical system could be made to work properly was for each person to perform correctly his assigned role. "Let the ruler be a ruler and the subjects be subjects," he said, but he added that to rule properly a king must be a virtuous person, setting an example of proper ethical conduct. To Confucius, social stratification was a fact of life to be sustained by morality, not force. He laid much stress on the possibility of remolding men's minds through education (in which music and dance were important parts of the curriculum), and taught that proper inner attitudes could be inculcated through the practice of rituals (which, to be effective, must have proper ritual music) as well as through the observance of rules of etiquette and decorum.

In the twentieth century Meo Zedong, Chairman of the Communist Party from 1949 to 1976, like Confucius, viewed music and the arts as important educational tools. But Mao's practical application of this view was vastly different from that of the Confucianists. To Mao, music and the arts were important tools in the propagation of state ideology. Couched in the language of Marxism-Leninism as interpreted by Mao, the state ideology plays a key political role in the People's Republic; it defines, explains, and rationalizes the whole range of human activities and thinking in the society. Endowed with the sanctity of unchallenged truth, the state ideology constitutes the basis and substance of political values and is buttressed by the fullest extent of coercive power inherent in a sovereign political system. Few in China are able to ignore the all-pervasive influence of ideology. Propagation of ideology is a premier function of the Communist Party acting on behalf of the state, and music and the arts are important components of this propaganda machine.

Mao, like Confucius, also defined music as being of proper and improper kinds. The proper or "correct" kinds are those that have been sanctified by the state and which contain "correct" ideological messages. The "Songs for the Masses" that I sang as a student in the various politically charged contexts I have described belong to this kind. (When the students in the prodemocracy movement of the spring of 1989 sang these sanctioned songs at Tiananmen Square, the irony, to me at least, was inescapable—the students were singing these songs of high-flown political rhetoric to remind the Communist Party and the state of their failures and unkept promises after forty years of rule). Improper kinds of music are those which have been construed by the state to contain "poisonous" influence, either from the discredited "feudal" society of the past or from the capitalistic, decadent West, and as such they must be censored or eliminated. Until the early 1980s, pop music, including rock, certainly belonged to the "poisonous" category.

Authorship and the Creation Process

Only a few traditional Chinese pieces have any attributed authorship. The sources for most traditional Chinese music were anonymous folk or popular materials transmitted orally or through written notation in manuscripts rather than printed books, and the idea of an original composition identified with a particular person was foreign to the Chinese before the twentieth century. This may have something to do with the traditional method of composition, which involved rearrangement of often anonymous preexistent materials, resulting in a newly recomposed version of the older model. The rearrangement process, however, is genre-specific; that is to say, each genre has its own procedures and rules regarding rearrangements.

Some genres of music require a measure of improvisation during performance, such as the adding of improvised embellishments simultaneously in Jiangnan sizhu, which I have already described. By adding improvised embellishments and varying the dynamics and tempi of the music according to established conventions during a performance, and—most important of all—by extending or subtracting portions of the thematic materials in a spontaneous fashion, a performer is in fact acting as a composer as well.

With the introduction of Western ideas to China in the twentieth century came also the Western musical repertory, compositional processes, and techniques, and the idea of composership. Like their Western counterparts, modern Chinese composers nowadays regard themselves as individual creators of original music; the idea and emotion associated with a particular piece of music are regarded as the unique, individual expression of the composer alone.

Amateur and Professional Musicians

Before 1949 the status of a musician was determined by his education and his occupation. Professional musicians, who relied upon music for their livelihood and usually had little formal education, had rather low social status, particularly those who performed entertainment music catering to members of the unlettered class. Unlike the professional musician, the amateur—who did not rely upon making music for a livelihood but was accomplished in music, well educated, and cultivated—was regarded as the ideal gentleman. In Chinese history many distinguished amateur musicians, who usually came from the leisured class, were given high acclaim as musicians and mentioned in historical documents. Records of professional musicians, on the other hand, were few and far between until the twentieth century.

After 1949 the Communist government endeavored to create a classless society, and the stigma on professional musicians was removed. For nationalistic and propagandistic purposes, many forms of traditional entertainment music and folk music that had been frowned upon by orthodox Confucians in the past were elevated as China's national heritage, and the status of their practitioners was also elevated as a result. The government established many modern conservatories, whose curricula included Western art music as well as traditional Chinese music. Distinguished performers of traditional music, both amateur and professional, were hired as equals to teach in these conservatories.

REGIONAL STYLES

Although the Chinese people are relatively homogeneous, China comprises diverse ethnic groups and languages, and the many regional styles of Chinese music reflect this diversity. The Han ethnic community, which accounts for 95 percent of the population, speaks a number of related Sinitic languages that are known collectively as Chinese, of which the major form is Putonghua (Mandarin); other forms are Wu, Xiang, Min, Hakka, and Yue (Cantonese). These various forms are mutually unintelligible when spoken but use a common ideographic writing system that enables any literate Chinese to read them all by simply pronouncing the words in his own language. The rest of the Chinese population is made up of some sixty groups of non-Han people, the "minority nationalities" (chief among them the Tibetan, Mongol, Hui, Korean, Manchu, and Miao), whose homelands have been absorbed by the Chinese state. The languages of the minority nationalities also are unintelligible both to the other groups and to the Chinese.

Musically, each major linguistic region possesses its own vocal styles and forms. The major types of vocal music, such as musical narratives and musical theatricals, have been profoundly influenced by the linguistic characteristics of each region. According to Chinese statistics, there are about 317 regional dramatic genres in China today. Instrumental music is also regional in character; for example, the Jiangnan sizhu is predominantly a genre of the Jiangnan region, while Fujian province in the south has its own instrumental ensemble style called the Fujian nanyin ("Fujian ensemble"), and the Guangdong province in the deep south has its own Guangdong xiaoqu ("Guangdong ensemble"). Some of the same instruments, however, are used in most major instrumental ensembles—for instance, the dizi (transverse flute) and the yangqin (dulcimer).

In spite of the regional differences, there are some common stylistic characteristics shared by music of various regions, and one of the reasons for this commonality is the extensive borrowing of musical styles from region to region. When a particular regional style—like the famous Peking opera—becomes widely adopted throughout the country, a national style is formed.

PEKING OPERA

First emerging as a national style in the nineteenth century, Peking opera is probably the best-known Chinese traditional music theater in the West. A form of musical theatre combining plots, stylized gestures and movements, acrobatics, fanciful makeup, elaborate costumes, and simple props into a unified whole, it is a conglomeration of several northern and southern regional music-theater styles that was accomplished in the capital Beijing (Peking). Though known in the West as Peking opera, it is called jing ju in China—"jing" meaning "capital" (i.e., Beijing) and "ju" meaning "theater." It is a sophisticated genre offering diverse attractions such as virtuosic singing in romantic scenes involving young lovers, stylized battle scenes on land or at sea featuring breathtaking acrobatic skills, comical slapstick often having the bite of political satire, and dramatic scenes having themes of betrayal and revenge, retribution, and the triumph of loyalty and justice. Since its inception in the mid-nineteenth century, the Peking opera theater has been enjoyed by a wide spectrum of Chinese audiences all over the country.

The sources of the plots of Peking opera come mainly from popular legends, historical events, novels, and other narratives. At present there are some 200 traditional plays in the repertory that are still performed frequently, and new plays are also occasionally created. The nature of the individual plays varies; depending on their purpose or focus, the Chinese classify them as lyrical plays, warrior plays, acrobatic plays, virtuosic vocal plays, virtuosic acting plays, and so forth.

Personages in Peking opera are stock-character types divided into five main categories and their subcategories according to sex, age, social status, and character. Each role type is defined by the costumes and makeup the actor wears. All the characters sing, but each employs distinct vocal techniques and singing styles. The characterization of each role is thus defined by costumes, makeup, and timbral quality and style of singing and speech. The five main categories and their subcategories are described below:

1. Sheng: Male role.
   a. Xiaosheng: A young-male role; usually a romantic and dandyish scholar. A xiaosheng actor must have a good singing voice; he sings in a delicate manner and uses both falsetto and chest voice.
   b. Laosheng: A major old-male role; usually a serious, loyal, and just character who may be royalty, a minister, or a respected family retainer. A laosheng actor must possess good singing and acting skills; he sings with chest and throat voice, and his singing style should be steady and vigorous.
   c. Wusheng: Male warrior; someone with consummate acrobatic ability and extremely skilled with sword and spear. A wusheng actor sings with a throaty voice; acrobatic skills, however, are more important than singing ability.
2. Dan: Female role.
   a. Qingyi: A major female role for a mature woman. Qingyi literally means "blue gown"; the sedate color of her gown exemplifies the Confucian ideal of virtuous womanhood. A qingyi character sings in falsetto voice exclusively, in a steady and delicate manner and with clear articulation. He (i.e., a female impersonator) or she must be a consummate singer as well as a good actor or actress.
   b. Huadan: Young female role; usually a frivolous, flirtatious young lady, a prostitute, or a pert young maid. A huadan sings in falsetto voice in a manner full of infectious nuances and innuendos and

must possess both good singing and good acting skills.

    c. Daomaodan: Female warrior; someone with acrobatic skills.

    d. Laodan: Old female.

3. Jing: Painted-face role; played by a male whose face is painted with intricate colored patterns indicating his character and psychological makeup; a heroic character who may be a general or a leader of a rebel or bandit group. A jing character sings with a throaty voice and in a very forceful manner.

4. Mo: A minor old-male role.

5. Chou: Male comic role; someone with quick wit and verbal skills who is also a good mimic. A chou actor does not sing very often, and when he does, it is usually in an exaggerated and ironical manner (Figures 4–7 and 4–8).

Figure 4–7. Performance of a scene from the Peking Opera play *Huan Shan Lui* (Tragedy in the Deserted Mountain) in Beijing. The role-types are (from left to right): the *dan* role (*qingyi*, or "blue-gown"); the actor is the well-known female impersonator Mr. Zhao Rongshen, the *wa wa sheng* role (male child role), and the *jing* role (painted face role).

Figure 4–8. Students of the Peking Opera percussion ensemble of a training academy in Beijing rehearsing. The instruments are (from left to right): small gong, cymbals, gong, drum and clapper (hung on the drum stand).

The basic musical elements of Peking opera are arias, musical speech, and instrumental music. These elements, together with movements, are systematically organized into a simple structure making up a play. In the following, the individual musical elements are discussed in some detail.

Instrumental music in Peking opera has many functions—first and foremost, to accompany the singing and the physical movements and dance. To an audience familiar with the conventional musical code of Peking opera, it may also describe a dramatic situation and action, indicate the spatial dimension of the setting, convey the moods and psychological makeup of characters, and provide soundscape or sound effects connected with a particular dramatic moment. With musical clues, an educated Peking-opera audience will be able to form a mental picture of the temporal and spatial aspects of the drama and respond to it with appropriate emotion and understanding.

The instrumental ensemble is made up of two components: the melodic, or wenchang (civic instrumentation) ensemble, and the percussion, or wuchang (military instrumentation) ensemble. In the musical communication of information, the percussion ensemble plays a more important function than the melodic ensemble. In addition, the percussion ensemble also provides rhythmical punctuation for movements and singing, and it serves to combine all the discrete elements of a play—musical as well as gestural—into a complete whole.

The percussion ensemble is made up principally of five instruments: danpigu (a single-headed drum), ban (a paired wooden clapper; danpigu and ban are played by one person, who functions as the conductor), daluo (a big gong that produces a falling pitch), xiaoluo (a small gong that produces a rising pitch), and naoba (a small pair of cymbals). In addition, there are a few other percussion instruments for special effects: datangu (a big barrel drum), xiaotangu (a small barrel drum), several other gongs and cymbals of different sizes, a muyü (a "wooden-fish" slit drum), and a pair of small handbells.

The music of the percussion ensemble includes some sixty conventional rhythmic patterns, each of which is identified by a proper name and a specific onomatopoetic syllabic pattern. The five principal instruments are combined in different ways to indicate different kinds of dramatic situations, atmospheres, or moods. There are three basic percussion combinations:

1. A trio made up of the big gong, the small gong, and the cymbal, with the big gong being the principal instrument. This combination is usually employed in scenes of pageantry featuring a big crowd of actors, and also in dramatic scenes that require strong emphasis.
2. A duo made up of the cymbal, as the principal instrument, and the small gong. This combination usually accompanies tragic scenes.
3. A small gong solo. This is generally used in scenes of a tranquil or lyrical nature.

Besides these basic combinations, other additional combinations include a duo of the big and small barrel drums (used in acrobatic and fighting scenes), a duo of the small gong and the big cymbal (played in a specific way to indicate underwater and thunder sounds), and so forth.

The sixty-or-so named conventional percussion patterns, each requiring different instrumental combinations and varying tempi, perform many functions. The most common are:

1. to indicate entrances and exits of dramatic personages and their social status;
2. to indicate and emphasize certain emotional situations;
3. to emphasize a word, a phrase, a person's name, or a place name;
4. to punctuate sentences;
5. to increase the rhythmic liveliness of certain words or phrases;
6. to accompany an interlude between actions or arias;
7. to accompany specific stylized miming movements;
8. to accompany fighting scenes;
9. to produce special sound effects; and
10. to introduce arias and melodic interludes.

The instruments of the melodic ensemble of the Peking opera are mostly strings and winds, as well as a set of ten small, suspended pitched gongs called the yunluo. The strings are the jinghu (the leading melodic instrument, a two-stringed bamboo spiked fiddle with very high and piercing pitch), the erhu, the yueqin (a four-stringed plucked lute with a round sound box), and a small sanxian. The winds are the dizi transverse flute, the sheng, and the big and small suona (conical double-reed oboes).

The primary functions of the melodic ensemble are to play introductions and interludes for arias, to accompany arias, and to play incidental music for dance and miming movements. The strings and the winds perform somewhat different functions. The strings, with the jinghu as their principal instrument, accompany the two main types of Peking-opera arias known as the xipi and the erhuang, which were derived from some folk predecessors of Peking opera. (These arias will be explained further.) In addition, the strings also play various incidental pieces—all of which have proper names—to accompany some miming movements, such as sweeping, changing clothes, putting on makeup, walking, and to accompany scenes of banqueting and general pageantry, celebration, and dance. Each individual piece of named incidental music has an association with specific dramatic situations and moods, and each requires different playing techniques on the various strings for the production of varying volumes and timbres.

The winds—the dizi and the sheng only, without the suona—sometimes in combination with the sanxian and the erhu, accompany arias in scenes derived from the repertory of the aristocratic theater called kunju, another predecessor of the Peking opera, which uses the dizi as its principal melodic instrument. Kunju-derived scenes are usually lyrical in nature, and in these scenes the yunlo gong set is also used. The winds are also used to accompany arias derived from folk tunes that have been absorbed into the Peking-opera repertory. Furthermore, the winds play specific named incidental pieces to accompany dances derived from the kunju.

Finally, the big and small suona are always employed in combination with the percussion ensemble exclusively to accompany arias sung by a chorus. Named incidental pieces specially associated with scenes involving military maneuvers, fighting, marching, hunting, or processions are also played by the suona-and-percussion ensemble.

The instrumental ensemble of Peking opera is organized with great economy. There are only nine players in the entire ensemble. The performers, who are very versatile, usually play more than one instrument. For example, in the percussion ensemble, the conductor, who plays both the single-headed drum and the clapper, also plays the big or small barrel drum. One person plays the various sizes of cymbals, and another plays the various sizes of gongs. In the melodic ensemble, the jinghu and erhu players also play the big cymbals when the music only involves the wind players, and sometimes they may have to play the suona and the dizi as well. The yueqin and sanxian players also play the suona, the dizi, the sheng, and even the yunluo or the barrel drums.

Now let us turn our attention to vocal music. Vocal music in Peking opera comprises arias, recitative-like short phrases, and heightened speech, which is a type of stylized stage speech having steeply rising and falling contours. The arias express the lyrical sentiments of the character; the recitative-like phrases and the heightened speech propel the narrative of the dramatic actions. Heightened speech is used exclusively by important characters and characters of high social status, while everyday speech in the Peking dialect is used by the comics and characters of lower social status. In general, arias, recitatives, and speech are performed as solo numbers, but there are exceptions when these are done by an ensemble (Figures 4–9 and 4–10).

The term "aria" used in the context of Peking opera requires further explanation. All Peking-opera arias derive from a group of some thirty preexistent skeletal tune-and-rhythm pattern types called ban (literally "beat," but best translated "melody-rhythmic type"). By setting the same melodic-rhythmic type to a different text, a new aria is produced.

Most arias contain a two-phrase unit that sets a rhymed couplet; the constituent lines, which are of equal length, may have either seven or ten syllables. The syllables in each line are always grouped into three prosodic units; the prosodic grouping for a seven-syllable line is $2 + 3 + 2$, and that for a ten-syllable line is $3 + 5 + 2$. The melody for each phrase, however, is always arranged in a five-bar structure, juxtaposed with the three-prosodic-units-per-line textual structure.

Defined in terms of their rhythm, tempo, and corresponding dramatic functions, five main aria types can be identified:

Figure 4–9. The *jing* role (painted face) actor in the ghost play *Zhong Kuei Jai Mei* (Zhong Kuei Marrying His Sister)

1. the *narrative aria* in 4/4 meter and moderate tempo is usually used to provide narration in an unemotional manner;
2. the *lyrical aria* in 4/4 meter and slow tempo is used at lyrical moments and is usually melismatic;
3. the *animated aria* in measured rhythm and fast tempo is used to reveal a character's psychological state;
4. the *dramatic aria* in free rhythm, always accompanied by a steady beat from the clappers and the fiddle, is used to propel the dramatic action or to add tension to spoken dialogue; and
5. the *interjected aria*, usually very short (only one phrase) and in free rhythm, is sung at a highly dramatic moment as a signal or a call.

Musically, the melody-rhythm types of Peking opera are divided into more than ten categories, each of which has different melodic characteristics. The two most important ones are the xipi and the erhuang; the former derives from a northern regional theater, and the latter from a southern regional theater. In addition, folk tunes of various regions and arias of the Kun theater (kunju) have also been absorbed into the Peking opera.

Arias in the erhuang category are in a moderate tempo and are usually employed in tragic or lyrical scenes. Erhuang arias are arranged in a seven-tone diatonic scale, with a raised 4th degree and a lowered 7th degree (e.g., G-A-B-C♯-D-E-F-G); the raised 4th and lowered 7th are usually used as neighboring or pivotal tones, and they serve to identify erhuang arias. For erhuang, the two strings of the jinghu—i.e., pitches G and D—are considered to be the 1st and 5th steps of this scale.

Arias belonging to the other melodic category, the xipi, are rhythmically more varied and lively than those in the erhuang category and are used in a greater variety of dramatic situations. Xipi arias are arranged in either a five-tone or a seven-tone scale, which can be represented in comparison with the erhuang scale as G-B♭-C-D-F-G or G-A-B♭-C-D-E♭-F-G. For xipi, the pitches of the jinghu are still considered the 1st and 5th of the scale, but as can be seen, their relation-

Figure 4–10. The *dan* role (young female) actress in a scene of the romantic play *Mou dan ting* (Peony Pavilion)

ship to the rest of the scale is different from that in erhuang. The pitches G and D are always played portamento (joined to other notes with a slide or glissando), and this may be considered the most characteristic feature of xipi arias.

In Peking opera, the aural and visual elements are of equal importance. The conventions of Peking opera require that an actor should master highly stylized acting techniques just as thoroughly as singing. Just as knowledgeable Chinese audiences would not excuse bad singing, neither would they excuse bad execution of movements on stage. For a Peking-opera actor, the appearance demanded by his conventional role, his capacity for wearing the costume pertaining to it, and the scores of strictly defined movements and gestures are of vital importance. The actor is the focus of attention, the central point of that harmony of movement which is the essence of a theatrical performance. The costumes are designed to assist and emphasize that movement, together with instrumental music, speech, and arias, all inter-dependent on the others.

Such a highly stylized and conventional theater requires an audience that possesses "the art of watching and listening" to appreciate it fully. Unfortunately, in recent decades such audiences have been rapidly shrinking. The conventions of Peking opera are deeply rooted in an old society based upon Confucian moral precepts and political outlook, and these have been thoroughly discredited by the contemporary socialist state. It is small wonder that young people who have grown up in this state find the art archaic and alien; they prefer programs on television and pop music. The government has tried to remedy this situation by taking certain reform measures, which include the creation of libretti with modern themes, reorganizing troupes in order to streamline the companies, giving more financial incentives to able actors, and introducing electroacoustic instruments, but these measures appear to have met with little success.

CHINA BIBLIOGRAPHY

Gulick, Robert H. Van, *The Lore of the Chinese Lute*, rev. ed. (Vermont and Tokyo: Charles E. Tuttle, 1969); Pian, Rulan Chao, and others, "China," *The New Grove Dictionary of Music and Musicians*, ed. Stanley Sadie, 1980; Wong, Isabel K. F., "East Asia," *The New Harvard Dictionary of Music*, ed. Don Randel, (Cambridge, Mass., and London: The Belknap Press of Harvard University Press, 1986); Wong, Isabel K. F., "*Geming Gequ*: Songs for the Education of the Masses," in *Popular Chinese Literature and Performing Arts in the People's Republic of China, 1949–1979*, ed. Bonnie S. MacDougall (Berkeley and Los Angeles: University of California Press, 1984), pp. 112–43; Malm, William P., "East Asia: China," in *Music Cultures of the Pacific, the Near East, and Asia*, 2nd ed. (Englewood Cliffs, N.J.: Prentice Hall,

1977); Lieberman, Fredric, *Chinese Music: An Annotated Bibliography*, 2nd ed. (New York: Garland, 1979); Lieberman, Fredric, trans., *A Chinese Zither Tutor: The Mei-an Ch'in-p'u*, (Seattle: University of Washington Press, 1983); Scott, Adolphe Clarence, *Literature and the Arts in Twentieth-Century China* (New York: Anchor, 1962); Liang, Mingyue, *Music of the Billion: An Introduction to Chinese Musical Culture* (New York: Heinrichshofen, 1985); Liang, Mingyue, *The Chinese Ch'in: Its History and Music* (San Francisco: Chinese National Music Association and San Francisco Conservatory of Music, 1972); Mackerras, Colin P., *The Rise of the Peking Opera, 1770–1870* (Oxford: Clarendon Press, 1972); Yung, Bell, *Cantonese Opera: Performance as Creative Process* (Cambridge: Cambridge University Press, 1989); DeWoskin, Kenneth J., *A Song for One or Two: Music and the Concept of Art in Early China*, Michigan Papers in Chinese Studies No. 42 (Ann Arbor: Center for Chinese Studies, University of Michigan, 1982); Pian, Rulan Chao, *Song Dynasty Musical Sources and Their Interpretation* (Cambridge, Mass.: Harvard University Press, 1967).

CHINA DISCOGRAPHY

General: *Anthology of the World's Music: The Music of China*, Vol. 1: *Chinese Instruments*, ed. and with notes by Fredric Lieberman (Anthology); *Chine Populaire, Musique Classique* (instrumental music) (Ocora); *Chinese Classical Music* (instrumental) (Lyrichord LL 72).

Peking Opera: *The Chinese Opera* (Lyrichord LLST 7212 sides A and B); *The Peking Opera* (Seraphim SER 60201 sides A and B); *Ruse of the Empty City* (Folkways FW 8882 sides A and B); *Traditional Peking Opera* (Folkways FW 8883 sides A and B).

Kunju: *Youyuan Jingmeng (A Dream in the Garden)* (Art Tune Co. CO 228 & 229).*

Qin (Ch'in) music: *Ch'in Music of Ten Centuries* (Museum Collection Berlin MC7 A&B); *Chinese Master Pieces for the Ch'in* (Lyrichord LLST 7342 A&B); *The Drunken Fisherman* (Lyrichord LL 72 B/3); *"Youlan" ("Orchids in a Secluded Valley")* (Art Tune Co. ATC 73 A/1).

Jiangnan Sizhu: *"Chunjiang huasyueye" ("The Moonlit Spring River")* (Art Tune Co. ATC 16 A/1); *"Sanliu" ("Three Six")* (Art Tune Co. ATC 16 B/1); *"Huanlege" ("Song of Happiness")* (Art Tune Co. ATC 16 A/2); *Popular Jiangnan Music* (Hong Kong; under license from China Records Co., Peking).

Regional Ensemble Music: *Music of Amoy* (Art Tune Co. AST 4002 A&B); *Shantung Music of Confucius' Homeland* (Lyrichord, LLST 7112 A&B); *Chinese Masterpieces for the Erh-hu* (Lyrichord, LLST 7132 A&B).

"Songs for the Masses": *The East Is Red* (China Records M 982); *Commune Members Are All Like Sunflowers* (China Records M 2265).

*Recordings released by the Art Tune Company can be ordered through World Music Enterprises, 717 Avondale Street, Kent, Ohio.

5

JAPAN

Isabel K.F. Wong

HOGAKU PERFORMANCE IN TOKYO

Tokyo, Japan's capital, is a crowded, bustling modern city with almost twelve million people. It is the political and financial center not only of Japan but of Asia, and increasingly of the world as well. Although a formidable city at first glance, Tokyo can be seen at a second glance to be more like a conglomeration of small towns and neighborhoods clustered together, each with its own shops and narrow, winding streets.

Tokyo is both new and old, Eastern and Western. The variety of Japanese, Asian, and Western musical performances that take place in Tokyo during the concert season (spring to fall) is a reflection of this fact. When I visited Tokyo in early June, 1989, for example, many Western art-music concerts were being performed there, among them a concert of European baroque music performed by a New York Philharmonic ensemble conducted by Mamora Takahara at the famous Izumotaisha Shrine, one of Japan's largest Shinto shrines. Performances of hogaku, Japan's traditional music, were also plentiful. Some hogaku performances may take place in the concert halls clustered around the Tokyo Station, others in the recital halls inside great department stores in the Ginza area, Tokyo's chic shopping district, and still others in the National Theater, situated across the street from the grounds of the Imperial Palace.

During my 1989 visit, I attended two musical performances at the National Theater, which was opened in 1966 for the promotion and development of traditional Japanese performing arts. It actually comprises two theaters: a large one seating nearly 1800, which is used principally for the performance of kabuki musical drama; and a small one seating about 630, which is used to stage a variety of concerts of hogaku music and dance, as well as performances of puppet musical plays known as bunraku. There are also two restaurants attached to the National Theater: a larger one on the second floor that serves a set menu for dinner, and a smaller one at the front of the theater grounds that serves snack food.

A Mixed Concert

One of the hogaku concerts I attended at the National Theater was a gala event commemorating the sixtieth birthday of a respected hogaku master. It took place in the small theater and started at 6:30 P.M., but most of the audience arrived before curtain time in order to have dinner at the restaurants. It was a sold-out concert, and I was lucky to have obtained a standing-room ticket—the least expensive kind—at 4000 yen (equivalent to U.S. $28 in 1989). As in a Western concert, the audience was greeted by ushers at the door of the theater and handed program notes (in Japanese) about the four items to be performed; this included song texts and instrumentation, and was followed, as in the West, by many advertisements. The inside of the theater was very similar to a Western one, with a proscenium stage and rows of seats. The members of the audience were primarily well-dressed Japanese men and women wearing Western-style clothing, but there were some older women who wore the kimono.

The relatively long concert, lasting more than three hours, began with three pieces for a chamber ensemble consisting of six musicians. The final piece of the program, coming after an intermission of about twenty minutes, called for a chorus and orchestra each consisting of a dozen or so performers, as well as dancers. All the performers wore traditional attire and knelt on the floor of the stage with low music stands placed before them.

As each piece began, the performers picked up their instruments from the floor in front of them in a deliberate and uniform fashion. Their erect posture and great decorum was complemented by the attentiveness of the audience. At the end of each piece the performers replaced their instruments on the stage floor in the same deliberate and uniform manner in which they had taken them up, and only then did the audience applaud. They acknowledged the applause by bowing very formally, and then remained stationary until the curtain had descended completely.

The first piece in the program was an ensemble played by three kotos (long thirteen-stringed zithers) and three shamisens (three-stringed lutes played with a plectrum). The musicians, who included both men and women, sang as they played; I noticed that the first and last sections were sung with instrumental accompaniment, while the middle section, which was the longest, was entirely played by instruments. I also noticed that the music was primarily pentatonic but with occasional auxiliary pitches. The voice, the kotos, and the shamisens seemed to share a basic melody, but each performed the melody in a somewhat different fashion, rhythmically as well as melodically, resulting in a texture that may be described as heterophonic (Figures 5–1, 5–2 and 5–3).

The second piece was a jiuta. Broadly speaking, the term denotes a type of vocal piece having a lyrical text which is accompanied principally by the shamisen, sometimes by a koto as well. This performance included both shamisen and koto accompaniment, the former being supplied by the vocalist herself. Like the previous piece, this too had three sections, of which the middle was a purely instrumental interlude.

Figure 5–1.   Timothy Barnes playing the thirteen-stringed long zither *koto*.

Figure 5–2.   Timothy Barnes playing the three-stringed plucked lute *shamisen*.

The third piece was a trio for solo voice and two shamisens that was derived from a narrative genre called the shinnai-bushi. The vocalist, who did not play any instrument, sang with a penetrating voice. The shamisen used in this piece had a thicker neck than those used in the previous pieces. One shamisen played the basic melody while the other played a lighter and higher part, heterophonically elaborating the melody. In contrast to the others, this piece was divided into six sections.

During the intermission, people who had not had dinner before the concert—I among them—went to the theater restaurants to have a quick bite. The food was delicious and was served in beautifully decorated lacquered bowls and plates; but when the bell rang, indicating that the curtain was about to go up, I hurriedly finished my dinner and returned to the auditorium.

The final piece, featuring some two dozen musicians, made me realize how much a foreigner to Japanese music I was. Despite the magnificent costumes of the dancers I had difficulty concentrating on the performance, yet I noticed how most of the audience appreciated the piece greatly. Many different types of instruments were used, including a number of kotos and shamisens and various types of flutes such as the fue (horizontal flute), shakuhachi (end-blown flute), nohkan (a horizontal flute closely associated with the noh drama), and ryuteki (a horizontal flute closely associated with the gagaku court music). In addition, there was a double-reed oboe called the hichiriki, which has a very distinct and penetrating sound; a mouth organ called the sho; plus a small percussion ensemble (a small pair of cymbals, a small drum, a paired wooden clapper, and a small gong). A modern attempt to combine various kinds of traditional music in a new composition, this piece included the jiuta (played by a trio made up of shamisen, koto, and shakuhachi) from the nagauta ensemble associated with kabuki, lyrical shamisen music with chorus, the Buddhist chang shomyo, a shamisen duet, and finally materials deriving from folk song and dance. At the end of what seemed to this foreigner a tediously long piece, the audience gave the performers a standing ovation. As soon as the curtain fell, however, the audience disappeared quickly, and clearly no encore was expected.

Figure 5–3.   Ralph Samuelson playing the end-blown flute *shakuhachi* (photo courtesy Mr. Ralph Samuelson).

A Kabuki Appreciation Class

The second performance I attended at the National Theater was an appreciation class for the kabuki theater, which was extremely interesting and educational.

Kabuki, Japan's main popular theater, is regularly performed in several theaters in Tokyo; among these the most famous and best known is the Kabukiza (za means "seat," but today it has come to mean "theater"), which is situated in the Ginza and contains, aside from the theater, *six* restaurants. The Kabukiza has about eight or nine kabuki productions a year, each of which lasts about twenty-five days. Usually two different programs are performed daily; matinees run from about 11:00 A.M. to 4:00 P.M., and evening performances run from 4:30 P.M. to 9:00 P.M. The Kabukiza was built in 1887 and has been reconstructed many times since then. It is an impressive theater with more than 2000 seats, a wide orchestra, and two balconies. The stage, almost ninety-three feet wide, is equipped with revolving platforms and trap lifts. In addition, there is a long runway connecting the stage with the rear of the theater, which is also part of the stage. In the lobby, various kabuki recordings and cassettes, books about kabuki (in both Japanese and English), and various souvenirs are sold. Foreigners who do not understand Japanese, or are novices to the theater, can rent earphones and listen to a simultaneous translation of the libretto.

Kabuki performances are also held several times a year at the larger hall of the National Theater, which also runs an annual "Kabuki appreciation class" every summer for young people. There are two appreciation classes daily, at 11:00A.M. and 2:30 P.M., and I bought a ticket for the morning one.

When it was time for the class to start, all the lights in the theater were turned off except those on the bare proscenium stage. An actor in a kimono appeared on the stage. "Hello everyone, I am a kabuki actor called Iwai Hanshiro. I am going to tell you something about the kabuki theater today so that you can appreciate it better," he said. "It is a pity that too many Japanese people nowadays cannot appreciate kabuki because they do not understand it. The purpose of this appreciation class is to tell you some of the fun and secrets of the kabuki theater, so you will come to the theater again and again.

"Let me first tell you a bit of the history of kabuki. The first kabuki performance was done entirely by females and took place in 1596 in Kyoto. The government immediately banned female performance of kabuki, so the stage was taken over by a troupe of young males. Since 1652 kabuki has been performed by adult males, as it still is today. Female roles are impersonated by male actors. In the eighteenth century, when Japan was ruled by a succession of military strongmen known as shoguns and entered a long period of peace, kabuki developed into a definite cultural form for urban dwellers (chonin). You must remember that kabuki is predominantly a dance theater with musical accompaniment; it makes use of extensive and elaborate scenery, costumes, and properties, which I will show you later. Kabuki borrowed a lot from other types of theater, such as the classical noh theater and the puppet theater bunraku. It has also absorbed folk dance and popular dance. How many of you have been to the noh theater?" Only a few hands were raised. "How many of you have seen the bunraku?" More hands were raised. "Let me demonstrate some kabuki gestures that were derived from the bunraku and the noh."

At this point our lecturer made a vigorous gesture with his arms and legs which was very masculine, abrupt, and angular. "This gesture is an adaptation of puppet movement of the bunraku theater, known as aragoto, meaning 'rough business.' " He then walked in stately, gliding steps, moving without any perceptible upper-body motion. "This gentle and refined movement came from the noh theater.

"Dance is very important in kabuki theater. A kabuki actor is primarily a dancer, and kabuki dance is essential movement toward a climactic static posture." He now struck and held a dramatic pose, and then turned to us and said, "Now, this is the time for you to applaud me. We kabuki actors like to know that you appreciate what we do!" The young audience, encouraged by the lecturer, giggled and applauded enthusiastically. At that moment, a middle-aged woman sitting next to me shouted "Bravo!" in Japanese, which was acknowledged by our lecturer with a deep bow in her direction. The young audience turned to look at her with puzzled expressions on their faces, whereupon our lecturer said, "This is a very appropriate and common way to give praise to actors. You may try it yourselves!" "Bravo! Bravo!" shouted the audience, greatly energized. Our lecturer bowed graciously to them.

"It is now time to show you something about the kabuki stage. The kabuki stage is equipped with several trap lifts which are used to bring scenery or musicians from below the stage to the level of the stage floor, and vice versa." As he spoke, several men who were holding musical instruments in their hands suddenly rose up through the stage floor on a trap lift. The young audience, obviously loving this, burst into applause. "There are more fun things to follow. The stage is also equipped with two revolving stages in the center, an outer one and an inner one, which are capable of being moved in opposite directions. These revolving stages are used to change the entire set at once and have been in use since the sixteenth century." As he spoke, a realistic set depicting a large rice field complete with stacks of grain, trees, and thatched huts suddenly revolved into the center of the stage. A few seconds later, this set disappeared from sight, and another one showing the inside of a house, with cooking utensils and straw mats on the floor, appeared in front of us (Figure 5–4).

Figure 5–4.   A scene in the Kabuki play *Kagami Hishi* (Lion Dance), with on-stage musicians (photo courtesy Mr. Shozo Sato).

Then our lecturer pointed in the direction of the raised runway connecting the stage to the rear of the auditorium, and asked: "How many of you know the name of this runway?" A few treble voices shouted "Hanamichi!" "Good!" our lecturer said. "You have been studying this in school, no doubt! The hanamichi is a unique feature of the kabuki theater. It serves as an additional acting space for the actors, and it also serves as a more intimate acting area. There is a passageway built beneath the floor of the theater for actors to go from the dressing rooms behind the stage to the entrance of the hanamichi without being seen by the audience." Suddenly, a man dressed in the costume of a peasant appeared on the hanamichi at the rear of the theater. He walked a few steps, paused, gently moving his head from side to side as if hesitating, and finally moved forward to the stage proper with an attitude of determination.

"Meet Hayano Kanpei, the hero of the play you are going to see after my lecture! Have you guessed that Kanpei is no peasant? He is really a ronin—that is, a samurai who has lost his master. He is disguised as a peasant in order to avenge his master's death. If you have been observant, you should have noticed that before he finally proceeded to the stage proper, he moved his head gently from side to side. A peasant does not move in such a refined fashion! The connoisseur would know from this gesture that his real social status is higher than that of a peasant." At this point the actor who portrayed Kanpei gave the audience a bow and exited.

"Another important element of kabuki theater is music, and it is time to introduce the musicians! Many musicians and instruments are used in the kabuki theater. I will show you some of them later. In general, there are two groups of musicians: those who appear on the stage, and those who do not. The onstage musician group is called the degatari, and the offstage group is called the geza." He gave a signal, and a pair of men were elevated from below to stage right. Both were kneeling, and one was holding a shamisen. "This is the chobo, a pair of onstage musicians borrowed from the puppet theater. One is a narrator; the other one accompanies him on the shamisen. Even though they may sometimes participate musically in the events taking place on the stage, the chobo musicians are not actors. Let me give you an example. Suppose that I am a character in a play who is sobbing; the chobo narrator can take over the sobbing for me without a break, and the shamisen player in turn can imitate the sound of sobbing on his instrument, while all the time the sobbing is supposed to be that of the character on stage and the accompanists do not participate in the action. The chobo musicians not only participate musically in the events on the stage, they also narrate and explain the plot to the audience; you could say that they are story tellers.

"Sometimes a character in a play may want to sing about his feelings, or another may want to perform a dance. Who will provide musical accompaniment? Another group of onstage musicians is called the debayashi, meaning 'coming-out orchestra.' These musicians are singers as well as instrumentalists, and their number varies according to the needs of the drama." He gave a signal, and from the rear of the stage a trap lift raised up a two-tiered platform covered with red cloth on whose upper tier knelt six men holding shamisens; below them, on the level of the stage, six singers knelt behind low music stands. "Let us hear their music!" the lecturer commanded, and the ensemble played nagauta, a kind of unison chorus with shamisen accompaniment.

"Now let us bring on the geza musicians." At this moment both the chobo and the debayashi musicians were lowered beneath the stage by trap lifts, and downstage right there appeared another group of instrumentalists and a large drum. "These are offstage musicians called the geza," we were told. "They normally sit in a room situated at stage left, where they can look out to the stage and the hanamichi through a bamboo curtain, and the audience cannot see them. Their job is to provide sound effects for the dramatic action. The instruments are: the o-daiko (big drum), shamisen, nohkan, and gongs and bells. Let me show you the strokes of the o-daiko." As he was talking he picked up the two drumsticks and hit the drum with several types of strokes. "Some strokes indicate curtain calls; others create different atmospheres and moods; some strokes represent raindrops, the sound of wind or thunder, and others represent the appearance of a ghost."

When the demonstration was over, the geza musicians disappeared from the stage. "I know you are very eager to see today's play, but I have yet one more important instrument to show you, and that is the hyoshigi." Immediately, a man appeared at the corner stage right, holding two rectangular woodblocks in his hand; he knelt and began playing the blocks in a series of accelerating beats. "The player is called the kyogenkata; he is a stagehand, and the rhythmic pattern he just played announces the rise of the curtain." With this final demonstration, the actor concluded his introduction and called for the play to begin.

The play, about Kanji's revenge, employed all the devices, mechanisms, and musical groups we had just learned about, and using the simultaneous translation of the dramatic dialogue and explanation of the plot in English transmitted through the headphones I wore, I found that I could readily understand the plot and enjoy the drama.

The music for the chamber vocal and instrumental recital described above and for performances of kabuki can be heard and seen in Japan nowadays with some frequency, particularly in the four major cities— Tokyo, Kyoto, Osaka, and Nagoya. These types of hogaku music are essentially products of Japan's most recent "ancient" period—that is, the time from the seventeenth to the nineteenth century known as the Tokugawa or Edo period, when Japan, ruled by the Tokugawa clan in the capital Edo (present-day Tokyo), experienced a period of uninterrupted peace. Cities such as Edo and Osaka grew into populous centers of trade and government where a large and prosperous bourgeoisie developed—tradesmen and artisans who vigorously supported the developing arts and culture. It was under the patronage of this bourgeoisie that the kabuki theater and the many chamber vocal-instrumental genres involving the koto, shamisen, and other instruments came into being and flourished.

THEATER MUSIC

The culture of the bourgeoisie, essentially urban and popular, was characterized by a taste for romantic or comic novels, for salacious or witty lampoons, for brightly colored prints and paintings, and above all for lavish theatrical entertainment. The kabuki theater, with its lavish costumes and staging, its elaborage stage machinery, and its fondness for plots of romantic love, is representative of this culture.

The Bunraku Puppet Theater

The other important popular theater of the Edo period, which can also be seen today, principally in Osaka and in Tokyo's National Theater, is the puppet theater called bunraku. Growing up at about the same time as kabuki and under the same circumstances and patronage—primarily that of the bourgeosie or chonin of Osaka—the bunraku both borrowed from and exerted influence on the kabuki theater.

The bunraku puppet, made of wood, is moved by three puppeteers who manipulate its arms, fingers, legs, body, head, eyes, mouth and even eyebrows. These movements are so realistic that the spectator can easily forget the actor is made of wood, even though the puppeteers are not hidden behind or above the stage. The two junior puppeteers are, however, completely shrouded in black and hooded, and only the senior puppeteer's face is visible.

The narration of the bunraku, both sung and spoken, is provided by a narrator/chanter who is accompanied on shamisen, a three-stringed, long-necked, fretless lute whose sound box is covered with cat or dog skin front and back, and whose strings are plucked with a large plectrum; this is the same combination as the chobo ensemble we encountered in the kabuki demonstration. When a kabuki play is derived from the bunraku theater, the narrative and music accompanying the dramatic actions are provided by the chobo, in the same manner as in the bunraku theater.

The narrative style used in bunraku is called gidayubushi, after its developer, Gidayu Takemoto (1615–1717) of Osaka. The vocal style of gidayubushi includes chants, heightened speech, and lyrical songs. The shamisen, whose music is made up of various arrangements of stereotyped patterns, plays preludes, interludes, and postludes to the singing. Bunraku rose to its artistic and popular height when Takemoto collaborated with the famous playwright Monzaemon Chikamatsu (1653–1717).

The Noh Theater

Edo-period musical theatricals are by no means the only kinds of traditional stage genres one can hear and see in Japan today. Among genres originating in other historical periods of Japan, the noh theater is particularly important. Combining various folk dances, musical theatricals, and religious and courtly entertainment of medieval times, the noh was transformed into a serious Buddhist art by the performer Kannami Kiyotsugu (1333–84), and into a refined court art by his son Zeami

Motokiyo (1363–1444). Wearing a mask, brocade robes, and white socks, the chief actor moves and dances slowly on a bare stage with perfectly controlled and restrained movements; accompanied by a male chorus and a small instrumental ensemble made up of a flute and three drums, he carries the spectator into the austere world of a medieval Japan deeply influenced by Zen Buddhism.

The noh was a product of the Muromachi period (1333–1615), which was marked by continuous military strife between the various clans of warriors (samurai). Exclusively an art of the ruling samurai class from the fifteenth to the nineteenth century, the noh, with its performing style of elegant simplicity and restraint and its major themes of redemption of human suffering through the love of Buddha, is a direct antithesis of the flamboyant, colorful, and lavish theatrical entertainments of the Tokugawa bourgeoisie such as kabuki and bunraku.

In Zeami's day, a performance of noh consisted of at least five plays—a god play, a warrior play, a woman play, a possession play, and a demon play—interspersed with comic plays called kyogen for a change of pace. Today the usual program consists of two or three noh plays (each lasting about an hour) and one or two kyogen (lasting about thirty to forty minutes).

Supported mainly by intellectuals now, noh is performed in major cities in special indoor theaters that are owned and operated by five traditional schools of noh performance. In addition, noh plays are performed on various festival occasions throughout Japan on outdoor stages that are built in the compounds of Shinto or Buddhist temples.

The main element and action of a noh play is linked closely with its major actor, the shite. The supporting actor, or waki, provides a foil for the revelation of the shite's character and the explanation for his actions.

Noh plays are typically in two acts. Thematically, these acts can be organized into five major dan (sections or units). The first act—comprising the first dan, which is an introduction, and the second, third and fourth dan, which together make up the exposition of the play—ends with a dance called kuse, its high point. The act provides a full exposition of the spirit of the shite. The second act consists of only one dan; in this denouement the shite is transformed into a new character (usually a supernatural being), sings a couple of songs, and performs another dance, called the mai, which reveals his new essence after his spiritual transformation.

Music for the noh consists of songs (solo and choral) sung by the actors or chorus, recitativelike heightened speech for the actors, and instrumental music played by an instrumental quartet (a flute and three drums). The functions of the instrumental ensemble are to play introductory music and interludes, to set the scene or mood of individual units within the two acts, to accompany entrances and exits of actors, to accompany songs and dances, and to provide a rhythmic background for dialogue and action. The songs (uta), sung by either the actors or the chorus, are of two types: the sageuta, which are short, slow, and in low range, and the ageuta, which are longer and higher.

The instruments making up the instrumental quartet for noh are a flute called nohkan and three drums of different sizes.

Unlike most bamboo flutes, which simply consist of a tube of dried bamboo, the nohkan is constructed from such a tube split lengthwise into strips that are then turned inside out, wrapped with cherry bark, and lacquered. It has seven fingerholes and a mouth hole. Other elements of its construction and playing technique lend this flute a distinctive, piercing sound, and rather than blending with the other components of noh, like them it retains a strong individuality.

The music of the nohkan is made up of various arrangements of a large number of stereotyped patterns; different pieces are produced by rearrangement of the sequential order of these patterns, and the use of certain sequences is determined by the dramatic conventions of the noh theater. The music for the nohkan serves as a marker for certain subunits of a dan, sets the tempo for the dances and accompanies them, adds a melodic layer to the drum patterns, sets the pitches for the chorus and accompanies it, and provides emphasis for certain lyrical passages of the songs.

The nohkan and the three drums used in noh are collectively called hayashi (a generic term for ensembles of flute and drums). The three drums are: the ko-tsuzumi, the o-tsuzumi, and the taiko. The first two are hourglass-shaped drums, while the taiko is a shallow barrel drum. Of the three, the smallest but most important is the ko-tsuzumi; although it derives from Chinese and Korean models, the manner of playing it in the noh theater is entirely a Japanese development.

All the noh drums have wooden bodies, with two skin heads that are stretched over iron rings and then stitched, and two sets of ropes that hold the skins to the body. The special tone of the ko-tsuzumi, is achieved by carving special patterns on the inside surface of the body and affixing bits of damp paper to the rear head, which is not struck, and the ropes holding the heads to the body may be squeezed to increase tension on the heads. The tension of the head of the o-tsuzumi is always at a maximum and thus cannot be altered by further tightening the ropes; in fact, before a performance the drumhead is heated over a hibachi to increase the tension still further, and during a performance a newly heated drum may be substituted. All this tension creates a dry, hard sound that may be increased by the use of hard thimbles on the player's fingers.

The taiko is played with two thick sticks instead of the hand. Instead of being held by one of the player's hands, the drum is placed on a special stand that grips the encircling ropes, lifting the drum off

Figures 5–5 and 5–6.   Sakiji Tanaka playing the Noh
drum *taiko* (photo courtesy Mr. Shozo Sato).

the floor for better resonance. The taiko is used sparingly, normally joining the other instruments for dance sections.

All three drums are capable of producing several basic sounds, and
their varying combinations form stereotyped patterns that are identified
onomatopoetically.

An additional but integral part of noh drumming is the use of drum
calls by the drummers. These kakegoe, as they are called, may have
originated as practice devices, but they are now part of the overall sound
of the music for noh and are certainly one of the distinctive elements
that add to its strangely rarefied atmosphere (Figures 5–5 through 5–9).

Figure 5–6.

Like the chobo ensemble of gidayubushi, the noh hayashi, too, has been adopted for some kabuki performances, where it always introduces a reference to classical, courtly culture.

The vocal part of noh, called yokyoku, is sung by both the actors and the onstage chorus. The melodic style of yokyoku is solemn and spare, betraying its origin in Buddhist chanting of medieval Japan. The articulation of every textual syllable is deliberate and prolonged, and their pronunciation is based on a stage convention different from everyday speech. Together with the actors' stately bodily movements and gliding steps, which I described in conjunction with the kabuki apprecia-

Figures 5–7 and 5–8.   Sakiji Tanaka playing the Noh drum *ko-tsuzumi* (photo courtesy Mr. Shozo Sato).

tion class, the music of yokyoku and hayashi contribute to the overall impression that the noh theater is ethereal and otherworldly.

Yokyoku has two basic styles: the heightened speech called kotobe (words) and the aria called fushi (melody). Fushi is sung in two basic ways: the yowagin (soft) style, which is delivered softly and is used in lyrical scenes, and the tsuyogin (strong) style, which is delivered with strength and is used in masculine and warlike scenes.

The tonal system of the yokyoku is based on the interval of the minor 7th, coinciding with the same interval when the uniquely constructed nohkan is overblown. (Most flutes produce the octave when overblown.) Within this minor 7th, three notes making a conjunct pair

Figure 5–8.

of perfect 4ths provide important tonal centers. If we designate the minor-7th interval as being from A down to B, then the three tonal centers are A-E-B, in that order of importance. Around each of these tonal centers there is a cluster of notes forming a tonal system for melody.

The rhythmic structure of noh singing, like that for the hayashi, is based on an eight-beat framework, but in a very flexible manner. The number of textual syllables in each poetic line to be sung within these beats varies, but a five-syllable line is most common.

The individual musical elements of noh are conceived in a linear fashion, and the key to appreciating noh is to follow the various lines of the voices and the instruments. For example, the chorus and the

Figure 5–9. The Noh drum *o-tsuzumi*. The ropes holding the heads to the body may be squeezed to increase tension on the heads (photo courtesy of Mr. Shozo Sato).

nohkan may be involved in two completely separate melodic lines, while the drums may be playing a rhythmic pattern of a different length from either. As mentioned, the strong individuality of the components of noh is a characteristic feature, and relying on this, noh can create a complex art from few resources. The center of this art is the poetic text, and the musical elements revolve around it.

Noh plays are produced by a group of people: the poet supplies the text, and the actors, the chorus, and the hayashi compose their own parts according to the text. Such a creative process works for noh because the music is highly systematized.

THE RELIGIOUS TRADITIONS

Shintoism and Shinto Music

Among the ancient types of Japanese music that can still be heard today are court Shinto music, or mikagura; court orchestral music, or gagaku; and the Buddhist chant, or shomyo. The latter two were originally Chinese-inspired, while the first one is entirely indigenous.

The earliest Japanese religion shared many elements with the religions of other peoples of East Asia, and only became designated Shinto ("the way of the gods") when confronted with Buddhism and Confucianism. Shinto is a loose agglomeration of local and regional cults with a diversity of gods and spirits, and it includes a variety of religious elements such as nature worship, animism, shamanism, ancestor worship, hero worship, fertility rites, phallicism, fortune-telling, and so on.

Constant change and adaptation is the norm of Shinto. It adopted and adapted gods and cults with ease, and there has seemed to be no clear conception of divinity and no real attempt to articulate a theology on a rational basis, nor is there an organized, hereditary priesthood.

Five elements or objects stand out in Shinto worship: the sun (or fire), water, mountains, trees, and stones. In ritual practice, Shinto ceremony consists essentially of attendance upon a god and offerings to him or her, accompanied by invocations and prayers. Festivals represent special occasions for honoring the gods and establishing good rapport with them by offering food, drink, and music and dance. Shinto rituals generally take place during important occasions of life and of the agricultural year, such as birth, marriage (always celebrated at a Shinto shrine), the New Year, plowing, planting, and harvesting. Shinto has nothing to do with death, however.

Until the Edo period, musical creation was regarded as a gift from god, and like the beauty of nature, a miracle. Thus in the Shinto view, an appreciation of music sprang from admiration and awe at what is "natural," pure, and simple, rather than from a rational admiration of the artfully organized.

One type of ancient Shinto music that can still be heard today is that performed in court Shinto ceremonies, called the mikagura. It is performed by a male chorus and accompanied by the wagon (a six-stringed zither), the kagura-bue (a transverse bamboo flute with six holes), the hichiriki, and the shakubyoshi (a pair of wooden clappers).

Fifteen songs are still preserved in the present-day repertory, and they are of two main types: the torimono, songs paying homage to the gods, and the saibari, songs meant to entertain the gods. Since the nineteenth century, mikagura songs have been performed by two choruses, each having its own repertory. The performance is initiated by the leader of each chorus, who sings the initial phrase of a song and accompanies himself on the clappers, followed by a unison chorus accompanied by the rest of the instruments. In Shinto ceremonies, dance is an integral part of the ceremony.

In folk Shinto rituals, the music used is called satokagura. There are two main types: the one used in shamanistic rituals paying homage to the gods involves a priestess who sings and dances and is accompanied by the wagon, the transverse flute, and the suzu (bell-tree); the other, used in Shinto festivals called matsuribayashi (festival music), is performed by a hayashi consisting of the o-daiko, two taiko, and a transverse flute. This music is characterized by a lively syncopated drum rhythm which accompanies a repeated melodic line played by the flute.

Buddhism and Buddhist Music

Buddhism came to Japan in the sixth century C.E. from Korea and China. By this time it was already a thousand years old, and a highly developed religion.

The essential tenet of Buddhism concerns suffering and the elimination of suffering through the cessation of desire—the achievement of Nirvana. When it came to Japan, Buddhism gave the Japanese a means of dealing with death and suffering, something that Shintoism had not provided. It affected the Japanese deeply, but their innate delight in the simple joy of life also modified Buddhism by infusing it with an appreciation for life and nature.

During the Nara (553–794) and Heian (794–1185) periods, when Japan's capitals were in Nara and Kyoto respectively, the great aristocratic clans adopted the Mahayana form of Buddhism. Great monastic systems were established and integrated into the court and its civil administrative system. The theology of Mahayana Buddhism asserted that salvation from suffering and death was open to all, and it attracted a huge following among the populace. The government decreed the building of many great monasteries and demanded religious services praying for peace and prosperity for the state. Sutras were chanted in these ceremonies to secure good harvests and the welfare of the state.

The chanting of Buddhist sutras is called shomyo; it is performed by a male chorus in responsorial style, and the texts are in several languages: those in Sanskrit are called bonsan; those in Chinese, kansan; those in Japanese, wasan. The music consists of a series of stereotyped patterns belonging to two different Chinese-derived scales, the ryo and the ritsu, each of which has five basic notes and two auxiliary notes. Shomyo chants may be syllabic or melismatic, and their rhythm may be more or less regular or free. A chant usually begins slowly and gets faster.

During the Nara and Heian periods, the aesthetic aspect of Buddhism predominated, not only because of native Japanese sensitivity but because the aristocrats admired beauty and elegance above all things. Aesthetic cultivation (the playing of music being one of the requirements), together with physical training and psychological discipline —all aspects of one personality—were involved in the attainment of Buddhahood, which was the goal of the Esoteric Buddhism practiced in the Nara and Heian periods. Consequently, ritual, art, and music were as important as scriptures and meditation. It was not just a matter of enlightening the mind but of affecting and transforming the whole world. This view of the world and of man gave great impetus to Buddhist art (including images of Buddha and mandala paintings) as well as Buddhist music.

The collapse of the Heian court and its civil administration in the eleventh century brought about profound changes in Buddhism. Religious institutions bound up with the fortune of the court nobility declined, while a highly aestheticized and sentimentalized religion, based on the refined enjoyment of beauty, could not meet the challenge of the difficult time ahead. With the constant warfare, famine, pestilence, and social disruption of the ensuing Kamakura (1185–1333), Muromachi, and Azuchi-Momoyama (1333–1615) periods, a new form of Buddhism arose, whose primary mission was to bring salvation immediately within reach. This Buddhism for the masses, called Amida Buddhism, had little to do with the arts and aesthetics.

Another form of Buddhism that arose during this difficult period was Zen Buddhism, whose roots were in China and India. Zen emphasizes personal enlightenment through self-understanding and self-reliance by means of meditation, using practices related to the yoga practice of ancient India. In Japan, Zen Buddhism was supported by the military class during the Azuchi-Momoyama period.

Aesthetically, Zen inspired many of the traditional arts of Japan, such as landscape painting, landscape gardening, swordsmanship, the tea ceremony, and noh drama. It was under the patronage of the Ashikago shogun that Zen and its allied arts, including noh, evolved and developed.

A CONCERT AND A COURT TRADITION

Sokyoku

Popular koto-and-vocal music of the Edo period is known under the generic name of sokyoku. The koto is a long zither whose thirteen strings are stretched over movable bridges. The player places the instrument on a mat or low table and plucks the strings using plectra on the thumb and the first two fingers of the right hand. With the left hand the player presses on the strings to the left of the bridges in order to create ornaments and new pitches by altering the tension of the strings.

There are two types of sokyoku. The first, kumiuta, is a koto-accompanied song cycle; the verses of each individual song, called uta, are derived from preexistent poems whose subjects are unrelated. Typically, an uta has duple meter and is in eight phrases, each divided into four measures. The second type, danmono, for koto alone, is in several sections (dan), each consisting of either 64 or 120 beats. The structure of danmono is akin to a loose rondo-variation form. Jiuta, the third type, is an important hybrid form of koto music that combines the techniques of both kumiuta and danmono. It is sometimes called tegotomono, after the tegoto, the important instrumental interludes between vocal sections. Tegotomono usually contain three parts: a foresong (maeuta), an instrumental interlude (tegoto), and an aftersong (atouta). This basic structure may be extended.

Today, jiuta is played by an ensemble called sankyoku (trio) consisting of koto, shamisen, and shakuhachi (an end-blown bamboo flute with four fingerholes and one thumb hole, with a notch cut in the lip to facilitate sound production). The koto plays the main melody, while the shamisen and shakuhachi play an elaboration of the main melody, producing simple heterophony. The koto tradition is perpetuated by various schools, the most important of which are the Ikuta School of Kyoto and the Yamada School of Tokyo, while the Meian and Kinko schools, also based respectively in Kyoto and Tokyo, are the main traditions of shakuhachi performance. The latter have an interesting and colorful origin; they were founded in the Edo period by masterless samurai who combined the profession of street musician with that of spy and informer and used their heavy bamboo flutes not just as musical instruments but also as clubs!

The music of the koto and the shamisen best represent the music of the Edo era. While the shamisen belongs primarily to the world of the theater, with its colorful and exciting entertainments, the koto, by contrast, developed out of a court tradition and gradually entered the home, played by members of the rising merchant class as an emblem of cultural accomplishment. In the modern era the koto maintains a position in Japan similar to that of the parlor piano in nineteenth-century America. It is a popular instrument for middle-class Japanese girls, who play it as a sign of good breeding.

Gagaku

Gagaku, meaning elegant or refined music, is the instrumental and choral music and dance that has been under the continual patronage of the imperial court for more than a thousand years. Influenced by the ancient music of China, Korea, and Sinolized-Indian music, it has been carefully transmitted by generations of court guild musicians to the present day and is perhaps the oldest ensemble music in the world. Gagaku is also used to accompany dance; in this role it is called bugaku.

Gagaku was first initiated in the Nara period (553–749)—the first major historical period in Japan, during which the Japanese struggled to establish a national government modeled after the Chinese government of that time. Prior to the Nara period, Japan was ruled by various rustic clans, among which the Yamato, who originated from the southern island of Kyushu, were dominant. Up until the Nara period, the history and mythology of Japan were concerned primarily with the gradual northern extension of the imperial Yamato power and the justification for Yamato hegemony over other lesser clans of the land.

The construction of the city of Nara was begun in 708, and the court was moved there in 710. Fashioned as a miniature of the Chinese capital of Changan (present-day Xian), it captured perfectly the spirit of an age in East Asian history dominated by the pervasive influence of the great empire of the Chinese Tang dynasty. Nara was the first urban center in Japanese history.

The founding of Nara was accompanied by a great burst of economic, administrative, and cultural activities. One of the administrative measures taken was the establishment of a music bureau staffed by musicians from Korea and China. Musicians in the music bureau performed music and dance for court entertainments and rituals.

The founding of Nara also ushered in the age of the court nobles, a period that lasted until the later twelfth century. Members of the imperial household, court ministers, and Buddhist priests contended for political power at court. The constant court intrigues suggest a fundamental instability in the ruling institutions. A century later this instability was exploited by one dominant court family, the Fujiwara, who were able to dominate the throne and subsequently the political affairs of the country for a long time.

The emperor Shomu and his consort, who was a Fujiwara, were fervent Buddhists, and they greatly helped the perpetuation of this foreign faith. In 737, Shomu ordered the construction of the Todaiji (Great East Temple) in Nara. Housed within the central building of the Todaiji is the huge bronze statue of the Buddha. The casting of the Great Buddha was an impressive technological feat for eighth-century Japan, and it also represented the first Japanese artistic representation of the human form.

At the "eye-opening" ceremony for the Great Buddha in 752, during which the statue was symbolically given life by having the pupils of its eyes painted in, all the great dignitaries of the Nara court were in attendance. In addition there were visitors from China, India, and other distant lands, and some 10,000 Buddhist priests. It was without doubt one of the grandest occasions in all of early Japanese history. Hundreds of musicians and dancers performed, and many instruments dating from this occasion are still preserved in the imperial treasury of Nara, the Shosoin. Music thus became a part in important rituals pertaining to religious and court affairs.

The court music of the Nara period was all of foreign origin and was played primarily by foreign musicians in its original style. In the subsequent Heian period (794–1185), there were signs that the Chinese influence was beginning to be assimilated and modified.

Heian (Kyoto), the newly constructed city to which the government moved in 794, remained the capital of Japan for more than a millennium (until the Meiji Restoration in 1868). At the end of the Heian period in 1185, a new military national government was established in Kamakura by the warrior family of Minamoto, bringing an end to the age of the court nobles and ushering in nearly seven centuries of domiance by the warrior class, until the restoration of the Meiji emperor in the late nineteenth century.

During the Heian period great changes occurred in the governmental system, with the power of the emperor becoming eclipsed by that of the regent, who was controlled by the Fujiwara family. Buddhism continued to flourish in the Heian period, and it had become the principal intellectual system and one of the most important institutional systems in Japanese life. The nobles of the Heian court were preoccupied with etiquette and ritual, and they lived in a world governed by formal standards of beauty and the cultivation of poetry and music.

The court music of the Heian period still employed a host of Chinese instruments and forms, but the musicians themselves were mostly Japanese. In the ninth century a standard gagaku orchestra was created under order of the emperor, and a repertory of two main categories was standardized. The togaku repertory includes music of Chinese and Indian origin, while the koma-gaku includes music of Korean and Manchurian origin.

Gagaku music was extremely popular in the Heian court. Not only was it a necessary component of all court ceremonies, but it was also practiced by the court nobles themselves. Amateur gagaku clubs flourished at court. The famous novel of the Heian period, The Tale of Genji, is full of descriptions of musical activities of the noblemen. Today there are about twenty gagaku musicians maintained by the emperor who are descendants of musicians of the professional guilds, and there are also amateur ensembles outside the court.

The ensemble for gagaku consists of percussion, strings, and winds. The various instruments used in gagaku are described briefly below under separate headings:

Percussion:

1. The da-daiko, a huge drum struck by two thick sticks. It is only used in bugaku.
2. The tsuri-daiko, a suspended two-headed drum, only one side of which is struck with two sticks. It is a "colotomic" instrument—that is, it serves to mark off the larger phrase units.
3. The shoko, a small suspended gong played with two sticks. It is usually played on the first beat of every measure.
4. The kakko, a small drum whose two heads are struck with thin sticks. The kakko is the leader of the toganku ensemble. Its three basic rhythmic patterns are two types of rolls (a slow roll done with both sticks and a faster roll done on the left skin) and a single tap with the right stick. These patterns are played to regulate the tempo of the piece, and they are found mostly in free rhythmic sections; they are also used to mark off beats or phrases. The kakko is only used in togaku.
5. The san-no-tsuzumi an hourglass-shaped drum with two heads, only one of which is struck. Korean in origin, it is played only in koma-gaku, by the leader of that ensemble.

Strings:

1. The wagon, a six-stringed zither used in kagura.
2. The gaku-so, a thirteen-stringed zither, a predecessor of the koto. The strings are plucked by the bare fingers or with finger picks. The music for the gaku-so is made up of two basic patterns which are played to mark off sections;
3. The biwa, a pear-shaped lute with four strings and four frets played with a small plectrum. It is also used to mark off sections in a piece. The music for the biwa consists primarily of arpeggios, which may end with short melodic framents. The effect of biwa music in gagaku is primarily rhythmic.

Winds:

1. The hichiriki, a short, double-reed bamboo oboe with nine holes, originating from China. Through use of the embouchure and fingering technique, tones smaller than a half-step can be produced, and this is the salient characteristic of the hichiriki. Its tone quality is penetrating and strong, and it is the center of the gagaku ensemble.

2. The kagura-bue, a six-holed bamboo flute which produces a basic pentatonic scale; other pitches may be produced by using special fingerings. The length of this flute varies, and thus also its actual pitch. It is used for Shinto ceremonies.
3. The ryuteki, a seven-holed bamboo flute of Chinese origin used for togaku music. It is the largest of the gagaku flutes.
4. The koma-bue, a six-holed flute of Korean origin used for koma-gaku music. It is the smallest of the gagaku flutes.
5. The sho, a mouth organ with seventeen reed pipes (two of which are silent) in a cup-shaped wind chest with a single mouthpiece. Its predecessor was the Chinese sheng. Chords are produced by blowing into the mouthpiece and closing holes in the pipes. Its primary function is harmonic. Typically, each chord is begun softly and gradually gets louder, whereupon the next chord is produced with the same dynamic swelling; this process is repeated continuously by inhaling and exhaling air.

The wind instruments are the heart of the gagaku ensemble; they play roles analogous to those of the strings in a Western symphony orchestra.

Different instrumentations are used for togaku and koma-gaku. The former uses three sho, three hichiriki, three ryuteki, two biwa, two gaku-so, one kakko, one shoko, and one taiko. Instrumentation for koma-gaku is basically the same, except that the komabue is used instead of the ryuteki, the san-no-tsuzumi is used instead of the kakko, and the strings are not used.

The musical style of gagaku is characterized by smoothness, serenity, and precise execution without virtuosic display. The major melody, played on the hichiriki and the flutes, is supported by chords produced on the sho. An abstraction of this melody is played on the gaku-so in octaves and on the biwa in single notes. While smaller sections of a piece are marked off by a biwa arpeggio, larger sections are delineated by tsuri-daiko and shoko strokes. Drum patterns played by the kakko or san-no-tsuzumi serve similar colotomic functions and also regulate the tempo of a piece. When a chorus joins in the major melody of gagaku, it sings in a natural voice using very little ornamentation.

The melody of the gagaku is based on six modes theoretically based on the Chinese-derived ryo and ritsu scales; the rhythm is organized so that slow pieces have an eight-beat rhythm, moderately fast pieces have a four-beat rhythm, and fast pieces have a two-beat rhythm.

Gagaku music, like most music that came after it, was conceived in an aesthetic scheme of introduction—exposition—denouement known as jo-ha-kyu, which has also influenced the aesthetic of noh. In gagaku, jo is the netori, a slow beginning section that is meant to set the mood of the mode in which the piece is written. In a full-blown gagaku piece the sho generally starts the netori, followed in turn by the hichiriki, the flute, and finally the kakko. The mood of the netori is generally subtle and serene and has a tentative feeling like a warming-up.

During the ha section the rhythm becomes regular. Here the main body of the composition begins. The hichiriki and fue play the basic melody, the sho provides a harmonic background, and the percussion provides accompaniment; shortly, the strings also join in. Once the entire ensemble is playing together, there is no further change in the full ensemble sound.

Kyu is the rushing to the end. Here the tempo gets very fast; toward the end, the pace slackens, the instruments drop out one by one, and the texture becomes thinner. Finally, only the biwa and the gaku-so are left; they play two or three very slow notes, the biwa ending with plucking the dominant or the tonic of the mode, and the gaku-so completing the composition with one stroke on the tonic.

Listening to the archaic sound of the gagaku, one may imagine going back into the rarefied time of the Heian court nobles and sharing with them, for a brief moment at least, their profound preoccupation with aesthetic self-cultivation.

GENERAL TENDENCIES AND CHARACTERISTICS OF HOGAKU

Before closing it may be helpful to provide some summary observations on the general tendencies and characteristics of traditional Japanese music, hogaku.

The rise and fall of a particular style of music through Japanese history has been closely linked with changes in political life, social conditions, and religious developments. For example, the gagaku of the Nara period was regarded as a symbol of authority and power of the newly evolved imperial and national government, and no effort was spared to increase its grandeur.

The noh theater, with its themes of redemption of human suffering through the love of Buddha, was exclusively an art of the ruling samurai during the long ages of military strife; it is in particular an expression of the samurai class's preoccupation with Zen Buddhism, which emphasizes simplicity and personal enlightenment through self-understanding and self-reliance. Noh was also a political symbol of the samurai class. During the Edo period, it continued to be performed in the Edo castle, the political center of the Tokugawa military government. Finally, the popular rise of the kabuki and the bunraku theaters was due entirely to the rise of the urban bourgeoisie and their patronage. As the bourgeois arts par excellence, they represent a fondness for popular entertainments, and in particular, lavish theatrical entertainments.

Japanese music is closely tied with ritual, literature, and dance, and these ties have remained unbroken through the ages. It was said that in ancient times, when the emperor or his courtiers asked for the pronouncement of an oracle, it was habitual to offer a musical performance first; therefore the court has always kept musicians in its service.

In hogaku, vocal music predominates. Music serves primarily as a vehicle for words and literature. All Japanese instruments were developed to emulate the human voice. It is noteworthy that the first significant instrumental solos, the tegotomono, were created to serve as interludes to the verses of songs.

Among Japanese music genres, theatrical music is the most important. The course of Japanese music history is marked by a steady growth of theatrical music. This is due again to the Japanese love of storytelling and preoccupation with ritual.

Finally, we have already noted at some length the basic Japanese aesthetic concept of jo-ha-kyu, and the application of this concept in various kinds of music. We have also noted the propensity of the Japanese to use stereotyped melodic patterns in creating new compositions. It remains to be noted that Japanese music is predominantly a chamber music in its conception; even the gagaku ensemble is essentially a chamber orchestra.

JAPAN BIBLIOGRAPHY

Malm, William P. *Japanese Music and Musical Instruments* (Rutland, Vt.: Charles E. Tuttle, 1959); Malm, William P., *Six Hidden Views of Japanese Music* (Berkeley: University of California Press, 1986); Malm, William P., *Naguta: The Heart of Kabuki Music* (Rutland, Vt.: Charles E. Tuttle, 1963); Piggott, Francis Taylor, *The Music and Musical Instruments of Japan*, 2nd ed. (London: B. T. Batsford, 1909; repr. New York: Da Capo, 1971); Tanabe Hsiao, *Japanese Music* (Tokyo: Kokusai Bunka Shinkokai, Society for International Cultural Relations, 1959); Harich-Schneider, Eta, *A History of Japanese Music* (London: Oxford University Press, 1973); Kishibe Shigeo, *The Traditional Music of Japan*, 2nd ed. (Tokyo: Japan Foundation, 1981); Garfias, Robert, *Music of a Thousand Autumns: The Togaku Style of Japanese Court Music* (Berkeley: University of California Press, 1975); Adriaansz, Willem, *The Kumiuta and Danmono Traditions of Japanese Koto Music* (Berkeley: University of California Press, 1973); Wade, Bonnie C., *Tegotomono: Music for the Japanese Koto.* (Westport, Conn.: Greenwood, 1976); Kunio Komparu, *The Noh Theater: Principles and Perspectives* (New York, Tokyo, Kyoto: Westherhill/Tankosha, 1983); Ernst, Earle, *The Kabuki Theater* (Honolulu: An East-West Center Book, University Press of Hawaii, 1974); Brandon, James R., William P. Malm, and Donald H. Shively, *Studies in Kabuki: Its Acting, Music, and Historical Context* (Honolulu: University Press of Hawaii, 1978).

JAPAN DISCOGRAPHY

General: *Nihon No Ongaku,* 2 disks (Polydor MN-9041–9042) (notes in Japanese).

Instruments: *Traditional Music of Japan,* 3 disks, with notes in English and Japanese by Shigeo Kishibe (Nihon Victor, JL 52–54); *Japan: Semi-Classical and Folk Music,* with notes in English, French, and Italian by Shigeo Kishibe (Odeon 3 C064–17967); *Classical Music of Japan* (Elektra EKS 7285).

Shomyo: *Shomyo-Buddhist Ritual from Japan, Dai Hannya Ceremony-Shigon Sect* (UNESCO Collection Musical Sources, Philips); *The Way of Eiheiji, Zen-Buddhist Ceremony* (Folkways FR 8980) (everyday chanting of shomyo).

Shinto Music: Edo No Kagura To Matsuri Gayashi (Nihon Victor SJ 3004) (shinto festival and dance music).

Gagaku: Gagaku Taikei (Nihon Victor SJ 3002) (instrumental gagaku; another disc (SJ 3003) contains vocal gagaku); *Gagaku: Ancient Japanese Court Music* (Everest 3322); *Gagaku* (The King Record KC 1028).

Noh: *Noh,* 2 disks (Nihon Victor SJ 1005, 1006) (the most complete albums for noh; with history, music theory, libretti, photographs, and explanatory commentaries for each piece); *Hogoromo <and Kantan>* (Caedmon TC 2019) (contains two major noh dramas, sung and performed by players of the Komparu and Kanze School of Noh, Tokyo); *Japanese Noh Music* (Lyrichord LL 137).

Koto Music: *Sokyoko To Fiuta No Rekishi,* 4 disks (Nihon Victor SLR 510–513); *Japanese Koto Music, With Shamisen and Shakuhachi* (Lyrichord 131) (performed by masters of the Ikuta School).

Kabuki: Azume Kabuki (Columbia WL 5110); *Kanjincho* (Nihon Victor JL 105) (a complete Kabuki play); *Kabuki Geza Uta Shusei,* 4 disks (Nihon Victor SJL 2091–2095) (off stage kabuki music explained in detail).

6

THE MUSIC OF INDONESIA

Charles Capwell

JAVANESE MUSIC IN CHICAGO

A subtly glowing array of bronze ingots, pots, and gongs in intricately carved wooden cases painted indigo and red with flashes of gold leaf—this was the dazzling sight that greeted us, a small group of university students and faculty who had come to the Field Museum in Chicago for an afternoon's introduction to the performance of gamelan music (Figures 6–1 and 6–2). Gamelan—an Indonesian word meaning "musical ensemble"—can be variously constituted, but the one at the Field Museum is representative of those used at the princely courts on Java, the most heavily populated island in the nation of Indonesia. Nowadays, similar gamelan are to be found in many universities and colleges in the United States and Europe. The Field Museum gamelan, however, has a special history: a couple of Dutchmen who owned coffee and tea plantations on Java brought the gamelan to Chicago, along with a group of Javanese musicians and craftsmen, for the Columbian Exposition of 1893, a great world's fair. The same entrepreneurs had arranged similar contributions to an exposition in Amsterdam a decade earlier and to another in Paris in 1889. At the latter, the composer Claude Debussy was enchanted by the music he heard and later tried to capture what

134

appealed to him in pieces of his own such as some of the *Preludes* and *Images* for piano (Figures 6–1 and 6–2).

Now that dozens of Indonesian gamelan of various types are to be found scattered around the United States in private and institutional collections, dozens of Americans have become competent performers and scholars of different types of Indonesian music. At the time of our visit to the Field Museum, Dr. Sue Carole DeVale, an ethnomusicologist with a special interest in the study of musical instruments (organology), took charge of our instruction. She had been fundamental in getting the museum to restore the gamelan, which had been more or less forgotten in storage for many decades, and had convinced them to make it available for use under her direction.[1]

Figure 6–1.   The Sundanese *gamelan* at the Columbian Exposition in Chicago, 1893. (Photo courtesy of the Field Museum of Natural History, neg #A106223).

[1]Dr. DeVale now teaches at UCLA, and the Field Museum, afraid that the gamelan might become damaged with further use, has returned it to storage.

Figure 6–2. The Columbian Exposition *gamelan* as it looked after it was restored in 1978. (Photo courtesy of the Field Museum of Natural History, neg #A106838c).

THE JAVANESE GAMELAN

Instruments in the Javanese Gamelan

Like most high-quality gamelan, this one consists largely of metallophones—in this case, instruments of gleaming bronze, but it also includes a chordophone (rebab, a two-stringed fiddle), a xylophone (gambang), an aerophone (suling, a notched vertical flute), and a couple of membranophones drums (kendang) (Figure 6–3).

Sitting among the metallophones, we became aware that the bronze had been fashioned in several different ways to make the various types of instruments. The sarons, for instance, had keys shaped like rounded ingots; these were pinned through the holes in their ends to the edges of a shallow trough made in a wooden case that thus served both to hold them in place and to increase their resonance. There were three different sets of sarons, each in a different octave. The highest, the peking, had a delicate but piercing tone; that of the middle range, barung, was mellower and longer-lasting; and the set in the lowest range, demung, had a powerful clang. The peking was sounded by striking the keys with a mallet of water-buffalo horn, but the others were played with heavier and less bright-sounding wooden mallets.

A similar three-octave range was found in the differently constructed bonangs, although there were only two of these. The lower pitched b. barung and the higher b. panerus each spanned two octaves, with the higher octave of the lower instrument duplicating the lower octave of the higher one. The "keys" of the bonangs resembled overturned bowls with knobs protruding from the tops, which is where they were struck with a pair of batonlike mallets wrapped with string. Each

Figure 6–3. F. X. Widaryanto, playing the *gender barung.*

instrument had two rows of bowls resting on strings that were stretched in wooden frames.

The kenong also had bowllike individual components, but these were fewer and much larger than those of the bonangs, and each one was supported in its own case on a web of string. A single bowl, closer in size to one from the set of bonangs but flatter in contour, sat by itself and contrasted with all the other instruments mentioned so far because of its curiously dull-sounding "clunk"; this was the kethuk.

The most impressive bronze instruments, for both their size and their sound, were the hanging gongs. ("Gong," by the way, is a Malay— that is, Indonesian—word.) The largest, gong ageng, was nearly a meter in diameter, and its slightly smaller mate, gong siyem, hung by its side. These can be seen in the 1893 photo presiding over the whole ensemble from their privileged position at the back and in the center. On the end of the same rack that holds these gongs, a smaller gong has been suspended that is named kempul; like other names such as gong or kethuk, kempul is onomatopoetic and calls to mind the sound of the instrument it names.

In addition to these common instruments, the Field Museum gamelan also contained two others—the jenglong, similar to the kenong, which is found in gamelan from Sunda, the western part of Java; and the gambang gangsa, similar to the wooden gambang but having bronze keys like those of the saron instead of wooden ones. All in all, this original group of about twenty-four instruments was as impressive for its size as for its beauty; nevertheless, it lacked certain other instruments at the time of its use at the Columbian exposition that have since been added.

Perhaps the gender could be considered the most important of these. Coming in two sizes (g. panerus and g. barung, like the bonang), they group thin, slablike bronze keys in a slightly larger range than the saron (Figure 6–4). Much thinner than the ingots of the saron, the keys of the gender are struck with a pair of mallets having padded disks at their ends, and they produce a delicate, muffled ringing that makes up for their soft volume with longer-lasting resonance. The secret to the long-lasting sound is that each key has its own individually tuned amplifying resonator in the form of a tube, above which it is suspended by strings so that it is not damped by resting directly on the case (the saron keys rest on pads of rubber or rattan to lessen the damping).

Originally, the kempul in the Columbian Exposition gamelan, as described above, had been a single hanging gong, but additional gongs have been added to complete a full scale, as was also done for the kenong.

Figure 6–4. F. X. Widaryanto, playing the *rebab*.

While the two-stringed fiddle, the rebab, was part of the original ensemble, the plucked string instrument celempung, a type of zither, was among the additions.

Tuning and Scales

Having familiarized ourselves a bit with the components of what at the start had seemed a bewildering array, we still had one further thing to learn before taking up our mallets to attempt our first piece: the instruments came in pairs. A complete Javanese gamelan is in fact two orchestras in one, for there are two different types of scales used in Javanese court music, one of five tones (pentatonic) and another of seven tones (heptatonic). Since the gaps (intervals) between pitches in one scale are different from those of the other, it is not possible to select five tones from the heptatonic scale to produce the pentatonic, and therefore there is a separate collection of instruments for each tuning system (laras). To play in laras slendro (pentatonic system), for example, the saron players faced front, and to play in laras pelog (heptatonic system) they had to make a quarter-turn to the left. (You could get a general idea of the contrast between these by playing on the piano C-D-E-G-A as 1-2-3-5-6 of slendro and E-F-G-B -B-C-D as 1-2-3-4-5-6-7 of pelog.)

Although the Western scale, like that of the white piano keys, is heptatonic, too, we soon discovered that the seven pitches in pelog formed a different set of intervals from the regular half- and whole-tones on the piano. The difference was not so simple as merely being one between Javanese and Western scales, however, because each gamelan has its own unique slendro and pelog scales, unless it has been constructed purposely on the model of an existing gamelan. It's a bit as though the Boston Symphony Orchestra and the New York Philharmonic played slightly differing forms of major and minor. Just imagine how interesting Beethoven's Ninth Symphony would be if it took on a new tonal flavor with each orchestra that played it!

Instrument Functions and Formal Principles

When we finally took up our mallets to play, we began with a piece in pelog. As the sarons attempted the first section of their melody, we sang along with them using numbers for the pitches and following our instructor: "6-5-3-2" we sang out as the sarons sounded the tones, all of equal duration. After repeating this phrase, we learned the third, "3-3-2-3," and then returned to the original for the conclusion. On the last tone, the player of the gong ageng was given the signal to strike, and the awesome sound left little doubt that we had arrived at an important juncture. The role of the gong was just to furnish this most important punctuation at the end of every completed melody—in this case sixteen beats long, with a single pitch on every beat. Two distinct musical functions were illustrated in this beginning: the sarons provided a "skeletal melody" (balungan) whose periodic punctuation (the "colotomic structure") was provided by other instruments like the gong ageng (Figure 6–5).

The other colotomic instruments were the next to join in as the sarons grew more confident: the kenong sounded the appropriate pitch at the end of every group of four beats (gatra), and so every fourth kenong stroke sounded with the gong; in the same manner, the kempul sounded the pitch every fourth beat midway between strokes of the kenong, omitting the second beat, however, so as not to interfere with the continuing resonance of the gong. Finally, on every odd-numbered beat the "clunk" of the kethuk was heard, so the beats in between kempul and kenong were marked, too.

The next instruments to be added were the bonangs, which added a third functional component to the music, that of elaboration of the balungan. Because their music was more elaborate, it also required more dexterity and skill to play than did the other instruments, and while we had been pleased at the ease with which we had picked things up

Figure 6–5.   The University of Illinois *gamelan* performance group during a rehearsal.

to start with, it became clear as we patiently waited for the bonang players to start getting the hang of their parts that things were getting rapidly more complicated and demanding. While the bonangs required more skill to play, the principle behind their basic method of melodic elaboration was easy enough to understand: as the kenong and kempul played every fourth beat, the b. barung did the opposite and divided the beat in two, and the b. panerus divided it into four, doubling or quadrupling each pair of balungan pitches. The peking (highest-pitched saron) was also told to double the number of pitches to a beat by anticipating each balungan note. Thus, the first gatra (four-beat phrase of the balungan) came out like this:

```
bonang panerus      6 5 6 . 6 5 6 5 3 2 3 . 3 2 3 2
bonang barung         6   5   6   5   3   2   3   2
peking                6   6   5   5   3   3   2   2

SARON                     6       5       3       2

kempul                            5
kenong                                            2
gong                                              X
```

When we got the whole sixteen-beat phrase together, it sounded like a marvelous clock whose music was the actual time-keeping mechanism, and just as with a clock, the sounding of the gong signaled a conclusion that could also be the taking-off point for another cycle.

Whether we were to repeat or not was indicated to us by the drum player, our instructor, who, in regulating and supporting the pulse and rhythm of the music, fulfilled the fourth function in the ensemble so that the melody, its elaboration, and its punctuation were controlled from this instrument rather as the conductor in a Western orchestra controls the rest of the group. (In the eighteenth-century Western orchestra, in fact, the "conductor" was actually a performer, too—usually the first violin or the harpsichord player.)

When we had at last become comfortable with this first phrase, we went on to complete the piece with a second, similarly constructed phrase (7567 5672 2765 6765) which we now learned to call a gongan,— that is, a phrase punctuated with a stroke of the big gong. As we have seen, each gongan was divided into four 4-beat kenongan (punctuated with a kenong stroke), and each of these was further subdivided by a kempul stroke on the second beat and kethuk strokes on beats 1 and 3. Because this colotomic pattern is a fixed structure, it is common to a number of pieces differentiated from one another by, for example, their balungan, but similar in their colotomy, and these make up a general category of small, simple pieces called bubaran (sometimes called lancaran mlaku). The particular piece we had learned has the title "Udan Mas" ("Golden Rain") and is used to send people off at the end of a ceremony or concert. It served as our farewell, too, as we had used up most of the afternoon and decided not to press our luck in attempting another piece.

The Variety of Styles and Forms

Although we came away feeling we had accomplished quite a bit in one afternoon, we had, of course, barely scratched the surface of this one type of Indonesian music. We hadn't even touched some of the instruments such as the genders, for example, because we played a "loud-style" piece in which gender, rebab, celempung, gambang, and suling do not participate; these difficult instruments are used for the elaboration of "soft-style" pieces, which may also include singing by a chorus of men (gerongan) and one or two female soloists (pesindhen).

We had naturally learned to play a short, simple type of piece, but among the types of other pieces for gamelan there are some whose gongan, for example, have sixteen times as many beats as our sixteen-beat buburan! And instead of playing just twice for each beat, the saron peking might play four times in order to fill in the great gap between one beat and another—so it might be as much as ten minutes between strokes of the gong ageng instead of the approximately ten seconds of our bubaran.

As an example of a small-scale, soft-style piece, we could consider ketawang "puspawarna" laras slendro pathet manyura. This is a work entitled "Kinds of Flowers" (Puspawarna) that has a gongan of sixteen beats, like a bubaran, but it is divided into only two eight-beat kenongan, and therefore it falls into the class of ketawang. It employs the scale of the pentatonic tuning (laras slendro) in one of three particular ways or pathet, that is called "peacock" (manyura). (There are also three distinct pathet for laras pelog.) For this ketawang, all the soft-style elaborating instruments join in along with the gerongan and pesindhen vocalists.

"Puspawarna" is a very popular piece played not only on the precious gamelan of princes but also on the modest two- or three-piece ensembles of itinerant street musicians. Despite its wide use for a variety of circumstances and audiences, however, it is not merely a piece intended for listening pleasure; it also has particular associations and prescribed uses, and even its title can tell us something about the political and cultural history of Java.

THE CULTURAL AND HISTORICAL SIGNIFICANCE
OF JAVANESE GAMELAN MUSIC

Ketawang "Puspawarna": A piece for the Prince

Just as "Hail to the Chief" played by the Marine Band has sometimes been used to announce the arrival of the President at a function or ceremony, "Puspawarna" was played by the gamelan of the two subsidiary central-Javanese courts to announce the presence or the arrival of their respective princes. The main courts of the Sultan of Yogyakarta and of the Susuhunan of Surakarta (Solo) were established in the mid-eighteenth century when the Dutch succeeded in supporting their trade interests by asserting political control over much of the Indonesian archipelago. The central-Javanese kingdom of Mataram was divided at that time between two ruling families centered at Yogyakarta and Solo, with a secondary court, the Mangkunegaran, attached to Solo. Later, in the early nineteenth century, the Paku Alaman court was established as an adjunct to Yogyakarta, and the various princes all had their own particular identifying pieces of music, "Puspawarna" serving both of the subsidiary courts and symbolizing a family connection between them.

Since political power was largely in the hands of the colonial overlords, the wealth and energy of the courts was expended on the development of cultural matters like music and dance as a means of both establishing and justifying their precedence and prestige. Mataram had been the last great native power in Java, a Muslim kingdom in a land where Islam had steadily been increasing its influence for several centuries. As the Sanskrit words in the title "Puspawarna" and in the name of pathet "Manyura" reveal, however, the culture of India and its Hindu and Buddhist religions had considerable influence on the elite and ruling classes in Java and other parts of the Indonesian region for a millennium or so before the establishment of Islam, which itself had been introduced in large part by traders from northwestern India. While a segment of Indonesian society may follow a strict and conservative Islam that, among other things, condemns most musical and performing arts, the aristocracy of Java, while accepting the "new" belief, continues to prize the older spiritual and cultural concepts and also to accommodate indigenous practice and beliefs that antedate any of the imported ones.

Some Spiritual Aspects of Javanese Gamelan Music

We may discover something of the complex relationship between Islam and music that obtains in Java by citing some observations the ethnomusicologist Jaap Kunst made about sixty years ago:

The gamelan, found by the Islam on arrival in Java as an indispensable element of all Hindu ceremonials, has never become . . . an integral part of Mohammedan religious rite. Accordingly during the month of fasting, as well as on Fridays, all orchestras in the whole of the Javanese territory are expected to remain silent. (This rule is not strictly adhered to in the kraton [court]. All that is done there is to avoid beating the gong agentg, and to play the gong kemodong [a substitute gong] instead. The princes, for that matter, are regarded as above the adat [customary law]. When, for example, one of their memorial days falls in the fasting month, then the prohibition of gamelan-playing, it seems, is raised entirely. Then, however, a sum of money is paid into the mosque cashbox as a compensation of this breach of the religious adat.)[2]

Princely privilege was partly related to the use of music in rites and ceremonies, and to do away with music altogether would have undermined the privilege as well; yet acceptance of Islam required some recognition of its precepts. So a fine was paid to the mosque when a princely anniversary requiring musical performance to ensure its success violated the prohibition against playing the gamelan, or alternatively, the most imposing and important instrument in the ensemble was kept silent and a simpler substitute was used. In the latter case, the gong agentg no doubt stood as a metonymical symbol for the whole ensemble which could be considered silent, too, if it were absent.

The Power of the Gong

But another reason for silencing the gong might also be offered. In many cultures the blacksmith has had a special position, not simply because of his technological expertise but also because of his spiritual power.[3] Metallurgical skill was considered to require supernatural cooperation, and the smith, therefore, had to be possessed of special powers to accomplish his extraordinary task of converting earth and stone into metal. In Java, the smith in charge of forging a new gamelan used to prepare himself by fasting and other acts of purification so that he could become fit for possession by the spirit of Panji, a culture hero who figures in many traditional Javanese stories. If the forging of the instruments were successful, they too would become the abode of a spirit, and the gong agentg, the most difficult instrument to make, would contain the greatest spiritual power. Especially fine old gamelan—or their spirits—have even been ennobled; one at the Yogyakarta kraton, for example, that actually antedates the founding of the Sultanate in 1755 and that is used for special celebrations like those accompanying the birthday anniversary of Mohammed, is referred to as "Kangjeng Kyai Guntur Madu," or

[2]Jaap Kunst, *Music in Java: Its History, Its Theory, Its Technique*, 3rd enlarged ed., ed. Ernst Heins (The Hague: Martinus Nijhoff, 1973), Vol. 1, pp. 266–67.

[3]Mircea Eliade, *The Forge and the Crucible*, 2nd ed., Chicago. Univ. of Chicago Press, 1978, 238 pp.

"Venerable Sir Torrent of Honey." For this reason, it remains proper etiquette when entering the gamelan to remove one's shoes and to avoid the rudeness of stepping over an instrument. Further, the spirit of the gamelan, embodied in the gong ageng, is paid homage with offerings of food, flowers, and incense. A rigidly orthodox Muslim might find such behavior to be verging on idolatry, so it is not surprising that even in the more flexible attitude found at the kraton, the gong ageng should be singled out for silencing on the Sabbath.

A Christian, too, might object to venerating the spirit of the gong, but just as different attitudes prevail among the Muslims, Christians can also accommodate old patterns of behavior. Consider, as an illustration, a story told to me by a dancer whose family had been performers connected with the Yogyakarta kraton and whose father had converted to Christianity. Once when he was rehearsing with a gamelan, the gong was disturbing him by its poor tone quality, even though it was supposed to be a very fine instrument. It was suggested that the spirit of the gong was disturbed and that an offering of incense and flowers should be made to it; when this was done, the dancer was pleased and surprised to notice that the gong began to sound resonantly and clearly again.

The spiritual power that is invested in old gamelan by tradition in turn invests power in their owners, for which reason they are important components of princely regalia (pusaka), over which battles have been fought in the past. The gendhing (musical work) played on these gamelan, too, may have such power that, for example, it was in the past forbidden to hum them casually; in transcribing them into notation—a practice initiated as a result of European influence in the nineteenth century—it used to be considered advisable to make an occasional mistake in order to prevent the power of the tune being used inappropriately.

The Sacred Dance Bedhaya

The tunes accompanying the sacred dance bedhaya, for example, are considered especially powerful because of the reputed origin of the music and dance and their association with kingship, as recounted in this paraphrase of a story from the History of Gamelan by Warsadiningrat:

> One night in the year 1643, Sultan Agung (the last great ruler of the kingdom preceding the establishment of Yogya and Solo) was meditating when he heard music that was so beautiful it gave him goosebumps. The next day he decided to form a dance troupe and called together musical experts to arrange the melodies for the accompaniment. Suddenly Kanjeng Sunan Kalijaga appeared; one of the nine saints legend credits with introducing Islam into Java, he was a noble Hindu by birth who first became a notorious bandit and then converted to Islam after a lengthy

period of continuous meditation in the manner of a Hindu holyman. Kalijaga congratulated the Sultan on his plans to create the *gendhing bedhaya*, for it was clearly a gift from He Who Is Great and Holy and meant to be a *pusaka* for the kings of Java that would bring blessings of peace, supremacy, and strength until the end of time.

Nine young girls from noble families were selected for their beauty and grace to dance the *bedhaya*. The *bedhaya* dance is important because: 1) it contributes to an understanding of Javanese culture by providing a guide to meditation; 2) it explains certain strategies of war; 3) it contributes to an understanding of music that portrays deep and noble emotions.

Just as the dance lessons were to begin, Kanjeng Ratu Kencana Sari, queen of all spirits, good and evil, suddenly arrived from her palace in the South Sea, in the dress and make-up of a bride. She appeared every day at dusk for three months to teach the dance because she loved the noble and majestic melodies, and she still appears for this reason. Because of this, when the *bedhaya* is performed, complete offerings of many kinds are prepared and a great deal of incense is burned continuously throughout the performance, and all the performers—dancers, singers, and musicians—must be pure and clean.[4]

As we see in this story, bedhaya is a remarkabe example of the eclectic nature of Javanese elite culture and the way in which it is used to assert status. Music and dance that conjure an indigenous Javanese goddess from her home in the sea and receive the blessing of a legendary Muslim saint whose conversion was accomplished through yogic meditation constitute one of the special heirlooms that buttress the powers of the king (Figure 6–6).

The Shadow-Play—Wayang Kulit

The shadow-puppet theater, or wayang kulit, is another Indonesian performance medium using music that has achieved special prominence in Javanese culture and that may also be associated with extraordinary power. While stories of Javanese and Islamic origins are performed in shadow plays, the stories derived from the Indian epics the Mahabharata and the Ramayana have the greater popularity and prestige, particularly the Mahabharata. Performed during the course of a whole night, the plays generally depict a battle whose turmoil is reflected in a disturbance of nature that, towards morning, is resolved when order is restored to human society and the world.

While the stories of the wayang kulit revolve around Indic

---

[4]Paraphrase of pp. 80–83 of "Wedha Pradangga" by Raden Tumenggung Warsadiningrat, trans. Susan Pratt Walton, in *Karawitan: Source Readings in Javanese Gamelan and Vocal Music*, Vol. 2 ed. Judith Becker, Michigan Papers on South and Southeast Asia No. 30 (Ann Arbor: Center for South and Southeast Asian Studies, University of Michigan, 1987). Description of Kalijaga based on pp. 25–29 of Clifford Geertz's *Islam Observed: Religious Development in Morocco and Indonesia*, University of Chicago, Chicago: 1973.

Figure 6–6.   A performance of *bedhaya* at the *kraton* of the Sultan of
Jogyakarta (Photo from *Tari di Mangkunagaran . . .,* M. A. Thesis (1990) for
Gadjah Mada University by B. Suharti).

characters, they have been Javanized by the introduction of a number
of comic characters who act as servants to the protagonists and incidentally serve as translators for the audience, since their masters speak a
Sanskritized and highfalutin poetic Javanese that is not commonly
understood. This differentiation according to language reflects the situation in contemporary Javanese, which has many styles of speech based
upon social class distinctions. (In Indonesia, whose motto is "Unity in
Diversity," the Indonesian language—Bahasa Indonesia—has rapidly
gained acceptance throughout the country as the lingua franca, since
it helps to overcome regional, ethnic, and class differences.) The chief
of the clowns, Semar, is a fat, lazy, wily, lascivious, and obstreperous-
ly flatulent fellow, but he is also a mysteriously all-knowing sage who
even takes precedence over the Hindu god Siva himself. Java may have
been awed by exotic Indian culture, but it seems that autochthonous
wisdom still earns the greater respect. Since Semar speaks colloquially,
he has the advantage not only of entertaining the audience with his wit
and shenanigans but also of giving good advice and wise counsel.

In fact, all the familiar characters in wayang communicate, at least by their actions, the various modes of human existence and manners of behavior; the shadow play has thus long been a medium for moral and ethical instruction and for discussion of contemporary events, and today it is often a medium for explaining government social programs as well.

All the different skills and knowledge needed to perform the shadow play come together in the dhalang, the puppeteer, a man (rarely a woman) who commands a thorough knowledge of karawitan (musical repertory and practice), who is familiar with the many different stories of the plays and their appropriateness for particular occasions, who speaks with a host of voices suited to everyone from the most refined gentleman to the crudest villain, who can skillfully move his puppets to convey an equal range of refinement and crudity, who knows archaic languages and the full range of contemporary social dialects, who is a repository of spiritual and cultural values, and who is acquainted with the latest political events and social problems—no wonder he is often thought to be a kind of superman!

Seated between a light source and a thin screen, the dhalang casts the shadows of flat leather puppets against the screen, all the while giving the appropriate signals to the gamelan for the pieces of music needed to accompany the scene, be it a moment of comic relief with Semar dancing or a tremendous battle between the forces of good and evil. Sometimes he sings, too, to set the mood for an upcoming scene.

Now that dhalangs can learn their art in schools (just as gamelan musicians do), an abbreviation and standardization of the wayang stories and of the puppeteers' skills is occurring. This inevitably lessens the special aura of the wayang and of the dhalang but helps to ensure them a continuing role in the cultural life of modern Indonesia.

MUSIC IN BALI

The arts of Indonesia, especially music and dance, have undergone many changes over the centuries as political and social circumstances have created different requirements and possibilities for performance. Among recent influences, the impact of tourism is certainly one of enormous significance, particularly for the arts of Bali, the small island just to the east of Java in the Indonesian archipelago. A jet airport that was opened there in 1969 has made possible easy accessibility to Bali for tourists from around the world, who since then have come in ever-increasing numbers. Not that tourism is new to Bali: some of its most famous visitors—painters, composers, anthropologists—arrived there in the decades prior to World War II and often stayed long enough to leave their indelible imprint on Balinese life.

Some Historical Events Influencing Balinese Culture

Before we touch upon the impact of tourism on the music of Bali, let us first consider a couple of political events of singular importance in the history of Bali. Earlier, we mentioned the Islamic kingdom of Mataram in the discussion of bedhaya. This kingdom was the predecessor of the central Javanese courts, founded in the eighteenth century through intervention of the Dutch, that still continue to exist in a ceremonial way in the present-day Republic of Indonesia. Mataram itself had earlier displaced the Hindu kingdom of Majapahit, refugees from which migrated to Bali in the fifteenth century. The culture these refugees brought with them casts an attenuated shadow over the arts of Bali today, but the aura attendant on all things connected with Majapahit casts all other cultural criteria into the shade. The elite Hindu-Buddhist–based culture of Majapahit introduced a new layer into the cultural fabric of Bali, and those who resisted its caste-based hierarchy and monarchical organization retreated to remoter areas of the island where so-called Bali Aga or "old Bali" villages continue many of the pre-Indic ways.

The other overwhelming event in Bali's history took place in 1908 when the kingdoms that had dominated the island for the last several centuries were finally dissolved by the Dutch, who invaded the island and took over its administration. The effect of Dutch intervention on Bali was quite different from its effect on Java. In Java the newly established courts, provided with financial resources but given limited responsibilities of governance, evolved an elegant way of life that fostered the development of the arts as the most effective means of retaining exalted status. In Bali the courts were dissolved, and the descendants of nobles, who were often employed as agents of Dutch rule, rarely had the financial resources to maintain the elaborate musical establishments associated with courtly life.

Music in the Balinese Courts

Among the several different ensembles maintained by Balinese kings, with their different instruments, musicians, repertories, and functions, was the gamelan gambuh, a kind of opera derived from Majapahit models. Quite unlike the large gamelan of metallophones we encountered in discussing Java, this one is smaller and consists of several extraordinarily long, vertical flutes (suling gambuh) and a rebab, with a few percussion instruments for punctuation and rhythmic control. The melodies of the flutes and fiddle are elaborately ornamented like those of the corresponding instruments in the Javanese gamelan, but rather than being part of a much denser and richer texture that competes with them, these flute melodies are the sole focus of attention. The flutes, whose tone has an ethereal and otherworldly quality, are played in such a manner that the melody is never interrupted when the player takes a breath. Using his cheeks as a kind of bellows, he inflates them before taking a breath so that he can continue to sound the flute with air from his cheeks while breathing in. The long-winded melodies and unfamiliar orchestra, the stately progress of the action, and the archaic language of the actors and general lack of comic episodes have given gambuh the status of a venerated relic of the past, even though it has recently undergone something of a revival. Much more popular today is the gamelan arja theater, another type of operatic performance not associated with courtly ceremony. It too has a small ensemble with flutes of a shorter, more common type and a few percussion instruments, but it also employs a greater variety of stories (including some on modern, topical subjects), female as well as male actors, and a lot of comedy.

Now rather rare, the "gamelan with the big gongs" (gamelan gong gede) is another ensemble that played an important role in the old courts. In its construction, it is more similar to the large instrumental gamelan of central Java than the g. gambuh is. It was regularly played for public ceremonies and temple festivities and performed pieces with regular structures whose melodies, elaboration, colotomy, and rhythm were realized in ways broadly similar to those discussed earlier for Javanese gendhing. An important difference, however, is the fact that, like the majority of Balinese ensembles, the g.g. gede is a single orchestra with but one tuning system, pelog; further, the version of pelog used is pentatonic—a selection of five pitches from the heptatonic pelog system scale. Like gambuh, this gamelan has a more popular and modern version that we will discuss a bit later.

A third court ensemble, gamelan Semar pegulingan, is a sizeable orchestra consisting largely of metallophones that was used to play purely instrumental arrangements of gambuh for the private enjoyment of the court. Since gambuh melodies employ heptatonic scales, some g. Semar pegulingan used to have fully heptatonic instruments, but others played pentatonic versions of the melodies. Today this ensemble, with its peculiarly delicate sound, has been revived to play a variety of old-style, classically structured pieces as well as new compositions and arrangements.

A very modest ensemble, the gender wayang, has not suffered a loss of popularity or been in need of revival because of its association with the shadow play based on stories of the Mahabharata and Remayana. This quartet of gender, similar in construction and playing technique to the gender of Java and tuned in laras slendro, is the sole accompaniment, other than the voice of the dhalang, for the Mahabharata; some percussion and colotomic instruments are added to it for the stories of the Ramayana. The quartet consists in fact of two pairs of gender distinguished from one another by being in different octaves. Within each pair, moreover, one instrument is distinguished from the other by being slightly "out of tune"—that is, a particular key on one instrument is purposely made slightly higher or lower than its twin in order to create a sensation of acoustical beats that gives a shimmering quality to the pitch when the keys are struck simultaneously. As the instruments of a pair are often played in unison, the result is a constantly throbbing resonance that almost seems to be breathing. While particularly effective in the Balinese wayang quartet, this principle of purposeful "mistuning" is evident in other bronze ensembles as well, and is especially noticeable when an octave is played.

The gender wayang continues to be a vitally important component of Bali's musical life, but the gamelan gambuh, Semar pegulingan, and gong gede have a more attenuated role as reminders of the past. With the passing of the courts, the patronage needed for the maintenance of the large numbers of instruments and for the support of the musicians, actors, and dancers disappeared. The common people of Bali, however, responded by filling the gap left by the absence of noble patrons, and this provided the impetus and stimulus for developing new types of performing arts. When Western intellectuals began to discover Bali between the World Wars, there was an efflorescence of the arts as they adjusted to the passing of old forms while accommodating new influences from the people and from contact with foreigners.

A Modern Form of Dance and Music—Kebyar

The most vibrant of the new styles was the result of the reshaping of the gamelan gong gede into the gamelan gong kebyar, by dropping some instruments and modifying and borrowing others. Village gamelan clubs often bought older-style gamelan no longer maintained or needed by the courts and recast them into the new form, and the new music developed for these was a revolutionary departure from the sedate and majestic pieces of the repertory for the g. gambuh or g. gong gede. In the latter, predictably familiar formal structures, conventional instrumentation, stable rhythms, and relatively unvaried dynamics created a sense of classical elegance; but the music of kebyar was a revolutionary change—virtuosic, mercurial, flashy, and unpredictable (Figure 6–7).

In an old-style gendhing for the gamelan gong or g. Semar pegulingan, the introduction would normally be a somewhat tentative solo on the trompong, an instrument similar to the Javanese bonang. Kebyar music, on the other hand, immediately asserts its independence of older formal traditions by beginning with a loud, confident unison for the whole ensemble. Instead of the classical elegance and refinement of former times, it displays a willful exuberance, progressing in fits and starts with sudden dynamic contrasts, jerky syncopations, and breathtakingly rapid figuration. No wonder many older connoisseurs found kebyar a disturbing phenomenon when it first took Bali by storm around the time of World War I.

Figure 6–7.   The *gamelan gong kebyar* "Tjarman Wati" of Sebatu, Bali. (Photo reproduced courtesy of Mel Howard).

Originally a purely orchestral music ideally suited for musical competitions among different villages, kebyar was given a new twist when it began to accompany dance. About 1925, a young dancer named Mario made a particular impression with his version of a dance to go with this exciting music. Like the fixed structures of the classical gendhing, the various dances done by trained court dancers or by people making offerings at the temple were based on traditional movements and gestures, and the stock characters of dramas like gambuh were confined to expressing the limited range of moods suited to them. But Mario's kebyar mirrored the fleeting moods and unpredictable contrasts of the music. Performing in an unusual crouched position, the dancer was on the same level as the seated musicians with whom he sometimes interacted directly, seeming to tease and cajole. Alternately rising onto his knees and squatting, playing with a fan, flashing a bizarre series of glances that registered astonishment, pique, enticement, and fury in rapid succession, the dancer would interpret the music's every change, and to top things off he might conclude by joining his accompanists in a choreographically performed solo on the obsolete trompong, all the while continuing to bob up and down and back and forth on his knees, twirl his mallets like a drum major, and register a bewildering series of moods on his face (Figure 6–8).

The individual nature of kebyar gave a new importance to the role of the composer and choreographer, and for a while compositions were jealously guarded as the special property of a particular club. The concept of the "composition" in the view of the Balinese gamelan club, however, is hardly equivalent to the Westerner's idea of a piece, say,

Figure 6–8.   A typical dance pose in *kebyar*. (Photo reproduced courtesy of Mel Howard).

by Beethoven. We can get an idea of how a Balinese composition is realized and treated from a memoir written by John Coast, an impresario who arranged the first world tour of the gamelan from Pliatan village in 1951. For this occasion, Coast wanted a special new piece for the repertory of the tour, and he commissioned Mario to choreograph a new dance to go with it. Here is his account of how the gamelan learned the piece:

> When we arrived about nine o'clock that night in the village we found the gamelan well into the first melody of the new dance [which they were learning by having each part demonstrated, as is customary, rather than from a score]; and it was Kebiar music, though new, Mario told us, having been composed originally by Pan Sukra for a club in Marga, near Tabanan, but it had never been used. And anyhow, these tunes were arranged for a girl dancer, while the original ones had been for a man.
>
> It took about three weeks for the thirty minutes of music to be perfectly mastered by Pliatan, and at the end of that time Pan Sukra went home to his village. Then Anak Agung, Made Lebah and Gusti Kompiang grinned freely. "Now it is our turn," they said.
>
> "What do you mean?" we asked.
>
> "Aggh! This is crude music. Now it is a matter of tabuh—style. You will see. It must be rearranged and polished by the club.[5]

In light of this, we might think of the Boston Symphony Orchestra playing a composition originally composed for the New York Philharmonic and, when the composer had turned his back, rewriting it according to their own tastes! No doubt some instrumentalists in Boston would respond with that expressive "Aggh!" to a newly commissioned work, but it is highly unlikely they would have the temerity to suggest altering the piece once it was completed, even if the composer had once asked for their advice on how to arrange the parts for their particular instruments.

Even in matters of interpretation, the initiative is apt to be that of the music director and conductor rather than of the rank-and-file instrumentalist. But in Pliatan as in other Balinese gamelan, the repertory was shaped by the contributions of all the club members although decisions may have been made by acknowledged leaders like the Anak Agung, a nobleman, and Made Lebah, a commoner, both of whom were respected performers and teachers.

In his account of the creation of the dance to go with the new music, Coast again reveals the cooperative nature of the work:

> And we saw the story of the dance unfold, as Mario had told us it would, creating itself bit by bit, with ideas thrown in from us all. We saw Raka as the little bumblebee sunning herself in a flower-filled garden, in moods of surprise, delight and fear; we saw the gaudy male bumblebee enter,

[5]John Coast, *Dancers of Bali* Putnam, N.Y.; 1953, p 109.

and Sampih could pick up Mario's ideas with the speed with which a western ballet dancer follows an enchaînement in class; we saw him spy the delectable little bee, zoom toward her, court her, frighten her by his advances till she fled from him. Then Sampih danced alone in baffled fury as the Kebiar music raged around him, and in the last rollicking melody he danced a Kebiar of sheer frustration around the whole gamelan, flirting desperately with its members. This was a development out of Mario's original Kebiar, and he called it now: Tumulilingan Mengisap Sari—the Bumblebee Sips Honey.

Luce was meanwhile busy with the costumes. . . . All our Pliatan family were engrossed in this dance, for it was a new thing and it was ours.[6]

To the creation of this new piece—which soon became a standard item in the repertory of the gamelan gong kebyar—even Coast and other members of the entrepreneur's retinue were able to make contributions as part of the "Pliatan family."

THE INFLUENCE OF FOREIGN ARTISTS AND TOURISTS

The Revival of Gamelan Angklung

Coast and his entourage were hardly the first outsiders to have an influence on Balinese arts, though. In 1938, for example, the Canadian-American composer Colin McPhee had, among other things, inspired the resuscitation of a moribund type of gamelan angklung. This multipurpose ensemble, often having only a four-tone scale, was a common feature of most village ceremonies and festivities, and at the time McPhee was in Bali only a few gamelan angklung in remote villages any longer included the instrument for which it was named. A kind of bamboo rattle, each angklung produces a single pitch in two, three, or four octaves, depending on how many bamboo tubes are loosely mounted in the frame that is shaken back and forth to make them sound. Ingeniously constructed, each tube is sliced in half over the greater part of its length to form a "key" that produces the desired pitch while the remainder of the tube is left intact to form a tuned resonator. Taking an interest in this obsolete instrument, McPhee attempted an experiment that he recalls in his book *Music in Bali*[7]:

Bright young musicians from central Bali who accompanied me on my expeditions to these remote villages found their old-fashioned orchestras utterly absurd. They would sit in polite silence while the musicians played, but could hardly wait until we drove off to comment on the "plain" . . .

[6]Ibid, p 110.

[7]Another of McPhee's books, *A Club of Small Men*, is a full account of the history of this ensemble. Written for children, it is an enjoyable read for adults, too. Colin McPhee, *A Club of Small Men*, New York J. Day Co. 48, 61 pp.

style of the music, the "stiff" . . . way of playing, and to gaily parody the preposterous accompaniment of the angklungs.

Nevertheless, when in 1938 I organized in Sayan a gamelan angklung composed entirely of small boys, I decided to include a set of angklungs in the orchestra. At first the children ignored these instruments entirely, but they soon became intrigued with their unusual sound, and there was much discussion—in which I took no part—as to who should play them. I engaged a young musician from Karangasem [the remote area where angklungs were still used] to teach the club and train the four boys to whom the angklungs had been assigned. These latter caught on to the unfamiliar style with surprising rapidity. Within a few months this club of children—a complete novelty in Bali—had acquired a repertory of compositions, some short, some of considerable length, which they played with complete assurance. Their first public appearance at a temple odalan [festival] in Sayan created a local sensation, partly because of the youth of the musicians, some of whom were no more than five or six, but especially because of the novelty of the angklungs. The word spread, and soon the club was in demand for festivals in other villages; the gamelan with angklungs had proved a success. Today [1966], I am told, these almost forgotten instruments have become familiar to everyone, and have been adopted by other angklung orchestras in central Bali.[8]

While the angklung may have been on the verge of extinction in Bali when it was revived by McPhee's intervention, in Sunda (where the Columbian Exposition gamelan came from) the angklung has always retained its popularity. But there, too, it has experienced interesting changes. Often combined with oboelike tarompets in ensembles accompanying street entertainments such as martial-arts duels or trance dancers, the angklung is now also found in school orchestras, where it is tuned to the Western diatonic scale for performing tunes like "Waltzing Matilda" in complete harmonic arrangements.

The evidence for change as a result of external influence in the Sundanese use of the angklung is obvious, but in the Balinese example it is hidden, since the music it performs had a continuous tradition. Without the intervention of McPhee, however, the angklung might have remained an archaic curiosity in Bali.

A Ramayana Performance—Kecak

McPhee's friend Walter Spies, with whom he toured Indonesia playing two-piano recitals, was also involved in bringing about changes in the arts of Bali. Primarily a painter, Spies had a profound influence on the visual arts as well, but his involvement in the development of kecak is of particular interest because this unusual performance medium has become a "must-see" item for tourists, who are often unaware that they are witnessing an art form specifically created to satisfy them. Being

[8]Colin McPhee, *Music in Bali*, New York, DaCopo 1976, p 243.

strange and disturbing in terms of the Westerners' usual experience of performing arts, it has indeed satisfied millions of tourists as an experience of something powerfully exotic, without which the time and money we spend in getting to new and distant places might seem poorly spent.

The kecak takes its name from the brusque, staccato monosyllables shouted by a large chorus of men in rapid and intricately interlocking rhythmic patterns. A few other men imitate with their voices the sound of a small gamelan, and these two elements accompany a drastically shortened version of the Ramayana acted out by a few actor-dancers. The basic story is this: Sita, wife of King Rama, an incarnation of the god Vishnu, has been abducted by the demon Ravana, who carries her off to his palace in Sri Lanka, but Hanuman, general of the monkey army and devotee of Rama, pursues them and rescues Sita. Since the chorus of men intermittently takes on the role of Hanuman's monkey army and sounds like chattering monkeys, the performance is also called the "Monkey Chant."

The rhythmic shouting of the men is traditionally associated with rituals of divination, in which young girls are entranced in order for questions to be put to the spirits (sanghyang) that take possession of them. While music and dance are frequently part of these rituals, dramatic stories from the Ramayana are not. Thinking that the kecak was an exciting and unusual kind of music, Spies suggested using it as the foundation for a concise presentation of the Ramayana that would give tourists, who were already discovering Bali before World War II, a professionally arranged and attractive means of experiencing it.

A Trance Dance—Barong

Performers in the Ramayana form of kecak do not go into trance as do the mediums in the sanghyang type, and in fact there is no indication in the former of the original association with trance. Barong, another kind of trance ritual adapted as a regular performance medium for tourists, is a kind of dramatic presentation accompanied by the gamelan gong or kebyar that represents the struggle between Good (in the being of the barong, an awesome but benevolent lion) and Evil (impersonated by a horrendous and malevolent witch). At the high point of the story, the supporters of the barong attack the witch with their krises (wavy daggers) and are forced by the witch's magic to turn them instead upon their own bodies, but the magic of the barong protects them from injuring themselves. During performances at village temples, many participants may fall into trance during and after the battle; indeed the spirits that are normally thought to reside in the masks of the barong and of the witch may possess the men who wear them as well.

In temple rituals for the Balinese themselves, the barong is certainly an event of supernatural import, but that does not prevent it from being an entertainment as well. One village, in fact, may visit another to perform its particular version of the barong and be appreciated for the style with which it performs as well as for the evident power of its barong and witch. There are, in fact, trance performances in Bali and elsewhere in Indonesia in which the trancers are said to be possessed by animals or even inanimate objects and that seem to have as their sole or main purpose the presentation of a bizarre entertainment. In such circumstances, the entertainment of tourists with a barong performance seems to fit in with the Balinese view of things, but it should be clear that such a performance cannot mean the same thing as one in which the primary object is to create a sense of well-being and security for the community rather than to satisfy the curiosity of outsiders for economic gain. While many of the tourists may regale their friends back home with stories of the "authentic" rituals they witnessed, the Balinese probably have a clearer idea of the distinction between the different types of authenticity involved in the performance of barong for themselves and for tourists.

Although changes in the motivations and presentation of performances like kecak or barong may be regretted by many for whom their original associations have strong meaning, such regret is surely an inevitable part of human experience, as no society is static and all culture must evolve and change or cease to exist. As the Sun Dance and other festivities of the Plains Indians in North America evolved into pan-Indian powwow celebrations or as the Medicine Dance of the San people of Botswana has evolved into a performance for others as well as for the San themselves, barong may be undergoing an evolution from an organic and vital part of specific Balinese communities to a "cultural performance" meant to help shape the idea of "Baliness" for the modern Balinese and for the outside world. Musical performances like barong, after all, can help mediate not just the contact between the human and the otherworldly but also the contact between groups of human beings, and we may hope that this latter role is no less powerful a validation of an art form than the former.

FOUR KINDS OF POPULAR MUSIC IN JAVA

Gambus

Entertainment and monetary gain are often thought of as the only reasons for the existence of many types of popular music. But when we think, for example, of how some people enjoy rap and willingly pay for the pleasure of listening to it while others dislike it but are vehemently devoted to reggae or heavy metal, it becomes clear that more powerful motivations must also be involved. Like barong, such music can shape an identity—for an individual or a group—and present it to the world.

In Indonesia, one of the pop musics that succeeds in doing this as well as providing its consumers a good deal of enjoyment is gambus, a genre named for an Arabic instrument that signifies connection with the homeland of Islam. Nowadays the gambus may be present only by virtue of having lent its name to the genre, the instrument itself having been replaced by the 'ud, which has wider currency in the music of the Middle East.

Not just the instruments of gambus—which may include, for example, nay and duff (Middle Eastern type of flute and drum)—but the musical style itself reflects Middle Eastern origins, with its short, often sequentially repeated phrases and simple, catchy, and danceable rhythms; even the vocal timbre is more that of Middle Eastern than of Javanese singers. And the dress of the performers as depicted on the sleeves of cassettes may include such articles as the kaffiyeh and agal, the Arab headdress worn by men (Figure 6–9). Although the texts of gambus may have Islamic subject matter, the songs are very much appreciated for their musical qualities—too much so, in the view of the more puritanical Muslims. As one Javanese Muslim told the anthropologist Clifford Geertz in response to a query about gambus, "It's like Africa in Java," by which he meant to say (being ignorant of the spiritual value in much African music) that the music was not conducive to leading a proper Islamic life since it was primitive and sensual. Perhaps one could imagine a similar confrontation in the United States between supporters of Christian rock and their adversaries.

Dangdut

Even more reprehensible in the eyes of the orthodox is dangdut, another popular music that is an extraordinary mix of Western rock and Indian film song. Its Indonesian texts range from love lyrics to homilies on leading a better, more productive life and the hope for a prosperous future. Its infectious rhythms have earned it the onomatopoetic name dangdut that represents its characteristic drum sounds and, for those who deride it, its suspiciously worldly appeal. Under the influence of the superstar Rhoma Irama (originally called Oma, he added the "R" and "h" from Raden Haji, a title given those Muslims who, as he did, perform the pilgrimage to Mecca), it became the dominant pop music in the late seventies and early eighties, and like the Indian songs from which it borrowed so much, it also was featured heavily in films.

Kroncong

While dangdut, a relatively recent phenomenon, has had a fairly swift rise in popularity in the manner of many kinds of commercial pop, kroncong, another popular style, has a long history in Indonesia stretching

Figure 6–9. Cover for cassette recording of *gambus*.

back to the first contact with European colonialism. The Portuguese ports in the East, such as Goa in India, Macao in China, Malacca in Malaysia, and the Portuguese areas of southern Africa and the Azores, linked Europe of the sixteenth and seventeenth centuries to the spice-growing areas of Indonesia. Before the Dutch established colonial hegemony in the Indonesian archipelago, the Portuguese outposts on the islands served as entrepôts for the shipment of spices to Europe; of mixed ethnic and racial background, these communities nevertheless maintained aspects of Portuguese culture such as the Christian religion and some types of folk music. In Indonesia, this music came to be called kroncong, and during the late nineteenth and early twentieth centuries it had a somewhat unsavory reputation associated with urban violence and glamorous toughs called buaya kroncong ("kroncong crocodiles"), who were like the Malay pirates of some Hollywood movies in the twenties and thirties.

The typical instruments accompanying kroncong are of European derivation—violin, cello, flute, and plucked strings of various types; one of the strings, similar to a ukulele, has given its name to the genre. These provided a simple, harmonically based accompaniment to vocal melodies sung with a mellifluous sweetness Americans might think characteristically Hawaiian, but the tunes often had disjunct progressions that exaggerated their crooningly sentimental quality in a distinct way. When kroncong began to attract the interest of a more polite section of middle-class Javanese society in the twenties and thirties, it underwent a kind of acculturation to central Javanese style, and while the instruments were the same they took on functional qualities similar to those of gamelan music. The flute and violin became like the suling and rebab, providing free, heterophonic elaboration of the melody; the cello, while continuing to provide a foundation for the harmony, was played pizzicato in rhythms resembling kendang-like drum patterns; and the kroncong, with its regular offbeat plucking, had a resemblance to the kethuk.

Some kroncong during this period also took on the typical 4 × 8-bar structure of Tin Pan Alley ballads, with a repeated first phrase that also returned after an intervening and contrasting second phrase—AABA; and, too, they acquired a jazzy feeling with the addition of "blue notes." What had been an indigenously evolved, traditional popular music, based on very old importations, had evolved into a more internationalized commercial music at the same time that it was becoming more "Javanized."

With its variety of styles appealing to different ethnic groups and social strata, kroncong became a music of broad appeal, and its popularity was consolidated during World War II when the Japanese banned foreign popular music, thereby helping it become a vehicle for the expression of national solidarity and nationalist sentiment. While newer styles like the rock-oriented kroncong pop have developed more recently, the powerful nostalgia evoked by the music from the war and prewar period gives it a strong appeal for an older crowd, even as the young turn to more sensational music like dangdut.

Jaipongan

Or *jaipongan*. This style of pop music has the unique characteristic of being derived from a type of professional folk entertainment of Sunda (West Java) and does not betray the foreign derivations or influences of gambus, dangdut, or kroncong. The Sundanese kethuk tilu ("three kethuk") is a small ensemble of musicians playing rebab, gong, three kethuk, and drums, who accompany a female dancer/singer (and sometimes prostitute) in a kind of audience-participation performance during which various men get up to dance with her. Many similar types of dance entertainments exist or existed in Java and Bali as well as other parts of Indonesia, and troupes were often hired for private parties or for celebrations connected with occasions like weddings or circumcisions.

Like "dangdut," the word jaipongan was made up from syllables representing drum sounds, and flashy Sundanese-style drumming is basic to jaipongan. To the instruments derived from kethuk tilu a saron is generally added, and this accounts for another characteristic equally as attractive as the drumming and as typically Sundanese, for the saron is in slendro while the singer and rebab usually perform in another tuning such as pelog, adding ornamental pitches as well. According to Philip Yampolsky, it was a young musician named Gugum Gumbira who was responsible for introducing the amalgamation of various Sundanese musical components that started the jaipongan craze in 1974, and the popularity of the style soon caused it to spread beyond his original troupe to other parts of Java outside Sunda, as well as to take on the nature of a popular dance fad for couples:

> [*Jaipongan*] was taught in schools and private dance classes, and was per-
> formed in dance-halls and nightclubs, at parties and festivals, in the streets
> and on TV. A 1982 newspaper report describes some of the places in Jakar-
> ta and Bandung where one might find Jaipongan: a dance-hall, where
> the women hired by the management danced with paying customers; an
> exercise club for rich women; an open-air stage near the railroad tracks
> in a seedy area, where peddlers and pedicab drivers danced with
> prostitutes.[9]

While the social-dance fad has waned in recent years, Gugum Gumbira has concentrated on creating staged performances, and as Philip Yampolsky remarks later in the disk-jacket notes also quoted above: "Today, Jaipongan is accepted as a 'national' stage dance." It is even included in cultural performances by Indonesian students in the United States for national-day celebrations.

UNITY IN DIVERSITY

"Unity in Diversity," as we pointed out earlier, is the national motto of Indonesia, a nation created within the memory of many of its present-day citizens. Creating unity is a primary concern in any attempt to form a nation—or to maintain one, as events in the Soviet republics, Germany, Korea, India, and Great Britain remind us every day. But the

---

[9]Notes by Philip Yampolsky for *Tonggeret*, compact disc Nonesuch 79173-2, [4].

chore is a remarkably daunting one in a country with the topography of Indonesia and a population ranging from the industrialized city dwellers of Java to recently contacted groups of former headhunters in Irian Jaya (the Indonesian part of Papua–New Guinea) and Kaliman-tan (the Indonesian part of Borneo). In the scholarly view of music, the unity of the area is often related to the use of bronze-casting technology and cyclical musical structures that also link Indonesia to the Southeast Asian mainland, to southern China, to northeastern In-dia, and to the Philippines. Valid and interesting as such a system of relationships is, it does not accommodate many other types of musical phenomena in Indonesia such as, for example, the various pipe ensembles of people in Kalimantan, whose music might be reasonably discussed in comparison with that of similar ensembles among the Andean Aymara or South African Venda.

The necessity of national "unity," evidenced in music by the establishment of government conservatories with standardized curricula, will present a challenge to the more marginal components of Indone-sian society and to their cultural forms; these components of Indonesia's "diversity" will likely be neglected—as we have neglected many of them in this chapter—but their lack of importance for the national or na-tional scene does not necessarily indicate the inevitability of their disap-pearance or impoverishment. Thanks to the inexpensive and widespread technology of audio-cassette recording, many types of regionally cir-cumscribed musics find a locally supportive market that helps to perpetuate them at the same time as it may alter their uses and associa-tions. Rather than propagating a narrow range of musical product, the cassette industry in Indonesia has in effect created the audio equivalent of the country's motto, a wide range of music in the uniform medium of the audio cassette.

Recorded sound has demonstrated the variety of Indonesia's music today, but it has also made a record of the sound of its past as well, for the gamelan brought to the Columbian Exposition of 1893 was recorded not only on film but also on wax cylinders, the audio-recording medium of the day. Although these are not the first recordings of an ethnomusicological nature—some earlier ones were made of American Indians—they are among the earliest, and they help to lend a special aura to the instruments now housed in the collection of the Field Museum. What would those musicians recorded in 1893 have thought, I wonder, if they had been able to hear the performance of bubaran *"Udan Mas"* that was described at the start of this essay?

INDONESIA BIBLIOGRAPHY

Java: Judith Becker, ed., *Karawitan: Source Readings in Javanese Gamelan and Vocal Music*, 3 vols., Michigan Papers on South and Southeast Asia No. [29?], 30, 31 (Ann Arbor: Center for South and

Southeast Asian Studies, University of Michigan, 1984, 1987, 1988); Mantle Hood, *The Nuclear Theme as a Determinant of Patet in Javanese Music* (New York: Da Capo, 1977); Susan Pratt Walton, *Mode in Javanese Music*, Monographs in International Studies Southeast Asia Series No. 79 (Athens, Ohio: Ohio University Center for International Studies, 1987); Claire Holt, *Art in Indonesia: Continuity and Change* (Ithaca, N.Y.: Cornell University Press, 1967); Judith Becker, *Traditional Music in Modern Jave: Gamelan in a Changing Society* (Honolulu: University of Hawaii Press, 1980); Jaap Kunst, *Music in Java: Its History, Its Theory and Its Technique*, 2 vols., ed. Ernst Heins (The Hague: Martinus Nijhoff, 1973); Peter Manuel, *Popular Musics of the Non-Western World* (New York: Oxford University Press, 1988); Bronia Kornhauser, "In Defence of Kroncong," in Margaret J. Kartomi, ed., *Monash Papers on Southeast Asia No. 7* (Clayton, Victoria: University of Monash, 1978).

Bali: Colin McPhee, *Music in Bali: A Study in Form and Instrumental Organization in Balinese Orchestral Music,* (New York: Da Capo, 1976); Colin McPhee, *A Club of Small Men* (New York: John Day, 1948): Colin McPhee, *The Balinese Wajang Koelit and Its Music* (1936; repr. New York: AMS Press,; I Made Brandem and Frederik deBoer, *Kaja and Kelod: Balinese Dance in Transition* (Kuala Lumpur, New York: Oxford University Press, 1981); Urs Ramseyer, *The Art and Culture of Bali* (New York: Oxford University Press, 1977).

INDONESIA DISCOGRAPHY

Java: *Java Palais Royal de Yogyakarta: Musiques de Concert* (Ocora 558 598); *Java Historic Gamelans*, Art Music from Southeast Asia IX-2 (Philips 6586 004); *Musiques et Traditions du Monde: Une Nuit de Wayang Kulit Légende de Wahju Tjakraningrat* (CBS 65440); *Java Court Gamelan from the Pura Paku Alaman Jogyakarta* (Nonesuch H-72044); *Java Court Gamelan Istana Mangkunegaran Surakarta* (Nonesuch H-72074); *Java Court Gamelan Kraton Yogyakarta* Nonesuch H-72083); *Sunda: Musique et Chants Traditionnels* (Ocora 558 502); *Tonggeret* (Jaipongan) (Nonesuch 79173-2).

Bali: *Semar Pegulingan: Golden Gong of Bali* (Grevillea Records GRV 1020); *Gamelan of the God of Love: Gamelan Semar Pegulingan* (Nonesuch H-72046); *Bali: Musique et Théâtre* (gender wayang, gambuh) (Ocora OCR 60); *Golden Rain* (kebyar) (Nonesuch H-72028); *Bali: Le Gong Gede de Batur* (Ocora 585 510); *The Balinese Gamelan: Music from the Morning of the World* (Nonesuch 72015); *Gamelan Music of Bali* (Lyrichord LLST 7179).

7

THE MUSIC OF SUB-SAHARAN AFRICA

Thomas Turino

A SHONA MBIRA PERFORMANCE IN ZIMBABWE

Arriving near the roundhouse door after dark, we heard hand clapping, singing, talking, and the shuffling of dancers coming from inside. The people playing hosho (maracalike shakers) provided an additional musical layer, but there was still another sound—an instrument we had not heard before—which was deep and moving like the combination of water and bells. This was the mbira. Two men, leaning against the far wall, sat with their hands hidden inside large calabash gourds playing mbiras. They were the center of the musical activity, and the singers, dancers, and hosho players created their rhythmic patterns and improvised vocal parts based on the many simultaneous melodies that the mbiras played.

During a break in the music we asked the mbira players to show us their instruments. Twenty-two slightly rusted metal keys were tightly fastened over a metal bridge on a wooden soundboard, with bottle caps attached to a metal plate on the board (Figure 7–1). A necklace of bottle caps was also strung around the gourd resonators, creating the buzzing sound a torn stereo speaker makes. The musicians explained that, without

Figure 7–1.   Shona Mbiras (left to right): Karimba; hosho rattle; 22-key mbira in calabash gourd; 22-key mbira, side view.

the gourds, the mbiras were too soft to be heard in occasions for communal music making, such as the bira ceremony that we were attending, and without the buzzing of the bottle caps they would not sound like mbiras. Though the mbira is referred to as "thumb piano" and thought of as a toy in the United States, the type of mbira that they were playing is one of the most important and sacred instruments of the Shona, Bantu-speaking people of Zimbabwe in southeastern Africa. It is one of many mbira types used by the Shona and throughout sub-Saharan Africa. Shona mbira players often specialize on one variety of instrument, each with its own distinct scale pattern and playing techniques; changing between mbira types is like switching from a guitar to a mandolin or a banjo.

The musicians sat down and began another piece. Listening more closely to the mbiras this time, I could hear several distinct bass, middle, and high melodic parts coming from the two instruments. I watched their hands closely. They would play the same patterns for a long time before changing, perhaps, only one or two pitches by striking different keys, and then would repeat the new variation many times. But even when they were playing the same patterns, I sometimes thought that I heard changes in the melodies. During their next break the musicians explained that it was always like that. Even simple mbira pieces contained many "inner melodic lines" that resulted not from changes in the keys played but rather from the particular combination of right- and left-hand parts that the listener focused on. They explained that mbira music was an art of creative listening as well as playing, and that the mbira itself seemed to continually suggest new inner melodic lines to the musician even when his hands continued to play the same keys. They told us that this was one reason why mbira players can perform the same pattern for a long time without getting bored or feeling the need to create constant contrasts. It was almost as if the mbira itself magically created its own variations; one simply had to have patience and learn to hear what it had to offer. We enjoyed talking to these musicians, and were learning something of the art of listening to Shona music, but it was time for them to return to playing for the ancestral spirits in the bira ceremony (Figure 7–2).

Figure 7–2.   Shona mbira player: Mr. Chawasarira. Photo: Patricia Sandler.

The Bira

According to the ethnomusicologist and mbira player Paul Berliner, the Shona believe that one's ancestors continually interact with, and affect the lives of, the living. A good relationship must be maintained with the ancestors. Misfortunes such as illness or sudden death are sometimes interpreted as resulting from having offended a particular spirit, or that ancestor's desire to call attention to a specific problem or misdeed within the family or community. Communication between people and their ancestors takes place through spirit possession when an ancestor enters and speaks through the body of a living person—a spirit medium. The bira is a communal ceremony in which the members of a family seek the aid and advice of a particular spirit.

As the bira begins, people arrive and begin talking and drinking together to the music of the mbira ensemble, which will play all night. These musicians are often part-time professional specialists who are invited to perform at the ceremony. But as the evening progresses, family and community members join in with the ensemble by clapping different patterns and dancing in the center of the room. Men and women also may contribute to the performance by singing verses, singing melodies that weave in and out of the mbira's bass part, or performing in a high-pitched yodeling style to complement the mbira ensemble's singer. Both well-known verses and improvised words are sung to fit the occasion, and the poetry moves people as do the dance and the music itself. After one piece has ended, the two mbira players, each with his own specific part, begin again, and again the different participants add what they will, until the performance becomes a dense, rich fabric of sound, movement, and feeling. The length of a given piece varies, but frequently the four short phrases that constitute its basic structure will be repeated and gradually varied over a long period of time, the repetition itself heightening participation.

Good mbira playing and concentrated communal effort are essential to the success of the bira, because it is the music that calls the spirits into this world and into the ceremony. As the intensity mounts and the energy within the room becomes right, the spirit enters the body of the medium. Since specific spirits respond to different pieces, playing the right tunes is also crucial for bringing on possession. The mbira players, however, should not become possessed while they are performing because they must keep their attention focused on the music. Once possessed, the spirit medium is dressed by his or her attendant in a black robe and feathered headdress.

The medium then follows the will of the spirit and may continue singing, dancing, or playing the hosho. She or he may become quiet and withdrawn, or wild and physically out of control, or may act in any number of ways. The powerful mbira playing and group participation that brought on possession must be sustained to hold the spirit. After the spirit has participated in the event for some time, the music comes to a halt and the people consult her or him about the problem that occasioned the bira. Different opinions regarding the given issue may be offered by the participants, but it is the ancestor that serves as the final judge and arbitrator. After the consultation, the music, singing, and dancing start up again and continue until morning.

The Mbira and Some Principles of African Music

Unlike Western instruments such as the piano on which the pitches are arranged in a linear fashion from low to high moving from left to right on the keyboard, the low keys on most mbiras are found in the center and the keys become shorter and higher as they fan out to the two sides. Depending on the type of mbira, the keys on the left side are played by the thumb of that hand and the right thumb and forefinger play the keys on the right side.

The pieces are constructed so that the right and left hands play different complementary melodies or motives that are *interlocked* to create resultant, "inner" contrapuntal melodies. Shona mbiras such as the large twenty-two-key dzavadzimu, and the smaller fifteen-key karimba, have an upper row of higher keys and a bottom row of lower ones, so a bass part and higher melody can be played simultaneously in interlocking fashion. The actual pitches played by each hand frequently alternate, fitting together like the fingers of folded hands. The bass, higher, and resultant inner lines are heard as relative to each other, and the variation of one part changes a listener's perception of the other lines as well.

Each musician has his own part. One part is called the kushaura, ("to lead the piece" to play the basic piece), and the other is called kutsinhira, a second interlocking or complementary accompanying part. The hand-clapping patterns, dance movements, and vocal melodies provided by the participants at the bira and other types of performances frequently do not simply reproduce the basic beat or division of the beat and are not performed in unison. Rather, each participant may add his or her own clapped patterns, sung parts, or dance movements, which may fall in between or around central beats and pitches of other people's parts, thereby providing another series of interlocking aspects.

The final polyphonic, polyrhythmic character of a communal Shona performance, then, results from the interplay, layering, and interlocking of the participants' contributions. The same principle, however, is found even in solo mbira performance, where the parts of the two hands, of the upper and lower manual keys, and of the vocal and mbira melodies are made to interlock. Given the rhythmic tension created by the simultaneous performance of multiple rhythmic and metric parts (e.g., people playing patterns in groups of two beats against groups of three), a performer must concentrate on his or her own part, but at the same time must listen carefully to the other performers. A basic musical value among the Shona, and in many African societies, is the ability to add your own distinctive part to the ensemble while making it blend with the whole. This illustrates an important conception of the individual's relation to the community.

The Shona, like many African peoples, prefer dense, rich sounds. Bottle caps or shells attached to gourd resonators and mbira soundboards create a buzzing aura around the discrete pitches which contrasts with the clear, "pure" instrumental timbres (tone qualities) preferred in the European classical tradition. The multiple layers produced in ensemble performance also add to the density of sound, as does the very nature of the mbira, on which keys previously struck continue to ring through the following pitches sounded, each key producing multiple overtones.

The Shona have a way of conceptualizing the relation between variation, contrast, and repetition that is commonly found elsewhere in the sub-Saharan region, and which might be considered basic to a more general African musical aesthetic. This conception informs their basic musical organization of a piece. The compositions played on the twenty-two-key mbira usually consist of four short segments or phrases that are repeated in sequence and together form the basic pattern or ostinato of a composition. This basic pattern is repeated over and over again, the piece being cyclical and open-ended in conception rather than having a linear and closed-form organization with a decisive beginning and end.

As a mbira performance progresses, small variations, including traditional formulas and improvised lines, are gradually added to, and over, the basic pattern. Mbira players say that a skilled musician must have patience and not rush the variations. It is not considered good playing to use overly apparent or dramatic contrasts; rather, one variation must be built on the last and subtly lead to the next within the ostinato cycle. Usually each variation will be repeated a number of times before further development is attempted. The cyclical-repetitive nature of Shona mbira music points to a distinctly African worldview and conception of time.

The very definition of what constitutes a "piece" in Shona culture, and in many sub-Saharan societies, suggests another characteristically African feature. Although mbira pieces are sometimes associated with specific composers and all have titles, the composition is conceived as an aggregate of musical resources that may be put together and improvised upon in different ways, making each performance recognizable as "the piece" and yet unique. Such resources include: the harmonic, temporal, and melodic character of the basic ostinato, or repeated pattern; a series of stock variations and motifs associated with the piece;

and certain sung melodies and lines of text. But the length of a given performance, the number of variations used and the order in which they are performed, the speed and character of development, and the improvisations on the basic patterns make each performance fundamentally distinct, so that, in a sense, a new piece is created in every performance. This approach resembles that of jazz, blues, and some rock performers, indicating one way that people working in these genres may have been influenced by the African heritage.

For the Shona, "the piece" and music itself are conceptualized as a process linked to specific people and a particular moment or context, whereas for some musical traditions in the West, music has become a reproducible sound *object* that can be, and is, isolated and abstracted as a thing in itself. Recordings and written scores perhaps facilitate thinking about music as an object that can be purchased, consumed, collected, and copyrighted. It is significant that the Shona words for the two basic parts of a mbira piece—kushaura and kutsinhira—are not nouns, referring to things, but rather are verbs ("Kushaura" means literally "to lead the piece"), underlining the notion of music as an interactive process.

AFRICA GENERAL AND AFRICA SPECIFIC

In the previous section I have tried to link certain features of Shona mbira playing with more widespread African musical characteristics, and indeed there is a tendency among North Americans and Europeans to think of Africa as one place, and African music as a single, identifiable phenomenon. Yet, the continent of Africa has over fifty countries, and linguists have identified at least 800 ethnolinguistic groups; 386 different languages have been identified in Nigeria alone. The organization of sub-Saharan Africa into modern nation-states is primarily a colonial legacy based on the way the continent was carved up by the European powers at the end of the nineteenth century. It has little to do with internal ethnic divisions within these territories or with the single linguistic groups that cross national borders. (People who speak different forms of the Manding language, for example, live in parts of Senegal, Gambia, Mali, Burkina Faso, Ivory Coast, Guinea, and Sierra Leone.) Because many musical traditions are linked to specific ethnolinguistic groups and cultures, it is often better to think about African music in these rather than in national terms.

In contrast to the stereotypic vision of small, so-called primitive tribes in Africa, it has been shown that there were various kinds of traditional indigenous political organization including: (1) complex, hierarchical, centralized states with political authority vested in the hands of hereditary rulers; and (2) more decentralized, smaller-scale societies where political power was regulated by interactions between kinship groups such as clans or lineages. Centralized kingdoms with highly developed political organization have existed in Africa from early times. As only one example, the state of Zimbabwe (the modern nation being named after this early empire) was thriving by the twelfth century. On the other hand, small egalitarian bands of hunters and gatherers such as the BaMbuti Pygmies have lived for centuries in the central African rain forest. Hunter-gatherer groups such as the Pygmies and the San (Bushmen) are in a small minority, however. The majority of traditional African societies depended on agriculture and animal husbandry for subsistence—stable agriculture being important for state formation. And just as political and economic systems differ widely between specific African societies, family and social structure is also diverse.

Ethnomusicologists have begun to find that sometimes there are important correlations between economic modes of production, social structure, and musical practices and style. Given the socioeconomic diversity among African societies, we would expect musical diversity as well. Indeed, there are important differences in the styles, processes, and functions of music making between different African societies, just as there are differences in conceptions about music, the role and status of musicians, and the types of repertory, instruments, and dances performed. Yet there are some basic similarities in musical style, practices, and aesthetics that span the sub-Saharan region, even between such diverse groups as the Shona in southeastern Africa, the BaMbuti Pygmies in the central rain forest, and the Manding-speaking peoples in the northwestern savanna region. Taken at the most general level, it is these similarities that allow us to speak of "African music" (much as the European harmonic system, among other general traits, allows us to identify mainstream "Western music"), although it is the facets that distinguish the different African musical cultures rather than the similarities that will probably appear as most significant to Africans themselves.

In the sections that follow, similarities with the major characteristics outlined for Shona mbira music will serve as a focus for the discussion of several specific African musical cultures. At the same time, differences between the musical cultures discussed will be emphasized, and these will be considered in light of the distinct ways of life and worldviews that characterize different African societies.

MUSICAL VALUES, PRACTICES, AND SOCIAL STYLE

The Pygmies

Groups of Pygmies are found in the equatorial forest area stretching from Gabon and Cameroon in the west to Uganda, Rwanda, and Burundi in the east. The Ituri Forest, bordering on Uganda to the east and

Sudan to the north, remains a major stronghold for Pygmies, and about 40,000 live in this region. The majority of groups maintain a semi-autonomous hunting-and-gathering existence. Centuries ago, the Pygmies found their central forest region invaded from the north by Bantu (a major linguistic category in sub-Saharan Africa) and Sudanic groups who were cultivators and pastoralists. The Pygmy languages were abandoned for those of the neighboring groups, with whom they entered into types of patron-client relationships. The anthropologist Colin Turnbull, however, suggests that the BaMbuti Pygmies of the Ituri Forest lead a kind of double life, maintaining their own traditional ways (with the exception of language) when alone in the forest and taking part in Bantu ritual and musical life on their visits to the villages. Here we will concentrate on Pygmy life and music in their forest home.

The BaMbuti net-hunters maintain a nomadic existence, setting up camps for a month or so in different places in the forest as they continue their search of game. Net-hunting, like most aspects of Pygmy life, is a communal affair, with male family members stringing their nets together in a large semicircle and the women and children beating the brush to scare game into them. The catch is shared. Bands are composed of nuclear families, and while certain individuals are considered to have more expertise in some realms of activity than in others, there is little specialization of social and economic roles within age and gender categories. A formalized hierarchical system of leadership is not present. Because survival is dependent on cooperation rather than competition, the keystones of Pygmy society are egalitarianism, consensus, and unity. Because of their nomadic existence, the ownership of goods and property is minimal among most Pygmy groups.

All of these aspects strongly influence their musical culture. The Pygmies have few musical instruments of their own. Pygmy instruments include whistles and end-blown flutes made from cane. They may be used to accompany singing, or in duets for informal music making. In flute duets, one instrumentalist plays a repeating ostinato pattern, while the other plays a part that interlocks and overlaps with the first, reminding us of the basic principles of Shona mbira performance. Rhythm sticks and rattles are found, as are several trumpet types such as the long, end-blown molimo trumpet. Some Pygmy bands also use a musical bow. A few other instruments, such as mbiras and drums, may occasionally be borrowed from their Bantu neighbors.

Vocal music is at the core of Pygmy musical culture. Some songs are sung by individuals informally, such as lullabies and game songs, but communal singing for collective ceremonies and occasions is much more important. Like most aspects of Pygmy life, musical performance is a nonspecialized activity. As in net-hunting, where men and women fulfill different roles, however, musical participation may be differentiated by gender, depending on the context. For example, men are the primary singers for the molimo ceremony, through which the benign relationship with the sacred—and living—forest is maintained. Women are the primary singers for the elima, a puberty ceremony. On other occasions, as before almost every hunt, men and women sing together.

Except for the ritual occasions when gender and sometimes age distinctions are made, musical performance involves anyone in the band who wants to sing. Song forms are varied but follow two basic principles that we have already encountered in the Shona mbira music and the Pygmy flute duets: the use of ostinato and and interlock. A standard organizational feature found among the BaMbuti Pygmies and in many other African societies is the use of a leader/chorus call-and-response format. The leader, or one group of people, sings a melodic phrase and is immediately answered by a second group singing another phrase so that the two interlock to create the entire melody. Pygmy vocal practice frequently uses the *hocket* technique (singers alternating short melodic fragments to create a melody), reproducing the same practice of interlocking parts. Yodeling is also frequently practiced by some Pygmy groups and is often considered a hallmark of their vocal style.

In its simplest form, the call (C) and response (R) phrases are simply repeated continually, creating a cyclical ostinato pattern like that described for Shona mbira music. Some songs among the BaMbuti have a more complex structure, such as ||:C1/R C1/R C2/R C2/R:||. People within a Mbuti chorus help to create a dense, layered sound by simultaneously singing a number of individual variations of the basic melodic parts. Among the Aka Pygmies of the Central African Republic, ostinatos without call-and-response organization constitute a basic structure. On top of the basic ostinato singers may add a second complementary ostinato, and others will perform variations on both melodies, thereby creating a dense, overlapping contrapuntal texture (a texture produced by simultaneous melodic lines). The time span of the basic ostinato serves as the reference point for various clapped and percussion parts. Thus, one percussion part may be a six-beat pattern and another may last eight beats, dividing the overall time span of the song, say of twenty-four beats, into different-length cycles.

Certain individuals may begin or lead a song, just as different individuals are considered to have particular expertise in other realms of life. Once a performance is in motion, however, musical roles and leadership may shift, different voices may move in and out of the background. Hence, Pygmy musical style and practice grows out of, and reflects, the specific egalitarian nature of Pygmy social and economic life just as certain features (e.g., ostinatos, density, and interlock) are consistent with African musical practice in other societies.

As in Shona culture, Pygmy musical performances often involve communication with the spiritual world. What differs is the conception of the divine and humans' relations with it. According to Colin Turnbull, the Pygmies recognize that they cannot see, truly comprehend, or give a single name to God. But since they view the forest as the benevolent provider of their lives and livelihood, they associate divinity with the forest, itself living and divine. They believe that the world and the forest are basically good, and if misfortunes—such as a bad hunting period, sickness, or death—come, it is because the forest is sleeping. Their response is to wake it by singing to it every night during a ceremony known as the molimo, which may last several months. The long, tubular, end-blown trumpet known as molimo is used to create the sounds of the forest and answer the men's singing, thereby realizing, through ritual, the relationship the Pygmies feel with their natural surroundings and the divine.

Unlike the Shona, who use elaborate and varied sung poetry in performances for the ancestors, communicating with the divine occurs among the Pygmies primarily through musical sound alone; song texts are kept to a minimum, even to a single line such as "The forest is good." Since the Pygmy conception of the divine cannot be formulated with words, it may be that music, whose existence and meaning are likewise both concrete and diffuse, provides a more direct mode of relating to and representing God. Nonetheless, it is interesting that the Pygmies emphasize singing much more than instrumental music and yet grant so little attention to sung poetry and the power of the word. In this and other important respects these people of the forest are the polar opposites of the Manding-speakers on the savanna in West Africa.

The Manding of West Africa

Manding speakers represent one of the most important ethnolinguistic groups in sub-Saharan Africa. A number of Manding subgroups, including the Mandinka of Senegal and Gambia, the Maninka of Guinea and Mali, the Bamana (or Bambara) of Mali, and the Dyula of the Ivory Coast all claim a common descent from the thirteenth-century Mali empire. Connected historically to the Mali state, Manding societies are still characterized by an elaborate, formal social hierarchy as well as by occupational specialization. An individual's social status and occupation are defined according to family heritage, family history thus being very important to the Manding. People of royal ancestry and commoners fall into the sula, or nonspecialist, category and are employed as merchants or farmers or in a variety of urban-based jobs. Alongside the sula are the nyamalo, or craft specialists, including metalsmiths, woodworkers, leatherworkers, and the jali, who has perhaps the most important musical role in Manding society. The jali traditionally functioned as an oral historian, musician, singer-bard, and praise singer, and the occupation demands a high degree of specialization in all of these areas.

People in the nyamalo category have traditionally been considered to be of lower status than the sula within the strict social hierarchy. In particular, an attitude of disdain toward the jali, who earns his livelihood by performing for higher-class patrons, has been widely reported from the seventeenth century to the present. But the status of the jali is ambiguous: he is looked down upon while simultaneously considered to be an important and valued member of the society. The reasons for this ambivalent social position are connected, as we shall see.

In Manding society, *words* are considered to be very powerful, as is knowledge about someone's lineage and about history itself, since one's current social status is traditionally based on that of one's ancestors. The jali frequently works as a praise singer recounting the good deeds of a patron as well as the glories of his forefathers. This enhances both the patron's social (and sometimes political) status and his latent spiritual force (nyama). Roderic Knight has observed that "When the jali sings the name of a past hero, he views what he is doing as waking him up, bringing him back to life." The jali's specialized knowledge about genealogies also makes him an important mediator in questions of succession and inheritance, thereby enhancing his own social importance. But the jali can and does turn the power of the word from praise to damaging insult if not paid adequately. His knowledge and verbal skills can be used for or against given individuals, and he is therefore someone to be both valued and simultaneously feared and despised.

If we think about the ambiguous status of musicians in our own and in many other societies ("I enjoy their music but I wouldn't want my daughter to marry one"), the social position of the jali is perhaps not that hard to fathom. But it clearly differs radically from conceptions about music and musicians within Pygmy society, where everyone is a nonspecialist, nonprofessional musician and there is certainly no negative stigma attached to music making. In contrast, the jali is a hereditary specialist working as a professional musician and verbal artist, and his status position derives from hierarchical rather than egalitarian social relations. Another distinction between these two societies regards the power of the word and the importance of song texts. But certain features of Manding musical style are consistent with the general traits discussed for the Pygmies and the Shona.

The main instruments played by the Manding jali to accompany singing are the balo (a xylophone), the kora (a harp lute), and the kontingo (a five-stringed plucked lute with a skin head like the banjo); musicians specialize on one instrument. The kora is unique to the Manding. It has twenty-one strings, with a range just over three octaves. A skin is stretched over the gourd sound box, and strings come off the neck in two parallel rows perpendicular to the skin face (Figure 7–3). The tuning is such that the scale series alternates for the most part between the two rows and the two hands (right hand—*do*, left hand—*re*, r.h.,—

Figure 7–3. Manding Kora. Photo: Thomas Turino.

mi, l.h.,—*fa*, etc.). The basic playing technique for the kora often involves the plucking of alternate notes by the right and left hands so that the melody results from the interlocking of these two, similar in principle to mbira playing and the principle of interlocking parts in general. Another striking similarity between the kora and the Shona mbira is the attachment of a metal plate with jangles to the bridge of the kora. This produces the dense, buzzing timbral effect favored in so many sub-Saharan societies.

Manding music performed on the kora consists of several components. Each piece has a basic vocal melody known as donkilo and a second kind of improvised, declamatory singing style called sataro. Sataro receives major emphasis in jali performance, as does text improvisation and the insertion of formulaic poetry appropriate to a given context. It was traditionally through the manipulation of sung poetry for a given occasion that the jali earned his living—praising a patron, telling a story, or recounting history. The use of songs to fulfill these social functions is widespread throughout West Africa and in other parts of the sub-Saharan region. The primary emphasis on song texts among the Manding is another feature common to many African musical cultures, the Pygmies and the Kalahari San being notable exceptions.

The jali accompanies his singing with the kumbengo part—a short ostinato, the most basic organizing feature of a performance—played on the kora. The kumbengo is played for long periods, during which subtle variations are gradually introduced, as in Shona mbira playing. Improvised instrumental interludes known as birimintingo are inserted between the long ostinato sections. Frequently, the birimintingo sections provide a greater degree of musical contrast than would be found in a typical Shona mbira performance or Pygmy song. Nonetheless, the conception of what constitutes a "piece"—that is, a series of stock resources that are uniquely arranged and improvised upon according to the needs of a given performer and occasion—are extremely similar between the Manding and the Shona. This conception of music as process rather than product seems widespread in many African societies.

The Ewe of Ghana

North Americans often have the general impression that African music primarily consists of drumming. As we have seen, vocal music, strings, and other types of melodic instruments such as the mbira and marimba may in fact have equally, or more, prominent positions in certain musical cultures. However, one of the most famous sub-Saharan regions for drumming is the West African coast, and among the Anlo-Ewe of Togo and the southeastern coast of Ghana dance drumming is the most important type of musical activity.

The Anlo-Ewe, who remain musically and socially distinct from other Ewe groups farther north and inland, work primarily as farmers and fishermen. Southern Eweland is divided into autonomous political districts, with the Anlo district having the largest population and cultural influence. The district, which traditionally functioned like an independent state, was ruled by a paramount chief with largely ceremonial and sacred status, although he had the important role of mediating disputes. The chief stands at the pinnacle of a political hierarchy over geographically organized territorial and town chiefs and finally over clan, lineage, and *ward* (village subdivision) leaders. The clans and lineages (tracing descent to a common male ancestor) and wards thus form an important basis of the social system. *Age sets*, groups of people of similar age who identify with each other on this basis, are another important feature of social organization. As we shall see, social organization is often a key to understanding basic aspects of a musical culture, because the formation of ensembles, the definition of genres, and even the organization of musical events are frequently shaped by local conceptions of social hierarchy as well as according to the groups (e.g., gender, age, lineage) that people use to define their social identity.

Among the Anlo-Ewe, voluntary dance clubs, organized by individual villages, wards, or age groups, are the primary institutions through which the all-important dance-drumming traditions are performed. As villagers migrate to the cities, new dance clubs are often created on the basis of hometown identity, and these clubs may serve as the basis for social networks and support systems in the urban environment. According to David Locke, an ethnomusicologist and performer of Ewe music, the organization of some dance clubs traditionally reflected the political structure of the ward and lineage, although European influences have also by now been incorporated.

The dance-drumming clubs are generally led by a committee of men and women consisting of a chairman, a secretary, and the leaders of different subgroups within the institution (i.e., dance leaders, and leaders of the drummers and the singers). Club organization, then, may be seen as resembling the broader Ewe political hierarchy, which involves a paramount chief who presides over the leaders at the more specific levels of social organization (territorial, village, clan, etc.). Living in a hierarchical society ourselves, this might appear as a normal way to organize things, and yet we must remember that to the egalitarian Pygmies such a modus operandi might seem very strange. Besides the officers already mentioned, another key figure in the club is the composer, who is responsible for creating the distinctive music and song texts which serve as identity emblems for his institution.

Unlike in a Pygmy band, where some kind of music is likely to be performed almost daily, musical performance is less frequent among the Ewe. Occasions for club performance include the welcoming of government officials, the promotion of a political party, the formal presentation of a new club, or occasions for recreation. One of the primary functions of the clubs is to support its members during crises, and especially upon the death of a family member. Like the Shona, the Anlo-Ewe place great religious importance on the ancestors and the spirits of the dead, who are believed to intervene in the lives of the living. The Ewe thus place major emphasis on providing honorable funerals for the new spirits, and it is considered extremely prestigious to have a dance club perform at such events (Figure 7–4).

In terms of musical specialization and professionalism, we might think of the Ewe dance clubs as midway on a spectrum between the highly trained, specialized, and professional jali and the nonspecialist, nonprofessional Pygmy musician. For example, rehearsing is an important part of an Ewe club's activities, and learning to perform the dance and music is relatively rigorous, whereas among the Pygmies learning to sing, like learning to talk, is a normal part of socialization. While the jali is a full-time musical professional, most members of the Ewe dance clubs can be thought of as semiprofessional at best. That is, except when fulfilling personal obligations of club members—such as performing for a funeral, or for recreation—the organizations expect payment for their musical presentations, but the members usually only derive a small portion of their income in this way.

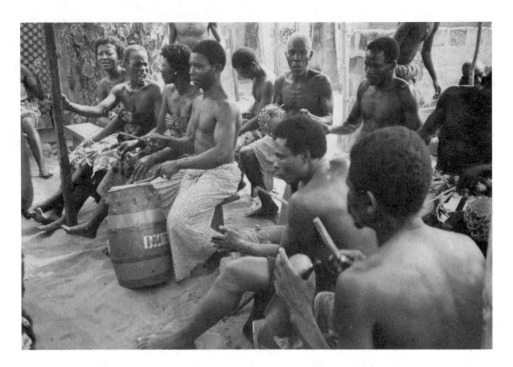

Figure 7–4.   Ewe Drum Ensemble: Gideon Foli Alorwoyie, lead drummer
for the Yewe Cult, funeral music. Photo: Art Davis.

As Alfred and Kobla Ladzekpo have suggested, the drumming,
dancing, singing, and hand clapping in an Ewe performance must be
thought of as a unified whole. If any individual part is changed the
perception of the whole changes, because each part is heard as relative
to and dependent on the others, in a mbira performance. This characteristic, common to many African musical traditions, is a result of
the practice of interlocking multiple parts.

Among the Anlo-Ewe there are a number of different dances.
Depending on the specific dance tradition performed, each club uses
various types of music. For example, clubs involved in the takada tradition have different genres for processions, for more leisurely types of
dancing, and for the vigorous styles of dancing that are accompanied
by the full drum ensemble. The specific instruments used also depend
on the dance traditions performed by a given club, although certain
instruments are widespread (Figure 7–5).

Typically, Ewe drum ensembles include a double-bell (gankogui),
which often plays a repeated ostinato within a twelve-pulse cycle, serving

as the organizational point of reference for the rest of the instrumental parts. A gourd shaker (axatse) performs a similar role. In addition, a series of four or more different sized barrel-shaped drums (made of wooden staves and hoops, ranging from 55 cm. to 124 cm. in length) are used for a variety of functions. The large drums (e.g., atsimevu, gboba) are used by the lead drummers to create the music from a repertory of established and improvised patterns. The middle-sized drums (sogo and kidi) serve the function of a chorus, playing a more limited variety of patterns in call-and-response fashion with the lead drummer; and they interlock their patterns with other percussion parts. In the takada tradition, the smallest drum (kaganu) plays a single repeated ostinato which, in combination with the bell and rattles, creates the ground of the overall rhythmic organization that consists of the combination of the different parts.

Within these ensembles we thus find musical principles and aesthetic values that have already been discussed for other African societies: call-and-response, interlock, ostinato organization, improvised

Figure 7–5. Ewe dondon drum player, member of the Brekete Cult. Photo: Art Davis.

variation based on stock formulaic patterns, and density in the resulting sound of the entire ensemble. The drum ensemble accompanies both the dancing and the singing, and it is the songs themselves that are considered particularly important to Ewe participants for expressing the distinctive identity of the club. As elsewhere in Africa, the dance steps performed can be considered integral to the polyrhythmic fabric of the total performance.

The Buganda Kingdom

In order to help us get our feet on the ground regarding basic African musical features, contexts, practices, and ideas, the descriptions of the musical cultures thus far have emphasized traditional features almost as if they were frozen in time. But of course culture and musical practices are never static, especially in an era of social upheavals caused by colonialism, nation building in the postcolonial period, and Africa's increased participation in international capitalist relations over the last century.

As briefly mentioned for the Ewe dance clubs, rural-to-urban migration has led to new musical styles, contexts of performance, and meaning for musical traditions in cities throughout Africa. It might also have been mentioned, for example, that beyond their traditional functions, Shona spirit mediums played an important part as popular leaders and legitimate figures of local authority during the Zimbabwean revolution. As we shall see, Shona musicians likewise used song as a tool in the struggle for Black independence in Zimbabwe. Among the Manding, colonial rule meant a limiting of wealth among the local nobility. This, in turn, signaled a change in the patronage system affecting jali performance practices and styles. Many jali now focus more on instrumental virtuosity and an entertainment function than on their traditional roles as verbal artists, historians, and political mediators. There are many more such examples, but nowhere are the changes in a musical culture resulting from recent sociopolitical events more dramatically illustrated than in the case of the royal music of the Buganda court in what is now Uganda.

Buganda is the name of the country or state that was formerly the most powerful independent kingdom in the Lake Victoria region in East Africa; Baganda is the term for its Bantu-speaking people. The kingdom was particularly well-off economically because of ecological conditions favorable to agriculture and particularly to the raising of bananas, the staple crop. Unlike many African kingdoms, the Ganda king, or kabaka, did not have "divine" or sacred status. His notably strong, centralized power was supported by a system in which the king directly appointed and could remove subordinate chiefs, and by his ultimate control over many estates. (This contrasts with other African kingdoms, where middle-level chiefs could appoint their own subordinates, thereby creating an independent power base.) While individual citizens belonged to clans and other social groups, primary allegiance was to the state and to the kabaka himself.

The kabaka's court was a major center for musical activity. The kabaka supported a number of different ensembles, and the musicians lived as retainers on land granted by the king. One important court ensemble consisted of at least five side-blown trumpets made of bottle-shaped gourds. The different gourd-trumpets each produced different pitches necessary to complete a melody and were thus played strictly in interlocking fashion. Like most of the Buganda instruments, the trumpets were associated with a specific clan. Another court ensemble, of less prestige than the trumpets, consisted of five or six end-notched flutes accompanied by four drums. Specific to the court was the akadinda, a large twenty-two key xylophone on which the keys were freely set on two supporting logs running perpendicular to the keys. A single akadinda was played by six different musicians, three sitting on each side of the instrument. The most important royal ensemble of all was the entenga; this consisted primarily of twelve drums carefully graded in size and tuned to the local pentatonic (five-tone) scale, thus actually serving as melodic instruments. These were played by four musicians; they were accompanied by three other drums played by two drummers. The performance of the entenga was strictly limited to the royal enclosure. The repertory of the entenga and akadinda ensembles were closely related to, and derived from the vocal music accompanied by an eight-string Ganda bow-harp known as ennanga. Thus, although the court ensembles usually did not include vocal performance, it is typical of many African musical cultures that their music had been modeled on a vocal tradition.

The same principles of interlocking parts and ostinato organization that have been described for the Shona, Ewe, Pygmies, and Manding are also basic to entenga and akadinda performance. Each piece contains two distinct melodic-rhythmic parts known as okunaga (meaning "to start") and okwawula ("to divide"), each of which is composed of two or more phrases. On the akadinda xylophone, the three players for one of the parts sit across the keys facing the three musicians who play the other. The pitches of the starter and divider parts literally alternate, thereby reproducing the basic hocket or interlocking technique between the players on opposite sides of the keys. The parts themselves involve ostinato patterns. A third part comprising only two pitches, called the okukoonera (or "binder") emphasizes composite patterns formed by the interaction of the okunaga and okwawula. The okukoonera helps the players orient themselves within the dense ensemble texture.

The political importance of the royal drums and the demise of an African court tradition in the postcolonial period is dramatically illustrated by the story of the Buganda kingdom. During the colonial period, African kingdoms were often left in place within the European colonies, since the native political systems could be used to rule African populations indirectly. Under an agreement with the British colonizers, the kabaka of Buganda was officially recognized in 1900 as the ruler of his semiautonomous state, with the provision that he obey the British Governor of the Uganda Protectorate.

After independence, many new African states had to deal with the threat to national unity and state sovereignty that independent kingdoms within their boundaries might pose. While such problems have been handled variously in different African countries, in Uganda violent means were used to suppress the powerful Beganda king. Only a few years after gaining independence in 1962, troops under Uganda's first leader, Apollo Milton Obote, stormed the kabaka's palace and sent him into exile in an effort to stamp out the independent kingdom.

It was no accident that the royal drums were among the things destroyed in the attack on the palace. Traditionally, the drums were such central symbols of the kabakaship that potential heirs to the throne were known as the "Princes of the Drum." In *Desecration of My Kingdom* (London: Constable, 1967), a book written in exile by the last kabaka, he says that

> Among the sad news of who is dead, who is in prison and what is destroyed comes the confirmation that the Royal Drums are burnt. I saw this work begun and feared that it must have been completed. These drums, of which there are more than fifty, are the heart of Buganda, some of them hundreds of years old, as old as the Kabakaship. To touch them was a terrible offense, to look after them a great honour. A Prince is not a Prince of the Blood but a Prince of the Drum and his status is determined by which Drum. They all had separate names and significance and can never be replaced.[1]

With the destruction of the former political system and way of life in the name of nationalism came the demise of musical traditions that were central symbols of that kingdom. Although often less dramatic in nature, transformations of African musical cultures have taken place, and are still occurring, throughout the sub-Saharan region under the pressures of nationalism, urbanization, and influences from the West.

A SAMPLING OF INSTRUMENTS

Judging from the few musical cultures already touched on, we can see that African musical performance includes all the major instrument types (percussion instruments, skin-headed drums, winds, and strings), and

[1]Mutesa II, King of Buganda, 1967, *Desecration of My Kingdom: The Kabaka of Buganda.* London: Constable, 193.

the importance of given instruments may vary from one society to another. Vocal music, however, seems to be emphasized by a great majority of African societies, with the sung poetry often considered as important as the musical accompaniment if not more so.

We have also seen that aspects of the social and economic organization influence the number and types of instruments used within a given society. For example, the Pygmies and the San of the Kalahari Desert have relatively few permanent instruments and a minimal material culture generally, because of their nomadic way of life. In societies where the royal court was an important site for musical performance, the number, size, and elaborateness of instruments may be greater because of both available wealth and a more stable environment for performance. This was the case for the large Ganda drum-chime (entenga) and xylophone (akadinda) ensembles as well as for court traditions of other East and West African kingdoms.

The tremendous variety of specific African musical instruments, either played solo or combined in various types of ensembles, makes even a partial list difficult. Here it may be useful to highlight some of the most important instrument types as well as some that are less well known.

Percussion Instruments

Classified as percussion instruments, the mbira or lamellaphone (also called kisaanj, likembe, and by many other names depending on the region) and the xylophone are two of the most widespread and important instrument types in the sub-Saharan region. Although it has diffused to the Americas, the mbira is an instrument uniquely of African origin. Rattles, bells, cymbals, rhythm sticks, stamping tubes (hollow tubes with an open end made to sound when struck against the ground), and scrapers are also among the most common instruments found. For each of these general types, however, there are many different varieties, each with a specific local name. For example, there are rattles with the seeds inside the gourd (the Shona hosho) and those on which beads are sewn into a net stretched around the outside of the gourd (the Ewe axatse, and the sekere of the Yoruba of Nigeria). New materials are becoming increasingly important for the construction of percussion instruments. Hence, while scrapers are often traditionally made from notched bamboo or gourds, Fanta soda bottles are now frequently used for scrapers as well as to play bell parts, just as tin cans filled with seeds or stones make wonderful rattles.

Although percussion instruments such as bells, scrapers, and rattles primarily serve rhythmic functions, the aspects of pitch and timbre are important considerations in their construction and incorporation into a given ensemble. The parameters of pitch and timbre allow the given percussion instrument to contrast with and complement the other instruments used. For instance, the clear, high-pitched, metallic bell in Ewe ensembles contrasts in both pitch and tone quality with the drums, and the hosho both provides a timbral contrast and serves to augment the density in a mbira performance.

Drums and "Drum Languages"

The variety of African drums and their social importance in many societies is striking. In Ghana, for example, the relative status of Akan chiefs of different communities and regions is indicated by the size of their atumpan drums; a subordinate chief cannot have drums larger than his superior's. Among the many Yoruba kingdoms of Nigeria, each court was said to have its own dance rhythms provided by a special set of royal drums. The very power of the drum music, and the styles played, were supposed to express the elevated nature of the aristocracy. But also among the Yoruba, some of the most important orisas (deities) have specific types of drums and repertories associated with them. Drumming is used to call the gods into their mediums during Yoruba spirit-possession ceremonies, much as was described for Shona ceremonies. Thus, in these societies, drums are tied to both political and spiritual sources of power.

African drums are usually carved from a single wooden log (e.g., the Ganda entenga, Yoruba dundun and igbin, and Akan atumpan) but may also be constructed with wooden staves and hoops, as described among the Ewe. Drums are also made from ceramics, gourds, and even tin cans and oil drums. Both double- and single-headed types are found in hourglass, conical, cylindrical, and bowl shapes, among others. Metal jangles, shells, or seeds are attached to drums among West African groups such as the Hausa, Dagbamba, Yoruba, and Akan peoples to create the same type of buzzing effect described for the kora and mbira.

The attention paid to the pitch of drums is notable in many African societies, and it may involve the combination of different-sized, fixed-pitch drums in ensemble. Some drums, like the Yoruba dundun and the lunga of the Ghanaian Dagbamba, however, are used to produce multiple pitches. These are hourglass-shaped tension drums; the different pitches are produced by squeezing the lacing that connects the two drum heads under one arm while the other hand beats it with a curved stick.

The importance of pitched drums goes beyond merely creating timbral contrasts; as we have seen, it is sometimes extended to making tuned drums serve as melodic instruments (e.g., the entenga). More interesting still, pitched drums are used in many African societies to "talk" or communicate over long distances using actual drum languages.

Many languages in the Niger-Congo family, including the Bantu languages, are tonal; that is, the meaning of a word depends on the relative pitches applied to given syllables. Drums, lamellaphones, and even instruments such as the guitar are used by the Yoruba of Nigeria to articulate verbal formulas—for example, proverbs or praise names—by imitating the tonal patterns of the words. Longer messages can be played by drumming the tonal contour of different well-known stereotypic verbal formulas. Since many words may share the same number of syllables and tonal contours, the meaning of a given "word" (drummed tonal pattern) can be clarified by following it with a formula of its own (e.g., "cat" might become "cat walks quietly at night"), the tonal patterns of the whole phrase being easier to recognize. The social and "linguistic" contexts are crucial to interpretation. The Akan atumpan, a set of two large tuned drums, are used as speech surrogates, as are the Dagbamba lunga, the Yoruba dundun, and wooden slit drums and paired skin-headed drums in the Congo region, among other examples.

Wind Instruments

In some societies, wind instruments, especially horns, are also used for signaling. Trumpets, made from metal or animal horns and often side-blown, are particularly prevalent throughout the sub-Saharan region, and are frequently played in interlocking fashion, as was described for the Baganda. Side-blown and vertical flutes are widespread African wind instruments. It is perhaps less well known that panpipes are also found in different parts of Africa, as among the Venda of southern Africa, the Soga of Uganda, the Yombe of Zaire, and the Shona. Ranging from a single tube closed at one end and blown like a bottle to instruments with multiple tubes and pitches, panpipes are usually played collectively in interlocking fashion, the tones of the scale being divided among the various instruments of the ensemble so that each performer inserts the pitches that he or she has with those of others to create a complete melody. Although not as common as African flutes and trumpets, the panpipes are worth noting because they were brought to the United States from Africa, and even in recent years the quills (as they came to be called) were still played by rural southern African-Americans.

Stringed Instruments

The quills were not the only instrument brought by Africans to North America. In fact, while we usually think of the banjo as the most American of instruments, it too was brought by slaves during the colonial period. The banjo was modeled on West African lutes, which are known by various names depending on the linguistic group and region (e.g., tidinit in Mauritania, xalam among the Wolof in the Senegambia area, kontingo among the Manding). The sound box is made from a gourd or a carved wooden back with a stretched skin for the face. A neck is attached, and these instruments have between two and five strings depending on the region.

A wide variety of harps exist in different African societies. The kora, which we have already discussed, combines features of the lute and the harp, and harp-lutes with both straight and curved necks are found all over the sub-Saharan region. Single- or multiple-string fiddles made with round sound boxes and skin faces are also important in West Africa (e.g., the goge of the Hausa people of Nigeria) as well as in central and eastern Africa.

The oldest and one of the most widespread stringed instruments of Africa, dating by some estimates to 15,000 years ago, is the musical bow. Like the bows used to shoot arrows, it consists of a single string attached to each end of a curved stick. Depending on the tradition, either a gourd attached to the stick or the mouth cavity of the player serves as a resonator. The string is either plucked or, alternatively, struck with another stick; it is stopped with a hard implement to raise the pitch. The playing technique results in a percussive and yet beautiful and delicate sound.

Contrasting with the longevity of the bow, one of the newest and equally widespread stringed instruments is the electric guitar. It has become a major instrument within the new urban styles that have emerged all over Africa and are now becoming popular all over the world.

URBAN-POPULAR MUSICAL TRADITIONS

Many African urban-popular musical styles that have emerged in the last sixty years may be seen as creative responses to the changing social identities and worldviews of Africans as their societies become transformed by European imperialism, nationalism, urbanization, and international economic relations. Like everyone else within a society, musicians have to make sense of changing situations, but unlike other people, they use musical style to reflect and shape new realities.

A large number of vibrant urban-popular musical traditions have sprung up all over Africa, each fusing local styles with Western musical resources. The local input makes the sound of each of these traditions unique, whereas Western elements—brass band instruments, electric guitars, accordions, basic European harmonic resources (e.g., I, IV, and V chords) North and Latin American rhythms—function as a common denominator that unites them. As we saw in the Buganda example, social and political changes have led to the disappearance of some precolonial musical traditions. Frequently, these have been superseded by newer urban-popular forms. While the creativity of urban-popular musicians and the music itself are to be celebrated and enjoyed, the process of westernization itself is not innocent but accompanies political and economic domination and images of the superiority of the dominant societies and classes. In considering the growing uniformity of urban-popular music—as compared to the more locally diverse musical traditions of former times—we must also consider the impact of the transnational recording industry itself, which not only responds to, but also shapes local taste and trends.

Attached to the institutions of military conquest and ideological domination, Africans first became widely affected by European music through the presence of brass bands and the activities of Christian missionaries. Particularly in the British colonies, Africans were trained in military band music. In East Africa, local dance-drama traditions such as beni were centered around band performance. Beni performers also imitated military uniforms and styles of movement in their costuming and choreography as an, at least partially, satiric response to colonial rule. In the drive for conversion, missionaries taught religious songs translated into local languages and set to diatonic melodies (i.e., melodies based on the standard *do-re-mi* scale) and harmonies with basic Western chords (I, IV, and V). Hymn-based music can now be heard all over Africa, and it is certainly an element in the style of the famous vocal ensemble Ladysmith Black Mambazo, as it is among the other urban vocal groups composed of Zulu, Xhosa, Swazi, and other migrants in South Africa.

West Africa

In West Africa, dance-band highlife music originated on the Ghanaian coast, where the training of local African musicians in the brass-band idiom had begun as early as the eighteenth century, and where port life had introduced the locals to many international musical styles. By the 1920s, big bands using brass instruments and playing European popular dance genres like the waltz and fox-trot began performing at upper-crust social affairs for the westernized African elites and Europeans. During this period local Akan melodies began to creep into the highlife repertory, thereby Africanizing what was more or less a Western musical style in terms of rhythm and orchestration.

But it was not until after World War II that the fusion of Western and African elements became more integral in big-band highlife. According to David Coplan, E. T. Mensah, the "King of Highlife," was the first to orchestrate both traditional themes and indigenous rhythms for dance band in conjunction with the use of North and Latin American genres such as swing, the samba, the Cuban son and calypso. By this time the electric guitar had been incorporated, and Mensah's group used that instrument as well as trumpet, trombone, saxophone, string bass, and a Cuban-style percussion section. While these groups were playing for higher-class patrons, a parallel development of "guitar-band" highlife grew up among the lower classes in urban centers. This style fused the techniques and repertories of local Ghanaian instrumental traditions with those of the guitar and songs learned from sailors. The music of West Indian sailors, whose rhythms were originally based in African lamellaphone and string techniques, came full circle and began to influence West African highlife.

"Palm-wine" music, played on acoustic guitar and accompanied by various percussion instruments, spread throughout British West Africa. In Lagos, Nigeria, palm-wine and other syncretic urban working-class styles served as a basis for juju music. Now associated with the names Ebenezer Obey and King Sunny Ade, juju has become one of the internationally best-known "African-pop" styles. Christopher Waterman suggests that after World War II, the use of amplification influenced juju's evolution to include both more modern and increasingly traditional African features simultaneously. With the use of electric guitars and amplified vocals, it became possible to reintroduce larger and more complexly organized percussion sections using the Yoruba sekere (rattle) and the hourglass-shaped "talking drum," among other instruments. The pedal steel guitar has also been added to juju instrumentation, an element that might be traced back to the popularizing of North American country and Hawaiian music on 78-RPM records in earlier decades. The highly polished "studio" sound of contemporary juju bands is also aided by the use of synthesizers. Juju groups combine the traditional functions of praise singing and social-dance drumming, and perform both at urban bars and neotraditional Yoruba ceremonies (naming ceremonies, weddings, funerals). Although Western harmonies are used, juju music is organized around a series of interlocking ostinato parts payed by the guitars and drummers and leader-chorus call-and-response singing.

Congo-Zaire

Within the sub-Saharan region, there is no doubt that the urban-popular guitar music of the Congo-Zaire region has had a more profound impact than any other single African style. Leading exponents of the style include Franco et l'Orchestre O.K. Jazz and Docteur Nico, among others. Local likembe (mbira) dance music (accompanied by struck bottles and a drum) and Afro-Cuban music served as the foundations of the Zaire-Congo style. By the mid-1950s, the likembe had been replaced by acoustic guitar, and by the late 1950s Caribbean music became a primary model, with electric guitars as well as saxophones, trumpets, clarinets, and flutes sometimes being used. Different international "dance crazes" involving Afro-Cuban music were fueled throughout the Americas, Europe, and Africa by the recording industry. For some reason, the Afro-Cuban son and the distinctive Cuban "clave" pattern (see Chapter 9) took hold in the Congo region.

At first, groups copied the Cuban recordings to the extent that some even imitated the original Spanish texts. But as time went on, the Congolese groups began to develop their own distinctive sound as well as incorporate new foreign influences such as riffs from North American soul music. Less rhythmically complex than juju, the Congo style is organized around one or more guitar ostinatos, which serve to accompany the high, sweet singing style of performers like Franco. A performance usually includes long improvised guitar solos as well as the sparse, orchestrated entrances of the horn section over a danceable rhythm in duple meter. Perhaps inspired by the Congolese sound, the use of Cuban-style rhythms and rhythm sections can be heard in East and West Africa as well as in the modern music of Mali where, as in the style of the Super-Rail Band, such elements are fused with electric-guitar ostinatos and solos that are clearly based on kora music.

South Africa

The urban-popular music of South Africa—a particularly early European settlement—differs in various ways from the styles created in other countries. The traditional music of the Nguni (Zulu-, Swazi-, Sotho-, Xhosa-speaking) peoples of the region is itself stylistically distinct from the music of other African areas. For example, in contrast to all the African musical styles that we have discussed so far, Nguni music is a prediminantly choral-vocal style using slower tempos and lacking the polyrhythmic percussion accompaniments found in, say, West Africa. The music taught by Christian missionaries, also a choral tradition, had a particularly strong impact in South Africa, as did North American urban-popular musical traditions.

Various related syncretic choral styles were created using these sources in the context of the dismal living conditions of rural African migrant workers, who were forced by harsh circumstances to seek employment in the mines and cities. Within the workers' compounds, vocal-dance groups formed and participated in competitions, which became a primary social outlet. Styles such as mbube, bombing, and isicathamiya blended the harmonies taught by missionaries with the slow Zulu choral style characterized by multiple overlapping ostinatos. The music of Ladysmith Black Mambazo and the earlier hit popularized internationally by Pete Seeger, "Mbube" ("Lion," or "The Lion Sleeps Tonight") are examples that come out of this line of development.

In addition to the vocal traditions, urban-Black South African music was also highly influenced by African-American instrumental traditions, including the music of minstrel shows, ragtime, jazz, and more recently rock. Black jazz and rock groups flourish in the cities, as do artists who play locally created variants blending indigenous and international styles. Some modern urban Zulu artists such as Aaron Mbambo, the Rainbows, and Shoba blend electric guitars, bass, and trap drums with accordians, violins, and pennywhistles for a relatively simple, driving dance beat in 4/4 time. At present, both traditionally based and modern-syncretic songs are heard at protest and funeral marches in strife-torn South Africa. While music explicitly opposing the apartheid system has been recorded and diffused by South African artists, largely outside the country, the white-dominated recording industry and mass media in South Africa have censored such forms of expression. Apolitical popular music is pushed by the media, as is the maintenance of distinct lines of musical-ethnic heritage so as to hinder the unification of Black resistance.

Zimbabwe

The role of modern-syncretic and traditional music in Zimbabwe's struggle for Black liberation provides a happier picture. In what was formerly known as Rhodesia, African peoples such as the Shona were defeated in a revolt against the Europeans at the end of the 1800s. John Kaemmer suggests that with their defeat the Shona belief in the ultimate power of their ancestral and tribal spirits was weakened and they began to adopt European religion and culture as a means of upward mobility within the new power structure. Consequently, the importance of mbira music diminished.

As elsewhere in Africa, it was the members of the African elite that particularly stressed European music and cultural style in their effort to associate themselves with the white rulers. In 1965 Rhodesia gained independence from England, but the country was still controlled by the white local elite. Frustrated by lack of access to power, the black elite within Rhodesia spearheaded a revolution that led to majority rule of the country (renamed Zimbabwe) in 1980. During the revolution against white rule, there was a revival of interest in Shona ethnicity, religion, and music. Spirit mediums took on political importance as indigenous sources of authority, and young men once again began to take up the mbira instead of the guitar, which had gained popularity during colonial rule.

In addition, revolutionary songs known as chimurenga (struggle) songs were created and sung by urban-popular musicians and in the guerrilla camps. The chimurenga songs were also used to express the goals of the revolution and politicize the peasant population. One of the main originators of chimurenga music, and probably the most important Shona urban-popular artist from that time to present, is Thomas Mapfumo.

Mapfumo began his professional career in the 1960s playing cover versions of English and American rock and soul music. But in the mid-1960s, Mapfumo began to compose songs in the Shona language, and in the 1970s he produced a string of recorded chimurenga hits with various bands. In spite of government oppression, Mapfumo's music was diffused through records, and chimurenga songs were also broadcast on the "Voice of Zimbabwe" program over Radio Mozambique. Telling of the suffering in the countryside and calling on the people to fight, Mapfumo's songs served as an inspiration and a rallying point for the revolution. With his most recent band, Blacks Unlimited, Mapfumo's music is a wonderful example of the blending of traditional African and Western-popular musical sources. The group uses electric instruments and a trap-drum set with the sparse entrance of horns on some pieces. Traditional mbira music is used as the basis for many of his pieces, with an electric guitar playing the ostinato that would be on the higher mbira keys and the electric bass playing the part of the lower keys. In recent recordings, according to Mapfumo, a keyboard player plays the kutsinhira (second accompanying) mbira part while the guitar and bass perform the kushaura together. The drummer plays a rhythm on the highhat that sounds like the traditional hosho (Shona rattle) used to accompany the mbira, and Shona hand-clapping patterns are also added. Mapfumo sings in various traditional Shona styles (including the high, yodeling style and a speaking or chantlike style) over a hard-driving, rhythmic, dance-music base. In a 1989 tour of the United States, an mbira player had been added for live performances.

While Shona people who have migrated to the cities still play mbira and hosho at spirit-possession ceremonies, Mapfumo's music, like that of urban-popular musicians all over Africa, illustrates the creativity and adaptability of African musical resources in the context of ever-changing social conditions and human needs. In a recent conversation, Mapfumo praised the mbira and its music as a foundation of traditional Shona culture. Given his love for the instrument and his goal of raising black pride and unity during the revolution, I asked him why he had not replaced the electric instruments with a traditional mbira ensemble. He replied that the electric instruments and urban-popular aspects of his music appealed to the young people in the cities, just as his use of traditional mbira ostinatos, Shona vocal style and texts, and hosho patterns pleased the older people in the villages. The fusion of these various elements allowed him to reach these diverse groups during the revolution, and his music continues to mirror the complex amalgamation of foreign and indigenous African cultural resources that is the new Zimbabwe.

SUB-SAHARAN AFRICA BIBLIOGRAPHY

African Music, General: Francis Bebey, *African Music: A People's Art* (New York: Lawrence Hill, 1975); Robert Kauffman, "African Rhythm: A Reassessment," *Ethnomusicology* 24(3), 1980; Alan P. Merriam, "Traditional Music of Black Africa," in Phyllis M. Martin and Patrick O'Meara, eds., *Africa* (Bloomington: Indiana University Press, 1977): J. H. Kwabena Nketia, *The Music of Africa* (New York: W. W. Norton, 1974).

Ewe and Ghana: John Miller Chernoff, *African Rhythm and African Sensibility: Aesthetics and Social Action in African Musical Idioms* (Chicago: University of Chicago Press, 1979); Alfred Kwashie Ladzekpo and Kobla Ladzekpo, "Anlo Ewe Music in Anyako, Volta Region, Ghana," in Elizabeth May, ed., *Musics of Many Cultures* (Berkeley: University of California Press, 1980).

Ganda Music: Lois Ann Anderson, "Multipart Relationships in Xylophone and Tuned Drum Traditions in Buganda," *Selected Reports in Ethnomusicology, [Volume 5:] Studies in African Music* (Los Angeles: Program in Ethnomusicology, Department of Music, UCLA, 1984), Peter Cooke, "Ganda Xylophone Music: Another Approach," *African Music* 4(4), 1970.

Manding Peoples: Roderic Knight, "Music in Africa: The Manding Contexts," in Gerard Béhague, ed., *Performance Practice: Ethnomusicological Perspectives* (Westport, Conn.: Greenwood, 1984).

Pygmies: Colin Turnbull, *The Forest People: A Study of the Pygmies of the Congo* (New York: Simon & Schuster, 1962).

Shona of Zimbabwe: Paul F. Berliner, *The Soul of Mbira* (Berkeley: University of California Press, 1981).

Studies in African Urban-Popular Music: John Collins, "Ghanaian Highlife," *African Arts* 10(1), 1976; John Collins, *African Pop Roots* (London: Foulsham, 1985); David Coplan, *In Township Tonight! South Africa's Black City Music and Theatre* (London: Longman, 1986); David Coplan, "Go to My Town, Cape Coast! The Social History of Ghanaian Highlife," in Bruno Nettl, ed., *Eight Urban Musical Cultures* (Urbana: University of Illinois Press. 1978); Veit Erlmann, "Migration and Performance: Zulu Migrant Workers' *Isicathamiya* Performance in South Africa, 1890–1950," *Ethnomusicology* 34/2, 1990; Ronnie Graham, *The Da Capo Guide to Contemporary African Music* (New York: Da Capo, 1988); Christopher Waterman, *Ju Ju: A Social History and Ethnography of an African Popular Music* (Chicago: University of Chicago Press, 1990).

AFRICA DISCOGRAPHY

Anthologies: *Musical Instruments 1: Strings*, Music of Africa Series No. 27 (GALP 1322); *Musical Instruments 2: Reeds (Mbira)*, Music of Africa Series No. 28, (GALP 1323); *Musical Instruments 3: Drums*, Music of Africa Series No. 29 (Kaleidophone KMA 3); *Musical Instruments 4: Flutes and Horns*, (Music of Africa Series No. 30 (GALP 1325); *Musical Instruments 5: Xylophones*, Music of Africa Series No. 31 (GALP 1326); *Musical Instruments 6: Guitars 1*, Music of Africa Series No. 32 (GALP 1327).

Ewe and Ghana: *Folk Music of Ghana* (Folkways FW 8859); *Drums of West Africa: Ritual Music of Ghana* (Lyrichord LLST 7307); *Ewe Music of Ghana* (Asch Mankind Series AHM 4222).

Ganda: *Uganda 1*, Music of Africa Series (Kaleidophone KMA 10).

Manding: *Malamini Jobarteh & Dembo Konte, Jaliya* (Rounder 5021); *Kora Manding: Mandinka Music of the Gambia* (Ethnodisc ER 12101); *Mandinka Kora par Jali Nyma Suso* (Ocora OCR 70); *Rhythms of the Manding Adama Drame (Jembe)* (UNESCO Collection, GREM DSM 042); *Sounds of West Africa: The Kora & the Xylophone* (Lyrichord LLST 7308).

Pygmies: *Music of the Rain Forest Pygmies* (Lyrichord LLST 7157); *Pygmies of the Ituri Forest* (Folkways FE 4457); *Music of the Ituri Forest* (Folkways FE 4483).

Shona: *The Soul of Mbira: Traditions of the Shona People of Rhodesia* (Nonesuch H-72054); *Africa: Shona Mbira Music* (Nonesuch H-72077); *The African Mbira: Music of the Shona People of Rhodesia* (Nonesuch H-72043); *Rhodesia 1*, Music of Africa Series (Kaleidophone KMA8); *Ephat Mujuru: Master of Mbira from Zimbabwe* (Lyrichord LLST 7398).

Urban-Popular Music: *Ju Ju Roots: 1930s–1950s* (Rounder 5017); *King Sunny Ade and His African Beats; Juju Music* (Mango 9712); *Zulu Jive* (Earthworks ELP 2002); *Viva Zimbabwe* (Earthworks ELP 2001); *Voices of Africa: Highlife and Other Popular Music by Saka Acquaye and His African Ensemble from Ghana* (Nonesuch Explorer H-72026); *Black Star Liner: Reggae from Africa* (Heartbeat 41556); *Mbube Roots: Zulu Choral Music from South Africa, 1930s–1960s* (Rounder 5025); Thomas Mapfumo and The Blacks Unlimited; *Corruption* (Mango MLP 9848).

8

EUROPE

Philip V. Bohlman

MUSIC IN THE LIFE OF MODERN VIENNA

Streets and Stages: A Musical Stroll

As we stroll through the streets of modern Vienna on a June evening, the sounds and symbols of music envelop us and persuade us that Austria derives some measure of its identity from the musical past and present of its capital city. Music is everywhere, and Vienna has found a remarkable number of ways to make its own musical persona obvious. Grandiose edifices, monuments, and statues attest to the masters of the past and the extravagant performances of the present. The sounds of street musicians intermingle with insistent scales wafting from an open window in a music academy, the placards on walls announce a surfeit of upcoming concerts, and individuals we presume to be musicians because of their violin cases or armsful of musical scores scurry into buildings on their way to rehearsals or concerts. Even restaurants and the foods they serve bear the names of composers and musicians. This is an image of Vienna as the quintessentially musical city in a fundamentally musical nation in the heart of Europe, an image to which we are well accustomed. It is an image reproduced by recordings and movies, history books and tourist literature alike, all conspiring to convince the world that Vienna is, above all, a musical city.

Continuing our stroll, we begin to see that the larger image of Vienna as a musical city is considerably more complex than we had inferred from its surface. The map of Vienna that we hold in our hands tells a great deal about the interaction between the cultural core—symbolized by the center of the city, the First District, which the Ringstrasse, with its governmental and cultural buildings, surrounds—and the concentric ring streets that ripple outward toward the Alps in the west, Czechoslovakia in the north and northeast, Hungary in the east, and Yugoslavia in the south. The major highways radiating from the center of the city connect it with these other countries and cultures, which until little more than a half-century ago constituted an empire ruled by Austria. The Habsburg Empire is no longer a political reality, but Vienna still has the look and the sound of an imperial capital, for we see on the streets many cars from the countries of eastern Europe, and we hear street musicians singing in Hungarian or playing the instruments of Slovenian folk music. Vienna, it seems as we listen to these contrasting musics, attracts musical diversity, even draws it toward the city's center, and provides it with ample opportunities to express itself (Figure 8–1).

The annual Vienna Festival is in full swing during June, so it is hardly surprising that, as we pass along the streets forming the ring around the First District in the direction of the Staatsoper, many people are funneling into the front doors to see one of the nightly performances. Opera is an elegant affair, and many who are attending this evening's performance have suspended other activities to do so, dining before the 5:30 P.M. curtain and going to the nearby Mozart Café for drinks and desserts between acts. We check a kiosk to see what opera is on this evening, thinking it might be *Le Nozze di Figaro*. It is instead Richard Strauss's *Rosenkavalier*, although we see from the schedule of Vienna Festival events that *Figaro*, a favorite in modern Vienna, will be staged later in the month.

Many of the symbols of Vienna's musical past lie within a few blocks of the Staatsoper, and we decide to explore. We walk a few blocks to the historic Gesellschaft für Musikfreunde (Society for the Friends of Music), today a large building with several halls for musical performances, a library, archives, even a showroom for the distinguished Austrian piano manufacturer Bösendorfer. We pass along Bösendorferstrasse (the Austrians do have a habit of giving musical names to just about everything) and enter the piano showroom. It is an imposing, even daunting place, filled with pianos so highly polished that one hesitates to touch them and draped with huge posters of great Austrian pianists (and a few non-Austrians) staring or smiling down at us. Somehow, we get the impression of music that we should see and respect, even worship, but touching and playing seem out of the question in this context.

We consider the possibility of attending one of the concerts in the Gesellschaft für Musikfreunde—it hosts several evening concerts during the Vienna Festival—but everything is sold out, and, anyway, we are more than a little underdressed. Still, it is early summer, and our disappointment fades quickly as we resume our walk through Vienna. Many people are walking in the direction of St. Stephen's Cathedral, roughly at the center of Vienna's downtown. The Kärntnerstrasse, Vien-

Figure 8–1.   The Ring Area of Vienna. Source: *Freytag and Berndt.*
Buchplan Wien. Vienna: Freytag-Berndt und Artaria, 1990. Pp. 14–15.
Printed with permission of the publisher. © Freytag-Berndt u. Artaria, 1071
Wien.

na's main shopping thoroughfare, leads in that direction, and it is not long before we encounter street musicians, in fact numerous street musicians. They are of many types, and accordingly they are performing a remarkable variety of musical repertories. Flower vendors are selling an array of plants from the countryside and some imported from Italy and Spain, and they hawk their wares with a singsong style befitting a tradition of work songs. Several groups of street musicians have obviously come to Vienna from Hungary, and it seems likely that they will return after earning a bit of money and enjoying a few evenings in the Austrian capital. The Hungarians perform in an amalgam of styles, mixing rural folk songs with contemporary popular hits, but everything bears the stamp of the Hungarian language and an awareness of Hungarian instrumental styles.

We encounter also the rather raucous sounds of a young American singing chestnuts from the folk-music revival of the 1950s and 1960s, and with some embarrassment we throw a few schillings in his guitar case. At the edge of the square surrounding St. Stephen's, we pause to listen to an Andean panpipe ensemble, performing songs of political protest in Spanish and attracting the largest crowd of all the street musicians. Whether or not anyone understands the lyrics, the Andean ensemble (no one seems to know whether they are Peruvian or Bolivian, though the difference is also not troubling for most observers) obviously earns a considerable amount of money, probably enough to draw them back to this square through the rest of the summer.

Finally, we conclude our excursion by entering St. Stephen's itself, there to be greeted by the magnificient sounds of an organ on which Bach is being played, the music of a North German Protestant in the cathedral of this largely Catholic Austrian city. The others in St. Stephen's seem rather unsure whether the music accompanies a religious service or not, but they respond meditatively, not speaking or only whispering nervously to their neighbors in search of an opinion that will correctly inform them about what is happening at this particular moment. Just as nervously, we leave the cathedral and decide to spend the rest of the evening at a local wine cellar, a so-called Heuriger, where we will enjoy the wine of the season and the urban music called Schrammelmusik, named after Johann and Josef Schrammel, two nineteenth-century musicians who made this style of volkstümlich, or "folklike," music famous and contributed to the compositions and performance practice of the tradition. By the end of the evening, we wonder whether there is any music that we did not encounter, and, if so, whether we might have encountered it had we chosen a different route for our stroll. Rumors fly about that even American country-western can be heard if one knows where to go. Just where are the limits of Vienna's musical life?

The Many Musics of Vienna

The musical life that we discover during an evening's stroll through the streets of Vienna sharply contrasts with many descriptions of this quintessentially Central European city. Music-history books, for example, contain labels for musical styles that are distinctively Viennese, and so we read of "Viennese classicism," "Viennese waltzes," and even the "Second Viennese School" of avant-garde composers in the early twentieth century. Could we also observe a similar "Vienneseness" in our encounter with the vibrant musical life of the city on a summer evening? Surely there was no question that our expectation that Vienna would be a "very musical" city was fulfilled. It would hardly be an exaggeration to say that music—its presence as sound and idea—was everywhere. And yet it is not that easy to pin down what was especially Viennese about it, or even any single aspect connected with style, repertory, or performers that unequivocally expressed something Viennese. The street performers were often not even Austrian, and the multitude of musical sounds and experiences were more often mixed than identifiably of Viennese origin. Vienna's presence, nonetheless, was essential to our musical encounter. The city attracted these musicians, sanctioned their performances, and brought together the conflicting histories and cultural contexts in a unique way. What we heard during our stroll—indeed, what we would have heard on another possible route through the city—all of this, too, was Viennese music.

Our firsthand encounter with Viennese music reveals to us that there are many possible ways of understanding just what it is. One view seems anchored in the existence of an historical canon, a series of repertories created by gifted composers who grew up in Vienna or settled there because of the ideal conditions it provided for both the creation and performance of music. Music, then, symbolizes something unbroken and persistent in the history of the city, and the language used to describe music's historical role—notably the stubborn word "classical"—tells us that the past has been important in the present.

Another view of Viennese music, in contrast to the first, concentrates not on the central core but rather on the periphery, on the tendency of Vienna to attract outsiders. Relatively few of the composers generally associated with Vienna were originally from the city or received their musical education there; Mozart, Haydn, Beethoven, Brahms, and Mahler were outsiders, and their biographies demonstrate vividly that being accepted as an insider was no easy task. Clearly, the modern street musicians are not so different from the pantheon of Viennese composers in their relation to the city; the outsider status of the Hungarian folksingers or the Andean panpipe ensemble at once privileges and impedes, while making their presence almost unexceptional.

A third view of Viennese music challenges the historicism of the first two and poses what we might call postmodern arguments, though in fact these arguments may be no less relevant for the past than for

Figure 8–2. Contemporary Graphic of French street music, early nineteenth century. Vastly different styles and repertories—from colportage to hurdy–gurdy to military music—are juxtaposed in the urban environment. (Graphics collection, Deutsches Volksliedarchiv, Freiburg i.Br., Germany).

the present. Vienna, according to this view, forms the sort of cultural backdrop that permits unexpected, even jarring, juxtapositions. There are, accordingly, certain conditions that foster Viennese musics at particular moments, but these are almost random. Such a view helps to explain why the old and the new, the classical and the avant-garde, opera and street music exist side by side. Vienna is no less important to the various juxtapositions, for it provides a cultural template that encourages them. Its concert halls, its music academies, and its streets all become the stages for a music that, whatever else it might be, is unassailably Viennese (Figure 8–2).

EUROPE AS A MUSIC CULTURE

Europe as a Whole

There is no more commonly held assumption about music's relation to cultural and geographical areas than that something called "European music" exists. Other categories are created in contradistinction to European music—for example, Middle Eastern and Oriental music, whose positions in a world culture are determined by Europe's position, not their own. Throughout the world, students study European music; they call it by other names at times, perhaps "Western music" or "Euro-American music," but generally the term "European" has become common parlance in the twentieth century.

Just what European music is, of course, is another question. Despite the probable lack of consensus, relatively few writers on music concern themselves with stating the limitations of European music or defining what it is. It might be easiest to suggest that it is the music of Europe or the music created in Europe. Would, then, the Andean panpipe ensemble we heard in Vienna be European music? And would the music of Islamic Spain in the Middle Ages be European music? If we answer "no" to such questions, we seem to argue that Europe is more a shared culture than a unified geographic entity. If we answer "yes," we place greater importance on what happens within the geography, allowing even that the geography shapes the culture.

Europe is indeed unified in several ways. Europe is, for example, a continent, largely though not completely bounded by water. Linguistically, most peoples of Europe are related, closely in several cases and more remotely in others. Those languages not related to the larger Indo-European family, such as Hungarian and Finnish, may demonstrate European interrelations of their own. The cultural history of the continent, too, has a sort of unity, although sometimes that unity results only from attempts to barricade the continent from the cultures of Asia and Africa. Religion unifies Europe. Europeans are largely Christian, certainly to a degree that distinguishes certain aspects of shared culture; to travel from Europe toward Asia, the Middle East, or North Africa brings one immediately into contact with peoples who are not primarily Christian. All of these cases for unity contain exceptions, but together they reveal that there is considerable justification for studying Europe as a whole.

Europe as an Amalgamation of Cultural Areas and Peoples

Despite the acceptance of Europe's cultural wholeness, individuals do not always—or even most of the time—identify with it. Instead, individuals identify more often with the culture of the town, region, or nation in which they live. Similarly, at the individual level, most would identify more closely with a regional musical style than with a more abstract European unity. It has been characteristic of music in Europe that patterns of regional and cultural identity have remained especially pronounced, even as so-called mass culture encroaches in the twentieth century. The geographic area surrounding Lake Constance (in German, the Bodenseeraum) in Central Europe, for example, belongs to a single cultural area in which a single dialect of German is spoken, and its multitude of styles and repertories is related by a long history. This relatively small area nevertheless includes parts of four nations (Germany, Switzerland, Austria, and Liechtenstein). Even though the folk musics of Germany, Switzerland, and Austria are distinct at a national level, the Lake Constance region plays a more decisive role in determining musical unity.

The musical areas of Europe also result from groups of people who share a way of life and a distinctive music, even when these have little to do with national and political boundaries. Gypsy, Jewish, and Sami music cultures in Europe, for example, are circumscribed primarily by boundaries that arise within these communities. Gypsy communities exist throughout Europe, adapted to many different socioeconomic settings. On one hand, Gypsy musicians have traditionally adapted to the music in the European countries where they settled, often fulfilling very specialized roles as performers in the musical life of the non-Gypsy society. On the other, this flexible response to music in the surrounding, external society has not erased a distinctively Gypsy musical life. Bolstering that musical life have been the customs, languages, and social functions unique to the Gypsy community. It is, in fact, not quite proper to speak of "Gypsy" culture as if it were a homogeneous whole. Instead, we must always keep in mind the distinctive linguistic and cultural communities that make up the whole—for example, Roma and Sinti, the two largest groups.

If we were to generalize about the music of Gypsies in Europe, we would always need to take into consideration a process of negotiation between the Gypsy community and the larger nation or cultural area of which the individual community was a part. We would also need to incorporate the ways in which Gypsies make distinctions among their own musics and create their own typologies. Each supranational community undertakes such negotiations and typologies in different ways. The Sami in northern Europe have traditionally responded relatively little to the music cultures of Norway, Sweden, Finland, and the USSR, whereas Jewish communities in many parts of Europe have often been active participants in the musical life outside the community, so much so that many distinctions of style and repertory have disappeared.

European Unity and Europeanness in the Music of Modern Europe

For various reasons many genres of European music reflect an underlying belief that unity of musical style is important. Hungarian and German folk-music scholars have created classification schemes that assert the historical presence and importance of Hungarian and German folk music. European folk music in general falls into repertories that have national, linguistic, or cultural designations, suggesting that those who describe such repertories feel that these qualities of unity are fundamental to what folk music really is. Scholars in several countries have gone so far as to recognize patterns of relatively unified history in their national folk musics. This historicization of a national music is particularly evident in the models of Hungarian and English folk music; but elsewhere, too, we witness the ascription of unity on the basis of a belief that the music of the past is related to the music of the present in identifiably salient ways.

Folk music can reveal and articulate history in both musical and cultural (or, better, political and nationalistic) ways. The classification of Hungarian folk song was derived on the basis of whether musical style was relatively unbroken since the time Hungarian people were resident in Asia ("old style") or whether it had absorbed influences from surrounding European peoples ("new style"). Musically considered, an "old-style" song exhibited most of the following characteristics in one form or another: (1) a five-note, or pentatonic, scale, in which no half-steps were found; (2) melodies or phrases that started high and ended lower; (3) a melody in two halves, in which the second was a repeat of the first, only at the interval of the fifth lower (transposition by fifths); (4) a rhythmic style Bartók called "parlando" (speechlike); (6) a relatively steady tempo; and (7) ornamentation of the melody. The following example from Bartók's collections of Hungarian folk song demonstrates the characteristics of the "old style" in every way. Each of the seven characteristics is bracketed and numbered according to the preceding list to help you identify the musical arguments Bartók and other Hungarian scholars brought to their understanding of history in folk-song style (Figure 8–3).

Figure 8–3. "Imhol kerekedik"—Hungarian Folk Song in the Old Style.
Source: Bartók, Béla. *Das ungarische Volkslied.* Berlin: de Gruyter, 1925, P. 11, Example No. 40.

The musical characteristics of the "new style" contrast in virtually every way (at least in those ways that Bartók deemed most important) with the "old style." (1) Melodies are repetitive, and they form arches rather than descending contours, exhibiting four-line verses with structures like the following (A⁵ simply designates a phrase that is transposed a fifth higher): A A⁵ A⁵ A, A A⁵ B A, A B B A. (2) The rhythm is not "speechlike" but rather "dancelike," demonstrating what Bartók called "tempo giusto." (3) Whereas pentatonic scales are occasionally found, more common are heptatonic modes, either the so-called church modes (e.g., Dorian) or major mode. (4) Non-Hungarian musical elements have been incorporated. (5) The influence of popular song, particularly Hungarian popular genres from the nineteenth century, is evident.

One of the first things we notice when we compare the musical traits of the old and new styles is that there is much more flexibility in those traits recognized as new. To fulfill the requisites for old style is very difficult, but virtually any Hungarian song—folk, popular, or even religious—fits into the new style. Upon comparing the two even further, we realize that, in certain ways, they are not so different one from the other. The transposition by fifths, particularly in forms like A A⁵ A⁵ A, in which repetition is also found, is as much old as new style, excluding the fact that a falling melody should somehow be older. Pentatonicism, too, is not excluded from the new style, and one might argue that the ornamentation in the old style has a tendency to fill in the gaps in its characteristic five-note scale; "Imhol kerekedik," for example, is pentatonic when we consider only the main notes but heptatonic when we add the ornaments, marked in Bartók's transcription with small noteheads.

This Hungarian construction of history out of folk-song style has clear ideological and nationalistic implications, and these are important to understand as ideas about European music. Transposition by fifths was important to Bartók because it was quite rare in Western and Central European music, but relatively more common in Central and East Asian traditions. A style of music that utilized transposition by fifths therefore proved that the integrity of the Hungarian people had been maintained to some measure, at least since they left Asia to settle in Europe. The close relation of the old style to speech (Bartók's use of the term "parlando" was hardly an accident) also reveals an attempt to link music to the uniqueness of Hungarian culture, for the Hungarian language is not a member of the Indo-European family. Clearly, then, identifying songs in the old style provided a strong argument for Hungarian nationalism. Recognizing that songs in the new style had been influenced from the outside—that their rhythms were regularized and loosened from their connection to language—made an equally strong nationalistic appeal. This interweaving of musical style, national history, and cultural ideology is such that we find it difficult to determine which characteristic of a song was determined for musical reasons, which for ideological reasons, and which for both.

The concept of "music history," itself a particularly European notion, asserts that unity is somehow central to the formation of musical repertories. French music, then, is more than just music that utilizes the French language or music that happens to be created or performed in France; rather, it is music that occupies a position within French music history, in which successive musical styles develop in a consistent way, maintaining an essential quality of style that is French. If we look at virtually any European country, we will find similar associations of national unity with a belief that musical style plays a fundamental role in the singular paths music history can take.

The power of musical style to serve as the basis of a recognized unity is also evident in the case of cultural areas that do not have the political unity that most residents would prefer. Folk-song collections from the Südtirol, the German-speaking area of northeastern Italy, establish as many patterns of unity with Austrian folk music as possible, ultimately demonstrating in the eyes of the folk-song collectors that music history would justify the redrawing of the modern border. The Baltic republics of the Soviet Union (Estonia, Latvia, and Lithuania) similarly have musical repertories that reflect what is believed to be a unified style that undergirds cultural—and ultimately political—autonomy and independence from the Soviet Union.

Whether or not the patterns of stylistic unity sought by European scholars are real or not is, of course, open to question. Such patterns have also produced rather unfortunate historical distortions—for example, when some German musical scholars sought to equate pockets of German folk-music style (in the French Alsace, for instance, or in the so-called *Sprachinseln*, or "speech islands," in Eastern Europe) with colonialist expansion in the late nineteenth and early twentieth centuries. The need to equate musical style with national and regional unity in Europe remains one of the most noticeable traits of the continent even at the end of the twentieth century.

The "Europeanness" of music assumes many forms in modern Europe. We shall touch upon only a few here, keeping in mind that it would be possible to discover an infinite variety using these as points of departure. An initial survey of the way Europeanness in music is articulated suggests that more traditional notions have survived relatively untouched. We find in Britain and Ireland general acceptance that there are English, Irish, Gaelic, Cornish, and Highland folk musics; all of these recognize regions, population groups, and political aspirations in ways that could be extrapolated to Yugoslavia or Spain. Classical music and its institutions likewise seem no less codified by nationalistic designations than they were a century or two ago; we find many people who accept that there is Polish music or a Czech national opera, even though most would be hard-pressed to identify the precise musical traits that justify these assertions. European popular music, though heard across national borders, becomes undeniably nationalistic at certain levels—for example, when focused on a political agenda or performed in contests like the annual "Eurovision" competition, in which bands from one country are pitted against those from another.

The more we choose examples to illustrate the persistence of older patterns of unity, the more we recognize that these are functioning in different ways in modern Europe. Motivations for retaining and expressing nationalistic or regional musical qualities have changed, as have the audiences who listen to popular and classical musics. A Polish popular singer must sing part of her repertory in English to assure success in Warsaw, but that success allows her to sharpen the bite of the political message in her songs, both Polish and English. The mass media link the different linguistic regions of Europe in new ways, thereby empowering indigenous languages to claims of greater importance while permitting international languages to encroach at an increasing pace.

The religious underpinnings of many repertories have become extraordinarily important, albeit not necessary because the music retains an intimate connection with ritual and rites of passage. The German-speaking residents of northeastern Italy, for example, find it especially significant that the liturgy of the Catholic Church is in their vernacular German, in fact, a transformation that occurred only with Vatican II, almost a half-century after the Südtirol was absorbed by Italy in World War I. Their identity with the music of the Catholic Church has an increasingly politicized and nationalized meaning. The churches of Eastern Europe have also functioned in this way, providing a powerful voice—and in public, especially a musical voice—for East Germans, Poles, Lithuanians, or Ukrainians asserting the unity of their national identity.

The Europeanness of music today is not unlike the Viennese attributes we observed during our stroll through Vienna. Seemingly unrelated traditions are juxtaposed in unpredictable ways. Elements of indigenous and foreign music commingle, and in some cases they demonstrate an affinity for each other. Revitalizing old folk music is not an uncommon way of highlighting contemporary political issues. The old and the new coexist, as do different genres and styles of music. Just as Vienna shaped its conflicting musical parts into a unity that reflected the history and contemporaneity of Vienna, so too does the Europeanness of music today assert itself in such a way that the changing complexion of Europe has a powerful musical presence. That European music so often combines such diverse parts is, as we shall see, fundamental to the basic ideas that Europeans hold about music.

IDEAS ABOUT MUSIC

The Concept of "European Music"

Music is many different things to the people of Europe. Still, we recognize from many larger concepts that we employ in our speech about music that there are qualities that make music European and enable us to discuss a European music culture. We commonly employ the term "European art music" to describe the classical music of the Western concert hall. "European folk music," too, provides a way not only of stratifying shared forms of musical activity but also of ascribing boundaries to that activity and of suggesting ways in which folk music beyond those boundaries must be somehow different.

Earlier in the history of ethnomusicology, and to some extent today, music outside of Europe was defined by contrasting it with European music, calling it simply non-European. Implicit in such terms and categories was not the notion that music was so much the same in different parts of Europe, but rather that certain experiences, both historically and culturally, had produced musical activities and ways of thinking about music that were more similar to each other than to those elsewhere in the world. Hungarian and Norwegian folk musics, therefore, do not sound like each other, but both fulfill certain expectations of what folk music should be in rural European society and in the construction of national cultures, musical styles, and art musics.

Music in Peasant and Folk Societies

European ideas about music have a great deal to do with shared historical experiences and similar notions about how these experiences have led to the formation of modern European societies. At an early stage in these experiences the social relations of society were relatively undifferentiated and rural, and yet a common culture—consisting of language, folklore, and belief system—provided the cohesion for groups of people. Music, too, played a role in expressing the common culture of a people, and it could do so because it was in a language shared by the people and was a part of their daily lives and distinctive rituals. Music was thought to be inseparable from the essence of a culture. As such, it could express the culture's past, share traits of a language, and articulate religious belief. In doing so, music differentiated one society from another on the basis of national, regional, and linguistic styles.

Music functioning in these ways is, of course, what we call folk music. Folk music is a particularly European concept. It is hardly surprising that a German, Johann Gottfried Herder, actually coined the term *Volkslied* (literally, "folk song") in the late eighteenth century and that the collection and study of folk music spread throughout Europe by the end of the nineteenth century, encouraging the establishment of archives and anthologies and forming the basis for nationalism in music. The gap between a village folk song and a symphonic poem using that song as a theme was, of course, massive, but it is significant for our consideration of European music that folklorists, composers, and many other intellectuals found it vital to bridge that gap. Folk music, then, provided a means for understanding both the essence of, say, the Polish people and the ultimate expression of that essence in a national art music. Many twentieth century European composers, such as Béla Bartók and Ralph Vaughan Williams, have continued to combine collecting and writing about folk music with composing in nationalistic styles (Figure 8–4).

Figure 8–4. Peasant Wedding from Gotha (Germany) 1526. Bagpipe accompanies the meal; *Schalmei* accompanies the wedding dance. Text of the song is printed with the woodcut. Graphics collection, Deutsches Volkliedarchiv, Freiburg i.Br., Germany.

Music in Urban Society

Most European concepts of folk music portray it as the product of rural life. A certain irony lurks behind the need to privilege the music of rural life, because European society has a long history of extensive urbanization. Markets, seaports, monasteries, courts, and fortifications all served as the kernels from which great European cities developed during the Middle Ages. Ideas about music do, in fact, reflect this history as well. The urban centers of Europe have their own genres of music and forms of musical life, and many European ideas about music reflect these.

European cities, for example, have often served as the gathering points for people from other places—that is, people singing in different languages and performing on different instruments. As we might expect, musical "trade" has been as common in the city as the trade of goods and services. During the Middle Ages troubadours, Minnesänger, and minstrels emerged as highly skilled musical specialists who traveled to urban centers, courts, and fairs, picking up new styles and repertories. Urbanization has also affected the manufacture of musical instruments and the mass production of music in all forms, ranging from printed broadsides in early modern Europe to anthologies and recordings in the nineteenth and twentieth centuries. The European city, then, has become a meeting place for music and musicians, and the musical moments we encountered in Vienna at the beginning of this chapter embody processes of urbanization that take place in many different ways in all European cities.

Cities may bring the musics of many different groups together, but by no means do they eliminate the distinctive qualities of these musics. The survival of communities and societies that maintain musical lives relatively independent of national folk music or European art music—or even interact with these in highly individual ways—helps us to distinguish yet another fundamental European idea about music. Gypsy musicians, for example, not only have a distinctive music culture of their own but they also perform as musical specialists for events in a variety of settings outside of their own society, such as in the small courts of southeastern Europe. Similarly, a wide variety of musical styles and repertories exist in European Jewish communities, while Jewish musicians are known for the specialist roles they play in the musical activities of non-Jewish society. Even the Jewish klezmer ensembles that performed widely for the holidays and rites of passage in Yiddish-speaking shtetls of Eastern Europe occasionally traveled to play at events and celebrations among the Christian peasants.

Music within the Nation, Music outside the Nation

Music cultures such as those of the Gypsy and Jewish communities illustrate yet another characteristic of European music, namely the persistence of repertories and styles that belie national and political boundaries. The boundaries of Sami (formerly referred to by the derogatory term "Laplander") music culture, for example, are effectively the same as those represented by the reindeer-herding routes in northern Norway, Sweden, Finland, and the Soviet Union. The Celtic folk-music traditions of Western Europe—traditions unified by the Gaelic languages and related stylistic traits, among them the importance of the harp in the instrumentarium—stretch from Brittany (western France) north through Wales and Ireland to Scotland. Modern political boundaries have failed to eliminate these traditions, and in fact the unity of musical style characteristic of such traditions has ensured their cultivation during periods of revivalism and historicism.

The twentieth century political state has, of course, become a significant element shaping modern ideas about music in Europe. European governments have been particularly supportive of music, providing financial support for folk music as well as classical music and supporting festivals and broadcast media. When Bulgaria sought to create an international image of Bulgarian music in the 1980s, it could send its Bulgarian State Women's Chorus on tour throughout the world. State choral ensembles from the Baltic republics have also toured widely, promulgating an officially sanctioned Latvian or Estonian folk-song style and repertory. It is hardly surprising that there is no single model for national music in Europe. A national music may have a style that is the result of a consistent and unified history, or it may combine rather disparate styles and repertories from different parts of a country, symbolizing a modern kind of unity. Whatever the reasons for associating music with the state, politics has come to play a powerful role in the shaping of twentieth century ideas of European music (Figure 8–5).

Music and Religion

Religious concepts and experiences often provide keys for the understanding of music in European society. Both folk and scholarly classifications of music include categories that specify some forms of music as religious, not infrequently relying on just two large categories, sacred and secular music. Classification schemes that simplify, however, tend to mask a far more complex presence of religion in European ideas about music. If we consider the larger historical impact of Christianity on the formation of European culture, we also see that systems of musical patronage often reflect the structure of Christian polity, that is, the organization of society within the hierarchy of the Church. Indeed, much of the music studied as European art music was created for specific use in religious services or institutions. Choral composers of the Renaissance, Johann Sebastian Bach, and the contemporary French composer Olivier Messiaen produced many of their greatest works for performance in

Figure 8–5. Polish postcard from 1978, used to disseminate folk songs. Postcard in the collections of the Deutsches Volksliedarchiv, Freiburg i.Br., Germany.

religious services, and it was not uncommon for musical style to respond to the dicta of the Church hierarchy—for example, the call during the sixteenth century Counter-Reformation for a polyphonic style that could render text as audible as possible.

Folk music that accompanies ritual or that embodies spiritual themes is overwhelmingly religious in many communities. A harvest or wedding song, for example, may very well articulate some of the most fundamental sacred beliefs of a community. Not only are Norwegian folk songs predominantly religious in thematic content, but many are actually variants of hymns that have entered oral tradition. Religious occasions, such as pilgrimages, have served as the venue for the genesis of new songs and the formation of new communities that give such songs special meaning and function. At the end of the twentieth century, religious music has become a primary voice for protest and resistance, especially in Eastern Europe, where the church provides an historical link between the national culture of the past and an alternative social framework for the future (Figure 8–6).

Concerts and Concert Stars

When most of us think about European music, we think also of how and where music takes place. In short, we equate European music with concerts. The concert is a specialized musical event, one in which the difference between performer and audience is very great and the focal point of most activity is the singing or playing of music. At one level, the concert suspends the ritual of folk or sacred music by privileging the music itself, and social behavior dictates that one listen carefully

Figure 8–6.   Fasching musicians with *Narrenzünfte* ("fools' guilds") at the pre–Lenten celebrations in Gusswerk, Austria, February 12, 1991. Ethnomusicologist, Rudolf Pietsch, performs with Hans Martschin and the Mariazeller Sparkassenmusi. Photograph, Philip V. Bohlman.

to a particular musical text. At another level, concerts have generated their own form of ritual in European society, and audiences behave according to social requirements specific to the concert setting: dressing in a certain way, refraining from conversation, and listening attentively and critically.

Concerts have become a form of musical ritual particularly suited to modern Europe, and many ideas about music reflect the diverse ways concerts serve as an emblem of European culture. Some concerts may preserve one type of musical ritual, while others become the moment for radical innovation. The European concert empowers musicians to recontextualize music—to bring rural folk music to the streets of the city or to relocate sacred music in a public auditorium. Though an idea shared by all Europeans, the concert has nevertheless remained one of the major sources of musical diversity in modern times.

Concerts inevitably shift a certain degree of attention to the performer as a result of splitting musical participation into the two groups of music makers and audience. The performer therefore acquires importance because of the skill she possesses, because of the role the audience wants him to play. Virtuosity often becomes one of the markers of this role, and accordingly outstanding musicians have often emerged as extremely important in European ideas about music. The virtuoso has taken many forms. We think first of the performer who plays the most difficult passages in a concerto cadenza faster than anyone else—the early-nineteenth-century Italian violinist Nicolò Paganini, for example. There were those in the nineteenth century who speculated—a few even seriously—that Paganini's virtuosity resulted from other–worldly influences, perhaps some sort of pact with the devil. Stories about the nineteenth-century piano virtuoso Franz Liszt chronicle also his amorous skills, which were linked to his ability as a performer when he tossed broken strings from his piano to adoring women in the audience.

Although many stories about virtuosi are apocryphal, they reveal a great deal about European ideas about music. The virtuoso is somehow superhuman and can achieve things that no mortal is able to achieve. A sort of cult-figure worship develops around this superhuman quality, and the usual requisites for behavior are suspended. We find these ideas embedded elsewhere in European music, such as the association of certain instruments (for example, the Norwegian Hardanger fiddle) or musical structures (for example, the "devilish" interval of a tritone) with supernatural forces. The German philosopher Friedrich Nietzsche canonized these ideas in his writings about cultural supermen, and music historians have applied them to virtuosi in all aspects of classical music making—composer, conductor, and performer alike. In the twentieth century the notion that virtuoso musicians were extraordinarily important has been widely shared by adoring audiences and avid record buyers. European music making has been inseparable from the presence of individuals who stood out from the rest of society.

The Individual and Society, Creativity and Community

As a social counterpoint to the musicians who stand out as exceptional, more communal forms of music making continue to thrive in European society. Musical ensembles in which cooperation is preferable and the total musical product depends on a group's willingness to subsume individual identity into that of the ensemble reflect many of the ideals that Europeans associate with folk music. In the idealized form of folk society, all music theoretically belongs to the community, and because the means of producing music—family traditions, group interaction, community ritual—are shared, music becomes an aesthetic metaphor for communality. We recognize that this notion of communality is idealized, and yet we need not look far before discovering similar metaphors for other types of European music making. Chamber music, for example, is a genre of classical music in which each member of a small ensemble performs a part that is regarded as equal to all the other parts. The four voices of a string quartet, one of the most common ensembles, interact in such a way that competition to make one voice dominate the others—say, by giving the melody exclusively to the first violin—would undermine the performance. To symbolize this social equality, the chamber orchestra, the largest chamber ensemble in the classical tradition, often performs without a conductor. Not only does this avoid the symbol of power accruing to an individual, but it assures the performers that their musical and social survival depend on an ability to function as a whole with interacting parts.

The folk-music or chamber ensemble may appear as idealized models for European society, but the complexity of European society, in which the parts do not always function as a whole, can also be symbolized by the musical ensemble. Folk-music ensembles—the tamburitza of southeastern Europe, for example—derive their structure in part from the soprano-alto-tenor-bass structure of choirs. European classical-music ensembles became relatively fixed in this format in the late eighteenth century and so we see that the tamburitza and the string quartet both symbolize a perception of gender roles in an otherwise egalitarian society.

German male choruses in the nineteenth century became a symbol for the power of nationalism and Germanness as embedded in and expressed by the Volk, the German people. Similarly, large choruses in Eastern Europe at the end of the twentieth century have come to symbolize the achievement of the modern socialist state or, among those cultural groups without their own state, the national voice that survives despite the state-generated traits of national culture. Even though musical ensembles function in vastly different ways, their connection to the people as a collective society pervades European ideas about music. We witness a vivid portrayal of this in Mozart's *Le Nozze di Figaro*, in which the peasant folk together constitute the choruses, who gather on the stage at the culmination of significant scenes in the opera to serve as the final arbitrators of the actions of peasant, specialized laborer, and noble alike. In the end, it is the chorus that symbolizes the communal underpinnings of European society.

MUSICAL INSTRUMENTS

If we reflect back on our stroll through the streets of Vienna and take stock of the instruments we observed various musicians playing, we might be struck both by the importance of instruments and their variety in this vignette of European musical life. The pianos in the Bösendorfer show room were displayed as if in a museum—untouchable and expensive symbols of the musical activities of an elite. No less untouchable was the organ in St. Stephen's, whose sounds filled every corner of the Gothic cathedral, yet failed to help us locate the organist tucked away in a loft somewhere. The instruments of the street musicians were equally symbolic of identity and social function. The distinctiveness of the Andean panpile players emanates most directly from their instruments; once considered a measure of music's universality, panpipes now serve as markers of a few musical cultures, especially those of the South American highlands.

The institutions of music in Vienna also bear witness to the importance of instruments. Museum collections juxtapose the so-called "period instruments" of early music with the experimental models of more recent times (which, too, may someday be regarded as "period instruments"), and folk-music archives assemble folk instruments to classify them and run acoustical experiments on them. The music academies are, in fact, metaphors for the learning and specialization that musical instruments demand. Musical instruments, therefore, are inescapable symbols of the unity and distinctiveness of European musical life. They may tell us that a musical style or repertory is European on one hand but Austrian, Hungarian, Sicilian, or Macedonian on the other. Instruments act as a vital material representation of musical life in Europe and as such embody its history, its forces of change, and its great diversity.

Folk Instruments

Musical instruments have long served as some of the most commonly employed criteria for classifying music. The instruments of folk music, for example, were those constructed within the society or community where the particular repertory of folk music was performed. Indeed, many thought that a folk instrument was one built by its player, therefore functioning ideally for the player's needs in every way. An instrument imported from elsewhere, even another village a few miles away, did not belong to the musical life of the community in quite the same way.

In the idealized folk society of Europe, then, an instrument is somehow the extension of the individual musician yet at the same time a marker of the community's musical identity. It is a specific product that we should be able to trace to its maker and the particular roles it plays in a given community. If this understanding of the folk instrument is idealized, it nevertheless underscores the importance of the instrument as a measure of European folk music itself—that is, folk music as a product that comes into being according to a specified set of conditions.

There are performers of folk music who do make their own instruments, but today the norm is that instruments come from elsewhere and are probably the product of an unknown maker or an industrial manufacturer. The willingness of European musicians to borrow an instrument from elsewhere, moreover, is by no means a modern phenomenon. Instrument types and names reveal a long history of instrumental peregrinations, both within Europe itself and across its borders. European instruments such as the lute and the guitar came originally from Islamic North Africa, and the Ottoman presence in southeastern Europe induced a particularly rich exchange between that area and Turkey. The button-box accordion called the "Grazer" is no longer found only in Graz, a large provincial capital in southeastern Austria, but has become one of the preferred button-boxes in many regions of Europe where they are played, such as Slovenia in northern Yugoslavia. Instruments like the bagpipe and the violin exist in countless variations in folk-music cultures throughout Europe; local communities everywhere have adapted these instruments to their own music cultures and individual musicians have personalized them. The Hardanger fiddle of Norway, a fairly recent adaptation of the violin, is indisputably Norwegian; a Swedish hummel, or dulcimer, is as likely to bear witness to the individual who performs it as is the gusle, or bowed lap fiddle, of a Serbian epic singer. The ubiquity of such instrument types notwithstanding, they show that the tendency to use instruments to express individuality and community identity has not abated in the modern folk-music cultures of Europe.

When Instruments Tell Stories

If musical instruments illustrate certain ways in which music is a product, many also participate in the means of production, that is, in the processes that determine the product. Musical instruments become indispensable participants in a chain of events, and Europeans show a tendency to anthropomorphize instruments, to regard instruments as music makers with human qualities. We refer to the parts of an instrumental piece as its "voices," and it is fairly common to relate these directly to human voice ranges. Europeans, like peoples throughout the world, ascribe human qualities to instruments (think of how many instruments have "necks," that part of the human body in which the vocal cords are located) and decorate instruments with human or animal figurations (for example, by transforming the scroll at the top of a violin's neck into a face of some kind). Instruments become the musician's partner in music making.

Musical instruments in Europe often assist in telling a story. Narrativity is one of the functions that makes them humanlike. Among the earliest specialists who performed secular narrative song in Europe were those who sang by accompanying themselves on an instrument, usually a stringed instrument. The medieval Minnesinger, for example, recounted tales of history and great heroes, encounters with lovers and with enemies while wandering about the world, all the while relying on the narrative assistance of the lute. The importance of the lute to the German song tradition appears in a nineteenth-century interpretation in Richard Wagner's *Die Meistersinger von Nürnberg*, in which the mastersingers must prove themselves by playing correctly on the lute according to the rigorous rules imposed on the tradition.

Whereas Wagner's vision was particularly Romantic and German, the narrativity of epic traditions in southeastern Europe predate even medieval Europe, evolving from the Homeric epic traditions of ancient Greece, according to the great epic scholars Milman Parry and Albert Lord. The epic is a narrative genre in which the poet-singer performs tales from the life of a hero or heroine. The singer's instrument, the gusle, has become so closely identified with the genre that the singer's name, guslar (player of the gusle), is derived from the instrument itself.

The instruments of classical European music also demonstrate narrative functions, often in such ways that we recognize a close relation to rural society and folk beliefs. The twentieth-century composer Igor Stravinsky used the narrative potential of the orchestral instrumentarium in his early ballets to transform the pagan ritual of *Le Sacre du Printemps* (The Rite of Spring) and the Shrovetide folktale of *Petrushka* into classicized ballets. The narrative power of the piano, too, marks the work of many composers—for example, Robert Schumann, who told the tale of attending a pre-Lenten party (again, Shrovetide, although most readers will be more familiar with the French equivalent, *Mardi Gras*, or the German, *Fasching*) in his *Carnaval*. Narrativity also distinguishes the symphonic tone poems of late nineteenth-century composers and the nationalistic works of composers seeking to use the orchestra to tell those stories most characteristic of their own history and culture. Much of the aura associated by Europeans with instruments clearly is the result of their potential ability to be humanlike.

Musical Instruments in an Industrial Age

Although personal, communal, and human qualities continue to influence European concepts about musical instruments, the modern European instrumentarium would be inconceivable without technology. Technology's influence is evident in the development of new areas of musical life—for example, the dependence of rock musical instruments on mass-produced sound and means of dissemination. Perhaps less evident is the previous development of new instrument types during the rapid technologizing of European society from the end of the seventeenth century on, when instruments we now regard as standard—the piano, for instance—were invented and reinvented. The technology of musical instruments is also one of the primary musical exports from Europe, and we can often recognize European influences on non-European musics by the appearance of certain types of technology, such as the harmonium in North India and Pakistan. Technological developments have, moreover, directly affected the reception of music, making it possible for larger audiences to hear a piano with a more powerful cast-iron frame or the amplified sounds of a folk-music ensemble using microphones.

No instrument symbolizes the impact of technology on European musical instruments as fully as the piano. Invented at the beginning of the eighteenth century in Italy, the piano transformed the direct striking or plucking action of the clavichord and harpsichord into a more powerful action by employing a series of levers connected by joints. The new machinery in the piano not only allowed for a broader palette of sound colors but made it possible for the piano to dominate the other instruments with which it was played. As the piano grew larger, so did its sound; as its machinery grew more complicated, the factories that manufactured it became more sophisticated and efficient. The technology to create pianos kept pace with the demand for an instrument that had its own solo repertory and a role in many other repertories. The piano both appeared on the stage of the largest concert hall and stood in the parlor of the bourgeois home.

A product of technology, the piano became the preferred instrument of the European "everyperson" by the mid-nineteenth century. It was an instrument that resulted from mass production and was capable of attracting mass audiences. Pianos followed Europeans as they settled elsewhere as both immigrants and colonizers. And yet the piano did not lend itself particularly well to other musics. Its technology was so highly developed that it could not be easily adapted to nondiatonic and nontempered tuning systems. It stood apart in non-Western societies, effectively symbolizing the hegemony of European music in the colonial era.

Instruments and Musical Professionalism

Musical instruments often represent complexity in European music. Complexity is a musical quality highly valued in European society. Whereas both singers and instrumentalists do generally practice and study to acquire their skills, playing an instrument is often regarded as less natural, less a product of pure gifts than singing. The distinction between vocal and instrumental forms of music is, in fact, universal, and in many societies, such as those of the Islamic world, instrumental music may be criticized or even proscribed because it is less human—that is, not directly tied to words. Restrictions on instrumental music are not unknown in Europe, where periodic attempts to keep instruments out of Christian religious music are among the hallmarks of conservative religious movements. When they ascended to power in 1649, forming the English Commonwealth, the Puritans inveighed against instruments in churches and ordered that organs be removed and destroyed. The medieval division of music into *musica humana, musica mundana,* and *musica instrumentalis* was one of the first reformulations of a concept that was also fundamental to early Greek thought about music, and persists in European musical thought today.

Instrumentalists therefore acquire the status of specialists and, very often, professionals. They stand out as exceptional in society because of the skills they command, and the best—that is, the most skillful—receive financial rewards for their labors. The exceptional role of instrumentalists does not always reflect public sanction; instrumentalists like the becar in the Slavic lands of southeastern Europe are sometimes regarded as ne'er-do-wells or troublemakers (and, not insignificantly, attractive lovers). The outsider status of the instrumentalist also empowers her or him to move with ease from community to community, or even to perform within several distinct societies. We have witnessed this already in the Gypsy musicians of Eastern Europe. Medieval minstrels, generally instrumental musicians, were also distinguished by relative mobility and the license to travel to gather with other minstrels at great fairs in order to exchange repertories and learn new music. In more modern times, this has obtained also for the klezmer ensembles of Eastern European Jewish society, which have performed at various celebrations and rituals in the Jewish community but also historically played in non-Jewish communities (with varying degrees of anonymity, depending on just how important it was to establish the status of an outsider). The increased mobility further ensured the profitability of the instrumentalist's trade. We see again the European willingness to view music as a product, indeed one that a consuming society is willing to pay for.

HISTORY AND SOCIAL STRUCTURE IN EUROPEAN MUSICAL LIFE

The Underlying Historicism of European Musical Thought

We have seen throughout this chapter that history is one of the primary forces unifying European concepts of music, hence enabling us to understand the ways in which music reflects and participates in the musical life of the geocultural area encompassed by Europe. Just as Europeans are aware of these larger historical forces and moments—whether wars, religious transformations, or responses to other parts of the world—they also share a sense that an historical unity characterizes the musics of Europe. We witness such concepts of unity in phrases like "European art music" or "European folk music" (and conversely in phrases like "non-European music"). Though the presence of history in European musical life may seem an abstraction, we may observe the presence of history in our very concepts of music.

At least since the Renaissance, those who have written about music have largely concerned themselves with some musics of the past and the relation of these musics to a more recent time. It is hardly surprising, then, that we commonly refer to the professionals who write about European art music as music historians. The professional study of European folk music has been no less motivated by the urge to construct historical patterns for the relations between individual folk songs and among larger repertories. As we saw in an earlier example, Béla Bartók and Zoltán Kodály created a model for Hungarian folk song in which the notion of musical style was entirely historical, emerging as "old style," "new style," or a mixture of these two styles and outside influences. The "War between the Ancients and Moderns" in early-eighteenth-century France, with its evaluative claims that either "ancient" music or "modern" music was better, suggests an historical model for the interpretation of music that was not so very different from that formalized by Bartók and Kodály two centuries later.

Music as a Component of Mentalité

History does take a number of distinctive forms in European concepts of the relation of music to a given community, society, or nation. From what might be considered a prehistorical perspective, music is inseparable from the cultural profile of one of these social constructs; in other words, music is a part of and serves as a voice for what the *Annales* School of French historians call the *mentalité*. In contemporary usage, the mentalité of a people is that cultural profile existing apart from the actions of armies and political figures; instead, it forms from the everyday acts, aspirations, and belief systems of an entire society. The concept seems to apply particularly well to an interpretation of musical life that emphasizes folk music as a corpus of expressive activities shared by an entire cultural group; in effect, folk music becomes the product of the group's mentalité.

By no means is this a twentieth-century concept in folk-music scholarship; in fact, its development is coeval with Herder's eighteenth-century model for the shared music of a people, *Volkslied*. Herder and nineteenth-century folk-music scholars steeped their concept in historical potential, for it provided a means for determining the ideal origins of music and its gradual development according to a model of organic change into other forms of music which necessarily retained characteristics of the group's mentalité. The "everyperson" in European society, therefore, continued to contribute to music history by sharing in a musical collective. Even attempts to reformulate the assumptions of folk music—stating that it is really "people's music" (a Marxian turn of phrase), or the music of "groups" (a formulation associated with the German scholar Ernst Klusen)—retain the basic premise that it is a collective that shapes the formation, transmission, and history of music.

The Individual in History and the Political Economy of Music

Despite the widespread dissemination of music within a group, creativity enters the process of music history, and with it the role of the individual in history emerges. Few modern interpreters of European music history accept the notion that a folk song or any other form of popular music came into existence simply because of the will and collective action of the community, a notion clearly evident in Herder's formulation, "Das Volk dichtet." Instead, an individual, usually a musician with some specialized role in the musical life of the community, creates a piece of music, "composes" it, and therefore establishes its position in a particular music history. Folk songs, for example, might begin their history in oral tradition by first being printed on a broadside and sold on the street, largely to earn profit for the composer, printer, and hawker. The broadside ballad, which often appeals because it trenchantly captures the news of the moment or tells an intriguing tale in verse, is only possible if it embodies certain aspects of the community's mentalité and relies on the community's knowledge of a store of common melodies, yet it is the individual who establishes the nature of these relationships.

The broadside composer is often anonymous and represents one end of a continuum of positions of the individual in music history. Perhaps at the other end we find the twentieth-century recording virtuoso, whose status as a cult figure would seem to stand outside of history (fans will regard the virtuoso's interpretations as superior to those fixed or limited by historical performance practice), except for the mediating role that history has also played in creating and utilizing technology in such a way that individual interpretations can be widely disseminated and idolized. The history of European music has gradually shifted more emphasis toward the individual. The notion of the individual musician standing out from his or her community was virtually unknown in the Middle Ages, and it was still inchoate in the fourteenth century, when minstrels began to acquire designations such as "Fiddler" or "Pfeiffer" [Piper]) that help us to understand the relation between the musical specialist and the community. The designation of the individual as potentially exceptional, a musical genius, began only in the late Renaissance, but quickly became a primary impetus in European music history, and by the nineteenth century music historians were using "great men" to mark the epochs of historical change.

The musician's role in music history also reminds us that it is the actions of the individual that result in the shaping of music as a product, a commodity that others pay for and that results in remuneration for the individual. Accordingly, the history of European music lends itself to interpretation from the standpoint of a political economy, in which the individual and the community are counterposed. East German scholars such as Wolfgang Steinitz have employed this fundamental contraposition to historicize folk music, sketching a centuries-long tradition of folk music as the historical voice of the people. Other Eastern European scholars in the second half of the twentieth century have made similar cases for the historical tensions between individual and community that command the political economy of music, and the result has been widespread institutionalization of many forms of musical life in Eastern European nations. In essence, the socialist European nations have sought to arrest the historical slide in the nineteenth century in order to place emphasis on the individual and to shift the individual back to the larger society, where it can again articulate a shared mentalité. This modern institutionalization of musical life, however lasting it may prove to be during the decline of Eastern European communism at the end of the twentieth century, nonetheless serves as a vivid example of the power of historical concepts to shape the fundamental structures of European musical life.

Modern Nations, Modern Histories, Modern Musics

Twice during the twentieth century world wars have radically redrawn the map of Europe, creating new political entities while splitting and eliminating many old ones. The new face of Europe has had a profound effect on musical life in the continent. Just as new nations and cultural boundaries have developed, so too have new music histories emerged to interpret and, in some cases, to justify the widespread change. More than at any previous moment, the diversity of Europe's music at the end of the twentieth century is a result of conscious historicism, the revitalization of a musical past and its reformulation in the present. On one hand, historicism interrupts and negates the path of steady historical development by altering traditional social contexts. On the other, it collapses the differences between past and present, making it possible to combine musical styles and repertories in ways particularly appropriate to the political reality of Europe at the end of the twentieth century. Musical historicism recaptures the past in distinctly modern ways (Figure 8–7).

Figure 8–7. Paris Street Music, 1991. Singer performs chansons and accompanies himself by cranking a mechanical organ. In front of the Centre Georges Pompidou, which houses the Museum of Modern Art and IRCAM, a center for experimentation with electronic music. Photograph by Philip V. Bohlman.

Just what can musical historicism capture from the past? In what ways do elements from the past effectively serve as the music of the present? There are no simple answers to such questions; rather, modern European musical cultures have employed historicism in quite different ways with quite different motivations. One of the most common motivations is nationalism. This reflexive impulse explains the urge to search for Czechness in the music of Czechoslovakia. A nation of quite distinctive regional and minority cultures, Czechoslovakia has nevertheless endeavored to establish the criteria that make music Czech, finding, however, little consensus among composers or folk-music styles of the past. Slovakians, moreover, resist the notion that Czechness is a valid criterion of a national music, for they would view such a category as containing that music which was not Slovakian; Czech music would be only that music found in the western half of the nation.

If Czechness in music is itself elusive, the motivation to discover a distinctive nationalism is not unique to Czechoslovakia. We find similar tendencies among the inhabitants of the Südtirol in Italy, who have carved out repertories of music that consist entirely of German-language songs and pre-Italian Latinate dialects, which also survive in the region today. Südtiroler songbooks simply do not contain songs in Italian, and the examples in German, Latin, and English (the last usually from the American folk-song revival) reveal a clear pattern of choosing selectively from the past to build the repertory of the present. European institutions of classical music also arise because of the historicist impetus of the modern nation. The state or national academy of music, orchestra, or chorus has become normative throughout Europe. The new map of modern Europe, then, has relied on the historical underpinnings of musical life to reformulate that life—that is, to modernize it and link it to new historical conditions. In so doing, the musical life of modern Europe has come to express its fundamental Europeanness in new ways which nevertheless take account of the past.

EUROPEAN MUSIC IN THE LATE TWENTIETH CENTURY

The Eurovision Song Contest

Each spring television viewers from all over Europe gather in front of their sets on a Saturday evening to watch the Eurovision Song Contest. The television program they will watch is, in fact, only the culminating stage of a series of contests that begins locally in each competitor nation and concludes when the singer or singing group that is the best and most representative of the nation is sent off to the final contest to represent the nation. The Eurovision Song Contest is broadcast throughout Europe by an international network in which national television networks participate when there is some occasion to employ continent-wide coverage. Musical competitions of various kinds are common among these—for example, the annual *Wettbewerb der Volksmusik*, in which performers of volkstümlich music from Germany, Switzerland, and Austria compete. In the European world of popular music, however, nothing is more important than the Eurovision Song Contest, which not only assures a singer or band financial success but brings a measure of musical pride and glory to the nation whose musicians are victorious.

The evening's program lasts many hours and utilizes a format that will be familiar to American readers as a sort of cross between a Miss America Pageant and the Academy Awards ceremony. Set in a large auditorium, usually in a metropolitan center or resort city of England or France, filled with glamorous guests, the program progresses through the competition country by country. First we watch a short vignette about the country; then we meet the singers and learn something about their lives and aspirations; and finally we hear them perform their song live for the program itself. It is apparent that not all the nations of Europe send competitors to the contest; notably absent are several East European countries, though Hungary and Yugoslavia are predictably among the competitors. Also performing are a few nations that do not properly belong to Europe—Cyprus, Turkey, Egypt, Israel—although we have no difficulty recognizing a stylistic link in the popular music presented by the winning ensembles from these nations. Indeed, such countries seem to have more at stake by asserting a musical connection to Europe, and it is commonly understood that they take their participation in the contest rather seriously. Israel, for example, won the contest several times in the 1980s and always manages to place very high in the final standings.

The lineup of songs played by the national winners is rife with contradictions. A Norwegian guitarist quietly performs what at least sounds like a folk song; a highly electrified Finnish band plays a loud and out-of-tune piece, an intentional symbolic subversion of the international popular-music scene; the bands from Israel, Turkey, Italy, and France all sound alike; and the singers from England and Germany produce a homogenized rock sound pulled together from the past two decades, but perform in a style that enables them to exude sex appeal. Some performers wear approximations of national costumes; others flaunt a punk look. Some use national instruments; others, it would seem, avoid them. In the end, the winning band tends to be the least controversial one with the most compromised sound. On one hand, this sound is "European," but, on the other, it cannot completely fail to capture some nuance of national flavor. Over the years, the Eurovision Song Contest has always produced its winners in this way, and those countries wanting to win or place well—Israel, for example—have little trouble choosing their own winners, that is, those who will come closest to approximating the winning European popular sound.

The immense popularity of the Eurovision Song Contest assures us that the interest in a European musical identity has abated little at the end of the twentieth century. We witness popular music in its many forms throughout the evening of the contest: international, national, regional, and local or folklike. Those ensembles judged as winners combine characteristics from all these levels, establishing a complex nest of identities, all of them European in their different ways. There is therefore a European component in the international sound, just as the folklike sound has certain traits that have a currency throughout Europe. Even those bands that flaunt their disdain for the musical homogeneity promulgated by the contest and those that come from Mediterranean countries consciously play off the European musical community symbolized by the contest. Accordingly, they define their identities in relation to the larger European musical identity that the contest embodies.

Each year the victors and those who have not fared quite so well return home, perhaps to launch their careers using the winning sound, perhaps to return to the repertory and setting of the tradition closest to their individual aesthetics. Next year, other performers will be competing for the right to represent their town, region, and eventually nation in the Eurovision Song Contest, and they will be discovering yet other ways in which the musical identity of Europe can be forged from the panoply of musics that constitute the musical life of the continent.

A Viennese Waltz in Conclusion

The musical Europe we witnessed while watching the Eurovision Song Contest was not so very different from the musical Vienna we encountered during the excursion that opened this chapter. Issues of cultural identity were important, and music served to articulate these in varied yet ineffable ways. The contest showed that to belong musically to Europe was important, but no more so than to belong musically to one's own nation. The vital musical life of Vienna, too, was essential to its identity as a quintessentially musical city in the heart of Europe, but the more we listened to Viennese music the more we realized it was not one style or repertory but many. Just as the Eurovision Song Contest could incorporate Cyprus into the continent's musical life, the shoppers on the Kärntnerstrasse adopted the Andean panpipe ensemble into the musical life of their city.

Does this portrait of European and Viennese musical diversity bring us any closer to an understanding of the music of Europe? In a sense, we have posed this question throughout the chapter, taking as a point of departure a set of initial queries about Viennese music. It is only fair to return to Viennese music, then, to see what it tells us about the music of Europe. After all, the musical label "Viennese" has been applied repeatedly. The style period in the history of European art music bridging the end of the eighteenth and beginning of the nineteenth centuries is often labeled "Viennese Classicism." The "Second Viennese School"—loosely, Arnold Schoenberg, his students, and his associates—harkens back to that earlier period. In the nineteenth century, the "Viennese waltz" burst upon the popular-music scene and spread throughout the world. By the beginning of the twentieth century, popular music drama, namely "Viennese operetta," had become synonymous with the Austrian capital. We could broaden our search to the other arts—to the "Wiener Moderne" (Viennese Modernists), a theatrical and literary movement at the turn of the century, and the "Wiener Werkstätte" (Viennese Workshop), a firm that led a movement in the visual and plastic arts early in the century. The importance of identifiable "Vienneseness" in music is no less evident in the other arts.

And still, identifiable Vienneseness is a construction, a whole with parts that are sometimes compatible and at other times contradictory. The classicism denoted by the Viennese label in European art music suggests a conscious awareness of the past, even a return to the past. Yet neither Mozart nor Schoenberg was a musical conservative. Were they both not progressives, visionaries, even radicals? Moreover, were not both ill at ease and outsiders in the musical milieu of Vienna? The Viennese waltz, too, combines and reformulates musical styles, namely the diverse styles of Central European folk dance with the urbane Biedermeier culture of nineteenth-century Vienna. Again we see that the non-Viennese elements are at least as significant as the Viennese. On the way to acquiring the Viennese label, music also undergoes complex processes of negotiation: between past and present; between rural and urban; between Austrian and foreign; between the individual and the collective; between one musical style or genre and another; between one form of musical life in the social framework of Europe—say, folk music—and another.

The Viennese waltz is surely all of these; we can understand it as folk, popular, or classical, typically Viennese or international, socially conservative or liberal. As a juxtaposition of all these traits, it reflects a balance, and it is the nature of that balance that eventually establishes the relation of the Viennese waltz as a musical style to Vienna as a cultural setting. That balance—struck and forged among the conditions of history, society, politics, geography, language, style, performance, instrumentarium, and repertory—assumes myriad forms in the musics of other European cities and nations, and, complex as it is, seems to undergird European music history. That balance, in fact, provides the dynamic tension that makes it possible to understand the music of Europe as a whole that achieves its identity only from its diverse, composite parts.

EUROPE BIBLIOGRAPHY

Europe as a Whole: Theodor W. Adorno, *Introduction to the Sociology of Music,* trans. E. B. Ashton (New York: Seabury, 1976); Jacques Attali, *Noise: The Political Economy of Music,* trans. Brian Massumi (Minneapolis: University of Minnesota Press, 1985); Constantin Brăiloiu, *Problems of Ethnomusicology,* ed. and trans. A. L. Lloyd (Cambridge: Cambridge University Press, 1984); Bruno Nettl, *Folk and Traditional Music of the Western Continents,* 3rd ed. (Englewood Cliffs, N.J.: Prentice Hall, 1990).

Cultural Life in Vienna and Austria: Walter Deutsch and others, eds., *Volksmusik in Österreich* (Vienna: Österreichischer Bundesverlag, 1984); Carl Schorske, *Fin-de-Siècle Vienna* (New York: Pantheon (?), 1980); Michael P. Steinberg, *The Meaning of the Salzburg Festival: Austria as Theater and Ideology, 1890–1938* (Ithaca, N.Y.: Cornell University

Press, 1990); Stephen Toulmin and Allan Janik, *Wittgenstein's Vienna* (New York: Touchstone, (?), 1973); Gotthart Wunberg, ed., *Die Wiener Moderne: Literatur, Kunst and Musik zwischen 1890 und 1910* (Stuttgart: Reclam, 1981).

Folk Music: Ralph Vaughan Williams, *National Music* (New York: Oxford University Press, 1954); Walter Wiora, *European Folk Song: Common Forms in Characteristic Modification* (Cologne: Arno Volk, 1966); Philip V. Bohlman, *The Study of Folk Music in the Modern World* (Bloomington: Indiana University Press, 1988).

Music of Eastern and Southern Europe: Béla Bartók, *Hungarian Folk Music*, trans. M. C. Calvocoressi (London: Oxford University Press, 1931); Béla Bartók and Albert B. Lord, *Serbo-Croatian Folk Songs* (New York: Columbia University Press, 1951); Béla Bartók, *Rumanian Folk Music*, 5 vols., ed. Benjamin Suchoff (The Hague: Martinus Nijhoff, 1967–75); Rolf Wilhelm Brednich and Wolfgang Suppan, eds., *Gottscheer Volkslieder*, 2 vols. (Mainz: B. Schott's Söhne); Stephen Erdely, *Methods and Principles of Hungarian Ethnomusicology* (Bloomington: Indiana University Press, 1965); Zoltán Kodály, *Folk Music of Hungary*, trans. Ronald Tempest and Cynthia Jolly (London: Barrie and Rockliff, 1960); Boris Kremenliev, *Bulgarian-Macedonian Folk Music* (Berkeley: University of California Press, 1952); Albert B. Lord, *The Singer of Tales* (Cambridge, Mass.: Harvard University Press, 1960); Bruno Nettl, *Cheremis Musical Styles* (Bloomington: Indiana University Press, 1960).

Music of Central Eruope: Max Peter Baumann, *Musikfolklore and Musikfolklorismus: Eine ethnomusikologische Untersuchung zum Funktionswandel des Jodels* (Winterthur: Amadeus, 1976); Ludwig Erk, ed., *Deutscher Liederhort*, 3 vols., ed. and expanded by Franz Magnus Böhme (Leipzig: Breitkopf & Härtel, 1893–94); Wolfgang Steinitz, *Deutsche Volkslieder demokratischen Charakters aus sechs Jahrhunderten*, 2 vols. (Berlin: Akademie-Verlag, 1954, 1962).

Music of Western and Northern Europe: Frances James Child, *The English and Scottish Popular Ballads*, 5 vols. (Boston: Houghton, Mifflin, 1882–98); Svend Grundtvig and others, eds., *Danmarks Gamle Volkeviser*, 12 vols. (Copenhagen: Akademisk Forlag, 1853–1976); Olav Gurvin, *Norwegian Folk Music* (Oslo: Universitetsforlaget, 1958–   ); Dave Harker, *Fakesong: The Manufacture of British "Folksong" 1700 to the Present Day* (Milton Keynes, Eng.: Open University Press, 1985); A. L. Lloyd, *Folk Song in England* (London: Lawrence and Wishart 1967); James Porter, *The Traditional Music of the British Isles: A Reference Guide* (New York: Garland, 1989); Cecil J. Sharp, *English Folk Song: Some Conclusions* (1st ed., 1907), 4th ed., rev. Maud Karpeles (Belmont, Calif.: Wadsworth, 1965); France Vernillat and Jacques

Charpentreau, eds., *Dictionnaire de la chanson française* (Paris: Larousse, 1968).

Music of Ethnic Groups or Communities Stretching Across Several Nations: Samuel G. Aristead, Joseph H. Silverman, and Israel J. Katz, *Judeo-Spanish Ballads in Oral Tradition* (Berkeley and Los Angeles: University of California Press, 1968); Walter Deutsch, ed., *Dörfliche Tanzmusik im westpannonischen Raum* (Vienna: A. Schendel, 1990); Bálint Sárosi, *Gypsy Music*, trans. Fred MacNicoll (Budapest: Corvina, 1978); Mark Slobin, ed. and trans., *Old Jewish Folk Music: The Collection and Writings of Moshe Beregovski* (Philadelphia: University of Pennsylvania Press, 1982); Eric Werner, *A Voice Still Heard. . . . The Sacred Songs of the Ashkenazic Jews* (University Park: Pennsylvania State University Press, 1976); Walter Wiora, *Europäischer Volksgesang* (Cologne: Arno Volk, 1953).

European Musical Genres: Hermann Bausinger, *Formen der "Volkspoesie,"* 2nd rev. ed. (Berlin: Erich Schmidt, 1980); Rolf Wilhelm Brednich, Lutz Röhrich, and Wolfgang Suppan, eds., *Handbuch des Volksliedes*, 2 vols. (Munich: Wilhelm Fink, 1973, 1975); Werner Danckert, *Das europäische Volkslied* (Bonn: H. Bouvier, 1970; first publ. 1937); Richard Middleton, *Studying Popular Music* (Milton Keynes, Eng.: Open University Press, 1990); Leopold Schmidt, *Volksgesang und Volkslied: Proben und Probleme* (Berlin: Erich Schmidt, 1970); Leslie Shepard, *The Broadside Ballad: A Study in Origins and Meaning* (Hatboro, Pa. Legacy, 1978); Lajos Vargyas, *Hungarian Ballads and the European Ballad Tradition*, 2 vols. (Budapest: Akadémiai Kiadó, 1983).

Instruments: Walter Deutsch and Gerlinde Haid, eds., *Die Geige in der europäischen Volksmusik* (Vienna: A. Schendl, 1975); Erich Stockmann, ed., *Studia instrumentorum musicae popularis* (Stockholm: Musikhistoriska Museet, 1969–); Stig Walin, *Die schwedische Hummel* (Stockholm: Mordiska Museet, 1952).

Individual and Society in European Musical Life: Ernst Klusen, *Volkslied: Fund und Erfindung* (Cologne: Gerig, 1969); Heinrich W. Schwab, *Die Anfänge des weltlichen Berufsmusikertums in der mittelalterlichen Stadt: Studie zu einer Berufs- und Sozialgeschichte des Stadtmusikantentums* (Kassel: Bärenreiter, 1982).

Nationalism and Music: Sidney Finkelstein, *Composer and Nation: The Folk Heritage in Music*, 2nd ed. (New York: International Publishers, 1989); Dieter Rexroth, ed., *Zwischen den Grenzen: Zum Aspekt des Nationalen in der Musik* (Mainz: B. Schott's Söhne, 1979); Ralph Vaughan Williams, *National Music* (New York: Oxford University Press, 1954).

EUROPE DISCOGRAPHY

Discographical Note

Among the best surveys of national folk musics are those released on the Folkways label. Many music libraries, both public and university, have a selection of recordings on this label, and the Smithsonian Institution is currently rereleasing these recordings, often with new critical notes that will help the student. A particularly good selection of Eastern European traditions is to be found on the Nonesuch Explorer label. The suggested recordings on both Folkways and Nonesuch Explorer labels that follow in this brief discography are therefore only a few of those recordings that are available.

European academies of science and ethnological museums often produce recordings of extraordinarily high musical and educational quality, and these can often be recommended. During the 1970s and 1980s, a period of widespread folk-music revival in Europe, trade labels also produced voluminous recordings of local and national folk-music traditions.

Students will also wish to consider recordings of European art music and popular music, which are available in large numbers in libraries and record stores. Specific suggestions are therefore not necessary here. When studying and listening to these recordings, however, the student may wish to make comparisons in new ways and to examine new issues that their mass production reveal—for example, just how are these genres marketed in different ways, or how do different nations produce the "same" music but in different ways?

Deutsche Volkslieder,   2 disks (DGG 004-157, 004-160); *Electric Muse: The Story of Folk into Rock,* 4 disks. (Folk 1001); A. L. Lloyd and Ewan MacColl, *English and Scottish Popular Ballads.* (Washington 715–723); *Folk Music of France* (Folkways P 414); *Folk Music of Hungary,* collected by Béla Bartók (Folkways P 1000); *Folk Music of Portugal,* 2 disks (Folkways 4538); *Folk Music of Rumania,* collected by Béla Bartók (Folkways 419); *Islamic Ritual from Yugoslavia: Zikr of the Rafa'i Brotherhood* (UNESCO Collection, Philips 6586 015); *Le Mystère des Voix Bulgares,* 3 volumes (Electra/Nonesuch 79165-2); *Liturgical Chant for Lent and Easter: Armenian Mekhitarist Community of Venice* (UNESCO Collection, Philips 6586 025); *Songs and Dances of Holland* (Folkways 3576); *Songs and Dances of Norway* (Folkways FE 4008); *Songs and Dances of Spain,* 5 disks, with notes by Alan Lomax (Westminster WF 12001-5); *World Collection of Recorded Music,* 6 disks, based on collections of Constantin Brăiloiu (VDE 30-425-430).

9

MUSIC IN LATIN AMERICA

Thomas Turino

AN ANDEAN MESTIZO FIESTA IN PAUCARTAMBO, PERU

Most of the year the rural Andean town of Paucartambo seems almost empty. Many people have migrated to the nearby city of Cuzco, ancient capital of the Incas, or to larger cities on the Peruvian coast in search of employment and what they are told is a better way of life. In the weeks before the festival for the town's patron saint, the Virgen del Carmen (July 15–18), however, the place begins to stir in preparation. All the houses are freshly whitewashed, the streets are cleaned, and people who now live elsewhere begin returning home. The men who have accepted the roles of fiesta sponsorship visit the homes of relatives and friends who have promised financial contributions. Through tremendous expenditure, the main sponsor hopes that his lavishness will make this fiesta one that people will always remember. Meanwhile, more than enough food, liquor, beer, and fireworks are brought in, truck after truck—there is never enough. The primary participants in the fiesta are mestizos (people of mixed Spanish and indigenous *cultural* heritage) from the town itself; the people of the surrounding Quechua-speaking indigenous communities are excluded from taking part, and come mainly to watch.

In the weeks before the fiesta, the members of the various dance ensembles begin to rehearse for long hours on patios behind closed doors. They practice so that they may please the Virgin with their dancing and so that, this year, their group will be considered the finest. Meanwhile the women sew the elaborate costumes and older men make the masks. The townspeople say "Paucartambinos were born to dance," and for four days a year they do little else—in honor of their beloved saint and simply for the joy of it. For four days a year the plaza and cobblestone streets are transformed into a stage for a music drama that turns the normal order of daily life upside down, but that at the same time expresses some of the most important things that Paucartambinos have to say about themselves. These things are too old or too complicated or too deep to say directly with words, and so they dance.

The Dance Groups and Bands

Twelve or more costumed dance ensembles perform during the fiesta, and each one tells part of the story. The heros of the fiesta drama are a dance group known as the Qhapac Chunchos, the "rich and powerful jungle Indians." (Paucartambo is located in a beautiful river valley on the eastern slopes of the Andes near the jungle region.) Their costume includes the feathered headdress associated with Peruvian jungle Indians, and spears indicating their role as warriors. Within the fiesta drama, the Chunchos represent the home team, and throughout the fiesta the Chuncho king and his soldiers express the nobility of the town through dignified behavior and disciplined martial dance. During the processions of the statue of the Virgin, the Chunchos dance around her litter serving as an honor guard (Figure 9–1).

The other main protagonists are the Qollas, representing uncivilized outsiders, the traders of the high plateau of southern Peru. These mestizo dancers act out their part as savages from the puna (places of extremely high altitude) in various ways. They lead their llama (loaded with the goods that actual Qolla traders would carry) in and out of stores upsetting things as they go, they whip each other in one part of their dance, and they conduct themselves in an unruly manner throughout the fiesta days. Their dramatic persona thus contrasts fundamentally with the reserved, disciplined, dignified behavior of their rivals, the Chunchos (Figure 9–2).

According to one legend told in Paucartambo, the statue of the Virgen del Carmen originally belonged to the Qollas of Puno, Peru, but through battle the Chunchos won her and brought her to Paucartambo, where she remained as the provider of prosperity, health, and all good things. In another version, I was told that the Virgin originally belonged to Paucartambo. On one occasion the Qollas tried to steal her (the statue) away but were attacked by the Chunchos, who defended her and, by winning the battle, kept her safe in Paucartambo. As a

Figure 9–1. Chuncho Dancers—Paucartambo, Peru.

Figure 9–2. Qolla Dancers—Paucartambo, Peru.

reminder of these and other legends surrounding the Chunchos, the Qollas, and their special relationship to the Virgin, a dramatic mock battle is fought during the fiesta, and each year the Chunchos win.

The Saqras (or "devils," in the native Quechua language) are also central to the meaning of the fiesta, since they serve as foils to the holy saint. The Saqras' costumes include clothing representing the colonial Spanish, blonde wigs alluding to Europeans, and ceramic animal or monster masks. Their choreography is reminiscent of a genteel European contradance, and this fortifies the satiric portrayal of Europeans. These devil dancers thus combine imagery that expresses Peruvian attitudes about the evil that comes from beyond this world, as well as the evil that arrived in ships from beyond the Andean world beginning in the 1500s. During the two fiesta processions, the statue of the Virgin is carried through the streets accompanied by dancers, music, and the people of the town. At these times the Saqra dancers climb to the red-tiled roofs and, as the saint passes, shield their eyes from her brightness and slowly disappear behind the rooftops. Both in the drama and according to local beliefs, the Virgin rids each house of evil as she passes during the processions (Figure 9–3).

Most of the other dance groups in the fiesta likewise represent and parody outsiders. The Doctores, for example, represent lawyers and government officials who are known for their exploitation of rural Peruvians. As the Doctores move through the streets, they frequently capture people of the local indigenous communities who have come to town to watch the fiesta. Once the dancers have encircled the unfortunate man, they begin beating him with the heavy law books that they carry as a part of their costume while shouting a thousand abuses. The nature of the law book as weapon against common people is enacted by making it a concrete weapon—much to the hilarity of onlookers lucky enough not have gotten caught.

The cast also includes: the Negros, a dance ensemble representing black slaves brought during the colonial era; the Chilenos, expressing the enmity towards the devastating Chilean army of the War of the Pacific (1879–1884); the Chuk'chus, or malaria carriers from the jungle; the Majeños, exploitative liquor traders from the city of Arequipa; and the Maqtas, or clowns, who serve as the policemen during the fiesta, among other dance ensembles. As a wonderful addition, some dancers have lately begun to dress up as young hippie tourists. They wear backpacks and floppy hats, and stick toy cameras into people's faces as they move through the streets, thereby commenting on the most recent invasion of outsiders and indicating the ongoing creativity of these fiesta dance traditions.

Each dance group is accompanied by its own band and a series of distinctive pieces that, through association over the years, have become as important to the characters presented by the groups as their

Figure 9–3.   Saqra (Devil) Dancers—Paucartambo, Peru.

costumes, choreography, and dramatic behavior. Some of the music is particularly pictorial, such as the staggering melody played by a brass band to fit the Majeño liquor traders' drunken dance. Other music may be in the style of major local genres such as the mestizo wayno, or more European in form like the contradance music used by the Saqras and other groups. Unlike the dancers, who are mestizo town dwellers from Paucartambo, the bands are hired by the dance groups and usually comprise semiprofessional musicians from elsewhere.

Mestizo Culture

Throughout Latin America, the term mestizo must be understood as a relative concept that indicates a blending of Amerindian and European *cultural* heritages and worldviews. The fiesta in Paucartambo clearly illustrates the nature of mestizo culture. In regard to religious meaning, for example, the festival celebrates the Catholic saint, but for many people in the town her significance is fused with that of Pachamama, the pre-Columbian earth mother and provider of life. The Catholic festival also contains elements of indigenous harvest rituals, but nowhere is the blending of cultural heritages more evident than in the bands that perform music for the event.

Three types of ensemble are heard. Several European-style brass bands, representing a tradition that has become ubiquitous throughout Latin America during this century, are hired (for the Majeños and the processions). The Chunchos and several other groups use side-blown flute and drum ensembles; the combination of flutes (of many different types) with drums is a tradition that hails from pre-Columbian times in the Andes, Mexico, and other regions of Latin America. The major ensemble type used to provide mestizo dance music in the state of Cuzco, however, combines European and pre-Hispanic Andean instruments. These groups, known simply as orquestas tipicas ("typical orchestras"), feature a large diatonic harp and two violins, European instruments diffused throughout Latin America by colonial missionaries. Indigenous vertical end-notched flutes known as kenas, however, are also included, as are drums and accordion—the latter having come to the rural highlands before the middle of this century.

The musical style combines European (triadic) harmonies with Andean syncopated rhythms and styles of instrumental performance, including a dense, breathy tone quality on the flutes. Like most Andean musical genres, the majority of dance pieces consist of between two and four short phrases that are repeated over and over, often in forms such as AABB. Also consistent with music throughout the Andean region, a variety of scales ranging from five to seven pitches are used, and duple meter (as opposed to triple or "waltz time") predominates. The songs sung to the Virgin by some of the dance groups are in Quechua, Spanish, or sometimes both, and therefore clearly illustrate the blending of cultures that defines Andean mestizo identity generally.

Upon entering the town of Paucartambo during the fiesta days, one is struck by the apparent chaos and intensity of multiple bands playing simultaneously and strange costumed characters roaming the streets as if they had taken over the town. The plaza is filled to capacity with drunks, dancers, fighters, lovers, and spectators. Beneath the surface, many stories are being told, woven together, by the dance groups and their musicians, who are essential to the meaning and the very existence of the festival. Like a Mozart opera with its heroes and villains, slapstick and tragic characters, supernatural intervention, and final triumph of Virtue over Evil, the fiesta creates a time of special reality when all is as it should be. Unlike the European musical culture that Mozart represents, however, the central genesis of creation in Paucartambo is not a group of musical specialists but rather the people of the town themselves.

SOCIOCULTURAL HERITAGES AND HISTORICAL BACKGROUND

The mestizo fiesta just described, with its blending of indigenous Andean and Spanish elements, represents only one type of amalgamation that characterizes contemporary Latin American musical cultures. At the most general level, three major heritages are involved: Amerindian, differentiated according to a vast number of lowland and highland groups; the Spanish and Portuguese (via Brazil) traditions of the Iberian peninsula; and African traditions of the slaves brought during the colonial era. Except for Indian groups in relatively isolated but sometimes extensive regions of Mesoamerica, the Amazon, and the Andean highlands, it is the Iberian culture of the colonizers that provides the oldest common denominator—to the extent that one exists—for Latin American societies and musical cultures.

The importance of Iberian influence, of course, must be understood in political terms, since, through institutions such as colonial and contemporary states and the Catholic Church, people of European heritage have largely controlled the indigenous and African-American populations since the colonial era. Until the present century, the Catholic Church was the primary institution involved in the conscious transformation of Amerindian and African musical practices throughout Latin America. The conversion of Indians and African-Americans to a European worldview and European cultural behavior was fundamental to colonial domination, and music, dance, and drama proved to be powerful tools for attracting new followers to Christianity. Missionaries taught European music, but they also in some cases allowed for the inclusion of non-European practices under the guise of Christian trappings to aid conversion. The religious and musical syncretism described for Paucartambo's fiesta is typical of the result. As another example, in places like Cuba and northeastern Brazil the divinities of West African religions have been fused with Catholic saints, and African and European musical styles and practices have likewise been blended.

These examples illustrate that the nature of the cultural mix differs dramatically according to region in Latin America. Different musical cultures, however, do not necessarily fall neatly within the boundaries of the modern Latin American nation-states, but rather must be understood in localized terms. For example, the Andean countries of Colombia, Ecuador, Peru, and Bolivia all have territory in the Amazon, and all but the last have lowland areas on the Pacific side of the mountains where there are substantial black populations. Hence, distinct lowland Indian and African-American musical cultures frame the music of the Andean highlands, which itself is quite distinct from one region to another and varies according to ethnic/class divisions between indigenous Andeans and mestizos within the same region.

Various indigenous groups of the Amazon maintain the greatest distance from European influence, although contact with missionaries, white settlers, and capitalists has a long and in many cases disastrous history. The major pre-Columbian states of the Aztecs, Mayas, and the Incas were located in Mesoamerica and the Andes. Large native populations supplied much of the necessary labor for the Spanish colonizers, and it is in these areas where highland Amerindian cultural styles and resources remain vibrant in some communities, or have combined with Iberian elements to form the clearest examples of Latin American mestizo musical cultures. African influences remain the strongest and have fused most prominently with the Iberian in the Caribbean and along the coasts of Venezuela, Colombia, Ecuador, the Guiana region, and Brazil, where slave labor supported the plantation economy. Other Latin American countries such as Argentina, Chile, Uruguay, and Paraguay, as well as the major urban areas of most countries, are characterized by the predominance of European heritage and cultural style, although northern Chile and Argentina belong to the Andean culture area.

Beginning in the early decades of this century, nationalistic movements, the activities of urban intellectuals, and state cultural policies became the most prominent forces for the continued syncretism of Amerindian, Afro-American, and European musical resources. Since at least the middle of this century, the expansion of mass media and education and the tremendous flow of rural migrants to urban areas have rapidly and profoundly diffused urban-Western musical ideas and styles to the countryside, while the musical traditions of rural migrants have simultaneously influenced Latin American cities. Also in this century, musical instruments (e.g., electric guitar) and styles (jazz and rock) from North America have become important new resources for Latin American musicians, and U. S. influence (many Latin Americans would say imperialism) has begun to represent a new "common denominator" for the southern continent.

MUSICAL VALUES AND SOCIAL STYLE

Two Amerindian Cases

One of the first things that we learn by studying the music of other societies is that radically different conceptions about music are to be found, and that these form a coherent part of other people's different modes of social, economic, and political life. A brief comparison of several distinct societies found in Latin America will illustrate the diversity between groups and the cultural coherence within them. The Aymara (a major indigenous Andean linguistic group) of Huancané, Puno, in southern Peru will serve as our first point of reference (Figures 9–4 and 9–5).

Figure 9–4.   Aymara Pinkillu (Flute) Ensemble—Huancané, Puno, Peru.

The Aymara have a heightened collective orientation to social life. The desire for community solidarity, reciprocity, and egalitarian relations constitute core values for approaching and ordering the social world. It is therefore not surprising that ways of thinking about music and approaches to performance emerge from these same principles. For example, Aymara-speaking peasants in this region generally only play music in large community wind ensembles (twelve to fifty musicians, with either panpipes or vertical flutes accompanied by drums) for public communal festivals; even practicing music by oneself is rare. During festivals any male community member is welcome to join in playing regardless of his musical knowledge or ability. Also, Aymara musicians do not usually comment on or correct other players in their group. Within typical community ensembles, there is no fixed hierarchy of authority or power—in contrast, for example, to a Western symphony orchestra directed by a conductor. Ultimately, among the Aymara in Huancané equal access to musical experience and the maintenance of amicable communal relations are granted more importance than attempts to strictly control the quality of an ensemble's musical performance.

In these peasant communities, individuals generally do not like to stand out or be singled out in social situations, both because the collective is granted greater importance than individual identity and perhaps for fear of arousing jealousy. Likewise, in musical performance there is no place for the soloist. Rather, the primary aesthetic ideal expressed by Aymara musicians is that ensembles should "play as one" or sound

Figure 9–5.   Aymara Sikuri (Panpipe) Ensemble—Huancané, Puno, Peru.

like a single instrument, and no individual's instrument should stand out from the dense sound of these Andean wind ensembles. The preference for a dense, well-integrated sound is also reflected in Andean instrumental performance techniques and instrument construction. Flutes and panpipes are blown to create a breathy sound, which aids group blending, and instruments are tuned slightly differently so that a rich combination of overtones will result. The act of "playing as one" and creating a thick, well-blended sound with no soloists thus becomes a clear musical articulation of the central ways of being for this egalitarian, collectively oriented society.

Musical aesthetics and conceptions about music among various Amazonian Indian groups share some of these elements but differ radically in other ways. Whereas Aymara musical culture centers around wind instruments and drums, and singing is unimportant, the music of the Suyá Indians of the central Brazilian Amazon is predominatly vocal, sometimes accompanied by rattles. As with the Aymara, collective participation in musical performances during festivals is a vital way to represent and maintain social unity within a village, and the blending of voices in unison singing embodies an important aesthetic value. But the Suyá also have songs that are individually owned and sung, indicating that there is more room for individual expression than among the Aymara of Huancané, where solo performance is basically nonexistent.

To take this one step further: While the Aymara stress "playing as one," some Suyá performances include a variety of individuals singing their own songs simultaneously, along with shouts, laughter, and bird-call imitations. This type of Suyá performance results in what to our—or Aymara—ears would be cacophony. Yet for the Suyá all these sounds contribute essentially to the total creation of a performance. We might speculate that the Suyá aesthetic, which in certain instances favors the dense combination of multiple, relatively independent sounds to form the whole, might be related to the sonic landscape of the forest itself, which similarly consists of a dense composite of independent sounds—insect, bird, and animal. It also reflects a different conception, relative to the Aymara, of the relationship of individuals to the community.

That Suyá musical production might be in part modeled on the soundscape of their natural surroundings seems probable given their belief that songs come from and are learned from animals, insects, fish, and plants of the forest. As with other Amazonian groups, important Suyá festivals and song types are named for and involve the representation of natural species. These have symbolic importance in relation to the ecological environment that sustains the Suyá through hunting, fishing, and agriculture. Many indigenous Andean festials and song types are similarly related to the specific environment and Andeans' occupations as agriculturalists and herders (e.g., songs for animal and earth fertility).

In addition to ecological-economic issues, musical styles and genres are used to distinguish and represent distinct groups within societies almost universally. For the Suyá, gender and age are central criteria for delineating important social categories and status within a village, and musical genres and singing styles are likewise differentiated according to gender and age. In Aymara society, the strictly separated gender roles in all realms of life are articulated in musical practice: women participate as singers and dancers, while instrumental performance is solely a male activity. Within Aymara communities in Huancané, social distinctions beyond gender and age are not marked; however, musical style and competition between performing ensembles (each representing a specific village) explicitly identify and separate the different local communities.

Mestizo/Criollo Musical Orientations

Musical thought and aesthetic values among the mestizo and criollo (Spanish-heritage) populations of Latin America vary according both to region and to rural versus urban locale; but overall they strongly partake of the European orientation and hence are closer to our own ways of thinking about music. In contrast with the Aymara, the primary criterion for judging a musical performance among criollos and mestizos is the quality of the sound produced. Thus, in Euro-American society, the musical personnel will be regulated toward the goal of producing the best sound possible. Like many orchestras and musical ensembles in the United States, this requires a hierarchy of control by which a leader or director has the authority to limit participation to competent musicians and direct their participation. This in turn is made possible by the hierarchical, specialized nature of the society as a whole. While this approach is logical given a European orientation, and to our ears might result in a more pleasing musical performance, this modus operandi would be rejected among the Aymara, for whom such control and limitations on participation would be highly offensive. Among the Suyá, the limited, controlled music might be considered incomplete—not beautiful—without the heterogeneous sounds of community participation.

In criollo-mestizo musical cultures there are specialized professional or semiprofessional musicians like those hired for the Paucartambo fiesta, and there are also amateur musicians who make music for their own enjoyment. Both of these musical roles are absent among the Aymara of Huancané, and although Suyá individuals make music for their own enjoyment the concept of professional musician does not pertain to their society either.

As in North American society, the status of professional criollo and mestizo Latin American musicians varies according to—and is indicated by—the fame and salaries that they command. The musicians hired for rural mestizo events are often treated like low-status servants, as is the case in Paucartambo. The strolling mariachi musicians who work the streets and restaurants in Mexico would also be considered low-status, as would most who perform in bars and clubs throughout the continent. Particularly in rural regions, mestizo parents often do not want their children to take up music since it is associated with drinking and lowlife activities. This contrasts with Aymara peasant society, where the musicians are granted prestige and thanks for making the community fiestas come alive. In Suyá society, singing is simply a normal part of social behavior, and if people refuse to sing it is generally understood that they are unhappy or angry. The negative attitudes toward musicians in many rural mestizo-criollo contexts are carried over to the urban areas among the lower and working classes. Nonetheless, in the urban areas there are a minority of professional musicians who are considered "artists," usually those who perform European classical music or, less frequently, urban-popular music. Such performers are granted prestige, fame, and money.

The higher prestige granted European classical music and urban forms in Latin America mirrors the highly stratified class divisions found in most Latin American countries, just as age-group and gender distinctions are musically marked in Suyá society. The prestige of musical forms and the musicians that play them derives from that of the social classes with which the music is associated. In much of Latin America, class position involves ethnicity, rural versus urban residence (with the upper classes in the cities), education, and wealth. Generally, European styles form the top of a musical hierarchy, with Amerindian and African-American styles representing the bottom rungs, thereby reproducing the class structure in musical terms.

MUSICAL INSTRUMENTS, GENRES, AND STYLE

Lowland and Highland Indigenous Musical Instruments

As has already been seen in the Aymara-Suyá comparison, different Latin American societies vary widely in their musical practices and values. The prominence of vocal music among the Suyá is typical for lowland Indian societies. Different vocal styles are found even within the same Amazonian group, depending on the occasion. In general terms, a loud shouting or chantlike style, as among the Suyá (akia) and Xavante (daño're) of Brazil, is widely diffused in the Amazon. Another common style performed includes soft-high-pitched singing, as among the Shipibo of the Peruvian Amazon.

In addition to vocal music, however, panpipes, side-blown and vertical flutes (end-notched or with a recorderlike mouthpiece), and various types of trumpets (often made from a long hollowed-out log or tree branch) are used throughout the Amazonian region. Double-headed drums to accompany wind and vocal performance are ubiquitous among Amazonian groups, as are a variety of shakers and other percussion instruments such as stamping tubes (hollowed-out branches used to stamp the ground). Stringed instruments such as the musical bow are played, and local copies of the violin have become important among some Amazonian groups in Ecuador.

Like Amazonian Indians, the indigenous groups of highland regions in South America and Mesoamerica traditionally performed vocal music, wind instruments, drums, and percussion primarily. The pre-Columbian Mesoamerican societies had numerous multiple-flutes on which several tubes, each with its own fingerholes, were attached to the same whistle mouthpiece, thereby making solo polyphonic performance possible. Long wooden and conch-shell trumpets were also used, as were ocarinas, different types of whistles, gourd rattles, and bone rasps in preconquest Mesoamerica. Central instruments in Aztec musical culture were the teponaztli (a slit or tongue drum producing two pitches) and the huehuetl (a single skin-headed drum). A wooden two-toned slit drum known as tun (tunkul) is still played in Guatamala, as are turtleshell and slit drums in Mexico. Flute-and-drum performance remains the most traditional type of Indian musical expression in contemporary Mexico.

In the Andes, panpipes (antaras and sikus), trumpets, and vertical end-notched flutes (such as the contemporary kena) were common in the preconquest period. The performance of conch-shell trumpets has been maintained since pre-Columbian times, as has the use of curved trumpets (e.g., the contemporary wakrapuku made of animal horn). Stringed instruments were not used in the Andes before the Spanish conquest.

Among the Quechua and Aymara speakers of southern Peru, Bolivia, and Chile, double-row panpipes (a single scale alternates between the two rows) are divided between pairs of players who perform in interlocking fashion. This musical practice, among many others, illustrates the Andean value of reciprocity and collective activity. (A double-row panpipe, siku, cannot be properly played solo.) Vertical end-notched flutes approximately two feet in length are still played in large ensembles accompanied by drums, as are side-blown flutes and various kinds of vertical duct flutes apparently of postconquest origin (e.g., pinkullus and tarkas). In contrast to mestizo and criollo ensembles, an important feature of contemporary Indian musical performance in the Andes is that wind-instrument types are not mixed within ensembles. Although vocal music is relatively unimportant among the Aymara of Peru, it is central among the indigenous majority of Quechua speakers in the Andean region. Andeans show a preference for high-pitched singing and instrumental performance (this seems to have been a pre-Columbian trait both in Mexico and in the Andes), and the vocal performance involves nasal head and throat singing.

Strings and Other Musical Instruments

Highland Indians, mestizos, and criollos throughout Latin America use a large variety of stringed instruments introduced from the Iberian peninsula. The violin and diatonic harp, diffused by colonial missionaries, have produced important Indian and mestizo musical traditions in Mexico (e.g., along the Atlantic coast and among the Purépechas of Michoacán and the Yaquis of Sonora) as well as in the Andean region from Ecuador to the state of Cuzco, Peru. Diatonic-harp performance is also a major tradition in Paraguay and in Venezuela (Figure 9–6).

Spanish guitars are used widely and have spawned the greatest number of local variants. These include the Andean charango (guitar-shaped, about the size of a ukulele, with five groups of strings and a

Figure 9–6.   José Romero, Purépecha, violinist from Michoacán, Mexico.

Figure 9–7.   Bandurria players accompanying a Carnival Dance in Canchis, Cusco, Peru.

round or flat back) among both indigenous and mestizo players in southern Peru and Bolivia. In Mexico we find the vihuela (smaller than a guitar, with five strings and a convex back), the huapanguera (slightly wider and deeper than a guitar, with eight strings in five courses), the jarana (smaller than a guitar, with five strings), and guitarrón (a large four- or five-stringed bass guitar with a round back). Other guitar types include the Venezuelan cuatro (smaller than a guitar, with four strings), the highland Colombian tiple (slightly smaller than a guitar, with four courses of three strings each tuned like the four highest strings of a guitar), and the five-stringed viola of Brazil (usually with five double courses), among many other examples. A particularly beautiful descendent of the European guitar family is the guitarrón of Chile (with twenty-five strings, deeper than a guitar, used to accompany ballad singing). In addition to these stringed instruments, mandolins and other instruments resembling them (e.g., the bandúrria and the Colombian bandola) are found throughout Latin America (Figure 9–7).

Different varieties of accordions (piano accordions and single- to multiple-row button accordions) have become popular in a number of rural and urban regional dance and song traditions, including the *conjunto* style of the Texas-Mexican border region and throughout much of Mexico, the *vallenato* cumbia music of Colombia, the mestizo fiesta

orchestras in Peru, the *tonadas* and *cuecas* of Chile, *merengue* performance in the Dominican Republic and other genres throughout the Caribbean, and the baião/forró style of dance music in northeastern Brazil.

In southern Mexico and Central America the African-derived
marimba has been taken up by both Indian and mestizo musicians as
a central tradition. In Guatemala, for example, it is considered the national instrument. Marimbas have buzzing gourd resonators and vary
in size, often requiring multiple players on a single instrument. As already
mentioned, the brass-band tradition has become extremely important
in both Indian and mestizo community festivals throughout Latin
America, as have saxophones and clarinets.

Indian Genres and Style

Lowland Indian song and instrumental genres and their musical
characteristics are so varied that it is difficult to make generalizations.
Everything from two-tone scales to scales with more than seven pitches
are found among the Shipibo of the Peruvian Amazon, for example.
Songs may have a range within a third (from *do* to *mi*), or may span
several octaves using both stepwise motion and large leaps. Monophonic
singing and instrumental performance is most common among Amazonian groups, but there are many exceptions such as the Suyá practice
of singing multiple songs simultaneously. Amazonian music tends to
feature many repetitions of short phrases, and melodies are often united
by the constant repetition of a few rhythmic motives. In similar fashion,
the song texts also exhibit a high degree of repetition. Generally, duple
meter predominates. Song types seem to be primarily identified by their
functions or performance occasions. These types include drinking songs;
festival dance songs (often evoking or named for different plants or
animals); songs used for curing; songs related to work, hunting, and
agriculture; and epic or mythic songs.

As in the Amazonian Indian cultures, genres and characteristics
of highland indigenous music are too varied to summarize beyond a
few general points. Among highland peoples, genres tend to be con-
cretely associated with and named for specific festivals, dances, and
functions. Among indigenous Andeans, music and dance are generally
linked conceptually, the same name being used to refer to both the music
and the dance. Indians and mestizos throughout highland Latin America
perform costumed fiesta dances similar to those described for Paucartambo. For example, blacks and other groups of "outsiders" are
represented in fiesta traditions by the Purépecha of Michoacán, Mexico, just as "devil dances" are found in highland Colombia and much
more widely. After the musical repertories that are named for particular
dances, the specific fiesta or ritual is the second most important criterion
for defining musical categories in highland indigenous societies. In either

case, a given group of pieces within the same local category may or may not be unified in terms of musical style. Among indigenous Andeans, some musical terms such as kashua (a circle dance) and harawi (today usually an unaccompanied agricultural song) are of pre-Columbian origin. But these genres are not stylistically unified even within the same region, and such terms are usually further defined by context: "tuta kashua" (kashua used for a courting dance at night in Canas, Cuzco), "kashua of Chiaraje" (a song-dance performed by women during a ritual battle in Canas), and so on.

Most traditional highland indigenous music is monophonic, but again exceptions abound. For example, the large Aymara wind ensembles of southern Peru and Bolivia use parallel 4ths, 5th, and 3rds; the harp-violin duets of the Yaqui Indians of Mexico and Quechua performers in the state of Ayacucho, Peru, involve polyphony. Duple meter predominates and syncopated rhythms are a common feature in Andean Indian music. Generally, highland Indian melodies comprise relatively few short phrases that are repeated in an open-ended fasion (e.g., ||:AABB:||, ||:ABAB:||, ||:AABBCC:||, etc.), with internal motivic repetition often taking place between phrases. Ostinato (the steady repetition of a given pattern, serving as the structural basis for a piece) and strophic forms are also found throughout Mesoamerica and the Andean region. Scale types must be considered according to specific locations and even according to the different instrumental and vocal traditions of a single locale.

Mestizo Song-Dance Genres

Within many Latin American countries, certain mestizo genres are more widely diffused and exhibit greater unity as stylistic complexes than the localized Indian musical forms. The specific metric-rhythmic underpinning of a given mestizo genre is frequently the clearest criterion for identification. In Peru and Bolivia, the *wayno* (huayno, or wayñu, pronounced "wino" or "wiño") is the primary mestizo song-dance genre. Its distinctive rhythmic underpinning fluctuates between an eighth-note triplet and an eighth and two sixteenths. It is a strophic song in duple meter in which the text-musical phrases are repeated (e.g., AABB). The wayno can be either a couples or a group circle dance, but in either case it involves partners. The themes of the texts (sung in Spanish, Quechua, or both) cover a wide range of topics including joking songs, protest songs, and songs of departure, but they are most frequently about love. Mestizo waynos usually conclude with an independent fuga section with its own short, distinct melody and text.

In Mexico the term son refers to a dance-song genre with a number of regional variants, and like the Andean wayno it is performed by a variety of regional ensembles. For most regional sones, the combination of 3/4 and 6/8 meters (both simultaneously in different instrumental parts and sequentially in the bass and melodic parts) played in a relatively fast tempo serve as unifying stylistic features, as does the fast foot tapping (zapateo) in this couples dance. Mexican sones are generally strophic love songs, most frequently using coplas (stanzas with four octosyllabic lines, although more lines may be added). Like the Andean wayno, sones often include instrumental introductions, interludes (sometimes improvised), and conclusions.

The cueca, a strophic dance-song genre using coplas and in 6/8 meter, has long been considered the national dance of Chile, and it is related stylistically to the mestizo marinera of Peru and the *zamba* of Argentina. The bambuco is a central mestizo dance-music genre of the Andean region of Colombia. Like the Mexican son, it is a couples dance in which the partners use handkerchiefs and flirtatious motions. Like the son and many Latin American mestizo song-dance genres, it simultaneously juxtaposes 3/4 and 6/8 meters—employing, for example, a bass line or drum part playing in three and a strummed guitar or melodic part in 6/8 in rapid tempo. In highland Colombia, bambucos may be performed by string ensembles consisting of guitars, tiples, bandolas, and requintos (smaller six-string guitars), or by side-blown flute and percussion ensembles known as chirimías.

The music used to accompany the national dance of Venezuela, the joropo, also juxtaposes 3/4 and 6/8 meters in rapid tempo with a great deal of syncopation. Joropos are typically performed with diatonic harp, cuatro, maracas, and vocals. The bassline of the harp is in triple meter, and the strummed cuatro and maracas usually in 6/8, although both include rhythmic improvisation and varied accents. The vocal and/or harp melody moves between a duple and triple feeling, and the ensemble as a whole creates an exciting rhythmic tension. This combining of 3/4 and 6/8 meters also characterizes a number of song-dance forms in Argentina, Paraguay, Chile, and elsewhere. The most common alternatives in South America are genres in 3/4 meter such as the pasillo (Ecuador and Colombia) and the waltz, and pieces in duple meter reminiscent of the polka and marches.

Iberian and Mestizo Lyrical and Narrative Genres

Besides instrument types and the introduction of European scales and triadic harmony, which have become standard for most mestizo music, Iberian musical influence in Latin America is perhaps most strongly seen in the verse forms and narrative song genres. Song forms derived from the Spanish romance (ballads sung since the Middle Ages) and even some old romances themselves have been preserved in different parts of Latin America. Romances usually treated subjects of an epic, historical, or religious nature, in stanzas of four octosyllabic lines (coplas).

Other Iberian text forms such as the décima (with ten-line stanzas and varying rhyme or assonance schemes) have also been extremely influential in Latin America.

Closely related to the romance tradition is the Mexican corrido, a ballad type that comments on current and historical events. In the Texas-Mexican border region there is a whole corpus of corridos recounting the trials of migrating to the United States and the dismal living conditions found there by migrant laborers. Many corridos were composed following the death of John F. Kennedy (a hero of Mexican-Americans and Mexicans). Corridos that tell of the Mexican revolution and the exploits of heroes such as Gregorio Cortez are still sung. Corridos are usually accompanied by guitars; they may be sung solo, but they are typically sung by at least two singers in parallel 3rds. The use of parallel 3rds for singing and in instrumental performance is a hallmark Iberian trait found ubiquitously in Latin American mestizo and criollo musical cultures.

Another prime example of the legacy of Spanish ballads in Latin America is the Chilean verso. Versos are often composed of six stanzas: an opening quatrain followed by four décimas on historical, epic, religious, or topical themes, and a fifth décima known as the "farewell." The rhyme scheme of the décimas usually approximates an ABBAACCDDC form, of seventeenth-century Spanish courtly origin. These ballads are accompanied by the twenty-five-stringed Chilean guitarrón in the "canto a lo pueta" ("poet's song") tradition. Both the melodies and the guitarrón accompaniment are fairly stereotyped, with the latter primarily alternating between the tonic and dominant (do–sol) chords. To the accompaniment of a single guitarrón player, a number of singers may alternate the décima stanzas of their own distinct songs until each has performed his farewell verse. If a number of singers participate (alternating their stanzas in turn), a single performance will normally last up to four hours, but for certain special festivals a performance can continue for days. If a rivalry emerges between established singers, they may take each other on in song duels and include ironic or mocking verses aimed at their opponent. Many of the aspects that characterize verso performance in Chile, including the song duels, are found in Argentine ballad traditions. In both the Argentine and Chilean traditions, ballads are broadly divided between a lo humano (about men) and a lo divino (religious themes).

Afro-Latin American Instruments and Musical Practices

As might be expected from its derivation, the marimba used by Indians and mestizos in Mesoamerica also has a central place in certain African-American communities in Latin America. Along the Pacific coast of Ecuador and Colombia, an area with a large Afro-American population, the marimba is used for the currulao, a community dance where women and men may meet and form new relationships. A currulao performance exemplifies a variety of African musical features. For example, the marimba (similar to a wooden xylophone, having twenty to twenty-eight keys with bamboo resonators, played by two musicians) is accompanied by single-headed conical drums (like conga drums) of two different sizes and classified as male and female, as is often the case for African instruments. The currulao ensemble also includes two deeper double-headed drums (bombos) and bamboo shakers. As in most sub-Saharan African music, the basis of the marimba music is an ostinato with improvised variations. The drums and shakers play separate but interlocking rhythmic parts, often in duple and triple meter simultaneously. This African-derived style of ensemble performance is used to accompany a solo singer, who interlocks his improvised or set vocal part with a female chorus in call-and-response fashion—another typical African musical practice.

Along with the marimba, drums, other percussion instruments, and the musical bow (e.g., in the Caribbean and the berimbau of Brazil), another important African instrument, the lamellaphone (e.g., the mbira, or "thumb piano"), also made its way to the Americas. In the Caribbean, a large box-lamellaphone (marímbula) serves a bass function in a variety of ensembles. A smaller hand-held lamellaphone of Angolan character was used in Brazil in the last century, and the smaller type is still played among the Saramaka of Suriname. Runaway-slave communities established in the forests of Suriname maintain their own amalgamation of African cultural practices to this day. Among these is the playing of papai benta, a lamellaphone with reed keys mounted on bridges on a flat board. Held between the knees and played with the index fingers, the instrument is used to perform pieces which are ostinatos with variations, as is the case with African mbira music. After lamellaphones, drums are the most prominent instrument type found among the Saramaka of Suriname, used to accompany dancing and historical songs, and to call the gods and ancestors.

The use of African-derived musical styles, concepts, and instruments is perhaps best exemplified in Latin America by certain religious traditions in the Caribbean and the Candomble religions of Bahía in northeastern Brazil. In Candomblé, music and dance are fundamental to worshiping various orixas (deities) hailing largely from the Yoruba religion of Nigeria. The music is performed vocally with a trio of different-sized single-headed drums (atabaques), also of Yoruba origin, and a double bell (agogo), for dancing, invocations to the gods, and to induce spirit possession. Even West African words are retained in the songs, although their meanings may be forgotten, and African rituals such as "the baptism of drums" (drums being considered sacred instruments, and dedicated to the divinities) are practiced in Bahía. Most striking, the roles of the double bell and of the different drums in the trio mirror those for the same instruments in Yoruba musical performance. The bell plays an ostinato pattern that serves to orient the other musicians, the two smaller drums play a separate ostinato part, and the largest, or "mother," drum is used for improvisation by a master drummer.

URBAN POPULAR MUSIC

To most non-Latin Americans, the concept of Latin American, or "Latin," music conjures up images of urban-popular styles stemming largely from the Caribbean and Brazil such as the mambo, the cha-cha, the tango (Argentina), the samba and bossa nova, calypso, and more recently reggae. The most widely known urban-popular styles were largely, or at least substantially, created out of the Afro-Latin American heritage in parallel fashion to the most famous North American urban-popular forms (ragtime, jazz, blues, rock). Becoming "dance crazes" at different times in the United States and Europe, various genres of Latin American popular music have been marketed and diffused throughout the world. Rhythms such as the clave part of the Cuban son (discussed later) have been incorporated in urban-popular music in as unlikely a place as China. As another striking example of the "global musical village," Afro-Cuban elements have become prime ingredients in Central and West African urban-popular music during this century—completing but not ending the circle of influence. It is also in Latin American urban-popular music that we find some of the clearest examples of the blending of African, European, and in some cases Amerindian musical resources.

Cuba

The Caribbean, and particularly Cuba, has produced some of the most internationally influential urban-popular musical styles. Various important Cuban genres evolved during the nineteenth and early twenieth centuries, including the habanera and the danzón, from the European-derived contradanza. A distinctive recurrent rhythmic pattern (♪♩ ♪♪ or ♪♪♩ ♪♪) in 2/4 called the "habanera rhythm" is related to this complex of dances and is also a basic feature of the tango. A fundamental component of the danzón is the cinquillo rhythm (♩ ♪♪♪♪♩), which some writers speculate is of Afro-Haitian origin. In Cuba, the danzón was in a form resembling the European rondo. It was performed by large orchestras comprised of European wind and stringed instruments and percussion, or with European salon instrumentation (flute, piano, bass, violins) accompanied by Cuban percussion (e.g., güiro or gourd scraper, and timbales, a type of Cuban drum set). By the end of the nineteenth century, however, Afro-Cuban and European musical elements had been combined in the danzón. Black danzón bands added greater syncopation into the more restrained European style, and often concluded danzones with a rhythically animated section comprising improvised solos.

Another important source for Cuban popular music was the Afro-Cuban *rumba guaguanco*. By the late nineteenth century, this genre was performed by a lead singer and chorus accompanied by drums and rhythm sticks. The rumba guaguanco has two main sections. Typically, after a brief vocal introduction, the main verses and chorus refrains are sung in the first part followed by the second call-and-response section in which the chorus repeats a single melodic phrase in alternation with the lead singer's improvisations. Characteristic of the guaguanco, the lower drum plays a $3 + 3 + 2$ pattern (4/4 ♩ ♩ ♩ ♩ 𝄾 𝄾 𝄾 ♩), and the sticks play a pattern which has become known as *clave*: 4/4 ♩ ♩. ♩ 𝄾 ♩ ♩ 𝄾

Features of the rumba guaguanco are heard in the Cuban son. Peter Manuel has pointed out that the latter incorporated the $3 + 3 + 2$ pattern (in the bass) and some variation of the clave pattern. Also like the Afro-Cuban rumba, the son was divided into two sections, with verses in the first part and improvisation and a call-and-response format in the second, or montuno, section. By the 1930s, the son had become the most popular dance genre in Havana, and it was soon to have a major impact internationally. In the 1940s and 1950s, Arsenio Rodríguez led a large ensemble consisting of tres (small guitarlike instruments with three courses of two or three strings each), piano, bass, trumpets and other winds, and Cuban percussion instruments such as timbales, conga drum, bongos, bell, and güiro. The son, as played by dance orchestras like that of Rodríguez (who worked for a time in New York), provided fundamental ingredients for modern salsa music. Salsa is now associated with musicians in Hispanic New York and elsewhere in the United States as well as in the Caribbean, and is currently enjoying a tremendous wave of popularity throughout Latin America.

Brazil

To mention Brazil is to recall images of Rio's carnival with its long parades, floats, elaborate costumes, and samba percussion ensembles. Samba, the music of carnival, has both rural and urban variants in Brazil, but it arose as an important urban-popular dance only after World War I. The special kind of urban samba heard at carnival comes from the predominantly black hillside slums of Rio. In keeping with its Afro-Brazilian roots, this type of samba is traditionally accompanied by huge percussion ensembles in which the different instruments—e.g., surdo (large bass drum), agogo (double bell), pandeiro (tambourine), tamborim (small hand-held drum), reco-reco (metal spring scraper), and cuica (friction drum)—all play their own syncopated interlocking parts. The songs accompanied by the percussion ensemble are sung in call-and-response fashion, also illustrating an Afro-Brazilian source. Carnival performance—percussion music, song, and dance—has been grounded in the escola de samb ("Samba school," referring to large social-musical organizations) tradition from the urban slum areas since the 1920s. In recent years Rio's carnival has become increasingly commercialized and controlled by outside economic and media interests, losing much of its grass-roots basis.

During the 1930s and 1940s an urban ballroom type of samba, performed by Western-style dance orchestras and a greatly reduced percussion section, became popular. In the late 1950s a softer, guitar-based type of music emerged on Brazil's popular-music scene. Known as *bossa nova*, this style maintained the syncopated accompaniment patterns of the samba (played on guitar, although also accompanied by other instruments) and included more elaborate harmonic schemes. The vocal style was understated, and some performers integrated improvisational jazz techniques. The song texts became quite sophisticated, as was fitting for the largely middle- and upper-class audiences of the style. Since the 1960s, a number of U.S.- and English-rock-influenced musical styles have become important in Brazil, and most recently U.S. "hip-hop" (e.g., rap, breakdancing) culture has become extremely popular with low-income urban Brazilians.

The Cumbia

Within Latin America itself, one of the most important urban-popular genres is the cumbia. Of Afro-Colombian origin from the rural Atlantic coastal area, cumbias were traditionally played with either a side-blown reed instrument known as pito or vertical duct flutes known in Colombia as gaitas (of lowland Amerindian heritage), several drums, and shakers. By the 1960s and in the decades to follow, ensembles playing a style that generally became known as "cumbia" were found in many Latin American countries from southern Texas (among Texas-Mexicans) to Chile. Cumbias were performed either with accordion or by urban dance bands (with electric guitars and bass, keyboard, horns, and percussion including the güiro and drums). The cumbia exhibits its Afro-American heritage in the distinct interlocking rhythmic parts played by the various instruments. The general metric framework is duple or quadruple; the bass emphasizes the downbeat, and the second half of the beat is generally emphasized by the scraper, a struck bell, or a high-pitched drum.

Another type of ensemble associated with cumbia in the Atlantic coastal region of Colombia is known as vallenato. Vallenato ensembles consist of an accordion (whose player also sings verses), bass, drums, and other percussion including a scraper (like a güiro, but known in the region as guacharaca). This type of ensemble plays a variety of genres such as the paseo and the merengue (distinct from the Dominican merengue). The melody, bass, and drum parts are often highly syncopated; in the merengue the bass plays triple metric patterns against the basic duple, whereas the paseo is more consistently duple.

The Creation of an Urban-Popular Genre: Chicha

Cumbia andina, or chicha (the term for Andean corn beer), has evolved in Lima since the 1960s. This genre may serve as a final example of the amalgamation of widely disparate musical resources within an urban-popular style. Chicha musicians fuse the cumbia rhythm (in the bass and percussion parts) with the form and phrase structure of the Andean wayno. Chicha bands include electric guitars, bass, and sometimes organ or synthesizer, with percussion including the güiro and the Cuban timbales. The style may be seen as truly representative of the identity of its fans and performers—young highland migrants in Lima, or the children of migrants—as Peruvians themselves frequently remark.

Throughout Latin America there have been tremendous waves of rural-to-urban migration, in part because of the economic crisis created by population expansion in rural areas. Since the 1940s, Peruvian highlanders have come to the capital city of Lima in great numbers. In many cases they recreated aspects of their highland culture in this Western-oriented city, in the face of ethnic prejudices against people from the mountains. In recent decades the children of Andean migrants are becoming one of the largest demographic groups in Lima, but their cultural identity remains ambiguous. Born in Lima, they are considered Limeños by their parents and other highlanders, but coastal Limeños do not fully accept them, and consider them highlanders. The style of cumbia Andina grows out of the ambiguous bicultural position of these teenagers. They represent the aspect of their Andean heritage with elements of highland music—the wayno—and combine this with the cumbia, which became a symbol of urban music for highland Peruvians by the 1960s. The use of electric instruments was influenced by North American rock music around the same time and fit with their teenage orientation. The final result of this synthesis was a musical style that precisely expressed the identity of the children of Andean migrants in the city: a musical portrait of who they are and where they are.

The use of music to construct and express social identity is, of course, almost a universal phenomenon. Different styles of rock music serve as identity emblems for North American teenagers, enabling them to join together with others of like mind. The Suyá of the Brazilian

Amazon consider a particular type of song, akia, to be basic to what it means to be Suyá, since they consider akia to be unique to themselves. Aymara communities in Huancané compete with other local communities and express social solidarity and uniqueness primarily through the performing style and original repertory of their village musical ensembles. Finally, a fundamental aspect of what it means to be from Paucartambo is the knowledge and ability to dance in the fiesta for their patron saint. "Paucartambinos were born to dance," the Suyá to sing, and the Aymara to play panpipes. There is tremendous cultural variation in the different regions and societies of Latin America, and this variation is expressed musically as well as in other ways. What remains constant is that people represent and recognize themselves through the music that they create and enjoy (Figure 9–8).

Figure 9–8.   Devil Dancers—Michoacán, Mexico.

LATIN AMERICA BIBLIOGRAPHY

General: Gerard Béhague, "Folk and Traditional Music of Latin America: General Prospect and Research Problems," *The World of Music* 25/2 (1982); Dale A. Olsen, "Folk Music of South America—a Musical Mosaic," in Elizabeth May, ed., *Musics of Many Cultures: An Introduction* (Berkeley: University of California Press, 1980).

Highland Indigenous and Mestizo Music: Max Peter Baumann, "Music of the Indios in Bolivia's Andean Highlands (survey)," *World of Music* 25/2 (1982); Robert Garfias, "The Marimba of Mexico and Central America," *Latin American Music Review* 4/2 (1983); Karl Gustav Izikowitz, *Musical and Other Sound Instruments of the South American Indians* (Göteborg, Sweden: Elanders Boktrycheri Aktiebolag, 1934); Manuel Peña, *The Texas-Mexican Conjunto: History of a Working-Class Music* (Austin: University of Texas Press, 1985); John Schechter, "The Diatonic Harp in Ecuador: Historical Background and Modern Traditions," Parts 1 & 2, *Journal of the American Musical Instrument Society* 10, 11 (1984, 1985); Thomas Stanford, "The Mexican Son," *Yearbook of the IFMC* (1972); Robert Stevenson, *In Aztec and Inca Territory* (Berkeley: University of California Press, 1968); Thomas Turino, "The Coherence of Social Style and Musical Creation Among the Aymara of Southern Peru," *Ethnomusicology* 33/1 (1989).

Amazonian Cultures: Anthony Seeger, *Why Suyá Sing: A Musical Anthropology of an Amazonian People* (Cambridge: Cambridge University Press, 1987).

African-American Traditions: William Aho, "Steel Band Music in Trinidad and Tobago: The Creation of a People's Music," *Latin American Music Review* 8/1 (1987); Gerard Béhague, "Patterns of Candomblé Music Performance: An Afro-Brazilian Religious Setting," in Gerard Béhague, ed., *Performance Practice: Ethnomusicological Perspectives* (Westport, Conn.: Greenwood, 1984); Harold Courlander, "Musical Instruments of Cuba," *Musical Quarterly* 28 (1942); Larry Crook, "A Musical Analysis of the Cuban Rumba," *Latin American Music Review* 3/1 (1982); Luis Heitor Correa de Azevedo, "Music and Musicians of African Origin in Brazil," *World of Music* 25/2 (1982); George List, *Music and Poetry in a Colombian Village* (Bloomington: Indiana University Press, 1983); Norman E. Whitten, Jr. and C. Aurelio Fuentes, *Black Frontiersmen: A South American Case* (New York: Schenkman, 1974).

Iberian-Derived Traditions: M. E. Grebe, *The Chilean Verso: A Study in Musical Archaism* (Los Angeles: University of California Press, 1967).

Urban-Popular Music: Stephen Davis and Peter Simon, *Reggae Bloodlines: In Search of the Music and Culture of Jamaica* (New York: Anchor, 1977); Peter Manuel, *Popular Musics of the Non-Western World* (New York: Oxford University Press, 1988); Charles A. Perrone, *Masters of Contemporary Brazilian Song: MPB 1965–1985* (Austin: University of Texas Press, 1989); Thomas Turino, "*Somos el Peru*: 'Cumbia Andina' and the Children of Andean Migrants in Lima," *Studies in Latin American Popular Culture* 9 (1990).

LATIN AMERICA DISCOGRAPHY

Highland Indigenous and Mestizo: *Musik im Andenhochland/Bolivien* (Museum Collection Berlin [West] MC 14); *Mountain Music of Peru* (Folkways FE 4539); *The Inca Harp: Laments and Dances of the Tawantinsuyu, the Inca Empire* (Lyrichord LLST 7359); *Your Struggle Is Your Glory: Songs of Struggle, Huayno & Other Peruvian Music* (Arhoolie 3025); *Kingdom of the Sun: Peru's Inca Heritage* (Nonesuch H-72029); *Music of Peru* (Folkways FE 4415); *Mexico: Fiestas of Chiapas and Oaxaca* (Nonesuch H-72070); *Texas-Mexican Border Music, [Vol 24]: The Texas-MexicanConjunto* (Folklyric 9049); *Marimba Music of Tehuantepec* (University of Washington Press UWP 1002); *Music of the Tarascan Indians of Mexico: Music of Michoaca and Nearby Mestizo Country* (Asch Mankind Series AHM 4217); *Music of Mexico: Sones Jarochos* (Arhoolie 3008); *Music of Mexico, [Vol 2]: Sones Huastecos* (Arhoolie 3009); *Amerindian Ceremonial Music from Chile* (Philips 6586 026).

Amazonian Cultures: *Why Suyá Sing* (cassette, Cambridge University Press); *Indian Music of the Upper Amazon* (Folkways FE 4458).

African-American: *An Island Carnival: Music of the West Indies* (Nonesuch 72091); *The Sound of the Sun: The Westland Steel Band* (Nonesuch H-72016); *Meringues and Folk Ballads of Haiti* (Lyrichord LLST 7340); *In Praise of Oxalá and Other Gods: Black Music of South America* (Nonesuch H-72036); *Afro-Hispanic Music from Western Colombia and Ecuador* (Folkways FE 4376); *Cult Music of Cuba* (Folkways FE 4410); *Music from Saramaka: A Dynamic Afro-American Tradition* (Folkways FE 4225).

Iberian-Derived Music: *Traditional Music of Chile* (ABC Command COMS-9003); *Chile: Hispano-Chilean metisse Traditional Music* (EMI Odeon 3C 064-18218); *Folk Music of Puerto Rico* (Library of Congress AFS L18).

10

NORTH AMERICAN INDIAN MUSIC

Bruno Nettl

"NORTH AMERICAN INDIAN DAYS"

A Modern Ceremony

The scene is the town of Browning, Montana, in the middle of the Blackfeet Indian Reservation. To the west are the rugged mountains of Glacier National Park, and in all other directions one sees the yellowish look and the curved contours of the high plains in late afternoon. We are on the edge of the small town with its handful of stores, boarded-up businesses, and streets with potholes, and have gone to the center of a large circle of tents, some the kind you can buy at any camping store but others canvas versions of the grand tepees of the Plains tribes with their ceremonial painted decorations. We are entering a kind of miniature stadium with entrances on four sides and an expanse of grass in the middle.

Some 300 people are sitting on benches or folding chairs; about half of them seem to be Indians, the rest whites, many with cameras and cassette recorders. There is a podium on one side, and a master of ceremonies is speaking over a loudspeaker, asking dancers (who are not visible just yet) to prepare for the grand entry. Around the edge of the grassy center several bass drums are spaced, each representing a singing group of a half-dozen men that seems to be collecting itself, setting up amplification equipment. Eventually, eighteen singing groups take their places; a few of them include one or two women, but one of them is entirely female. The MC proceeds to call the roll, naming and locating each group and giving it a number; each responds with a stroke on the drum. It turns out that the groups (called "drums") come from various locations on the reservation or from the Blackfoot reserves in neighboring Alberta; and about half of them are from other tribes, from Eastern Montana, the Dakotas, Arizona, and Washington. Their names indicate locations or family names, and it becomes clear that the members of a "drum" are often members of an extended family (Figure 10–1).

Grand Entry

The MC, who happens to be the chief of the tribal council and a well-known politician in the Indian world of the 1970s, engages in a bit of lighthearted banter and then calls on one of the "drums" to sing the

Figure 10–1. North American Indian Days in Browning, Montana, in the early afternoon.

song for the "grand entry," and they begin. The singers set up a steady rhythm by beating on the edge of their bass drum. The drum's leader sings a phrase in a falsetto voice, very tense, harsh, loud, and ornamented; the phrase is repeated by a second singer, and the whole group enters, singing a stately melody moving down the scale until it flattens out an octave below the beginning, then rising again, coming to the end of the song, and going on to repeat the whole form several times. The members of the singing group sit in a circle, facing each other but essentially looking at the drum or the ground, bent forward, singing with great concentration, ignoring the audience and also the dancers when they finally enter the enclosure. The song obviously has no words, only vocables or meaningless syllables, but all of the singers sing these in unison.

Then, rather suddenly, we see dancers in flamboyant costumes entering from all four sides of the enclosure, each group in single file, moving to the right and steadily clockwise around the center of the circle, eventually making a wide stream of bodies, perhaps 150, moving rhythmically to the drumming. The men wear brightly colored cloth-and-feather outfits, each unique; the women wear long dresses decorated in various ways with beads and colored cloth, simpler and more modest than the men's costumes. But each dancer has a costume in some sense of the word, while the singers wear blue jeans, T-shirts, and farmers' caps. From one entrance emerges a line of male dancers moving very athletically, with large steps and jumps; on the opposite side, men with more restrained movements (called, we find, "fancy" and "traditional" dancers, respectively); and the women, though with very much more restrained motions, divide themselves along the same lines in the other two entrances. All dancing is "solo"; couples do not dance, but while the men move singly and idiosyncratically, some of the women dance slowly, grouping themselves two or three abreast.

The song ends after seven or eight repetitions; the MC indicates that the next one will be sung by Drum no. 7 from Heart Butte (a small town thirty miles south of Browning) and that it will be (as most turn out to be) a type of song called "intertribal"; and the singing and dancing begins again. It goes on like this for several hours, each drum or singing group taking its turns, the series of songs frequently interrupted by related events such as a song and brief procession to mourn a recently deceased member of the community, different dances such as circle and owl dances (the latter danced by couples), dance contests, and brief ceremonies. The style of the music is very much the same throughout, and the singing groups from all locations sound similar and share a repertory. Members of the audience talk, walk in and out, speak with dancers and singers, take photos, and record the singing on cassettes. The scene is similar to that of a small-town sports event (Figure 10–2).

Figure 10–2. A Blackfoot singing group at North American Indian Days.

Ancillary Events

But while the main events of North American Indian Days take place
in the dance enclosure, there are other activities with music that are
worthy of attention. In a small hut, a traditional gambling game, played
by two teams facing each other and hiding a bullet or stick, is in progress.
The team hiding the object sings constantly, songs with a small melodic
range consisting of the alternation of only two brief musical phrases,
all the while beating rhythmically and rapidly on a plank. But the high,
intense, pulsating singing of the dance songs is here replaced with a
lower, more relaxed style. A couple of blocks away, there is a kind of
barn dance taking place in a parking lot, with a country-and-western
band composed of members of the Blackfoot tribe singing old Nashville
favorites. A half-mile further, south of the town, a small rodeo is in
progress. It is billed as an "Indian rodeo"; its content is like that of other
small-town rodeos in Montana, but the participants are all Indians.
Before and between the events there is recorded music, played over a
miserable speaker and attracting little attention; it is patriotic music—the
national anthem, "America, the Beautiful," and Sousa marches. The
next morning there is a parade with many dozens of floats representing
businesses and institutions of the area—some Indian, others white; this

is a central event in North American Indian Days. Some of the floats have music, live or recorded, and for once one hears traditional Indian music—the modern intertribal songs—along with rock, jazz, and Christian hymns.

North American Indian Days is a spectacle that characterizes North American Indian culture in several ways. First, it is a successor of the midsummer religious ceremonies that were held traditionally by many Indian societies. Further, as an intertribal event, it symbolizes to both Indians and whites the broad Indian identity that is important to native Americans all over. The fact that the same songs are known to singing groups from all over, that the same style (with some regional diversity) is used by many tribes, and that linguistic differences are submerged as the songs have no words (or occasionally English words)—all of this underscores that function of the powwow. The coexistence of several events, each with different music—gambling games from an ancient tradition, dancing from a modern Indian one, other events with Western music performed by Indians—symbolizes the present life of Indians as a separate population which nevertheless participates in the mainstream culture. The comparison of traditional and fancy dancers reflects the dual role of the event—traditional ceremony and modern entertainment. What is important for us to note is the way in which traditional Indian music is used to exhibit the old tradition but also to tie the various strands of the culture, old and modernized, to each other.

SOME OLDER CEREMONIAL TRADITIONS

The concept of "song" in most Indian cultures is a relatively short unit, rather like our nursery rhyme or hymn. But songs are ordinarily presented in large groups and sequences as parts of elaborate ceremonies and rituals. Most religious ceremonies are elaborate affairs, lasting many hours or even several days. In many ceremonies, the songs to be sung and their order are specifically prescribed. In others they are not; in the Peyote ceremonies of Plains tribes each singer must sing four songs at a time, but they may be any songs from the Peyote repertory, and only at four points in the ceremony must particular songs be sung.

Thus, the "Night Chant" (Yeibechai) of the Navajo, a curing ceremony, requires nine days and nights, and includes hundreds of songs and their poetic texts. The Hako, a Pawnee ceremony of general religious significance, required several days and included about a hundred songs. The medicine-bundle ceremonies of the Northern Plains peoples might consist of several parts: narration of the myth explaining the origin of the bundle; opening the bundle and performing with each of the objects in it; a required activity—dancing, smoking, eating, praying; and the singing of one or several songs (usually by the celebrant, sometimes by him and others present) for each object. The Blackfoot Sun Dance, the largest and most central of the older tribal ceremonies of this culture, required four preparatory days followed by four days of dancing. The Peyote ceremony, which became a major religious ritual in many tribes of the United States in the course of the late nineteenth and twentieth centuries, consists of a night of singing. Each participant—there may be from ten to thirty sitting in a circle—sings four songs at a time, playing the rattle while his neighbor accompanies him on a special drum.

Secular events too are structured so that songs appear in large groups. The performance of a Stomp Dance, a social dance of southeastern origin performed by a line of dancers moving in snakelike fashion with responsorial singing, leader and group alternating, includes a dozen or so songs. And the North American Indian Days powwow, described earlier, takes four days (Figures 10–3 and 10–4)

Figure 10–3. Plains Indian hand drum with drumstick covered with rawhide.

Figure 10–4.   Northwest Coast Indian drum.

THE WORLD OF NORTH AMERICAN CULTURES AND MUSIC

Native American Societies Past and Present

American Indian life today may be rather a mixed bag. There are some tribal societies that maintain their special identity, and there are also groups of tribes that were, through happenstance or force, obliged to share a reservation and have somehow fashioned a unified culture. There are activities and ceremonies, such as the powwow we have just described, of an essentially intertribal nature. Indians from various tribes find themselves in large cities and join together to establish for themselves a common Indian identity. In most respects, of course, Indians share the culture of their non-Indian compatriots, speaking English or Spanish. It is largely in music and dance that their Indian background is exhibited to themselves and to others.

Most of what is known about Indian music comes from the last hundred years, when recording techniques and ethnography were developed, and in this period Indians had already come into much negative and positive contact with whites. But in the early part of that period, one could still get a picture of what Indian music and musical culture may have been like before contact. It is clear, first of all, that each tribe had its own musical culture, its own repertory, musical style, uses of and ideas about music. There were between 1000 and 2000 tribal groups in North America, almost all speaking distinct languages. The average population of a tribe was around a thousand, but some were much larger and others had only 100–200 persons. Yet each tribe had a large number of songs and used them in many ceremonies, for curing, to accompany dances, and to draw boundaries between subdivisions of society such as age groups, clans, and genders.

Anthropologists have classified these cultures into six to eight units called *culture areas*, each with characteristic types of housing, ways of acquiring and preparing food, clothing, religion, and economic and political structure. Thus, for example, the peoples of the North Pacific Coast fished, built wooden houses, had a rigid class structure including slaves, had complex ceremonial sculpture such as totem poles and masks, and had special "potlatch" ceremonies to exhibit personal and family wealth and status. The Indian people of the Plains specialized in hunting buffalo as the prime source of food, housing, and clothes, doing this first on foot with the help of dogs and later on horseback. They were nomadic, lived in tepees, and had a rather informal and egalitarian political structure. Their religion was based on guardian spirits that were acquired by men in dreams, and their ceremonial life included many kinds of acts that showed personal courage. The Pueblo Indians of the Southwest, on the other hand, lived in towns of cliff-dwellings, grew corn and other plants, and had an extremely complex ceremonial life. In California there were a great many very small tribes who lived seminomadically, with complex ceremonial life but subsistence based on hunting small animals, including insects, and gathering plants (Figure 10–5).

Unity and Diversity in Indian Music

Comparing the sound of North American Indian music with that of Africa or Japan shows that Indian music is relatively homogeneous. It is almost always monophonic, and with very few exceptions it is vocal. While there are a number of distinct singing styles, they have in common a tense sound and the use of pulsations on longer notes. Two or three types of forms predominate. There are strophic songs, rather like folk songs or hymns in that a stanza of several lines is repeated several or many times; there are very short songs that consist of one or a pair of lines repeated many times; and there are forms in which two contrastive sections of music, one usually higher than the other, alternate. Almost all of the singing is accompanied by percussion, usually drums or rattles. Thus, the many Indian musical cultures have a good deal in common.

Figure 10–5. Blackfoot ceremonial objects: Two medicine bundle rattles, pair of gambling bones.

But if one goes into great detail, analyzing hundreds of songs and making a statistical study of their characteristics for each tribe, one sees that each group has a unique musical repertory and style. There are differences even between neighboring tribes. But the picture is not totally confusing, as there are units which we might call *music areas* which coincide roughly, though not always precisely, with the culture areas. It is worth mentioning that they do not coincide well at all with language areas; that is, societies speaking related languages often do not share either cultural or musical characteristics. There are about seven music areas.

Musical Areas

The *Plains area* coincides well with a culture area. It has the singing style most distant from standard Western singing, emphasizing high pitch, rhythmic pulsations on the long tones, tension, and harshness. Its characteristic form consists of stanzas internally arranged as follows: A short phrase is presented and repeated; there follows a descending line of three or four phrases ending with a low, flat cadence which is sometimes a version of the initial motif an octave lower; this long second section is repeated, so that the total may have the following scheme:

A A BCD BCD. This partial repetition of the entire song has given this format the name "incomplete repetition."

The Eastern part of the continent has a greater variety of forms, which usually consist of several short phrases in different arrangements; a rounder and more relaxed vocal sound; some singing in which a leader and a group alternate brief bits of music, the so-called call-and-response pattern; and resulting from this, occasional bits of polyphony.

A group of cultures representing the *Yuman-speaking peoples* of the southwestern United States and some cultures in *southern and central California* specialize in a form in which one section, a phrase or short group of phrases, is repeated several times but is interrupted occasionally by another, slightly higher and definitely contrastive section, called by some Yuman peoples and also by ethnomusicologists the "rise." Here also we have a very relaxed kind of vocal style.

Also in the southwestern United States we have the *Athabascan* style of the Navajo and Apache peoples. Its typical traits are a large vocal range, a rather nasal-sounding voice, and even rhythms that can almost always be written by using only quarter- and eighth-notes.

The style of the *Pueblo Indians* shares features with those of both the Athabascan and the Plains peoples but has a low, harsh, pulsating vocal style and long, complex forms.

The *Great Basin* style, found in Nevada and Utah as well as northern California, has songs with small range and a characteristic form in which each of a group of phrases is repeated once—e.g., AABBCC.

The *Northwest Coast* peoples and some of the *Eskimo* or *Inuit* peoples share a typical singing style and complex rhythms often pitting patterns in voice and drum against each other. The Northwest Coast is also the area richest in wind instruments and has a well-documented if not prominent polyphonic tradition.

IDEAS ABOUT MUSIC

What It Is and What It Does

If one asks how it was that Indian peoples, for all their interest in music and their large repertories, did not develop longer, more complex forms with greater interactions, the answer would have to be threefold. First, it is true that oral tradition places some limitations on the complexity of materials to be remembered. Second, there is really quite a lot more complexity, at a microscopic level, than the listener may at first perceive. But most important, the idea of technical complexity has never been a criterion of musical quality to Indian peoples. Rather, music is measured by such things as its ability to integrate society and to represent it to the outside, its ability to integrate ceremonial and social events, and its supernatural power. The rather athletic view of music taken in Western culture, where star performances by individual composers and performers and their ability to do very difficult things is measured, is replaced in Indian cultures by quite different values.

Music has supernatural power. In Blackfoot Indian culture, it is the songs which, as it were, hold the power. Thus, each act must have its appropriate song. In a ceremony in which a medicine man is trying to influence the weather, he will have a bundle of objects which he opens and displays, but their supernatural power is not activated until the appropriate song is sung. In many Indian cultures, songs are thought to come into existence principally in dreams or visions.

Composition and Creativity

In the Plains a man has visions in which powerful guardian spirits appear to him, and these are validated by the songs they sing to him. As many songs have no words, it is clearly not simply the texts but the act of singing—producing a kind of sound that has no other function in life—that embodies spiritual power. The strong association with religion, unusual even when we consider that religious music is a cultural universal, is characteristic of American Indian music.

Beyond the composition of songs in visions by Plains Indians, the creation of songs is viewed differently in American Indian traditions than in most European and Asian cultures. It may be that songs are thought to exist in the cosmos and need to be brought into human existence through dreams. In some tribes songs are extant in the supernatural world but need to be "unraveled" by humans in dreams in order to be realized. In an Eskimo culture there is a finite quantity of songs, and new ones can be made up only by combining elements of extant ones. In some tribes, making up songs is associated with emotional or mental disturbance. Except in modernized musical contexts, one rarely finds a situation in which humans are given credit for creating music. If there are specialists in making up songs they are ordinarily also specialists in religious matters, and their technical competence or aesthetic creativity seems not to be an issue.

Music, a Reflection of Culture

In Indian cultures even more than others, the musical system is a kind of reflection of the rest of culture. A Blackfoot singer said, "The right way to do something is to sing the right song with it"; and indeed, in theory at least, the Blackfeet have particular songs for all activities, and the more an activity is technically subdivided—as, for example, a ceremony—the more specific the association of songs with its various parts. In the Beaver Ceremony, the ceremonialist has a bundle of 168 objects, mostly dressed skins of many birds and animals of the environment but also some handmade objects, rocks, and sticks. For each he must sing the appropriate song. Traditionally, the men of the tribe divided themselves into seven societies by age, and a man was initiated successively into them roughly every four years. Each society had its ceremonies and certain duties in social life and warfare, and each had its separate group of songs. There were special songs for warfare, riding, walking. The most important social division, between men and women, was also reflected musically. Women had, so it seems, a separate and much smaller repertory, although they might join in singing certain men's songs; but more important, their singing style was different, with smoother and more nasal tone than the men's, and with the pulsations being not rhythmic stresses but melodic ornaments. In many Indian cultures, the major divisions in society are represented by major divisions in musical repertory and style.

MUSICAL INSTRUMENTS

Types of Instruments

North American Indian music is prevailingly vocal. Almost all instruments are percussive, and their function is to provide rhythmic accompaniment to singing. Solo drumming is actually rare. But there is a great variety of drum and rattle types. Large drums with two heads or skins, small hand-drums with a single skin, kettle-drums filled with water for tuning, pieces of rawhide simply suspended from stakes—these are examples of drum types widely distributed. There are container rattles made of gourds, hide pieces sewn together, or a turtleshell; others fashioned of strings of deer hooves; and more. Although the musical function of these instruments is essentially the same, a culture may have many types, distinguished in the details of decoration with beads, feathers, animal skins, carving, and painting, each type associated with a particular ceremony. There are other idiophones as well—notched stick scrapers, clappers, beaten planks, stamping tubes, jingles. Small metal bells, introduced centuries ago by Europeans, have become established and incorporated in some of the cultures.

Among the melody-producing instruments, the most widespread type is the flute. Various kinds of flutes are found, including true, end-blown flutes in which the player's pursed lips direct a ribbon-shaped column of air against an edge of the blow-hole, as well as duct flutes rather like European recorders. In some tribes, the repertory of flute music consists simply of songs which may also be sung. Elsewhere, particularly in the southwestern United States, flute music is separate in content though its style is not markedly different from that of the songs. Among the instruments found in small numbers among a few tribes, we should mention the use of simple reeds and trumpets for recreational and ceremonial occasions on the North Pacific Coast. The musical bow, similar to or identical with a hunting bow, appears to have been used as an instrument in the southwestern United States, and has been succeeded by the "Apache fiddle" or Navajo violin, a bowed instrument with one horsehair string and a cylindrical body about twelve inches in length, probably created as a combination of the bow and the Western violin (Figures 10–6 and 10–7).

Instruments, Singing, and Words

But most importantly, the instruments of American Indians are largely nonmelodic percussion instruments, and melody-producing instruments have very special and restricted functions. In this respect they are similar to other cultures with small populations, such as the tribes of Australian aboriginals, whose main instruments are percussion sticks of eucalyptus, struck against each other, and the didgeridoo, a long trumpet used mainly to play a single-tone drone. It is important to know, however, that the didgeridoo requires complex playing techniques such as circular breathing and changes in the shape of the mouth cavity for varying the tone color. In Polynesia instruments are used mainly to accompany singing, and in Melanesia and Micronesia the principal instruments are panpipes.

Figure 10–6. "Apache fiddle" or Navajo violin.

Figure 10–7. Singing and beating percussion plank at a Blackfoot gambling game.

     If the relative dearth of melody-producing instruments is noteworthy in North American Indian cultures, it is important to keep in mind that, in many of them, songs may not be primarily a vehicle for words. While some Indian song texts, like those of the Navajo and Pueblo peoples, are often highly elaborate poems, in Plains Indian culture songs may have no words at all but only vocables. Where there are words, they are usually brief and occupy only a short portion of the melody. Here are the texts of two Blackfoot songs: "Sun says to sing" (song of the Sun Dance ceremony); and "It is spring; let others see you" (sung at the beginning of a medicine-bundle ceremony, before the bundle is opened). In a sense, we could conclude that songs without words substitute for the absent instrumental music.

ASPECTS OF THE HISTORY OF AMERICAN INDIAN MUSIC

Reconstructing Prehistory

     There is little direct or written information about the history of American Indian music; yet various kinds of circumstantial evidence permit reasonable guesses toward a rough reconstruction. Indians have been in the Americas for at least 50,000 years, but they originally came, probably in waves, from Asia; thus, if there is musical material that they share with Asian cultures, it may be very ancient. The only thing to which one can reasonably point is the existence, in many Indian cultures, of a stratum of short, simple songs consisting of one or two repeated lines and built on a scale of three or four tones, associated with children, games, and love charms. This type of music is found in many parts of the world and may possibly be a remnant of a highly archaic stratum of human music. Comparison of North and South American Indian music may be indicative. There are musical styles shared by the two regions; peoples of the Gran Chaco have forms and a singing style not too different from that of the North American Plains. Ideas about music—the reflection of cultural categories in modes of performance, music's central role in myths about the origin of culture, music as a way of communicating within and with the supernatural world—often seem similar in the two regions. On the other hand, South American Indian music is, in most respects, very different from North American; there are more instances of major participation by women, and there is much more instrumental music. This suggests that the musical styles of North America developed independently and perhaps later. As cultures tend to hold on to their languages more tenaciously than to other things, and as language groupings do not often coincide with musical areas, the music of one society may have changed relatively rapidly and frequently. If so, the picture of Indian music history must have been quite variegated, tribes changing their music as they changed important aspects of their culture.

Archeological evidence is not very plentiful for the area north of Mexico. It is assumed that large ceremonies and massed populations generally give rise to complex musical structures, and thus Aztec and Mayan societies had choral music and probably polyphonic structures. But this kind of correlation is not found in East Asia, and as few instruments were either extant or preserved in archeological sites, little can be known about the music of the classical Mexican cultures. Similarly, archeological sites in the United States and Canada give us little information about musical life.

Since the Coming of Whites

American Indian history since the coming of whites is better documented, and aspects of it have been widely studied. On the one hand, the unhappy social and political history is accompanied by a great reduction in the content of musical culture. Clearly, as entire tribes were wiped out and virtually all Indian peoples were relocated, suffering cultural disintegration through devastating famines and epidemics, knowledge of ceremonies and rituals as well as social repertory decreased and much was simply forgotten. As Indians were motivated to take up Western lifestyles and religion, they also began to participate in Western music, and sometimes to adopt Western conceptions of music for their own musical culture. So in the Plains, for example, the notion that all songs have a supernatural origin has been replaced by the acceptance of human composition. And to the emphasis on music as a carrier of supernatural power has been added the concept of music as entertainment.

But the tragic history of the Indians also brought with it, as a happier kind of by-product, interesting new developments in music, as Indian people came to use music as a weapon to fight back against total absorption and for the preservation of their cultural identity.

Peyote and Other Intertribal Styles

One example comes from the Ghost Dance religion, a messianic cult that began in the Great Basin and was taken up by the Plains tribes as a way of combating and defeating the whites. Along with the Ghost Dance came the singing style and song forms of the Great Basin, which was thus added and enriched Plains music. But while the Ghost Dance songs are hardly ever sung any more, those of the Peyote religion, which came about similarly, are a major and distinctive element in the contemporary American Indian music scene.

The Peyote religion, based on the hallucinogenic buttons of a cactus native to Mexico, spread through much of the North American Indian world between 1700 and 1940. Its users developed a distinct song repertory using a singing style probably derived from that of the Navajo, a rhythmic structure using elements of Apache rhythm, the "incomplete repetition" type of form and the descending melodic contour of the Plains, and a kettle-drum filled with water that possibly originated in the southeastern United States. The songs use special vocables such as "heyowitsinayo" and "heyowanene," and each song ends with an amenlike "heneyowe." The origin of these vocable patterns is not known, but conceivably they came from the Comanche of the southern Plains. This is a religion which tries to tie Indian peoples together and takes a conciliatory position toward Christianity, and thus Christian texts in English are occasionally used. Here too we see the forced culture change resulting in the new musical style and the broadening of Indian musical culture.

The establishment of an intertribal style based on Plains music, and of a common song repertory for the powwow culture as observed in the Blackfoot North American Indian Days, is also a recent development. So is the development of Christian hymn styles based on traditional Indian music, and of a genre of Indian rock and roll, which uses some traditional tunes, the percussive sound of Indian songs, and texts derived from or referring to Indian culture. Just as important as the changes in musical sound are Western influences on contexts and ideas about music.

Indian music is very much alive. Indian peoples use it, and dance, more than anything else to show to each other and other Americans that they are a distinct ethnic groups. To them, music functions both as a way of maintaining their cultural integrity and as a form of mediating between themselves and other culture groups. In this sense it continues a tradition, for in earlier times too its function had been that of mediation, but between humans and the forces of the supernatural.

NORTH AMERICAN INDIAN BIBLIOGRAPHY

North America as a Whole: Marcia Herndon, *Native American Music* (Hatboro, Pa.: Norwood, 1980): Bruno Nettl, *North American Indian Musical Styles* (Philadelphia: American Folklore Society, 1952); Helen H. Roberts, *Musical Areas in Aboriginal North America* (New Haven: Yale University Press, 1936).

Blackfoot and Other Northern Plains Musics: Bruno Nettl, *Blackfoot Musical Thought: Comparative Perspectives* (Kent, Ohio: Kent State University Press, 1989); Frances Densmore, *Teton Sioux Music* (Washington, D.C.: Bureau of American Ethnology, 1918); Robert Witmer, *The Musical Life of the Blood Indians* (Ottawa: National Museum of Man, 1982); Alan P. Merriam, *Ethnomusicology of the Flathead Indians* (Chicago: Aldine, 1967).

Other North American Indian Peoples: Charlotte Frisbie, ed., *Southwestern Indian Ritual Drama* (Tucson: University of Arizona Press, 1980); David P. McAllester, *Peyote Music* (New York: Viking Fund Publications in Anthropology, 1949); David P. McAllester, *Enemy Way Music* (Cambridge, Mass.: Peabody Museum of American Archeology and Ethnology, 1954); Judith Vander, *Songprints* (Urbana: University of Illinois Press, 1988); Frank Mitchell, *Navajo Blessingway Singer*, ed. Charlotte J. Frisbie and David P. McAllester (Tucson: University of Arizona Press, 1978); Thomas Johnston, *Eskimo Music by Region: A Comparative Circumpolar Study* (Ottawa: National Museum of Man, 1976); Beverley Cavanagh, *Music of the Netsilik Eskimo: A Study of Stability and Change* (Ottawa: National Museum of Man, 1982); Ruth Murray Underhill, *Singing for Power: The Song Magic of the Papago Indians of Southern Arizona* (Berkeley: University of California Press, 1938).

Instruments: K. G. Izikowitz, *Musical and Other Sound Instruments of the South American Indians* (Götesborg, Sweden: Kungl. Vetenskap- och Vitterhets-Samhälles Handlingar, 1935); Thomas Vennum, Jr., *The Ojibwa Dance Drum* (Washington, D.C.: Smithsonian Institution Press, 1982).

NORTH AMERICAN INDIAN DISCOGRAPHY

Anthologies: *A Cry from the Earth: Music of the North American Indians* (Folkways FC 7777; 1979); *An Anthology of North American Indian and Eskimo Music* (Ethnic Folkways FE 4541; 1973).

Blackfoot: *An Historical Album of Blackfoot Indian Music* (Ethnic Folkways FE 34001; 1979); *Blackfeet* (Indian IR 220; ca. 1980); *Blackfeet Pow-Wow Songs* (Canyon C-6119; 1974).

Other Indian Peoples: *American Indians of the Southwest* (Ethnic Folkways P420; 1951); *Music of the Sioux and Navajo* (Ethnic Folkways P 401; 1949); *Kiowa Peyote Ritual Songs* (American Indian Soundchiefs Kiowa-590; ca. 1970); *The Great Plains* (Canyon ARP 6052; 1966); *Indian Music of the Canadian Plains* (Ethnic Folkways FE 4464; 1966); *Papago Dance Songs* (Canyon 6098; 1973); *Popular Dance Music of the Indians of Southern Arizona* (Canyon C-6085; 1972); *Inuit Games and Songs* (UNESCO Collection Musical Sources, Philips 6586 036; 1978); *Indian Songs of Today* (Library of Congress AFS L36; ca. 1960); *Omaha Indian Music* (American Folklife Center, Library of Congress AFC L71; 1984).

11

OLD WORLD CULTURES IN NORTH AMERICA

Philip V. Bohlman

MUSIC AT THE URBAN FOLK FESTIVAL

Performing Ethnicity in Pittsburgh

The Lithuanian folk dancers from Toronto have just concluded their program to the enormous, yet slightly reserved, applause of the audience assembled at the annual Pittsburgh Folk Festival. For the Polish folk musicians and dancers, a young Pittsburgh troupe from the community surrounding a Catholic church on the west side of the city, there will be only twenty more minutes before their performance. It's a time for nerves, and very understandably so. The Lithuanians always manage to give a very polished and professional performance. They are, after all, imported for the festival by the Lithuanian community in Pittsburgh, itself too small to form a sufficient folk-music ensemble, yet too proud of its presence in this city of countless ethnic communities not to display its culture with music and dance at the festival. From the standpoint of the festival organizers, this issue of fair representation is of utmost importance; the larger the number of ethnic communities displaying their culture, the greater the justification for the festival itself. But the politics of ethnic festival organization don't help to relax the nerves of the Polish troupe as the allotted time for their performance draws closer.

For several years, the Polish troupe had been attempting to reshape its repertory into a purer, more authentically Polish sound. Getting back to their roots meant finding specific pieces, dance forms, and ensemble combinations that were just like those their ancestors of a few generations ago would have known in Poland. The easiest part of this more Polish form of ethnic music was the identification of rural forms—not just the rural polka and its more syncopated duple-meter relative the krakowiak, but also a healthy portion of virtually forgotten mazurkas along with the now ubiquitous oberek, which by the 1980s had succeeded in winning a place for Polish dance forms in North America, albeit only at the cost of pushing out several other traditional dance forms. Also characteristic of the new sound the Polish troupe was searching for was a generally more asymmetrical phrasing structure and a more syncopated violin and concertina style. The musicians had worked hard over the past few years attempting to refine their sound, much to the chagrin of their parents and community sponsors, who had long found the urban Polish-American polka sound of Chicago effective as their banner of ethnic music distinction. Nobody—neither performers nor community members—was quite comfortable with the revived old-country sound that the Polish troupe was about to perform for the folk-festival audience.

Underlying the Polish troupe's nervousness was yet another area of tension, namely between the notion of ethnicity that the festival organizers wished the troupe to display and a notion that the troupe itself had formed through its understanding of the history of the Polish community of Pittsburgh. The festival had long relied on a philosophy that each group should present itself in the same way: food booths were to be the same size, displays of crafts should concentrate on similar items, and the music and dance performances should obey the same rules. No group should stick out, even though ethnic differences were essential to the reason that the festival existed in the first place.

The Polish troupe was uncomfortable being like every other performing group. First of all, in their performances in the community itself they were accustomed to relatively long suites, in which the complex forms of their dances could unfold according to tradition; here at the festival they had only twenty minutes, and if at all possible their performance should reflect variety, the key to holding the audience's attention, act after act. Second, this was again the year during which the festival planners requested that each group employ line dances, at any rate the preferred form of presentation because it filled the stage and brought the audience face-to-face with the performers. Line dances were particularly problematic for the Polish troupe, for the rural aesthetic and the dance forms they were attempting to revive stressed couple dances, many of which—for example, the oberek—relied on ring formations as well. Third, the Pittsburgh Civic Center required a big instrumental sound to fill the auditorium, with several musicians playing each part when possible and with traditional and nontraditional sounds mixed together, all of which together served as a public metaphor for the health of ethnic music and the ethnic mixture of the city.

The bigger-is-better aesthetic of the festival organizers was fine for the professional ensembles like the Duquesne University Tamburitzans, which represented Serbo-Croatian communities in Pittsburgh and had long played an indispensable role with the festival organizers in putting the festival together, particularly during the festival's fledgling years in the 1950s. The big-band sound encouraged by the festival, however, was precisely what the Polish troupe wanted to avoid. Their small ensemble of clarinet, violin, concertina, and double bass preferred a more refined and subdued style, one that could back up but not dominate the vocal parts, which the singers had practiced so hard to sing in reasonably correct Polish, a language none of them knew fluently. The festival organizers did like the idea of songs in Polish, but planning discussions often stressed that too many folk songs in ethnic languages would make the diverse audience uncomfortable because of their "foreignness" and because they supplanted the folk dances, which were by far more successful as display.

In the end, the festival was to symbolize Pittsburgh's ethnicity, not the ethnicity of individual communities. As uncomfortable as the Polish troupe was with the festival philosophy, it took to the stage anyway and conformed as well as it could to the twenty-minute frame provided for Polish folk music and folk dance in Pittsburgh. The Polish-American musicians and dancers were not as professional as the Lithuanians imported from Toronto, and they did not employ the slick acrobatics of the Tamburitzans. They managed to compromise, however, in ways that satisfied just about everybody's requirements. Between couple and ring dances, they managed to stick in a few line dances; by careful miking of their small ensemble, they avoided the need to enlist the heavy "dyno" sound that many polka bands used to give the feeling of mainstream popular styles; their songs were unobtrusive because they decided to forgo extra verses. Drawing upon their own sense of Polish revival, obeying the enjoinders of the festival organizers, and recognizing how to give the festival audience a good time while underscoring the essential diversity of Pittsburgh's ethnic makeup, the Polish troupe received enthusiastic applause, for it had used music to strike a cultural balance fundamental to the representation of ethnic diversity. During the Polish performance ethnic music had become not just a symbol of Pittsburgh's west-side Polish community, but of a large and pervasive ethnic presence in Pittsburgh and North America. Music had become the means of demonstrating the essential unity of cultural diversity.

Festivals and Ethnic Musics Today

Folk festivals, though they assume many forms and serve many different communities, might be understood as one of the most powerful metaphors for the music of ethnic North America. In fact, folk festivals have proliferated and grown in popularity at a time of sweeping transformation in most ethnic communities. During this period, largely since World War II, older ethnic groups, especially European, have formed a type of mainstream, while newer ethnic groups, particularly those from Asia, Latin America, and Africa, have established themselves as distinctive communities on the larger North American cultural landscape. The folk festival frames many of the changes and patterns of interaction that characterize this period of new ethnicity. The festival increasingly establishes a central position for the celebration of diversity in American and Canadian society.

The processes of ethnic transformation are acutely present in the music that we encounter at a folk festival. Music must change to fit the conditions of the festival much in the same way that immigrant traditions change to adapt to the conditions of a new nation, thus making the festival itself a context for the making and remaking of traditional musics. Musicians must shape and change their traditional performances to suit the purposes of the festival. Music, moreover, takes its place with other community activities, with organizations in any given community working together and strengthening their communal ties in order to make Filipino or Vietnamese ethnicity more palpable in the competitive world of a large city. The festival is a place in which music undergoes modernization, whether because of the need to amplify the Serbo-Croatian tamburitza orchestra for a large auditoriumn or to make a place for a Latvian rock band in Chicago that embeds its Latvianness in a highly amplified heavy-metal sound.

The music that we hear at the folk festival belongs specifically to the festival but more generally also to the experiences of modern North America. By the time the Polish troupe took to the stage, it was performing repertories that were totally different from anything in the old country. The instruments and social function had changed, and the sound would probably seem stranger to Poles in Warsaw than to Polish-Americans in Pittsburgh. The prerequisites of the festival, moreover, probably meant that the sound of the Polish performance was in some ways less foreign to the German- and Lebanese-Americans in the audience than it would be to those from the rural villages of Poland whose music the young Pittsburghers were consciously reviving. The different components of the music have a symbolic importance derived from the festival, not from original social function. A few songs in Polish are therefore important not because many of those in the audience understand the texts—not even the singers have any real sensitivity to the texts—

but because language provides a readily recognizable icon of ethnicity. Similarly, there is some music that is especially appropriate for the festival while some other musics are not and are therefore excluded. The festival becomes a cultural event that forces the musicians and the community to make decisions, providing them with the imperative and guidelines for expressing Polish-American ethnicity in Pittsburgh.

By choosing to perform at the festival, musicians juxtapose two seemingly contradictory tendencies. On one hand, the musicians accommodate to the festival requirement to perform in a way that resembles every other group. On the other, at the same moment they succumb to the requirement of similarity—performing line dances like every other ensemble—they must also assure their own community that it is unique and culturally distinct from all others. The festival thus turns ethnic culture on its head, confusing similarity and difference. It builds a larger culture with a reformulated vitality from many smaller subcultures. As such, it crystallizes the forces at work in the many domains of cultural activity in ethnic North America.

THE MULTIPLICITY OF MUSICS IN NORTH AMERICA

The Meaning of Ethnicity for Music in North America

In this chapter we examine the music of North America as a whole with many parts. The predominance of these parts, and the fact that we create the larger picture of music in North America only by first looking at the parts and then determining how they fit together, distinguishes this chapter in some ways from the other chapters. The musics of the culture area we are calling ethnic North America have historical origins elsewhere; by and large, they accompanied the influx of population groups from somewhere else in the world. The relation of these musics to concepts like "traditional music" or "indigenous music" or even "folk music" is necessarily problematic in ways unlike those the reader has witnessed in other chapters. In the continental music culture most comparable, Latin America, the interaction between imported and indigenous musics is quite different, as Thomas Turino has shown in his examination of the aesthetic and political undertow evident in the persistence of Andean Indian musical styles, instruments, and meanings. In North America the contacts among ethnic groups and between these and Native North Americans have been less likely to create hybrid styles in which specific ethnicity disappears than to stimulate change within the music, in effect reaffirming identity at all costs. Even musical styles that several ethnic groups share (for example, the polka), retain ethnic markers that continue to identify substyles (for example, Slovenian or Dutchman—German—polka). It will be one of our tasks in this chapter, then, to discover how the music of ethnic North America has remained a whole with many parts.

Ethnicity itself is a concept and set of cultural practices spread over many parts of society. Understood from the perspectives of ethnomusicology, ethnicity links music to culture in a multivalent fashion. Music that is ethnic, therefore, reflects patterns of organization within the group and reveals the ways in which the group understands and maintains its identity. Because the overriding concerns for organization and identity are products of the New World, ethnic music itself becomes connected ever more to the group after it has immigrated and resituated itself in the New World. Ethnic music as we shall seek to understand it in this chapter is therefore not simply music that clearly sounds French, Korean, or Ewe at a festival in Ottawa or in the clubs of Miami, but rather the music that particular groups of people have created to express the particularity of their identity and experiences in North America. We will not restrict ourselves to an understanding of ethnic music in the more usual sense—the product of occasional internal otherness—but rather as a more widespread phenomenon that also reflects the history and commonality of North America. More than any other music, then, ethnic music embodies the cultural experiences of the entire geographical area we shall be tackling in this chapter.

Venues of Musical Practice in a Multiethnic Culture

Where does one go to experience music in a multiethnic culture? In what kinds of places does one hear ethnic music? Is ethnic music really just folk music that has been relocated to another setting? These straightforward questions have rather complex answers that reveal important differences between the music of ethnic North America as we shall understand it and the usual concepts of folk music associated with a particular community and place. In contrast, the communities of ethnic North America have many musics, among them perhaps certain repertories of folk music from a particular place. However important folk music may be to the identity of ethnic groups in North America, it is seldom, indeed never, the only music one finds within those groups. It may provide only one set of practices and a single venue, thereby distinguishing only one aspect of musical identity. When new communities form upon immigration, they necessarily reformulate their venues of musical practice, both as a means of adaptation to their new cultural surroundings and as a form of aesthetic restructuring internally within the community. Repertories may be retained, but their role in community life necessarily changes as the settings and functions of their performance change.

We might effectively understand just how place and musical practice are linked by constructing a continuum and locating certain venues along it. Significantly, this continuum exhibits extremes that, at one end, reflect musical practices removed from direct contact outside the community and, at the other, describe conditions of considerable contact with other ethnic traditions. The place of musical practice, therefore, has a direct relationship to the different paths and speeds of change that accompany the transformation from immigrant to ethnic musical traditions. The continuum also illustrates a different metaphor for the juxtaposition of musics that a multiethnic society necessitates. All the musical styles and practices that we discover on the continuum might well be found in the same group, but not all interact with and influence the others in the same way. Those musical practices that characterize venues close to each other may therefore interact frequently, whereas those at great distance from each other may have little influence on one another.

At one extreme, musical practice centers largely in the home and accompanies the activities of family life. In the home there is little pressure on traditions to change, and preservation occurs without conscious effort, at least in the initial generation or two after immigration. Song serves as a means of preserving language, and the family musical traditions prescribe sufficient function. The venues for musical practice frequently encompass several generations, hence making the family a place where old-country, immigrant, and ethnic musical traditions coexist. As contact with others outside the home develops, musical practice also takes place at a level occupied by religious, social, or even cultural organizations. Again, the retention of tradition is a priority, and we can observe that many organizations form explicitly to provide a venue for ethnic (including musical) traditions; the choruses of German- and Scandinavian-American communities in the Midwest, for example, maintain musical traditions that distinguish shared ethnicities, but that would probably disappear without the organization itself. It is a quality of these organizations, moreover, that they overlap, undergirding ethnic culture at the organizational level. Religious organizations might maintain musical ensembles while relying on some financial assistance from an ethnic fraternal lodge with connections to insurance and financial services.

The physical presence of an ethnic community forms from its various institutions. Juxtaposition of musical practices is considerably more extensive at the level of the community than in the home or organization. Whereas the organization is the product of individuals who come together because of similarities, the community depends on the reconciliation of patterns of difference. The German-American community of Cincinnati, for example, can count among its members those with Catholic and Protestant Christian and Conservative and Reformed Jewish religious heritages. The German community of Cincinnati would be incomplete without any one of these distinct parts. The German-

American musical activity of the city, in turn, has historically depended on these different groups and their willingness to support particular musical practices and the institutions that supported them. It is also at the level of the community that contact with other ethnic groups is negotiated, with the result that external influences frequently appear. Strengthening the community might mean such forms of negotiation as the combination of musical activities by former residents from both sides of the common Polish-Ukrainian border, whose linguistic and musical differences are considerably fewer than those related by political and religious organizations. The ethnic community's musical identity, therefore, results from many different ways of working out the differences the community's residents bring with them in their search for commonality.

Ethnic communities often bolster their sense of identity by engaging in activities with communities elsewhere in a city, region, or nation. German choral activities in North America, to take one example of extensive intercommunity organization, form around leagues or unions at each of these levels. Several dozen German choruses in Chicago share a common home, namely the DANK Haus ("Deutsch-Amerikanischer National-Kongress") in a once-predominantly Central European neighborhood on the city's North Side. These many choruses not only represent different regions and cultural areas of German-speaking Europe (Rhineland Germans or Burgenländer Austrians) but also exhibit different social bases (religious, fraternal, or even émigré, as in the case of German-speaking immigrants from Czechoslovakia). The choruses maintain a variety of relations with other societies in the Midwest, and many are members of national organizations, such as the Nordamerikanischer Sängerbund, which periodically sponsors competitions and conventions.

Musical activity organized at this intercommunity level broadly recasts and restates the symbols of ethnicity, giving them a North American context. The German choruses that participate in citywide or national organizations, for example, adapt their practices to a core repertory while keeping the distinctive songs and dialect of a single region, thereby allowing them to maintain a specific identity. Intercommunity musical organizations inevitably bring about a certain form of juxtaposition. The result—say, the larger repertory of the Nordamerikanischer Sängerbund—may exhibit a certain homogeneity and yet admit far greater variety than any single German ethnic chorus would ever allow on its own.

Intercommunity contact has benefited considerably from the presence of the mass media as a stimulus to ethnic cultural activity. During the early centuries of settlement in North America, the print medium was the most powerful means of providing music and other forms of aesthetic expression to those at a great distance from a critical mass of fellow immigrants. The proliferation of ethnic hymnody throughout the nineteenth century and the ready availability of hymnbooks in Swedish, Danish, or Czech, for example, made it possible for those who were parishioners of ethnic churches to couple linguistic and musical literacy, and to do so through musical practices in the home. Ethnic sound recordings in the twentieth century reached an extraordinary number of North American homes, keeping the sounds of Spanish, Arabic, and Ukrainian music alive and doing so at affordable costs. Ethnic records continue to provide one of the most vivid means of documenting the musical styles and repertories shared by immigrants throughout North America. At the end of the twentieth century, ethnic radio and television have beome significant media for broadcasting music and establishing a place for it in the life of an ethnic community. In large cities many ethnic groups regard it as extremely important to their identity to support at least periodic programming in the mass media, thereby increasing the access of all to the sounds of ethnic music by creating new and more public contexts.

We now reach the other extreme of the continuum, at which ethnic musical activities stretch beyond the home, the organization, or the community, in fact to other ethnic communities. At this extreme we witness the ways in which the multiplicity of ethnic communities and musics reinforces the desire to retain and strengthen patterns of diversity. The folk festival, for example, offers a prime example of a multiethnic setting in which communities confront each other and emphasize their differences. Many communities may perform musics that otherwise are seldom heard or that have no real function other than to articulate differences when multiethnic musical performances take place. It is important for us to realize, then, that the growing importance of cultural activities that bring many communities together actually encumbers any tendency toward a melting pot. In order to participate in a folk festival or to contribute a performance to the series of ethnic Christmas shows at a civic museum, ethnic communities more commonly expand their musical repertories, engaging in both research and the reorganization of musical ensembles to create a performance that is convincing both to the community itself and those viewing it from the outside. The multiethnic cultural environment of North America, therefore, stimulates rather than stems the diversity of musical activity in its many communities.

IDEAS ABOUT MUSIC

Preservation

Preservation, survival, isolation—all are concepts that have surrounded North American ideas about folk music. These are concepts that are value-laden and freighted with notions of what North Americans want their folk music to be. Preservation allows the best of the past to survive; it establishes links between the generations; it isolates the differences between one group and another. Preservation, then, is an idea about music that stems from the tendency to idealize the past and to valorize differences. Preservation has driven folk-music scholars to collect only those pieces that survive and that prove that isolation has been good for a community. If a group preserves its music, it can also withstand the melting pot, the inevitable tendency to give in and capitulate to a different culture and homogeneous value system.

The valuation of preservation is an idea about music that we can find in every ethnic group in North America. It provides one of the ways for an ethnic group itself to define its cultural core and articulate those values it wants to survive. Preservation may, however, be more a reality in some groups than in others. The locus classicus of musical preservation in North America is the culture of the Amish. The Amish form a religious community that preserves not only language (dialects of German from the Palatinate in western Germany and from Switzerland) and folkways (e.g., avoidance of technology that broaches the ideal of community isolation by encouraging dependence on the world outside the community), but also musical practices that are unique to their areas of settlement, which are found largely in Pennsylvania and the states of the central Midwest.

Amish music, though largely in German, is only remotely comparable to other German-American genres of traditional music. Preservation results because the Amish themselves have deemed it of special value. Particular settings, usually religious and communal, prescribe musical practice, hence associating the preservation of music with the religious identity that provides central meaning in Amish society. The style of Amish hymnody may well preserve a musical style and even repertory characteristic of German pietistic Protestantism in the sixteenth and seventeenth centuries, although there is no way of proving this, for the long, lugubrious chorale tunes performed by the Amish are not to be found in written tradition, rather only in the oral traditions that form an important part of Sunday services in the home. Borrowing also takes place, but German folk and religious songs adapted by the Amish for more "secular" occasions also move toward a core of preservation, entering the repertory contained by the *Gesangbuch* ("Songbook"), which, in effect, transforms the change that might result from contact with other German-American traditions into a repertory that preserves and protects Amish values (Figure 11–1).

Preservation takes a quite different form when embedded in ideas about African music in North America. With the Amish it was the totality of their special religious subculture that survived. With African-Americans musical elements have survived to give music a fundamental link to the community. Again, preservation is inseparable from a system of values that music symbolizes and embodies. It is hardly surprising

Ausbund,

Das ift:

Etliche schöne

Christliche

Lieder,

Wie sie in dem Ge-
fängnis zu Baffau in dem
Schloß von den Schweitzer-Brüdern,
und von anderen rechtgläubi-
gen Christen hin,und her
gedichtet worden.

Allen und jeden Christen
welcher Religion sie seyen, un-
partheyisch fast nützlich.

Germantown:
Gedruckt bey Christoph Saur / 1742.

Figure 11–1.   Title page of the first Amish songbook/hymnal (*Ausbund*) published in North America. Publisher: Christopher Sour; published in Germantown, Pennsylvania, 1742.

that the growing awareness of African musical elements in the music of African-Americans accompanied an historical period in the mid-twentieth century when Americans of color most successfully resisted the hegemony of white cultural values and their political justification.

Remarkable as it may seem today, many scholars formerly insisted that the music and culture of African-Americans derived from the European-dominated mainstream society. Black spirituals, as some theories argued, derived from white hymn traditions; jazz depended on a store of white popular tunes and the harmonic structure that these provided as a basis for improvisation. The most forceful rebuttal of such aesthetic hegemony took the form of recognizing and identifying the ways in which African-American music preserved musical elements that are essential to the structure of African musics—for example, call-and-response structures and complex layers of rhythmic polyphony. As musicians and scholars recognized more and more genres that had maintained such elements from African music, it became possible to redress the cultural politics that privileged European musical and cultural transformation. Scholars increasingly understood African-American musical styles as a receptacle that could preserve distinctive musical qualities while enabling these to transform other musics in North America and elsewhere in the world.

Maintaining the Generations:
Oral Tradition and Ethnic History

If music can preserve and be preserved, it might also provide a link to the past. One of the most common ideas about music in ethnic North America is that it functions to recall another time and place: the old country in the age of our ancestors. The attempt to form this link is not merely a product of a conservative view of folk music—that is, the belief that it must be old, indeed several generations old, truly to be folk music. Clearly, my persistent use of a hyphen to separate one geographic location from another—Chinese-American, Ukrainian-Canadian—symbolizes that link as I attempt to represent it in this chapter. Ethnicity is unquestionably a construct that endeavors to maintain the generations and that undergirds the history of an ethnic community. Music, with its inherent quality of reframing time, serves as one of the most effective tools for recouping the other times and places so essential to a community's identity.

Many ideas about music depend on the importance placed on maintaining culture across the generations. Songs passed from generation to generation are valued not only because they reflect the integrity of the family but because they establish a claim for the tenacity of oral tradition. Oral tradition itself is regarded as vital because it establishes the contact between generations—that is, a physical, human contact that stretches back to the old country. The oral traditions of music accordingly symbolize the personal interactions that make an ethnic community possible. I do not mean to suggest here that ethnic music must be fundamentally oral, but rather that certain ideas about music assert the importance of oral tradition as a symbol of community strength and musical continuity. Even as groups revive ethnic musical traditions, they establish a place for these expressions of continuity, preferring to restore a truncated oral tradition rather then to perform what otherwise would seem like a frozen tradition of the past with no link to the present (Figures 11–2 and 11–3).

Boundaries: Music to Distinguish Us from Them

Identity has been one of the unifying themes throughout this chapter. The many musics in the multiethnic panorama of North America almost inevitably become banners of ethnicity, ways of telling others that difference is a significant way of achieving identity. Music often exists as a practice that has unique forms within the group, whether because

Figure 11–2. Norwegian Emigrant Song, "The Emigrant to Ottawa." Reproduced in: Svein Schrøder Amundsen and Reimund Kvideland, *Emigrant viser*. Oslo: Universitetsforlaget, 1975. Page 187.

O Susanne,

græd dog ej for mig!

Jeg gaar til Kalifornien og graver Guld til dig.

Ny Vise om den søde Susannes Lykke.

Figure 11–3.   Title page for Danish Emigrant Song for America, "O Susanne," which has the California Gold Rush as its topic. Published by the Strandberg Press, the largest Danish broadside publisher, 1980–81. This song sold 50,000 copies in 1881. Reproduced in: Lisbeth Steenstrup Jensen and Søren Koustrup. *Udvandrersange*. Munksgaard: n.p., 1976.

of its use of a language marking a contained linguistic geography, or whether it functions in ways that would be relatively meaningless in other contexts. Music assumes a salient position along the boundaries separating us from them.

Different musical styles may function as boundaries to varying degrees. Even within related ethnic groups it is possible to observe rather different ways of maintaining boundaries. Among French ethnic groups in North America, for example, two distinct forms of musical boundary maintenance have developed. The boundaries that are most firmly entrenched are those of the Québecois, the French of Canada. Here, the distinctiveness of identity has assumed political proportions. The musical culture of the Québecois, therefore, exhibits considerable centrality, focusing on the music of the community itself and the ways this differs completely from that of Canadians from other ethnic communities. Social dance, especially that which employs clogging of some kind, has great importance, thus allowing folk music to exhibit a form of public communality. Preservation is extreme, and the instrumentarium of ensemble music has solidified around a core of fiddles, accordions, and harmonica, with special ethnic accent provided by the addition of spoons and jew's harp.

In contrast, the music of the Cajuns—French-speaking residents of the American Gulf Coast, particularly the Bayou country of southern Louisiana—have created distinctive musical boundaries by allowing them to admit change, by recognizing that musical style can filter influences from the outside and reformulate them as Cajun. Cajun music is no less distinctive than Québecois, but it has incorporated elements of musical style from surrounding non-French communities, both white and black. The accordion of Cajun music, therefore, bears witness to German influences and accordingly lends itself to a style of social dance that is much less refined than French-Canadian social dance, taking place instead in public halls and being shared by the entire community. Cajun dance is more appropriately compared to the diverse forms of polka that one finds in Central and Eastern European ethnic communities in the United States. Cajun music reflects the music of the cultures outside the community's boundaries, whereas the performers of Québecois music equate its potential to differentiate us from them with an inviolable uniqueness.

Regionalism

Regionalism has long shaped North American ideas about music. People living within a region or those outside often speak with assurance of the musical styles and repertories that belong to the Canadian Maritime Provinces or the American South. Even within regions distinctions develop and persist—for example, in the Midwest, where the Upper Midwest has its own musical traditions. Musical regionalism grows for a number of different reasons which often interact. The distinctive histories of certain regions would appear to be one of the most obvious determinants of regional traits. Shaping each region are the patterns of immigration and settlement specific to it. The American Midwest, settled largely from the mid- to late-nineteenth century, has a significantly larger number of the Central and Northern European ethnic groups than the Southwest, where Hispanic communities predominate in many areas. Accordingly, the music of the Midwest reflects the influences of German and Scandinavian traditions, whereas the Southwest has a wide range of Spanish and Mexican traditions.

The distinctive character of regional musics is also a product of the patterns of mixture and change. Regionalism is therefore not an idea about music that depends on isolation or preservation. Inevitably, regional music styles form after musical contact between the different groups. The repertories that we recognize as characterizing the American South, for example, show that European communities have long interacted with African-Americans, and the coexistence of African-American and European-American musical traits is evident in a wide range of genres. Indeed, it is probably impossible to find any form of Southern music in which the centuries-long presence of African-Americans does not assert itself in identifiable musical traits.

There are regional styles that develop largely because of the particular contact between ethnic groups settling in the region. The American polka, for example, developed in that part of the United States in which large communities of Central European and Eastern European immigrants settled, forming what is often referred to as the "polka belt," which stretches from New Ulm, Minnesota, to Buffalo, New York. The polka itself is an amalgam of Germanic and Slavic folk-music elements, and contact across boundaries in Europe is often easy to identify—say, in German-Czech and Austrian-Slovenian styles. Interethnic contact became more prevalent in the American Midwest, especially in large industrial cities like Cleveland and Chicago. Polka was therefore ideally suited to the contact between ethnic groups that the Midwest and its economic and settlement patterns occasioned.

Ethnic Music and "Truly American" Music

Although ethnic music would seem to resist association with ideas about music that lay claim to "truly American" music, there have been more than a few attempts to associate ethnic forms with more sweeping Americanness. At one level, this results from a belief in representativeness. During the folk-music revival of the 1950s and 1960s, many enthusiasts believed that a common lode of American folk music was located in the Southern mountains. This music was rural and presumably had its origins in the British Isles before being relocated to the isolated areas of the South. Certain types of ballads received privileged treatment, and the revivalists often plumbed the Southern repertories for evidence of protest and class conflict. The musical instruments associated with Southern folk music, especially the guitar and the banjo, received most-favored status, and these, too, quickly became symbolic of an American folk-music instrumentarium. What is most interesting for our examination of music in ethnic North America is not whether the revivalists were right or wrong about the representativeness of Appalachian folk music. From our ethnomusicological viewpoint, we recognize that there is a certain motivation at work, namely the urge to find a musical voice for the entire nation, even if that voice had a heavy foreign accent in many other regions.

It is not only regions that have vied to use music to represent an overarching Americanness; ethnic groups have also contributed to domains of American musical life that extend far beyond the group itself. German-Americans, for example, have been particularly active in the building of American classical traditions, especially from the mid-nineteenth to the mid-twentieth century. German musicians filled the symphony orchestra of the nineteenth century, and the cultural life of many large cities was filled with German choral festivals, such as Cincinnati's well-known Maifest, that contributed significantly to the formation of a stable musical life. Music publishing, necessary for a healthy concert life, also developed in the nineteenth and twentieth centuries as a realm in which German-American printers predominated. Eventually, these contributions by German-American musicians did not remain anchored in the ethnic group, but spilled over into the mainstream of American art music. The values of the ethnic group were transformed to suit an idea about music that now belongs to the entire nation.

The contributions of African-American music to more comprehensive American ideas about music are especially notable. Not only do we hear African-American musical traits in many styles and genres no longer specific to African-American culture—the best-known example being rock and roll, though a rich store of other popular musics would also illustrate this phenomenon—but an aura of Americanness surrounds certain musical styles that have remained rooted in African-American music culture. The notion that jazz is the "true classical music" of North America is another—and perhaps the most widespread—reflection of the way in which ideas about music establish links between the particular and the general, between the music of one group and that of the entire continent. The classicization of jazz is even more remarkable, for it suggests that music in the intensely ethnic matrix of North America has the power to subvert some cultural values. Jazz has therefore succeeded in forging a position for African-Americans in the larger society that centuries of social struggle had not completely effected by the end of the twentieth century. Ethnicity, with its problematic questions of difference and identity, nonetheless plays an indispensable role in determining the most far-reaching yet culturally central ideas about music.

MUSICAL INSTRUMENTS

North America's Store of Musical Instruments

A secondhand store just about anywhere in North America provides a fine place to introduce ourselves to the musical instruments of the continent. Not that we shall find every kind of musical instrument here, but we can observe the care with which instruments are preserved, passed on to another generation, and transformed into artifacts and icons. The secondhand store reveals something of the way North Americans think about musical instruments—that is, the way they classify instruments according to function and social value and the way they willingly jumble instruments together to create new ensembles and the new mix of sound that these produce. Not every secondhand store yields the same instrumentarium—we would find more guitars in the Southwest, more concertinas in the Upper Midwest, more Ukrainian banduras in Manitoba—but it is precisely because the secondhand store's collection of instruments reflect the ethnicity and musical styles of its region and the people living there that we can turn to it to learn about the musical instruments of ethnic North America. For our purposes, let's visit a store in central Kansas, seeing what it can tell us about the musical instruments from the center of the United States.

The section devoted to musical instruments in the secondhand store quickly makes it clear that instruments are regarded with pride and that they acquire a value that makes it important to pass them from generation to generation, if even through the mediation of the store. As we look at the instruments displayed in the store, we notice that just about every conceivalbe type is to be found. A baby grand piano painted a smeary white stands in one corner; a sign on its lid proclaims that it was the house instrument of a local "ballroom," at which jazz and polka bands played five nights a week for forty years. Some brass and woodwind instruments sprawl across a big table, and the clerk tells us that these have accumulated over the years, having been traded to the store by several generations of musicians from the high-school band, the fireman's marching ensemble, and the band of the Swedish Lutheran Church. For someone who wants a cheap saxophone or euphonium and is willing to repair the pads and joints herself, this is the place to get a deal.

The clerk, knowing that we are in the area to learn about ethnic music, pulls us over to a wall of violins. "You might be interested to know that this area was well known for its Swedish fiddlers," the clerk tells us. "These fiddles, here, belonged to a family group that toured throughout central and eastern Kansas." There are other fiddles, too, most without the fine, laminated maple work of the Swedish fiddles, some obviously homemade. "The Russian-Germans used fiddles a lot, too," offers the clerk, "but never with the virtuosity of the Swedes. You'll see that their violins aren't so fancy. Still, did you know that they all came from Austria, where they really know how to make violins? If you want German instruments, let me suggest that you look at the accordions and button boxes on that table over there!"

On "that table over there" we encounter a completely different concept of musical ensemble: accordions of every shape, tuning, structure, and extent of mother-of-pearl inlay. Accordion heaven! Were there so many accordion players here in central Kansas? Anticipating our query, the clerk notes, "There used to be a German music store in town, and the owner was nuts about accordions. Always said the accordion was one of Germany's gifts to the world. Once, a German company sent one of its touring groups over, the sort that stopped with demo records and a trunk full of instruments at every little town. Well, this storeowner, he bought one of those trunks, and you're looking at about half of it right now."

Pride of place goes to the wall whose occupants are identified with a sign announcing "jazz instruments." This part of central Kansas was on a circuit for bands coming from Kansas City and other cities of the old "Southwest," cauldron for the development of swing during the 1930s and 1940s. The Bennie Moten band and the Count Basie Orchestra played fairly often in this part of Kansas, pulling into town in big touring cars and leaving before the night was over. A little note taped to one tenor saxophone says "played by Lester Young," and the store clerk is very proud. Whether or not Lester Young, one of the greatest of all Kansas City tenor-sax players from the Swing Era, ever did play this horn seems less relevant than the aura that now surrounds these instruments. They establish a musical link to another time and place, a musical culture that is different to imagine today in the town but one which distinguished its past. They may seem out of place, witnessing the vitality and social conditions of an ethnic group not likely to have much to do with the Swedish Lutheran band or the German accordion fanatic. And yet all of these instruments do belong to this store and its particular place in North America (Figure 11–4).

Musical Instruments in a Multiethnic Culture

The secondhand store is a metaphor for concepts of musical instruments in North America in a variety of ways. At first glance it seems like a hodgepodge, instruments discarded and assembled only in random fashion. The more time we spend with the instruments, however, the more that hodgepodge exhibits patterns that are themselves the products of the regional, socioeconomic, and ethnic history of the town in which the store was located. Juxtaposition has occurred, but it nonetheless belongs to the multiethnic community in which the store is located. It is, moreover, the juxtaposition itself that is such a persuasive metaphor for the relation between these instruments and the multiethnic culture of North America.

Instruments in many ensembles result from conditions not unlike those we found in the secondhand store. The old and the new mix, establishing links with both tradition and modernity. Instruments have many functions, depending on how they are used and who uses them. A fiddle, for example, may be Swedish, Cajun, German, or Appalachian. An accordion might have specific ethnic associations, or it might belong to a popular mainstream in which ethnic distinctions have disappeared.

Function—especially in the type of change one finds in the multiethnic culture—plays a fundamental role in determining just what musics can be adapted to particular instruments and ensembles.

The instruments in the secondhand store show that patterns of exchange are common, if not normative, in the multiethnic culture. An instrument may begin its life in North America as an artifact brought from the old country, only to cross ethnic boundaries to perform an entirely new repertory. Repertories and styles similarly participate in such patterns of exchange. Instruments may themselves undergo transformation during these processes of exchange. Musicians who attempt to authenticate Norwegian musical traditions in North America use the hardingfele as a symbol of Norwegianness. The "Hardanger fiddle"— actually a relatively new addition to the instrumentarium of Norwegian

Figure 11–4.   Boro Roganović, player of the single-string, bowed fiddle *gusle*. A Montenegran–American from Chicago, Roganović performs Serbian epics in ethnic communities of the Upper Midwest. Photograph by Randy Tunnell, used with permission of the photographer.

folk music, being relatively uncommon or localized prior to the nineteenth century—is itself a violin to which sympathetic resonating strings have been added. The hardingfele and the Swedish-American fiddles in the Kansas store demonstrate how related instruments can be used to express ethnicity in an immediately symbolic way.

The store is also suggestive of the ways in which ensembles form in ethnic North America. On one hand, the distinctiveness of an ensemble remains, perhaps because of the Swedish Lutheran church band or the big-band jazz collection. On the other hand, the store affects the blurring of the boundaries to which it admits. The accordions might seem to belong to a tradition of Dutchman polka bands, but there is no reason that they cannot cross the boundary to Slovenian or Polish groups. Musicians are more likely to base their purchasing decision on the sound, the construction, or the reputation of the manufacturer. Assembled in the store, the instruments are but stages in the transformation of the history of ethnic ensembles; their past is linked to their future by the catalytic moment that their sojourn in the secondhand store symbolizes.

The Fiddle and the Banjo

Few instruments are as ubiquitous in North American ethnic communities as the fiddle. Wide distribution notwithstanding, the fiddle is one of the most malleable of all instruments in ethnic music. Not only does it lend itself to membership in broadly different ensembles, but it can adopt the sound of just about any ensemble, whether the small group playing in a Lebanese club in Montreal or the fiddle-and-guitar duo accompanying folk dance in rural New Mexico. We might wonder whether this extreme adaptability is a possible explanation for the currency of the term "fiddle," as if to distinguish its many ethnic varieties from the stalwart violin of Western art music. Its name and its function underscore its familiarity; the fiddle is never a foreigner in ethnic musical styles.

Although the fiddle is adaptable, the ways in which it enters ethnic musical traditions and comes to function in them are quite distinctive. For some groups ethnicity seems almost to coalesce around the fiddle. The hardingfele is the most pronounced symbol of Norwegian-American music, much as painted wood handicrafts and furniture (*rosemaling*) occupy a position of extreme Norwegianness in the material culture of American folklore. In the revival of klezmer bands in Jewish-American culture, the fiddle also becomes the most Jewish of all the instruments, not least because of a long tradition of associating the violin with musical specialists in Eastern European Jewish society—specialists, that is, in both folk music and classical music. In Cajun music, too, it is the fiddle that verifies the link with French-Canadian music, whereas other instruments bespeak the influences from outside the French-speaking community in Louisiana.

The fiddle is an active participant in, even instigator of, musical change, realigning the stylistic markers of ethnicity. In Anglo-American instrumental music, an entire corpus of so-called fiddle tunes has solidified oral tradition and yet provided a conduit for the expansion of the corpus. During the years of transition from Anglo-American folk music to popular hillbilly or country music (roughly the 1930s, 1940s, and 1950s), the fiddle directed the processes of change, firmly holding on to the fiddle tunes, while staking out the possibilities for style change. Even before styles like bluegrass exploited the virtuosic possibilities of the banjo or the mandolin, the fiddle's role was one of stating and exemplifying the virtuosity that the Anglo-American instrumental tradition would tolerate. It was hard to play, and only the most accomplished musicians played it, affording it even more mystique within the tradition. As instruments all around it changed, the fiddle engaged in a process of stabilizing and retaining the core that anchored both the essential ethnic qualities and the history that effectively reshaped these.

From its twentieth-century contexts one would hardly suspect that the banjo came to North America with the Africans brought as slaves. The banjo now has almost no place among African-American musical traditions; it is an instrument that has largely been abandoned by one ethnic group to be adopted by others. During its peregrinations it has become an entirely new instrument, with new styles, repertories, and functions. It has crossed back and forth between genres, and it has enjoyed popularity in every sector of North America's musical life. Its ethnic qualities, then, derive from its remarkable adaptability, but also from its ability to ascribe a range of ethnic meanings to very specific styles of music.

An instrument characterized generally by the tight skin or plastic stretched over the circular frame of a long-necked lute, the North American banjo probably had its origins in West Africa. Accounts of slave musicians from the seventeenth century already describe instruments that are likely ancestors of the banjo. A variety of early names existed—banjar, bandore, banza—thus enabling historians to document a fairly consistent development of the banjo as an instrument accompanying African-American dance. In African-American slave society and in the South after the Civil War, the banjo largely served rural forms of music; to the extent that it has survived in African-American communities into the twentieth century, it has retained its association with folk music.

Ironically, it was because the banjo was such a powerful icon of African-American music that it crossed ethnic boundaries into white musical genres. During the 1840s and 1850s the banjo rapidly achieved enormous popularity in the urban North, largely because minstrels—white musicians smearing their faces with blackened cork and performing a repertory of popular songs that used parodies of black musical styles—incorporated the banjo into their ensembles, where it became the stereotypic minstrel instrument. In white society, the banjo first enjoyed success in urban areas, entering parlor music in the years following the Civil War. But the banjo lent itself also to a variety of other functions. It becamse an instrument of the rural South again, this time a favored instrument of rural whites. By the 1920s the banjo was crossing yet another boundary, this time into the urbanized styles of Dixieland jazz and early country music. Jazz largely dropped the banjo during the transplantation of musicians from New Orleans to Chicago and New York. As country music proliferated and developed into increasingly refined styles such as bluegrass, the banjo again moved toward the core of an almost entirely white music. Pete Seeger exploited rural connections again, touting the banjo during the folk-song revival of the 1950s and 1960s.

The banjo is an ethnic instrument that has demonstrated an ability to belong to many ethnic groups and many styles of ethnic music. Of the repertories that used the banjo, almost all represented some aspect of ethnicity, if only through parody. We might conclude, then, that the banjo played a role in ascribing ethnicity, in serving as a conscious symbol of some sort of association with another group's differences. We might also conclude that the banjo came to fulfill the need of musicians to represent the existence of difference, as if that established a link to the folk and popular culture of another community and therefore responded to the need to capture some fundamental quality of ethnic diversity. In so doing, the banjo may also have responded to a fundamental quality of the music of ethnic North America.

SOCIAL STRUCTURE/MUSICAL STRUCTURE

In what ways is the music of an ethnic community a reflection of the distinctiveness of that community? Does Filipino-American music *sound* Filipino-*American*? There is no question that it sounds different from, say, Korean-American music, but what distinguishes it as characteristic of the Filipino community in North America? How extensively, then, are social structure and musical structure in ethnic North America reflective of each other?

In this section we shall investigate a number of ways that social structure determines certain aspects of musical structure in ethnic music. From the different topics that follow it will be apparent that there are rarely simple correspondences between these aspects of structure. Far more often, we encounter mediating structures. Religion, for example, determines a set of institutions and practices that, in turn, play a role in the creation of distinctive musical styles and repertories. The ways in which ethnic communities tell stories about their pasts—even the ways in which they express a distinctive understanding of their own histories—take the form of narrative genres, which have traditionally employed certain musical genres that lend themselves particularly well to narrativity. The confrontation with modernity, clearly necessitating change in the social structure, also produces change in musical structure, rendering some forms more powerful and sweeping in their negotiation between past and present. By no means are social and musical structures really parallel. They do, however, influence each other in a myriad of ways that help us distinguish how music expresses the multiethnic culture of North America.

Music and Religious Community

Religious communities have consistently endowed music with an abundance of ethnic particularity. North American religious history is largely a chronicle of differences sanctioned both by political policies that made religion a matter of individual preference and by the intimate relation between ethnic and religious ideals. We are all aware that immigrant movements often have religious motivations and that settlement patterns reflect the continuation of those motivations. New immigrants frequently seek out coreligionists in order to move into a community where others already share their belief system. That the residents of such a community express those beliefs in a language and music that is equally familiar is but added motivation for focusing immigration toward the religious community.

The music of an ethnic religious community is highly codified. The church, synagogue, or mosque already provides both texts and contexts for music making that clearly delineates the community. Music accompanies the performance of standard religious texts and the rituals that the community enacts on a regular basis. Liturgies embody both music and the language of religion, wedding them in a metalanguage that the members of the community not only share but perform. Religion also determines a distinctive musical repertory—in fact, a body of musical pieces suitable for activities within and without the religious organization itself. Ethnic religious repertories are necessary for the celebration of rites of passage, holidays, and normal social gatherings. Religion, therefore, reinforces ethnicity while becoming itself the beneficiary of the particularizing force of music.

In many communities religious ethnic music predominates, replacing secular forms and even becoming secularized itself. This has been the case in many rural communities with Protestant German and Scandinavian ethnic groups in the Midwest. The particularity of religious denomination was so extreme in the nineteenth and early twentieth centuries (and, in some cases, at the end of the twentieth century) that Norwegians, Swedes, Danes, and Germans formed separate denominations of Lutheranism, with a surfeit of splinter groups even breaking away from these. Each group formulated its own religious and musical languages, which articulated its own doctrines and then began to function within the organizations of the town.

Larger religions may also subsume a great number of diverse ethnic communities. Muslims in a large North American city may come from musical backgrounds ranging from North Africa to southeastern Europe to the Middle East to India and Indonesia; Black Muslims, too, exert an important presence in urban North America, contributing yet another musical language to the larger Islamic community. At one level, the musical life of each Muslim ethnic group remains distinctive. At another, however, each group reckons with the central musical influence of the Koran and the recitation of religious texts and prayers. Widely divergent communities share certain paraliturgical genres, as well as forms of popular song like the ghazal. Where, then, do we find the musical life of an Albanian-American community or of Rajasthanis in Toronto? How do we interpret the nasal quality of Nigerian-American popular genres—for example, fuji—which distinguishes immigrants as Hausa, therefore more likely Muslim? Which is the more important distinction—Hausa, Muslim, Nigerian, or African-American? Religion, then, plays a direct if extremely complicated role in the creation and perpetuation of musical style. Unraveling that role is not always easy, but to investigate ethnic musical style without also examining the impact of religion is impossible.

Narrativity and History

The music of North America tells many different types of stories. These stories tell of the past, both historical and mythical, and address the realities of contemporary political and social conditions. Ethnic groups encode the experiences of their ancestors, while labor organizers use song as a powerful weapon in reminding workers of a history of struggle. Music possesses diverse and complex narrative qualities, and these often appear in the repertories of ethnic North America. Whether or not folk music can "tell the story" of Canada or the United States is impossible to know, but narrative genres nevertheless occupy a place in most communities that attests to the meaning and importance of the stories that they do tell. Perhaps more than anything else, narrative genres of music reveal the stories that a community tells about itself.

Ballads have long been among the narrative genres most prized by folk-song collectors. The British folklorists Cecil Sharp and Maud Karpeles searched through the American South in the early decades of the twentieth century, finding there the stories of an Anglo-Scottish past, presumably preserved in the F. J. Child collection of England and Scotland ordinary called the "Child ballads." Ballads tell their stories in very particular ways, and indeed a ballad takes its identity from the story it tells and the individual actors who play out the story. A ballad often has a protagonist, perhaps several, whose particular encounter at a moment in time constitutes the story. Most European-American ballads frame their narratives in a series of episodes, each one occupying a stanza or several lines of text. Musically, eposides also occupy a unit, often a four-line verse, which then repeats to articulate other episodes. Although ballads tend to form repertories according to linguistic and national region in Europe, they demonstrate a tendency to mix when ethnic groups come in contact in North America. The Child ballads, the richest single corpus of Anglo-Scottish ballads, are not uncommon in German versions in the American Midwest, where "Lord Lovell" and "Lady Nancy" may reappear as "Ritter Eduard" and "beliebte Lina" ("Sir Edward" and "beloved Lina") in a German version. Such exchange of ballads seems most common among ethnic communities in which narrativity is fairly widespread among other genres of music, in essence placing special value and emphasis on those songs that do tell stories (Figure 11–5).

To what extent do history and specific experiences from the past appear in these narrative forms? In the most important Mexican-American narrative genre, the corrido, both historical episodes and individuals are frequently celebrated, and some individual corridos with their variants may recount the history of a particular region or period of struggle between Mexicans, Mexican-Americans, and non-Hispanic Americans. Like the Anglo-Scottish ballad, the corrido usually comprises four-line stanzas, reflecting the structure of the Spanish literary unit known as copla. The melodic style, too, with its relatively narrow range and recitative quality, empowers the genre to function more directly as an expression of Mexican-American social and historical conditions. The corrido has rather more flexibility in its structure than the Child ballads, allowing singers to incorporate new stories into the genre. As a narrative genre, then, corridos are among the most specific in North America. The ceaseless border conflicts between the United States and Mexico during the nineteenth and twentieth centuries are common subjects of corridos in southern Texas. Other corridos have chronicled the lives of folk heroes, such as Gregorio Cortez, or contemporary social activists for Chicano rights, such as César Chávez. The narrativity of the corrido therefore lends itself to the political and social voice of Mexican-Americans, which in turn poignantly serves as a force to articulate the past and present of the community.

Mass-Mediated Ethnicity and the Commodification of Musical Style

Polka has become big business. A successful polka musician can earn fame and fortune, even a Grammy Award, for a record that has topped the polka charts for a long period. Polka clubs go on European tours and enjoy the videos of their idols. Polka is not far from earshot during

Figure 11–5.   Broadside of a popular emigrant's song from the fin-de-siècle Vienna stage, "Mondlied," from Bruno Zappert's *A Bohemian in America*. Graphic collection, Deutsches Volksliedarchiv, Freidburg i.Br., Germany.

the commercial breaks of ethnic radio and TV shows. Polka has become an ethnic music for all North Americans. Just why has polka come to occupy this central position among ethnic musics? Polka has a long history of remarkable musical and social adaptability. In many ways, these two forms of adaptability have enjoyed a reflexive relation, making it possible for polka to expand stylistically just as it expands into new ethnic and regional marketplaces.

   Polka in North America has largely developed in the industrialized North, especially in those regions of the Midwest and Middle Atlantic states in which large numbers of immigrants from Central and Eastern

Europe have settled. It is also a popular instrumental and dance form in smaller pockets where settlers from these areas established communities—for example, among the Czech and German towns of Texas's hill country. Polka's adaptability and malleability have even enabled it to cross unexpected ethnic borders—for example, from the folk-dance styles of Austrian settlers in Mexico to the "chicken scratch" music of Native Americans of the American Southwest. Polka has a long history in North America, occupying a place with other forms of genteel social dance by the mid-nineteenth century. The polka came to be widespread in North America, as it had found its way into the repertories of national folk musics at some distance from its presumed nation of origin, Czechoslovakia. As a dance form polka is not particularly difficult, consisting of slightly syncopated duple patterns that lend themselves to a wide array of permutations and functions. (By the end of the nineteenth century in the United States, polka was often associated with military marches and parades, for example.)

With mass immigration from Europe during the period from about 1880 until World War I, polka's European forms flooded the North American scene. Although polka was widespread among these rapidly growing ethnic communities, it nonetheless took forms related to the specific musics of the groups themselves. Each group adapted its own instrumentarium to the polka. Czech-Americans employed a rather full brass component, and German-American (or "Dutchman") bands settled heavily on the bass line with a blatty tuba. The Polish-American ensemble used piano accordions, while the button-box variety dominated the Slovenian-American sound and later that of groups from neighboring Austria. The polka as form remained intact, while more and more individual forms of expression proliferated within the genre—for example, Frankie Yankovich's introduction of the banjo into Cleveland's Slovenian style (Figures 11–6 and 11–7).

The polka illustrates a number of processes of change that musical style can engender. It tends toward popularity, serving as the conduit for the transformation of the particularity inherent in folk music to the broader appeal of music that thrives in and because of the mass media. Polka thus juxtaposes aspects of both unity and diversity in ethnic music. It lends itself to the commodification of style—yielding a product that all North Americans can enjoy—as well as the social conditions under which ethnic social dance thrives. Polka has long been a component of ethnic social gatherings, providing many groups with the opportunity to assert their ethnicity at weekend gatherings of fraternal clubs and labor groups. Musical structure and social structure enjoy an unusually close relation in the polka. Both remain resilient against the challenges to ethnicity, yet they combine to adapt ethnicity to those forms that most reflect the changing needs of ethnic North America.

Figure 11–6.   Photograph of the "Kurtz Orchestra," an ensemble performing salon music in the Burgenland-American communities of eastern Pennsylvania in the 1920s and 1930s. This "first-generation" Austrian-American
orchestra was the predecessor of the polka band of the late twentieth century. Photograph courtesy of Rudolf Pietsch, Vienna.

THE MUSIC OF AN AFRICAN-AMERICAN COMMUNITY

With this section we make a special excursion into the music of a single,
extraordinarily complex community: the African-American, particularly
in the city of Chicago. In many ways, this section deserves to be a chapter
of its own, indeed an entire book. By treating it as a case study within
the framework of a chapter on ethnic North America, I do not mean
to detract from the larger importance of the music of African-Americans.
Instead, I intend to underscore that importance by claiming, on one
hand, that African-American musical traditions have a remarkable
history and coherence that derives from the integrity and strength of
an ethnic community during three-and-a-half centuries of extraordinarily
difficult, often abhorrent social conditions. On the other hand, the importance of African-American musical traditions is not separable from

the enormous influence they have had on the musics of other ethnic communities and ethnic North America as a whole. It would be impossible to write a chapter on the music of this cultural area without emphasizing the music of African-Americans—without, in fact, recognizing the many ways in which African-Americans have contributed to the diversity of musics in ethnic North America far more extensively and profoundly than any other group.

I shall not pretend in this section to do justice to the enormousness of the special role of African-Americans in the music of ethnic North America. Rather I wish to turn our attention to African-American music in a single city, Chicago, whose complex ethnic makeup and vital African-American musical life are broadly paradigmatic for this chapter; we can understand Chicago as a microcosm for many of the ideas and

Figure 11–7. The Al Meixner Orchestra plays at a picnic of the Lehigh County, Pennsylvania, Burgenländische Gemeinschaft, an Austrian-American social club, in 1986. Trained in the traditions of the Duquesne University Tamburitzans, the band leader, Al Meixner (button box), now plays ethnic music professionally at EPCOT Center in Orlando, Florida. Photograph courtesy of Rudolf Pietsch, Vienna.

musics that we find throughout North America. Chicago is well known as a very "ethnic" city, an urban area whose cultural geography refuses to yield to any form of melting pot. The city is a complex of neighborhoods, each with a name and an identifiable ethnic history. Neighborhoods were originally the product of vast city planning in the wake of the Chicago Fire of 1871, which devastated much of the city. The organizations and grids of neighborhoods at the end of the nineteenth century quickly became home to the massive influx of immigrants, particularly from Europe, in the period of rapid industrialization prior to World War I. Each neighborhood has its own ethnic history—for instance, Andersonville, once Swedish, is now Korean, Chinese, and Assyrian—and the ethnic complexion of each is a commonly understood fact of cultural life in Chicago.

The history of Chicago's African-American community, too, has been one of neighborhoods and interaction with other ethnic groups. The influx of African-Americans from the South accompanied the rapid industrialization of the city, especially before and after World War I. The rural poor of the South saw in the expanding city a land of occupational opportunity, and they flooded into the city in search of jobs. The first major African-American settlement of Chicago, therefore, was comparable in many ways to that of the European-Americans, namely as the goal of immigration. African-Americans, too, recognized in the grid of urban neighborhoods the chance of building a community that was distinctive, yet no more or less exceptional in the urban landscape than that of other immigrant groups. There is no need here to rehearse the many reasons that the egalitarian grid of neighborhoods was often more exclusive than inclusive for African-Americans; the long history of racial prejudice in the United States and the extra burden of suffering that this history has wrought up to the present made Chicago's ethnicity as much an enemy as a friend for African-Americans.

The history of settlement in Chicago also channeled some extraordinary streams in the larger music history of African-Americans. Rural migrants brought with them rural musical styles: spirituals, Mississippi Delta blues, and folk-music repertories of many different types. Those who came from southern cities also brought distinctive musical styles with them: Dixieland jazz, ragtime, and gospel traditions from Nashville or Birmingham. For musics and musicians alike, the city was a catalyst and a cauldron, a center for the juxtaposition of styles, the mixing of repertories, and the transformation of musical life. The changes that African-American musics underwent in Chicago are therefore similar in many ways to those we have observed throughout the multiethnic culture of North America. During the first half of the twentieth century the music of African-Americans in Chicago thrived because of the extraordinary capacity of that music to adapt itself to new social conditions and musical influences. The several musical styles at which we look in this section, then, are no less African-American because of these changes, but they owe much of their distinctiveness to the community's history in Chicago.

Religious Music

The boulevards and avenues of Chicago's South and West Sides are lined with storefront churches. Some of these are indeed converted stores; others are conversions of a different type, namely from a church that was formerly mainstream (e.g., Methodist) to a religious center that more directly speaks to the African-American religious experience, say, by adopting the name of a religious figure like St. Charles Lwanga. Each structure, large or small, immediately bears witness to an extraordinary exuberance and form of religious expression that is personal yet rooted in public performance. The exuberance is evident in the many ways the building itself has been refashioned. Signs full of information about worship services, Sunday school, and choir rehearsals quickly reveal that there is almost no time in the week when the church is not the site of some kind of religious and musical activity. The signs proselytize, they aim to attract anyone into the community of performance and belief, yet they clearly reflect the depth of belief and experience that binds the community together. Each church among the thousands of these African-American neighborhoods has been a venue for religious musical practice.

It would be impossible to identify a single style or core repertory in this musical practice. That English Protestant hymnody has long contributed a store of musical texts is obvious; that African musical performance practice has molded these in distinctive ways is even more obvious. Rather than strict performances from a hymnal, those in the storefront church are spontaneous, improvisatory, shaped by the functions each congregation finds most meaningful. The structure of the new version of each hymn—obviously indebted to the spiritual tradition—has taken a Biblical verse and rendered it with the flexibility that call-and-response encourages. Rather than a sedate organ or piano accompaniment, the ensemble backing up congregational singing in the storefront church looks more like a small jazz band; guitar, drums, bass, and trumpet. It also sounds more like a small jazz band.

A fixed liturgy seems completely absent. The choir and, for that matter, individuals in the congregation have full license to sing when they wish, that is, when the spirit moves them to sing. Certain individuals do seem to exhibit authority, thereby assuming the role of leaders. The minister or the choir director, for example, may spontaneously break into song; even the band members can seize the moment when they feel the spirit moving in the congregations. The music is also performed in ways that obviously have special meaning to the congregation. Each individual has the right to feel the presence of God so deeply that she or he can move from singing and dancing into trance; the rest of the congregation supports this by suspending other acts of musical performance so that the feeling of spirit from the trance can engulf the community as much as possible. In all respects, then, the music moves through the personal acts of performance toward the core of the community, expressing the African-Americanness of its ideas about both music and Christianity.

The Chicago Blues

The migration of the blues from the Mississippi Delta to Chicago is one of the most powerful metaphors for the African-American experience in the twentieth century. The blues is a music of resistance—against racism, the degradation of poverty, the racial injustice that insists upon assuming new forms rather than disappear. Scholars such as Houston A. Baker, Jr., have argued that the blues has coalesced as a canon—a core of ideas and forms of expression—for African-American culture and the aesthetic representation of that culture. There are many theories about how the blues have come to exert such a powerful presence in African-American culture, most of which recognize the importance of the poetic and musical form itself and the adaptability of that form to the diverse experiences and arts of African-Americans. This combination of adaptability and particularity has appeared as a common theme in this chapter, and perhaps there is no better example of this theme than the blues. The blues is unquestionably one of the quintessential musical forms of ethnic North America.

The structure of the blues depends on aspects of both text and musical form. The text consists usually of three lines that assume an AAB structure. The first and second lines generally create a sort of question or establish a situation in need of solution, which the third line then revolves, hence always giving the three-line verse a dynamic impetus and an internal narrative quality. The following verses, the first and last two from a classic early Chicago blues piece, Blind Lemon Jefferson's "Long Lonesome Blues," show these aspects of poetic construction:

Blind Lemon Jefferson: "Long Longsome Blues."
Transcribed in Jeff Todd Titon, *Early Downhome Blues*.
(Urbana: University of Illinois Press, 1977).

I walked from Dallas, I walked from Wichita Falls,
I walked from Dallas, I walked from Wichita Falls,
After I lost my sugar, that was no walk at all.

Woman see you comin' man, go get the rocker chair,
Woman see you comin', go get the rocker chair,
I want to fool this man and make out he's welcome here.

* * *

Tell me what's the matter that I can't get no mail,
Won't you tell me what's the matter, papa Lemon can't get no
   mail,
I was sad last night 'cause a black cat crossed your trail.

I got up this mornin', these blues all 'round my bed,
I got up this mornin', these blues all 'round my bed,
Couldn't eat my breakfast and there's blues all in my bread.

Musically, the blues also takes advantage of the tension between the first and last lines, which the second line mediates. The most common harmonic pattern of the blues

(A)   I—I—I—I
(A)   IV—IV—I—I

shows a first line, in which relative harmonic stasis is maintained, followed by a second line, in which the stable feeling of the first line is disturbed by movement in the harmony. The harmony of the third line destabilizes the verse further by beginning with the tension of new harmonic relationships, which, however, the final part of the line then resolves. These points of tension and stability are often—but not always—stretched over the three lines in twelve measures, or "bars," hence the name "twelve-bar blues." Structure of any kind in the blues, however, is only the basis for variation and improvisation during performance, and again we witness the importance of individuality and performance context in expressing the essential African-Americanness of the genre.

The blues in present-day Chicago also embodies a number of tensions in the African-American experience. We can go to two parts of the city to visit blues clubs: the traditional, urban blues bars on the poor, black South Side and the affluent, upscale clubs on the largely white North Side. The blues experiences in these two parts of the city are worlds apart. On the South Side, the blues seem more at home; the symbols of struggle and poverty are no different from reality. The musicians and the audiences identify directly with the meaning of the music; social structure and musical structure are reflexive. On the North Side, audiences are largely white, even though most of the blues bands are still black. But here the gulf between the African-American experience and the audience is vast. The music is different here: more polished, but not really intended for listening. We see in both settings for the blues that the central themes and the basic forms remain present and retain their intimate association with the African-American community. The blues continues to embrace both the tragedy and the integrity of the community's history in ethnic North America.

The Art Music of African-Americans

African-American composers of art music have engaged in a long struggle to achieve appropriate recognition. There are many reasons to explain why recognition has not been forthcoming. First, the composers of art music have been no less the victims of prejudice and oppression than other African-Americans. Second, these composers have by and large written with a very distinctive voice, which, however grounded in the craft and aesthetics of American art music, too often remains foreign to the institutions and audiences of that music. Third, even scholars and critics trying to write favorably about music in the lives of African-Americans have frequently tended to ghettoize when making claims for the many ways in which distinctive black musical voices arise from the blues, gospel, and other vernacular traditions. We must ask ourselves, then, why should the art music of African-Americans be any different from that of any other community?

Asking just this question and providing increasingly convincing answers is the Center for Black Music Research, based at Columbia College on Chicago's most fashionable street, Michigan Avenue. It is a fundamental tenet of the Center and its director, Samuel A. Floyd, Jr., that African-American music must be viewed in relation to a historical mainstream, the traditions of which it enjoyed and participated in forming. This tenet radically redresses many prevailing ways of situating black music in the musical life of North America, certainly also the notion of ethnicity that underlies this chapter. There is probably no stronger body of evidence supporting this attempt to relocate the music of African-American composers than the biographies and literature they created. Accordingly, it is of central importance to the Center for Black Music Research to bring as much of this music to performance as possible and to expand the canon even further by recording it.

Just what type of musical voice did African-American composers in Chicago really seek? If we ask this question of the distinguished female composer Florence Price (1888–1953), we find considerable support for the form of redress advanced by the Center for Black Music Research. Born in Arkansas, Florence Price studied at the New England Conservatory and moved to Chicago after several years of teaching in both Arkansas and the East. She composed in many different forms and for numerous types of ensemble, winning prizes and performances with major orchestras. Her compositions that were best known during her lifetime were those that either set spirituals for voice or drew upon African-American literature, such as works by Langston Hughes. It was uncharacteristic of her writing simply to incorporate spiritual or folk melodies into her compositions; rather, she sought to find ways that her personal idiom might combine the several aspects of the American musical heritage. She recognized that African-American composers had a special role to play in the creation of art music, albeit one that bore witness to the mainstream and its institutions, in fact, serving as a means of integrating African-American and female musicians into these. Florence Price's voice did fall silent after her death, but it has been discovered again. In its discovery we also recognize that there were many other African-American voices that deserve our attention—for example, William Grant Still and William Dawson—and that give new dimensions to the music of African-Americans.

Chicago Jazz

Chicago jazz is really many different styles, repertories, and moments in the history of jazz. More than anything, it is perhaps cultural geography that has defined jazz in the city. Chicago became important in the history of jazz, first, because it was a momentary mecca for migrating musicians and, second, because the city itself provided that backdrop for the clubs and neighborhoods necessary for the support of jazz in an urban center. Chicago jazz, perhaps more than the other musics I have discussed in this section, has formed from complex ethnic interaction, with white musicians apprenticing with and learning from the black musicians who used the city as their base. Jazz therefore belongs to the African-American history of a very "ethnic" city.

Jazz lives today in Chicago with an aura of history surrounding it. By no means can one say that jazz is today a vital part of the African-American community. True, its influences are heard in other African-American styles, and some of the city's preeminent ensembles—for example, the Art Ensemble of Chicago—are important symbols of the presence of jazz in the African-American history of the city. Moreover, one can hear outstanding jazz at clubs and bars, not to mention colleges and universities. There is a summer Chicago Jazz Festival, and there is no shortage of jazz airtime on the radio. What one does not find is that jazz lives in the neighborhoods. Active jazz clubs are found downtown or on the Near North Side, intermingled with the blues clubs. Jazz is harder to find on the South Side or in the Austin neighborhood on the West Side, once home to the so-called "Austin High Gang," whose members formed several of the most important jazz bands of the 1920s and 1930s, such as the Wolverines. Chicago jazz has historically provided non-African-Americans the opportunity to participate in the vital vernacular traditions of African-American music, thus giving it an important cultural function in an urban environment marked by ethnic differences. It is hardly surprising that history has transformed Chicago jazz into so many different things (Figure 11–8).

Music Festivals in Chicago

Summer is a season of festivals in Chicago. The neighborhoods stage countless festivals in their parks and common squares. The city, too,

Figure 11–8.   Eddie "Clean Head" Vinson with the Frank Smith Trio, Kansas City, 1960.

supports a series of festivals, beginning in May and concluding by early October. In one way or another, virtually all of these festivals are ethnic; moreover, there is no more common way to highlight the role of ethnicity in a festival than to use music. The city's major festivals are also explicitly music festivals, and each of these bears witness to some aspect of Chicago's African-American music history. The festival season begins with the Blues Festival, moving on to the Gospel Festival and, on Labor Day weekend, the Jazz Festival. The festivals became immensely successful in the 1980s, each one drawing annually hundreds of thousands of listeners for a weekend's events. The neighborhood festivals, as well, are successful, although measuring success has less to do with adding up the spectators in a crowd than with assessing the relation between the festival itself and the community, which recognizes in the festival a means of reaffirming identity.

The large festivals are not so very different in general organization from the Pittsburgh Folk Festival. Each group has a specific allotment of time during which to present the most effective show possible. Music continues almost nonstop during the festival, and thus it behooves a performing group to make its show interesting in order to keep the assembled mass enthusiastic. To do otherwise is to risk losing an invitation to the next year's festival. Although the music and musicians of the major festivals are largely African-American, the crowds are not. There is no single profile of the crowds, but it is clear that they are at best distantly related to the sorts of blues supporters or storefront parishioners that one finds on the South Side of Chicago. And why should they be? This music—a professional gospel quartet from Philadelphia or a zydeco band from Louisiana (considered blues for the purposes of the festival)—is very different from that which they hear in their neighborhoods or from that which serves to move them in their quest for God. The festivals try to include Chicago musicians whenever possible, but that means that they have to fit in, one way or another.

The neighborhood festival provides a stage for a different African-American musical experience in Chicago. The festival is a fluid affair, utilizing the cultural geography of the neighborhood as much as possible. For the most part, whoever takes the responsibility for organizing the festival also has a responsibility to ensure that it includes as many people as possible. As far as the music is concerned, this means recognizing the fundamental performance nature of many African-American musics. The "performers," then, are not just those on a stage, but the community members who might want to dance or play a blues harp (harmonica) with a band playing at the end of a blocked-off street. No musician is much concerned about her or his "show," for there is not much to be gained financially and invitations for next year are as forthcoming as one's willingness to offer musical talents for the good of the community.

Chicago's festivals remind us of the complex presence of boundaries in the musics of African-American culture. Some of these boundaries exist within the community; others form between the community and other ethnic groups. As always, these boundaries bear witness to the omnipresence of change and the ways in which differences reinforce particularity. We cannot facilely say that the music at the annual Chicago Blues Festival is any less African-American than that of an ad-hoc block party in a neighborhood on the South Side. Nor can we say that one is more or less the product of Chicago and the ways African-American musicians have fundamentally shaped and reshaped their musical life for over a century. African-American music is intimately tied to each of these festivals and the experiences that they represent. African-American music is no less intimately tied to the whole of musical experiences in ethnic North America.

CONTEMPORARY AND POPULAR ETHNIC MUSICS

Of World's Fairs and Disney Worlds

Popular culture in North America regularly conflates past, present, and future, employing considerable doses of fantasy to erase any vestiges that boundaries of time might leave. Popular music, therefore, might be a style that proclaims itself innovative and on the cutting edge; it might be a style that revives the past, repackaging its symbols and sounds for a generation that has yet to know them; it might be the product of media adaptation, the quick and ready manipulation of sounds to effect an aura of contemporaneity and marketability. Popular music can address the needs of many people, whose experiences and communities are very different. These characteristics suggest some remarkable comparisons with the music of ethnic North America that we have been examining in this chapter. Although identifiable because of its distinctiveness, ethnic music unifies by providing symbols of identity, but also by establishing connections between the past and the present, the New World and the Old, with which a broad spectrum in a community can identify. It is hardly surprising that popular music abounds in ethnic North America. We shall travel a bit in a search to find ethnic popular styles. In fact, we shall take what for many North Americans serve as pilgrimages within popular culture. We shall visit some fairs and festivals that have historically served as venues for the musical practices of ethnic popular music.

Walt Disney World near Orlando, Florida, is home to one of the most grandiose experiments in popular culture. With its EPCOT Center, promising a "world of tomorrow," Disney World might seem at first glance to be the perfect model for a futuristic melting pot and the supremacy of technology over cultural differences. Music as a marker of the world's culture is also an important part of Disney World, and it is to the villages and pavilions that represent different countries that we go in search of music. Disney World seems to have a rather more conservative stance toward cultural differences than its predecessor, Disneyland in California, which took as its model for America the common street that all small towns had in Walt Disney's imagination, "Main Street USA." In the Florida world of Disney, however, the world and its differences have been restored, implying that the future will no longer be an American "Main Street" but a cluster of villages whose cultures are increasingly accessible to many, even though the boundaries between them are maintained.

The "world" of Walt Disney's fantasy in Florida is not that different from many others in North American history, in which links between the present and the past, one culture and another, were of prime importance. North Americans have used the world's fairs that they have staged to achieve similar ends—that is, to construct a multiethnic world by means of a magnificent festival. Traditionally, music has been one of the most vivid ways of creating this world of diversity. At the 1893 World's Columbian Exposition in Chicago, North Americans witnessed one of the first attempts—and in many ways, the model until the present—to assemble all the world's musics in one place.

Musicians, dancers, and instrumental ensembles arrived in the spring of 1893 from all over the world, which, however, largely meant Europe and the many cultures colonized by Europeans. Walking up and down the Midway at the Chicago world's fair, one heard music from Hungary, Java, Fiji, Dahomey, and "Old Vienna." Choruses from Sweden sang, and North African harems danced. The word "midway," meaning a place where the fairgoer undergoes a barrage of different stimuli, was a contribution of the Chicago fair, where the Midway was and is actually a parkway, again showing that the distinction between real and fantasy worlds virtually disappears at a festival. A thousand or more musicians from throughout the world regaled the visitors in the fair's world. At the very least, the world Columbus had presumably discovered only four centuries earlier was recreated for the world's fair celebrating that discovery as a sea of musical differences: a deliberate model for the musics of ethnic North America that we see again at Walt Disney World as celebrations of the quincentennial of Columbus's first encounter with North America draws nigh.

German-American Music at Disney World

The German band at Disney World plays a style of music that is immediately recognizable to most visitors as German. Surrounded by make-believe structures that might be Heidelberg or Munich or Vienna, depending on whom one asks, the German area takes a little bit from several places in German-speaking Central Europe. The band, too, takes a little bit from every place in Central Europe. The musicians are professionals, although many of them have traditional backgrounds. The accordion player, in fact, grew up in an area of eastern Pennsylvania where many from the rural area of Burgenland on the Austro-Hungarian border settled after the two world wars. He can play in a traditional Burgenland style, or the style of Burgenlanders in North America, or the style of popular German-American Dutchman music. The other musicians, too, can perform in a variety of styles. How about a Bohemian or Polish polka style? How about substituting a Slovenian button box for the piano accordion? How about beefing up the brass section to sound more Czech-German? Everything is possible.

Everything, however, is not done. Just as the German band can cross stylistic boundaries with considerable ease, they choose not to do so. Just as they could respond to the request for pieces from a number of different repertories, they have no need to do so. The repertory of the band has, in fact, formed a core of its own, with identifiable qualities of style and performance practice. There is no question that this core exemplifies qualities that are fundamentally German-American. The repertory itself derives from a corpus of folk melodies. Many of these have become standard as a result of the publication of voluminous folk song collections in Central Europe at the end of the nineteenth century and the subsequent adoption of these collections by German-American publishers. Others are more *volkstümlich* ("folklike") in nature, known because a popular singer or cabaret star made them famous on record. There are different sources for this repertory, but the band has reshaped it for its purposes.

Performance practice, too, has formed around a recognizable core. The instrumentation is far more North American than Central European. The heavy bass line, the seeming exaggeration of the tuba's "oom-pah"—these are the contributions of Hans "Whoopie John" Wilfahrt's band, the best-known Dutchman band of the Upper Midwest in the twentieth century. Though he based his band largely in rural Minnesota (anchored at one extreme of his circuit by New Ulm, at the other by Minneapolis and St. Paul), Whoopie John became tremendously influential by recognizing the potential of ethnic recordings and the wide range of nascent radio broadcasting in the years between the world wars. Like many ethnic musicians, Whoopie John discovered that these were halcyon years for ethnic popular music.

The German band at Walt Disney World took advantage of the styles of a different halcyon age, namely that in which polka had become big business. The band can depend on the direct experience many visitors have had with polka, and the indirect exposure of almost all to polka. Polka has various degrees of popularity. For the band, however, polka has the advantage of affording them the opportunity to play in very distinctive styles. They can experiment with a more Tyrolian sound, or they can reorchestrate their repertory to sound more Bavarian. The visitors largely do not understand these stylistic differences, but they sense that the band's skill has something to do with a more refined sense of ethnicity. The popular style of the band may bring about some unexpected combinations and commit some violations that European ensembles would find unconscionable, but accordingly new possibilities for German-American music emerge. Taking full advantage of the juxtaposition that the festival atmosphere of Disney World encourages, the German band reshapes German-American music, themselves juxtaposing processes that historicize, traditionalize, and popularize.

The Modernity of Traditional Music

Festivals have populated this chapter in a variety of ways, serving by and large as a unifying metaphor. The festivals we have visited have been of several different types—neighborhood affairs, annual civic events, world's fairs—but their similarities have been striking. Also striking is the fact that festivals are growing in popularity in North America. Visiting Toronto on most weekends during the year, one needs but to pick up the entertainment section of the newspaper to find abundant opportunities to visit an ethnic community's celebration of its culture. State tourist guides for Iowa have an extensive list of summer festivals; but if one wants a place to stay at the annual Norwegian Nordic Fest in Decorah, it is necessary to book rooms as much as a year in advance.

Festivals have proliferated, and so too has the music that is essential to their special character. Local groups are wont to stage pageants, and display booths for ethnic food and costumes also have several boxes of cassette tapes for sale. A quick look through these reveals that ethnic communities themselves are now recording on their own labels; there's no money to be made from recording this way, but reinforcing community identity through music has a value all its own.

The musical performances at the festival today belong more to the world reframed by the time and place of the event itself than to the "old country" or the customs of the past. Continuity may be constructed and a certain set of symbols may proclaim that "this is the way it was," but most participants at the festival are far more interested in making ethnic music a part of their own lives. Ethnic music is therefore modern music; it provides the sounds and symbols of a contemporary world. For North Americans of European ancestry, music increasingly needs to represent the sweeping changes that have transformed Europe on the eve of the twenty-first century; the Eastern European troupes at the Pittsburgh Folk Festival endeavor more to recapture the spirit of nationalism and political reform from the 1980s and 1990s than the imaginary pristine countryside of another century. Asian-Americans—the "new immigrants"—are no less concerned that their music be integrated into the festival and into the multiethnic culture of North America. African-Americans, too, turn to festivals to underscore the diveristy of their musics, not just more traditional styles but the sounds of a modern world and the virtual omnipresence of African influences.

The music of ethnic North America has truly become a world music. It is distinctive of the continent where it has developed; it embodies both the diversity and unity of that larger cultural area. The music of ethnic North America also has a resonance that is fundamentally modern and therefore traditional in the sense of a world whose cultural boundaries are increasingly traversed. Modernity is one of the most distinctive markers of all the musics we have encountered in this chapter, and modernity is one of the contributions of North America to a more expansive world music culture. The music of ethnic North America is, in effect, a grand mixture. It is not a mixture in which differences disappear, as in a melting pot, but rather a mixture in which the distinctiveness of individual styles and repertories comes to the sur-

face. The characteristic juxtaposition of musics has effectively sharpened
the awareness that each community, old or new, has of its own music
and culture. That heightened awareness has, moreover, provided musicians with the opportunity to reshape style and sound to reflect shif-
ting boundaries and changing cultures. The music of ethnic North
America is no longer just a means of remembering the past. It is very
much the music of a modern world and the complex, multiethnic culture
that will most certainly continue to characterize North America well
into the future.

ETHNIC NORTH AMERICA BIBLIOGRAPHY

North America as a Whole: Gilbert Chase, *America's Music: From
the Pilgrims to the Present,* rev. 3rd ed. (Urbana: University of Illinois
Press, 1987); Richard M. Dorson, ed., *Handbook of American Folklore*
(Bloomington: Indiana University Press, 1983); Charles Hamm, *Music
in the New World* (New York: W. W. Norton, 1983): H. Wiley Hitch-
cock and Stanley Sadie, eds., *The New Grove Dictionary of American
Music,* 4 vols. (London: Macmillan, 1986); Donald W. Krummel,
Bibliographical Handbook of American Music (Urbana: University of
Illinois Press, 1987); Terry E. Miller, *Folk Music in America: A Reference
Guide* (New York: Garland, 1986); Bruno Nettl, *Folk Music in the United
States: An Introduction,* 3rd ed., rev. and en. Helen Myers (Detroit:
Wayne State University Press, 1976); Nicholas Tawa, *The Sound of
Strangers: Musical Culture, Acculturation, and the Post-Civil War
Ethnic American* (Metuchen, N.J.: Scarecrow, 1982).

Music of Asian Ethnic Communities: Nazir A. Jairazbhoy and Sue
Carole DeVale, eds., "Asian Music in North America," Special Edition,
Selected Reports in Ethnomusicology 6 (1985); Ronald Riddle, *Flying
Dragons, Flowing Streams: Music in the Life of San Francisco's Chinese*
(Westport, Conn.: Greenwood, 1983).

Music of European Ethnic Communities: Roger D. Abrahams and
George Foss, *Anglo-American Folksong Style* (Englewood Cliffs, N.J.:
Prentice Hall, 1968); Samuel P. Bayard, "Prolegomena to a Study of
the Principal Melodic Families of British-American Folk Song," *Jour-
nal of American Folklore* 63 (1950); Alan Lomax, *The Folk Songs of
North America in the English Language* (Garden City, N.Y.: Double-
day, 1960); James Porter, ed., *Selected Reports in Ethnomusicology* 3/1
(1978) (Special edition devoted to the traditional music of Europeans
in America); Mark Slobin, *Tenement Songs: The Popular Music of the
Jewish Immigrants* (Urbana: University of Illinois Press, 1982); Robert
L. Wright, *Swedish Emigrant Ballads* (Lincoln: University of Nebraska
Press, 1965); Rochelle Wright and Robert L. Wright, *Danish Emigrant
Ballads and Songs* (Carbondale: Southern Illinois University Press, 1983).

Music of Hispanic-American Communities: Américo Paredes, *A Texas-Mexican Cancionero: Folksongs of the Lower Border* (Urbana: University of Illinois Press, 1976); Américo Paredes, *With His Pistol in His Hand: A Border Ballad and Its Hero* (Austin: University of Texas Press, 1958); Manuel Peña, *The Texas-Mexican Conjunto: History of a Working-Class Music* (Austin: University of Texas Press, 1985); J. D. Robb, *Hispanic Folk Songs of New Mexico* (Albuquerque: University of New Mexico Press, 1954).

Ethnicity and Ethnic History of North America: Larry Danielson, ed., "Studies in Folklore and Ethnicity," Special Edition, *Western Folklore* 36/1 (1977); Robert A. Georges and Stephen Stern, *American and Canadian Immigrant and Ethnic Folklore: An Annotated Bibliography* (New York: Garland, 1982); Milton M. Gordon, *Assimilation in American Life* (New York: Oxford University Press, 1964); Anya Peterson Royce, *Ethnic Identity: Strategies for Diversity* (Bloomington: Indiana University Press, 1982); Stephan Thernstrom, Ann Orlov, and Oscar Handlin, eds., *Harvard Encyclopedia of American Ethnic Groups* (Cambridge, Mass.: Harvard University Press, 1980).

Regional Studies: H. M. Belden, ed., *Ballads and Songs Collected by the Missouri Folk-Lore Society* (Columbia: University of Missouri Press, 1973); Robert Cantwell, *Bluegrass Breakdown: The Making of the Old Southern Sound* (Urbana: University of Illinois Press, 1984); Helen Creighton and Calum MacLeod, *Gaelic Songs in Nova Scotia* (Ottawa: National Museums of Canada, 1979); Helmut Kallmann, Gilles Potvin, and Kenneth Winters, eds., *Encyclopedia of Music in Canada* (Toronto: University of Toronto Press, 1981); George Korson, ed., *Pennsylvania Songs and Legends* (Baltimore: Johns Hopkins University Press, 1960); Timothy J. McGee, *The Music of Canada* (New York: W. W. Norton, 1985); Bill C. Malone, *Southern Music/American Music* (Lexington: The University Press of Kentucky, 1979); Vance Randolph, ed., *Ozark Folksongs*, 4 vols. (Columbia: University of Missouri Press, 1980); Howard N. Thorp, *Songs of the Cowboys* (New York: Clarkson N. Potter, 1966); David E. Whisnant, *All That Is Native and Fine: The Politics of Culture in an American Region* (Chapel Hill: University of North Carolina Press, 1983).

Music and North American Religious Communities. Michael Hicks, *Mormonism and Music: A History* (Urbana: University of Illinois Press, 1989); Donald R. Hinks, *Brethren Hymn Books and Hymnals, 1720–1884* (Gettysburg, Pa.: Brethren Heritage Press, 1986); Doreen Helen Klassen, *Singing Mennonite: Low German Songs of the Mennonites* (Winnipeg: University of Manitoba Press, 1989); Jeff Todd Titon, *Powerhouse for God: Speech, Chant, and Song in an Appalachian Baptist Church* (Austin: University of Texas Press, 1988).

Contemporary and Popular Traditions of Ethnic Music: R. Serge Denisoff, *Great Day Coming: Folk Music and the American Left* (Baltimore: Penguin, 1973); William Ferris and Mary L. Hunt, eds., *Folk Music and Modern Sound* (Jackson: University Press of Mississippi, 1985); Henry Glassie and others, *Folksongs and Their Makers* (Bowling Green, Ohio: Bowling Green University Popular Press, 1970); John Greenway, *American Folksongs of Protest* (Philadelphia: University of Pennsylvania Press, 1953); Robert B. Klymasz, "'Sounds You Never Heard Before': Ukrainian Country Music in Western Canada," *Ethnomusicology* 16/5 (1972); Judith McCulloh, ed., *Ethnic Recordings in America: A Neglected Heritage* (Washington, D.C.: Library of Congress, 1982); Neil V. Rosenberg, *Bluegrass: A History* (Urbana: University of Illinois Press, 1985).

Musical Instruments: James M. Borders, *European and American Wind and Percussion Instruments: Catalogue of the Stearns Collection of Musical Instruments* (Ann Arbor: University of Michigan Press, 1988); Miles Krassen, *Clawhammer Banjo* (New York: Oak Publications, 1974); L. Allen Smith, *A Catalogue of Pre-Revival Appalachian Dulcimers* (Columbia: University of Missouri Press, 1983); Akira Tsumura, *Banjos: The Tsumura Collection* (Tokyo: Kodansha, 1984).

African-American Music: Houston A. Baker, Jr., *Blues, Ideology, and Afro-American Literature: A Vernacular Theory* (Chicago: University of Chicago Press, 1984); Harold Courlander, *Negro Folk Music, U.S.A.* (New York: Columbia University Press, 1963); Dena J. Epstein, *Sinful Tunes and Spirituals: Black Folk Music to the Civil War* (Urbana: University of Illinois Press, 1977); Charles Keil, *Urban Blues* (Chicago: University of Chicago Press, 1966); Paul Oliver, *Songsters and Saints: Vocal Traditions on Race Records* (Cambridge: Cambridge University Press, 1984); Eileen Southern, *The Music of Black Americans: A History*, 2nd ed. (New York: W. W. Norton, 1983); Eileen Southern, *Readings in Black American Music*, 2nd ed. (New York: W. W. Norton, 1983); Jeff Todd Titon, *Early Downhome Blues: A Musical and Cultural Analysis* (Urbana: University of Illinois Press, 1977); Richard A. Waterman, "African Influence on the Music of the Americas," in Sol Tax, ed., *Acculturation in the Americas* (Chicago: University of Chicago Press, 1952).

ETHNIC NORTH AMERICA DISCOGRAPHY

Discographical Note

Because of the enormous number of recordings that document the music of ethnic North America, this discography will note some of the most important and comprehensive series of recordings rather than individual discs. Students interested in specific suggestions for recordings of the music of an ethnic group or in a particular genre can find these in discographies and special musical studies, for example, of jazz or the blues. A further source, in which new releases of ethnic and folk music are reviewed in brief, is the discography section of the *Journal of American Folklore*, a quarterly journal published by the American Folklore Society. A remarkably rich and detailed discographical source for American ethnic music is Richard K. Sottswood, *Ethnic Music on Records: A Discography of Ethnic Recordings Produced in the United States, 1893–1942*, 7 volumes (Urbana: University of Illinois Press, 1990.)

During the 1970s and 1980s a comprehensive collection of American music recordings appeared on the New World Records label. Funded by the Rockefeller Foundation and first conceived to celebrate the American Bicentennial in 1976, the first 100 releases on New World Records were distributed without cost to most college and university libraries, where students using this book will often find them. Although New World Records intentionally included all American traditions, folk and ethnic traditions are well represented, and the connections among diverse musical traditions are evident. Students will find it very helpful to compare these different traditions, their histories, and their cultural contexts. Comprehensive critical notes accompany each recording. Many standard studies of American music now refer to the musical examples on New World Records (for example, Charles Hamm's *Music in the New World*), further enhancing the value of these recordings as reference tools.

The Library of Congress has also produced excellent recordings of folk and ethnic music. Some of these document local and regional traditions, others specific genres. Students wishing to hear Child ballads recorded in the United States will find the Library of Congress recording *Child Ballads Traditional in the U.S.* (AAFS L57–58) very valuable. The fifteen-volume series *Folk Music in America* (LBC 1–15), edited by Richard K. Spottswood, is an excellent survey, particularly of early recordings and otherwise hard-to-find styles, such as folk music of rural southern African-Americans.

The Folkways label has recorded diverse traditions of American folk music, although ethnic music is not particularly well represented, with the exception of Anglo-American and some African-American traditions. Still, because many of the recordings released by Folkways were

made in New York City by immigrants and exiles in the decade following World War II, students have an interesting opportunity to study
the repertories maintained by a first-generation musician or ensemble.
A recording of "German folk music," therefore, might really contain
"volkstümlich" settings performed by a German-American. The Smithsonian Institution is releasing many Folkways recordings, often with
new and thorough notes.

The Smithsonian Institution has also produced several sets of
"classic" American musical genres, namely jazz, country-and-western,
and labor and protest songs. These multirecord collections are of the
highest quality, and the explanatory notes that accompany the sets are
at once scholarly and accessible. These recordings further help the student understand the ways in which different musical traditions interact
and ethnic music has historically influenced those traditions we might
not immediately consider as ethnic.

INDEX